Solidarity's Secret

Solidarity's Secret

the women who defeated communism in **poland**

shana penn

the university of michigan press   ann arbor

Copyright © 2005 by Shana Penn
All rights reserved
Published in the United States of America by
The University of Michigan Press
Manufactured in the United States of America
⊗ Printed on acid-free paper

2008   2007   2006   2005   4   3   2   1

A CIP catalog record for this book is available from the British Library.

Library of Congress Cataloging-in-Publication Data

Penn, Shana.
    Solidarity's secret : the women who defeated Communism in Poland /
Shana Penn.
        p.   cm.
    Includes bibliographical references and index.
    ISBN 0-472-11385-2 (cloth : alk. paper)
        1. Women political activists—Poland—History.   2. NSZZ
"Solidarnosc" (Labor organization)—Political activity.   3. Communism—
Poland—History.   4. Poland—Politics and government—1980–1989.
I. Title.

HQ1236.5.P7P46   2005
943.805'6'0922—dc22   2005002603

For My Parents

*You've come to learn about Solidarity women, so I will
tell you the truth, but who will care to publish it?
Everyone in Poland knows that women started the
1980s underground, but no one bothers to talk about it.
—Barbara Labuda, Wrocław*

Contents

Foreword

irena grudzińska-gross

Imagine the following situation: it is a severe winter, most of the people you used to work with are under arrest, all the telephones are cut off, the streets of your city are teeming with policemen and tanks, soldiers are warming themselves by street-side fires. What are you going to do? If you are Helena Łuczywo, and this is December 15, 1981, two days after martial law was declared in Poland, you walk out of the apartment in which you are hiding and look for people with whom you can rebuild the Solidarity movement. And, rather quickly, you find that some of the people with whom you used to conspire against the communist government before Solidarity even existed have not been apprehended and are ready to conspire again. Soon, you assemble seven people and organize—it is exceedingly difficult—the first meeting, in which the future course of the resistance is set up. The most important task is to preserve the voice and the authority of the Solidarity movement, to prevent its disappearance. One of the seven people present at that first meeting takes on the task of finding and contacting any elected Solidarity leader who escaped arrest. The safety of the leaders is to be carefully managed so that they can lead the movement. And because they need to have a platform from which their words can be heard, a newspaper must be created. Hence a decision is made to create the *Tygodnik Mazowsze* (Regional Weekly). The remaining six people sit down to plan how to accomplish this task. Such were the first steps in the long march that unseated communism.

What is rather surprising in this story is not only the courage, or should I say the audacity, of these seven persons, but the fact that all of them were women. They immediately found the formula for how to act against the political and human disaster of the introduction of martial law. And, what is even more remarkable, they persevered in their stubborn resistance for eight long and exhausting years. They hid in ever-changing apartments, evading arrest, missing their children's birthdays, working around the clock. Only one of them, Ewa Kulik, the one who went in search of leaders in hiding, became a member of the underground's decision-making structures. When in 1989 their activities bore fruit and the communist system collapsed, they went on to the next task without once receiving or demanding gratitude or simple recognition. They did not want to think about themselves as veterans of past battles and therefore marched right into new challenges. They also rejected any gender analysis, saying: we were all in it together, and we did what was needed, because it was the right thing to do. And while many people wrote themselves into the history of resistance against communism, the women of *Tygodnik Mazowsze,* as well as countless other women conspirators, are rarely mentioned. Today, barely fifteen years after the fall of communism, these are unsung, forgotten heroines of the Polish underground.

But, I should say, they WERE unsung heroines because the book you are about to read reconstructs their actions and secures their place in recent history. The story of the Solidarity movement has often been told: How, in the face of government-ordered price-raises, the young electrician Lech Wałęsa jumped over the wall of the Gdańsk shipyard and ultimately founded the Solidarity Trade Union; how that union demanded and won not only economic benefits for workers but demanded fundamental liberties; how it acquired ten million members; how it was then suppressed by martial law. But Shana Penn is the first to relate in detail what role a Gdańsk shipyard worker, Anna Walentynowicz, played before that famous Wałęsa jump, and what happened next. Expertly written by a sympathetic outsider, *Solidarity's Secret: The Women*

Who Defeated Communism in Poland is a thorough telling and deep analysis of the story of women in the initially legal, then outlawed, Solidarity movement in Poland. The book is multilayered. Part oral history, part historical and sociological reconstruction of the traditions governing Polish womanhood, it is also a political analysis of a national history that in itself is hard to disentangle. Penn pays very close attention to the particularities of the Polish situation and endeavors to communicate all its nuances. But the book's chief value comes from the fact that none of these traditions blinds her vision. She steps in with seemingly very innocent questions: What about the participation of women? Why weren't they noticed? Why were they absent from the formal leadership? Weren't they recognized as leaders as well? What did they do? How crucial were their actions for the survival of the movement? Why did they refuse to differentiate themselves as women from their male colleagues?

The responses to these questions produce a new and fascinating description of what was one of the most important mass movements of the end of twentieth century. Solidarity was a sort of protracted insurrection, and, like all great national upheavals, quickly developed into a mobilization against a common enemy. Polish history—at least the history that was actively remembered—offered many models of revolutionary behavior: that of a partisan, a negotiator, a rebel. But each Polish insurrection also had a supporting cast of wives, mothers, and sisters, who kept the fight alive, passed around (and often wrote) the movement's manifestos, supported the men, and fought the enemy on a multiplicity of fronts.

In August of 1980, when the Solidarity movement was brought into existence by men and women of the anticommunist opposition, its eventual membership of ten million was evenly divided between men and women. But the leadership was basically all men, and when on December 13, 1981, martial law was imposed, most of its leaders, who had come together at an important meeting, were rounded up and arrested. Many women were arrested as well, but their numbers had been underestimated by the police. As we see in this book, they hid the few remaining male leaders, founded underground Solidarity structures, and published the main Solidarity newspaper, providing the continuity to a movement that was in danger of extinction. And this is the untold history of the Solidarity movement in Poland.

Penn's perspective allows her to uncover an important element in Polish history, an element invisible to her subjects, blinded as they were by the persistence of the Polish romantic tradition, which valorized the activities of heroic men much more than those of women. In fact, in researching the book, she met with incredulous resistance by the women, who considered their activities to have been something completely normal and rejected any notion of heroism. They did not want to look at their struggle through a prism of gender, were afraid of being labeled "feminists," and were tired of any ideological affiliation whatsoever. With tact, persistence, and intelligence, Shana Penn pierced that resistance and here offers the reader the most complete and interesting history yet written of a social movement that shook the world. In *Solidarity's Secret* we see for the first time the complete cast of the movement that did not show much solidarity with its women. In this "family picture," men and women are seated side by side, their presence enhancing each others' roles. Only wise feminist scholarship could produce such a complete portrait and tell this important story of a group of brave, daring women, who took on a mighty state. And won.

Acknowledgments

Several institutions and individuals provided key resources without which this book and the Polish edition could not have been written. First, I wish to thank the Open Society Institute for awarding me an Individual Project Fellowship, which generously supported the last two years of my work on both *Solidarity's Secret* and *Podziemie Kobiet*. Open Society Institute also helped support the promotion of both books.

The Network of East-West Women's Book and Journal Project helped support the translations and book promotion, for which I am deeply appreciative. A Ludwig Vogelstein grant supported some of the research I conducted in the early 1990s.

Since 2000 the Women's Leadership Institute at Mills College in Oakland, California, has provided a beautiful setting in which to write and a community of colleagues from whom I have drawn intellectual and emotional support.

During my many years of travel between Poland and the United States, Peggy Simpson, an American journalist based in Warsaw, offered her apartment for use as my second home.

A book is a collective endeavor, an ongoing conversation between the author and the individuals who people her world—interviewees, mentors, colleagues, research assistants, editors, translators, interpreters, literary agents, publishers, friends, and family members. I wish to thank a diverse group of individuals who supported, inspired, guided, educated, informed, housed, fed, and otherwise assisted me in the development of this book over more than a dozen years.

A special thanks to the people closest to me in the writing and editing of this book: Ralph Benson, Agnieszka Graff, Jill Hannum, Marjorie Lightman, Isabel Marcus, Ann Snitow, and Bozena Uminska.

Mentors, colleagues, readers, editors, publishers, and friends include Agata Araszkiewicz, Janice Baker-Weil, Dagmara Baraniewska, Erin Barclay, Tressa Berman, Chris Caes, Kim Chernin, Roma Ciesla, Violetta Cywicka, Arwen Donahue, Kinga Dunin, Felicia Eth, Paula Fass, Dominika Ferens, Izabela Filipiak, Małgorzata Fuszara, Elinor Gadon, Kasia Gawlicz, Tomasz Głeb, Janet Greenberg, Irena Grudzińska-Gross, Anka Grupińska, Agnieszka Grzybek, Agnieszka Iwaszkiewicz, Maria Janion, Ewa Kulik-Bielińska, Hanna Jankowska, Joe Lamb, Cheryl Lehman, Barbara Limanowska, Bogna Lorence-Kot, Elzbieta Matynia, Jarosław Mikos, Mary Morrison, Bernard Osser, Elzbieta Oleksy, Karen Payne, Sarah Pick, Joanna Regulska, Iwona Reichardt, James Reische, Joan Ringelheim, Ruth Rosen, Jane Rosenthal, Andrzej Rosner, Katarźyna Rosner, Dorien Ross, Adam Rozański, Teresa Sasińska-Klas, Edward Serotta, Naomi Silverman, Peggy Simpson, Robert Soltyk, Kathy Sreedhar, Renate Stendhal, Każimiera Szczuka, Laurie Wagner, Sławomira Wałczewska, Lech Wałęsa, Susan Weidman-Schneider, Michael Weil, Adam Winiarz, and Carol Zemel.

Institutions include the Baltic Gender Center, Fundacja eFKa, Hoover Institution, Jagiellonian University Institute for International Journalism, Judaica Foundation, Karta Center, NEWW-Polska, OŚKA, Rosner and Partners, Warsaw University Gender Studies, and the United States Consul, Kraków.

Regarding research assistants, translators, and interpreters, I was fortunate that, when I began my research, several Polish colleagues were able to assist me, even though interpreting and translating were not their sole or primary professions. Between 1990 and 1992 research and interpreting services were provided by philosophy professor Nina Gładziuk, Holocaust researcher and author Anka Grupińska, feminist pioneer Jolanta Plakwicz, and human rights advocate Małgorzata Tarasiewicz. In recent years, translations of primary source materials were made by Renata Firek, Katarźyna Gawlicz, Nina Gładziuk, Agnieszka Graff, Ewa Meducka, Iwona Reichardt, Dominika Suwik, and Ewa Turyk. A special thanks to Ewa Meducka and Dominika Suwik, both students at Warsaw University in 2000–2003, for their diligence, competence, and friendship during the final stages of the book.

Interviewees include Magdalena Abakanowicz, Jolanta Banach, Dagmara Baraniewska, Anna Bikont, Teresa Bogucka, Zofia Bydlińska, Zsuzsa Dabrówska, Anna Dodziuk, Małgorzata Fuszara, Małgorzata Gebert, Nina Gładziuk, Irena Grudzińska-Gross, Anka Grupińska, Joanna Gwiazda, Anna Husarska, Monika Krajewska, Ewa Kulik-Bielińska, Zofia Kuratówska, Krystyna Janda, Maria Janion, Barbara Labuda, Barbara Limanowska, Wanda Nowicka, Jolanta Plakwicz, Agnieszka Maciejowska, Małgorzata Pawlicka, Barbara Pomorska, Zofia Romaszewska, Izabela Sierakowska, Joanna Szczęsna, Małgorzata Tarasiewicz, Anna Titkow, Anna Walentynowicz, Danuta Winiarska-Kuroń, Ludwika Wujec, and Krystyna Zachwatowicz-Wajda.

And finally, I'd like to extend my gratitude to my literary agent, Felicia Eth, and to my colleagues at the University of Michigan Press—James Reische, Pete Sickman-Garner, Mary Bisbee-Beek, Kevin Rennells, Felice Lau, and Amy Anderson—who've made the publishing process an enjoyable collaboration.

Introduction

Like so many other Americans, I avidly followed the media's accounts of Poland's Round Table discussions in the spring of 1989 that led to the sharing of power between the grass roots trade union Solidarity and General Wojciech Jaruzelski's very weakened Communist Party. Then, that autumn, revolutions thundered throughout Central and Eastern Europe, and I started looking for my passport.

I had it in mind to write a book that would explore the roles and experiences of Central European women in the communist labor force and in the family, with an emphasis on women who were active in the prodemocracy movements. I had connections that I thought could steer me to women I might interview in Poland, Hungary, and then-Czechoslovakia. At the time, I was working as an editor for the Elmwood Institute, an international environmental and human rights organization in Berkeley, California. Some of the institute's supporters had ties to opposition movements in the Eastern Bloc, and throughout the late 1980s they would return from their travels behind the Iron Curtain with reports of growing social unrest.

As I became increasingly caught up in the unfolding drama, I eagerly read the English translations of dissident writers such as

Adam Michnik, Václav Havel, and Gyorgy Konrad. I also read accounts by Timothy Garton Ash, Lawrence Weschler, Neal Ascherson, and other Western authors of Solidarity's rise, fall, and resurrection in Poland. What caught my attention and eventually inspired my first visit to Central Europe in June–July 1990 was that, whether written by Eastern Bloc insiders or by observers from the Western press, the accounts I was reading spoke only of the men who led the various opposition movements. Where, I wondered, were the women?

In the case of Poland, for example, if your information came only from the English-language Western press, you saw Solidarity portrayed as an anticommunist opposition that idealized the working class and was led by Lech Wałęsa, Adam Michnik, Jacek Kuroń, Zbigniew Bujak, and Father Jerzy Popiełuszko[1]—men representing workers, intellectuals, and priests, a unique coalition of Poland's social groups. We were told that these men and others had joined together *in solidarity,* beginning in the late 1970s, to bring an end to the communist state's one-party rule.[2]

This was, of course, broadly true. Brave men such as Nobel Peace Prize winner Lech Wałęsa and his cohorts did, indeed, create the first and only free trade union movement in the Eastern Bloc, as well as the largest mass-based opposition to communism in the Soviet-dominated region. The shipyards, coal mines, steelworks, and factories were centers of gravity for nationwide protests throughout the more than four decades of communist rule. In reality, however, Solidarity was more than a trade union movement made up of workers striking for higher wages and control of factories, for there were several other major loci of activism that shaped and sustained it. In addition, and possibly most important, Solidarity produced perhaps as many heroines as it did heroes.

But the Solidarity men consistently overlooked the movement's heroines, who, for their part, did not challenge the subordinate position they were allotted. And because the Western press reported news of the underground and the revolution as relayed to it by Solidarity, we were left with an unbalanced, unchallenged perspective on history. Together, Polish society and the Western press promoted the image of a male revolution, thus institutionalizing, at the very moment that a democracy was born, women's invisibility in the Solidarity movement.

Prior to my first trip to Poland in June 1990, I had familiarized myself with the widely disseminated accounts of Solidarity's beginning—accounts in which the Polish democracy's Founding Mothers play no role. The shorthand version of the established story (which is valid, as far as it goes) reads like this:

In August 1980, after a decade of protest and strikes, an estimated one million workers gathered in factory halls and shipyards across Poland to demand restoration of their human rights. Their collective apostasy created Solidarity, the first and only free trade union movement in the Eastern Bloc. By the first anniversary of Solidarity's creation, more than one-third of Poland's adult population, approximately ten million men and women, had joined Solidarity and helped to establish political clubs; adult education programs; legal services; an independent press; and an array of film, theater, literary, and artistic offerings. These were the makings of a veritable civil society, and Solidarity's was the largest and most successful display of social activism to emerge anywhere in the Soviet-dominated region. According to historian Padraic Kenney, "As a result of the Solidarity experiment, there were far more people in Poland than elsewhere with experience in independent political activism—perhaps by a factor of 100."[3] Solidarity also was the only movement to gain legal recognition by a communist government, which it achieved in 1980. The same government, however, soon decided that the grass roots movement it had endorsed would have to be stopped.

Sixteen months after Solidarity's creation, the Communist Party declared martial law. As Saturday, December 12, 1981, turned into Sunday the thirteenth, military troops moved across Poland, sealed the borders, isolated city from city, and cut telephone and telegraph lines. Tanks assembled in the streets. Police and army units broke down apartment doors, roused the inhabitants from their sleep, and hauled them off to prisons and internment camps in what U.S. journalist Lawrence Weschler called one of the most successful coups in late-twentieth-century history. Some ten thousand activists were arrested immediately—most of them men, including most of Solidarity's male leadership. In a matter of days, the Communist Party reversed the mandates that had ensured Solidarity's legal status.

The few male leaders who evaded arrest and went into hiding reconfigured a splintered Solidarity into an underground network that, between 1981 and 1988, connected hundreds of thousands of Poles to one another and to sympathizers around the world. Almost seven years passed before the subterranean movement resurfaced in full regalia, after nationwide strikes in the summer of 1988 had precipitated the pivotal Round Table negotiations between Solidarity and the government. By the summer of 1989, the communist system had toppled. Underground activists reemerged to declare Solidarity's successorship and the dawn of a new democratic era.

The Western media played an important role in the Polish drama, and the opposition regarded it as a lifeline, especially with respect to its support of political prisoners. Like other Eastern Bloc anticommunist opposition movements, Solidarity relied upon international attention to leverage pressure against the Polish government's human rights violations. Activists cultivated long-term connections with the foreign correspondents based in Poland as well as with the international press headquartered in the West. The resulting exposure—in every print and broadcast medium from Radio Free Europe, Agence France Presse, and the BBC to the *New York Times* and the *Wall Street Journal*—helped oppositionists gain crucial visibility and sympathy.

The power of communications first became strikingly evident during the strikes in the summer of 1980 that culminated in Solidarity's creation. As British historian Timothy Garton Ash underscored in his reports on the Gdańsk shipyard strike, Solidarity was a "telerevolution": "From the time in July 1980 when . . . activists started telephoning news of the first strikes to foreign radio stations, which broadcast the news back to Poland, the telephone, telex, tape recorder, radio and duplicating machine all played a vital role."[4] Garton Ash reported that, in opinion polls conducted during the ensuing sixteen months, Solidarity's legal period, "the demand for media which did not lie, and for the teaching of Poland's 'true history' in schools came second only to the demand for freedom."[5]

The Western press covered the telerevolution's achievements, questioned how long it would be before the Polish Communist Party and the Soviet Union would cease to tolerate the "democratic epidemic" that Solidarity spawned, and reported on the top tiers of action. It did not pay much attention to the civic and community leaders, many of whom were women, who were organizing people at the grass roots level and helping them transform their lives. The areas of civic activity where women could be found were considered only marginally newsworthy by the media.[6]

And so women in the opposition never made the headline news—with the single exception of Anna Walentynowicz, an outspoken, middle-aged crane operator whose firing from the Gdańsk shipyard in August 1980 sparked the nationwide strikes that catapulted Solidarity into existence.[7] The Western press allotted Anna her "fifteen minutes of fame," which lasted only until the 1980 strikes were victorious. Then Solidarity became a (briefly) legal trade union movement with men at its power center, and Anna fell below the radar screen of the daily press. Women's opposition exploits were not discussed in the more in-depth media accounts either or in contemporary historical accounts.

I had done a search through all the English-language books covering the decades before, during, and after Solidarity—including a perusal of the photographs and indices of such books published between the 1970s and early 1990s—and from these sources the only conclusion one can draw is that all of Poland's opposition leaders were men—handsome men, at that, and groomed to appeal to the Western press: bearded, brawny, big-shouldered hunks with the defiant, charismatic stance of heroes. Under the leadership of mustachioed working-class champion Lech Wałęsa —who represented the "voice of the people" inside Poland and presided as Solidarity's global voice before the international community— these articulate spokesmen defined where the "real" action was in Poland's courageous battle.

In an afterword to *Konspira*,[8] a collection of interviews with Solidarity men about their underground activity during martial law, Lawrence Weschler compared these Polish revolutionaries to the Founding Fathers of the United States: "In the same eerie way that a far flung colonial outpost on the farthest edge of the Empire, back in the 1770s and 1780s, managed to produce a generation featuring the likes of Washington, Jefferson, Franklin, Adams, Hamilton, Paine, and Madison, so Poland in the 1970s and 1980s had produced Wałęsa, Michnik, Kuroń, Borusewicz, Karol Wojtyła, Miłosz, Lipski, Frasyniuk, and the others."[9] Weschler never named a single woman. Either he and other journalists were not talking to women, or they did not credit the women who were their sources. Or perhaps they were protecting women's identities—a precaution I only later learned was very much a necessity for a core group of activist women in Warsaw.

Before I went to Poland, I wondered why Western journalists did not "see" women, did not ask the pressing question that came to my mind while reading their accounts—Where *are* the women? After I went to Poland, I realized that by neglecting to *cherchez les femmes,* the press had missed a huge story. Women had been active in the underground, working tirelessly behind the scenes to keep Wałęsa's face visible, to keep Solidarity's name alive, and to ensure that that face and that name stayed linked together.

In the press's defense, the women's story was not easy to uncover. Indeed, one of the women in question characterized it as Poland's "national secret."

And so I left for my first trip to Poland with my head full of Western books and media coverage, thinking I would find an anticommunist, male-dominated opposition that idealized the working class. I expected to meet workers who rallied for revolt from atop steam shovels and to hear tales of imprisoned intellectuals and of pacifist priests who sheltered dissidents. Instead I found an anticommunism that was cloaked in nineteenth-century romantic images and a country still entrenched in its communist infrastructure. The new, democratic Poland had a new creation myth—the history of Solidarity's victorious revolution—but that didn't cancel out the country's long and complex history of oppression and failed revolts.

In Poland a long tradition of resistance movements had spawned a popular saying, "Poles live by *unrule,*" which reflects the many periods of *unfreedom* during which Poles resisted foreign domination. Between 1792 and 1795 Poland was partitioned among the Russians, Prussians, and Austrians and until 1989 knew only twenty years of independence—between the end of World War I and the outbreak of World War II.

Poles grew adept at creating underground conspiracies—against the communist and Nazi occupiers in the twentieth century and against the Russian occupiers in the nineteenth. When tsarist authorities banned the use of the Polish language and the teaching of Polish history and culture, Poles everywhere began to fear that they would lose their national identity to their despised eastern neighbor, who had been at Poland's throat for nearly 360 years, invading its borders and holding the country hostage on thirteen different occasions: 1632, 1655, 1706, 1710, 1768–72, 1791–92, 1794, 1813, 1831, 1863, 1919–20, 1939, and 1944–45.[10] This ongoing cultural nightmare, intensified by the accumulated traumas and losses of World War II and its devastating aftermath, shaped Poland's postwar opposition movements and its hatred of the Soviets.

Thus, it gradually became clear to me that Polish resistance against the Soviet occupiers was on a deeper psychological level than just "anticommunism" and took place on a wider playing field than just the well-publicized factory strikes associated with Solidarity in the Western press. Actually, during the 1970s and 1980s there were three loci of activism in addition to the factories. One of these was the Catholic Church. Polish history began sometime in the tenth century with the baptism of King Mieszko I in the Latin rite, and over the next ten centuries, Catholicism and nationhood became intertwined. In the communist 1950s, the Church was too strong for the Polish Communist Party to destroy without provoking the hostile, mainly Catholic, population, and so Poland became the only Eastern Bloc country where the Church retained a measure of autonomy. Activist priests preached nonviolent resistance, harbored political fugitives, and provided rooms for illegal meetings, art exhibits, and theater productions. When Kraków cardinal Karol Wojtyła became Pope John Paul II in 1978, the country rejoiced, and his rousing pilgrimage across Poland the following year restored a long-submerged sense of national pride and dignity. Poles commonly said that the miracle of Wojtyła's election is what inspired the miracle of Solidarity.

The prisons and internment camps made up another major

locus of dissent. After the imposition of martial law, defiantly irrepressible intellectuals such as Adam Michnik and Jacek Kuroń communicated from their jail cells, appealing to the nation "to stop living lies" and, instead, to "live as if we are free." The imprisoned writers penned dazzling essays that were smuggled to the illegal press for publication.

It was the opposition press, which flourished illegally for most of the 1970s and 1980s, that was the third of the major, nonfactory sites of resistance. That enterprising, albeit clandestine, industry brought people together on the same page, so to speak, to get real news, not state propaganda, and to debate what an open society might look like. The illicit newspapers, magazines, bulletins, and books it published were called *bibuła,* the Polish term for illegal papers produced during periods of censorship. Analogous to the Russian word *samizdat,* "to self-publish," bibuła had the advantage of being a Polish word.

It was the illegal press that provided 1970s oppositionists with a practical vehicle to activate and coalesce support from the three, very different social groups that were fundamental to making change: the Inteligencja (a nineteenth-century way of saying "public intellectuals" and a term that continued to be used through 1989); the Workers, with a capital *W* (a purely communist term that the opposition brilliantly appropriated to argue for free trade unions); and the Polish Catholic clergy, the spiritual leaders most tolerated in the antireligious Soviet Bloc. (The political restraints on their power made the clergy unusually tolerant. They turned their backs on abortion and divorce, and they assisted women activists, even those who were single mothers, such as several of the protagonists in this story.)

Significantly, the illegal press was the chief playing field on which women were able to carve out distinctive, influential roles for themselves in the opposition. They distinguished themselves as editors, publishers, journalists, and communications strategists long before the world beyond Poland's police-patrolled borders had begun talking about the "Information Age." Much of my research leading to this book was to take place in the realm of the opposition press, but I had no inkling of that when I began my journey.

Arriving in Warsaw in the summer of 1990, I was aware that women made up approximately 50 percent of Solidarity's ten-million-strong membership—proportional to women's presence in the labor force. However, their political representation in the formal Solidarity structures was significantly smaller. "As one rose in the Solidarity hierarchy, the numbers of women diminished. Only 7.8 percent (69) of the 881 delegates to the Solidarity Congress [in September 1981] were women; only one woman sat on the National Executive [Committee]," reported U.S. historian Barbara Jancar.[11]

As I began collecting Polish women's stories, I kept the following questions in mind: If Solidarity's political leadership was male dominated, in what ways, then, had women participated? Were there particular issues or activities to which they gravitated? Did they demonstrate special organizing styles? Were there unsung heroines among them or any forgotten events?

The first clues surfaced when several women I interviewed in the summer and winter of 1990 made statements such as the following:

A group of women in Warsaw managed the Solidarity Press Agency after Solidarity was created; then they organized *Tygodnik Mazowsze* [Regional Weekly] during martial law; and after 1989, they created the first free press, *Gazeta Wyborcza* [Election Gazette].

When martial law was declared, women started the underground in Warsaw.

Men thought they were in charge, but women pulled all the strings.

Listening to first one woman's memories and then another's, I heard a subject ("a group of women"), a place ("the Warsaw underground"), an occupation ("the media"), and a date ("after the December 13 declaration of martial law") repeatedly linked. Alerted to the possibility that something of consequence might connect the individual stories being told, I formulated a new core interview question: "Where were you when martial law was declared, and what did you do?" The following picture emerged:

After Solidarity spent sixteen months flexing its newly legal political muscles, the government declared martial law and immediately arrested some ten thousand activists—around nine thousand men and one thousand women. With most of the male leadership either imprisoned or driven into hiding, a core group of women rose up to reconnect Solidarity's nationwide network of contacts, to protect the leaders in hiding from the secret police, to arrange meetings, and to smuggle money and equipment into the country. By January 1982 a uniquely all-female team based in Warsaw had pulled together unions and volunteers, moved typewriters and printing presses into attics and back rooms, and begun producing *Tygodnik Mazowsze,* which became the voice of Solidarity underground.

Working as a team, the women possessed the management skills, confidence, and media savvy to organize a large-scale, illegal publishing operation that served the entire nation, mobilized hundreds of thousands of individuals in support of Solidarity, and enlisted the help of thousands of supporting players—from reporters and printers to distributors and smugglers. The paper thus bolstered the growth of civil society under the repressive conditions of martial law, when it was humanly and technically almost impossible to coordinate nationwide activity.

Like nearly everyone else, the secret police were unaware that the leading newspaper of the 1980s underground was a female-run enterprise and that the thousands of people who helped produce and distribute it took their instructions from an all-woman editorial team. Blinded by sexism, the secret police hunted diligently for the men they assumed to be behind the newspaper— Solidarity men in hiding whose names had appeared in bylines. Keen to arrest and silence the paper's key personnel, the police completely overlooked its editors and publishers—Helena Łuczywo, Joanna Szczęsna, Anna Dodziuk, Anna Bikont, Zofia Bydlińska, and Małgorzata Pawlicka. They also overlooked Ewa Kulik, who coordinated the operations of the Warsaw underground in collaboration with *Tygodnik Mazowsze.* These seven women called themselves Damska Grupa Operacyjna (Ladies' Operations Unit), or simply DGO, and they form the core group of this study.[12]

Most of these women could trace their roots as oppositionists back as far as high school; many were involved in the brutally suppressed student protests of 1968; and by the mid- to late 1970s the majority had already anchored their activism in the arena of illegal publishing, which was just becoming a mainstay of the growing democratic opposition. When Solidarity became legal, many of the DGO women ran the Solidarity Press Agency, called AS, communist Poland's first uncensored news service and digest. During martial law they made *Tygodnik Mazowsze* a reality. And when it was time to clear the political ground for democratic governance in 1989, they founded the first postcommunist daily, *Gazeta Wyborcza.*

Beginning with their work at AS, the women shaped illegal publishing into an instrument of civic activism. They made a point of building up their communication channels so they could be used to foster a well-informed society. They planned media strategies on the premise that knowledge is power and communication is the underpinning of action. By December 13, 1981, they were already skilled at publishing and distributing newspapers, organizing protests, and petitioning the government, and when martial law cracked down, they reacted immediately. Determined to outmaneuver the military junta, these women were poised to lead the telerevolution.

Martial law was not a time for spectacular actions, for demonstrating, organizing public events, or making speeches. "To throw a bomb against [the authorities] would have been suicide," Polish émigré author Irena Grudzińska-Gross told me in 1991. "The road to salvation [was] in thinking and creating. . . . Without *Tygodnik Mazowsze,* the underground could not have existed. It was a forum in which political opinions and declarations could be made. It was a link among people in finding sympathizers in a dangerous time when people were dispirited."

In a 1999 interview that appeared in *Media Studies Journal,* Polish-born journalist Anna Husarska confirmed what Irena and several Solidarity women had told me years earlier. "The media and especially the print media *were* Solidarity. All right, Solidarity was a trade union and the workers had demands and the intellectuals supported the workers, but the civil society in Poland was built through the underground press. Almost everybody was involved in either the writing or the printing or the distributing or the trans-porting or even the producing of the ink. Everyone felt involved."[13] What Husarska did not note or explore, either in this article or in her 1989 piece in the Book Section of the Sunday *New York Times*,[14] were the identities of the women behind the underground press she described and analyzed.

In 1985 Barbara Jancar published an essay that discussed women's role in the Polish opposition in the 1970s and early 1980s.[15] She concluded that Solidarity's leadership was male dom-inated and that its reform agenda did not consider women's inter-ests outside the family. She also characterized women's activism at the time as having been spontaneous, symbolic, and endorsed by men. While her essay remains an important introduction to gender dynamics in the Polish opposition, it does not uncover the identities or the roles of women spearheading the opposition press, who were intellectuals, not working-class women. Jancar's main focus was on women workers because Solidarity was regarded as a working-class phenomenon. There was no indication in her findings that some women had already begun to institutionalize their distinctly female methods of operation at locations outside the realm of work-ers' strikes.

The view from inside the movement looked wholly different from what these outsiders had recorded. It came as a great sur-prise when I listened to Wrocław activist Barbara Labuda charac-terize women's role in the underground during our first interview in 1991. "Men didn't have the skills to manage the underground. Women were the brainpower," she declared. The women "chiefs," as she referred to the regional activists, rebuilt the communication channels, organized secret meetings, arranged for the transfers of money, found contacts at Western embassies, spoke to the press, and developed relations with local and foreign clergy. When Soli-darity members needed aid, they came to the women. When West-ern reporters requested interviews, they met with the women. "I gave a lot of the interviews but not in my name. I wrote all of the men's speeches," Barbara admitted. "My women friends in other regions share experiences similar to mine—we had to protect our own identities."

In order to protect their identities from discovery by the government or the secret police, the *Tygodnik Mazowsze* editors insisted on anonymity when speaking to the Western press and perpetuated the myth of working-class men as the superstars of resistance. They worked behind the scenes as invisible organizers in order to publicize the words, deeds, and leadership of their male colleagues. Strategically, they felt that this was the way to gain popular support and to rebuild the splintered movement. And they succeeded.

Journalist Lawrence Weschler was absolutely right to worry—in his 1982 collection of spell-binding reports entitled *Solidarity: Poland in the Season of Its Passion*[16]—that media coverage of underground activists could have jeopardized their lives in the final decade of one-party rule. However, this does not explain why the Western press did not return to the topic of women's contributions to the prodemocracy movement when they covered the 1989 changeover and the early transition years. One might surmise that *Tygodnik Mazowsze* was yesterday's news by 1989. But it wasn't, actually, because that was the year its staff and editors went public and declared the role they had played. Then several of them took another set of bold, pioneering, and equally newsworthy steps.

Having shed their anonymity, they announced the formation of *Gazeta Wyborcza,* the first postcommunist daily, and it should have been clear that these women editors were planting the seeds of an independent press in Poland. But their strategy of invisibility, so effective in the underground, worked too well, and somehow Adam Michnik got sole credit for starting *Gazeta Wyborcza.* For example, writing on the tenth anniversary of the 1989 revolution, Media Studies Center fellow Jay Rosen assigned credit as follows: "It is worth remembering that Solidarity was, among other things, a newspaper. Ordinarily, we would say that it *published* or put out a newspaper, but there was nothing ordinary about the act. The simple fact that the paper appeared and circulated meant that Solidarity stood for more than a struggling trade union. It was also an underground power capable of breaking into print, when print was supposed to be the stronghold of the state. It is no accident that one of its key figures, the writer Adam Michnik, is today the top editor of the leading—and most profitable—newspaper in Poland, *Gazeta Wyborcza.*"[17]

Not even Timothy Garton Ash's 1999 *New Yorker* profile of publisher Helena Łuczywo, the brains behind *Gazeta Wyborcza*'s popular and stock market successes, took seriously her leadership during martial law or the contributions of her all-female editorial team. He remembered Helena in the 1980s as a "pale, short, slightly built woman with untidy brown hair and intense gray-green eyes" and recalled the *Tygodnik Mazowsze* editors as "wan, intense women, dashing in with news of some crisis."[18] Appearance seems to have been more memorable than contribution.

It is perhaps a telling irony that the male-dominated Western press universally overlooked the significance of the birth of an independent press in Poland that was, perhaps uniquely, *not* dominated by men.

That may help explain why, here in the United States, we bought the Solidarity legend so thoroughly that, even when provided with concrete evidence, it was difficult to believe that women had played a Founding Mothers' role in the Polish revolution. Once the male myth had been entrenched, it was not easy to make room for a new story that included women. Even several U.S. feminists were incredulous and puzzled. I recall a particularly memorable conversation that took place in New Haven, Connecticut, in the spring of 1991. A small group of feminist academics and I were having lunch during one of those early 1990s conferences on what was commonly referred to as "The Transition." I had just completed my first round of interviews with several *Tygodnik Mazowsze* editors and other activists in Poland and described to my table mates the substantive role women had played, a role no one in Poland had formally acknowledged and no Western journalist had yet reported. Their reaction helped to shape a significant aspect of my subsequent research.

I had thought my feminist peers would welcome the news that Polish women had performed a leadership role in the Solidarity revolution, but my news was met by an unanticipated and vehement rejection. If women had taken charge, several women challenged, why hadn't they sought out international feminist support? Why hadn't they made contact with their Western sisters?

These Americans, all feminists who had helped organize the country's second-wave women's movement in the late 1960s and early 1970s, assumed that it could not have been possible for Polish women to make a powerful intervention without first undergoing a feminist awakening. It did not seem plausible that men would relinquish control or that women would assert themselves and move into positions of authority without first having gone through a power struggle. If Solidarity women had not thus come to terms with the patriarchal norms that colored their political movement and the society at large, then surely they must have spent their activist days making coffee for the men. That was what women in the U.S. civil rights movement and the New Left had been expected to do. The American feminists found it incredible that without challenging the patriarchal values that relegated women to brewing the coffee, without an attendant explosion, Polish women had been able to take command of a political crisis. How had they been able to do so? That was the underlying question these feminists highlighted for me, one that I realized I could not yet answer.

Clearly it bothered these American feminists that Polish women, who were invested in the radical political trends of the sixties, hadn't drawn the same two seminal conclusions as they had—that is, that societal ills are not only external but also internal and that a woman cannot access power without openly demanding it.

Because the experiences of Solidarity's unsung heroines embody such a radical departure from the American social change experience, it took me some time to penetrate Polish culture sufficiently to absorb certain of its inherent meanings, particularly regarding how women and men alike were both shaped and transformed by political resistance to authoritarian rule.

The reasons Polish women did not confront their men or develop a feminist consciousness stemmed from a cultural tradition that may sound like hyperbole or melodrama to Western ears but that Polish women have deeply internalized. This tradition stems from a historic link between Catholicism and nationalism that may have acted to rule out feminism in Poland.

A Polish woman's iconic duty, which began evolving in the late eighteenth century, is to mother the struggling nation. She must support her terribly disempowered men, who have martyred themselves in the quest to regain independence for a nation that has known so few years of freedom. A woman must carry out this culturally prescribed role heroically, anonymously, and without dreams of her own fulfillment. For her sacrifice, strength, and faultless virtue, she will be rewarded with an elevated status in her family, with odes to her moral authority, and with much hand kissing.

The role model for these expectations is the deeply embedded cultural icon of the Polish Mother, Matka Polka.[19] She first appeared in a poem by the celebrated Romantic poet Adam Mickiewicz (1798–1855). The poem, written in the wake of one of the nineteenth century's failed uprisings against the Russian occupiers, celebrates the heroic mother who raises her sons to martyr themselves for the nation. This icon defined a way of life for Polish women that lasted into and beyond the communist era.

After Poland was first partitioned by the Russians, Prussians, and Austrians, the question of cultural survival loomed large, given that no one could foresee how long Poles would remain stateless. It was then that the Polish Romantic myth was born—a myth in which Matka Polka figures prominently. Fused with Catholicism, Poland could then be reenvisioned as the "Christ of nations," which suffers humanity's burdens in its struggle for statehood. This image remained unchallenged for centuries.

At the center of the struggle, "surrounded with a halo of grandeur and beauty, stands the male hero—the knight, the soldier, the fighter, the unbroken prisoner, the leader," writes Maria Janion, Poland's preeminent scholar of nineteenth-century Romanticism.[20] Solidarity heroes such as Wałęsa and Adam Michnik were perfectly placed (in life and in the media) to fill the role of the romantic male figure. As the male's complement, there also is a perfectly realized romantic female figure, who carries her own halo of grandeur and beauty. She is the Black Madonna, recast in the nineteenth century as Matka Polka. The Black Madonna has been Poland's emblem of protection since 1655, when, presumably by the grace of her intervention, a battle against Swedish invaders was won in her name at the monastery at Jasna Góra. (During his days as the global voice of Solidarity, Lech Wałęsa took to wearing a tiny picture of the Black Madonna pinned to his shirt collar; and after receiving the Nobel Peace Prize in 1983 he placed the award at Jasna Góra.) Metamorphosed in the nineteenth century into Mickiewicz's hearth-tending patriot, Matka/Madonna has suffused the lives of Polish women ever since. Under her banner, women followed their husbands to Siberia during the partition era; filled in for men when they were imprisoned; armed themselves and fought the Nazis; and developed a repertoire of clever, pacifist tactics, often with religious themes, against the communists. The quiet anchor for her man and for the nation, she is also known as *bezmienne bohaterka* (nameless or anonymous heroine); she copes with hardships and pens letters to her incarcerated husband, reassuring him that "everything is okay."

Ingrained and bone deep, these mythic roles were, effectively, tools that reinforced the Solidarity ethos of "unity above all." For male and female oppositionists, that unity evolved from a network of loyalties forged, for some, as far back as their high school years. The power of these alliances became the brick and mortar of their activism—a liberating and defining experience. Women often described the opposition years to me with great poignancy—for them (and most of their peers) it was a time of intense, intimate experience, of belonging and loyalty to the group, and it represented wholly different personal experiences and cultural assumptions from mine or from those of others who participated in U.S. movements for social change. Thus, it took me years first to perceive and then to connect to the romantic structure underpinning the women's stories I recorded.

Eventually I realized that, without the operating romantic myths, the Solidarity women could not have accomplished what they did. They could not have found the energy to work twenty hours a week for over seven years, nor would they have been allowed to assume a strong central role in the opposition. Men stepped back and let women fill in because the supporting myth made women's activism socially acceptable and nonthreatening to the men, even when the women became larger than life—even larger than the ubiquitous tractor-driving heroines on Soviet posters. In their own eyes, the opposition women's underground achievements had not been revolutionary but necessary. Had they demanded recognition, they would have been making a revolutionary statement. They did not see the necessity of this.

In exchange for being allowed the adventure, Polish women

"agreed" to restrain their ambitions, to remain invisible, and to allow the men to reclaim power when the moment presented itself. I feel now that that culturally encoded agreement may qualify as having been the women's greatest unspoken sacrifice.

And, yet, though the Western press overlooked them, the Communist Party underestimated them, their male colleagues diminished their importance, and they themselves didn't demand recognition, none of these dynamic, unsung heroines emerged from the underground a victim. To the contrary, they were and are powerhouses. Each of them charged ahead into the post-1989 arena, driven by personal ambitions that have shaped prosperous careers and, for some, new families. Today, in their illustrious pursuits in the media, politics, and the foundation world, they are Poland's new liberal elite and resemble America's professional class, except that their successes came from overthrowing the old government and mining power from the new system they helped to shape. They all pushed hard for Poland's membership in the European Union (EU), which they think will strengthen liberal norms and practices, and they celebrated ecstatically on May 1, 2004, when Poland led the candidate countries into the newly expanded EU.

Although society's failure to recognize the *Tygodnik Mazowsze* women's crucial role in bringing democracy to Poland did not prevent their having achieved individual success, Polish women as a social group have borne heavy consequences in the new democracy, for the country's denial of women's political contributions in one era helped justify the marginalization of their participation in the subsequent one. Since 1989 women have shouldered a disproportionate share of the costs of privatization, such as the highest unemployment rates, and have suffered from policy reversals that have lost them many of the rights and benefits they knew under communism.

In the summer of 1990, when I first went to Poland, news of the political changeover's impact on women's social position was only just beginning to find mention in the United States, and I was still largely unaware of the implications. It was no easier to find information on the subject inside Poland, where, as in other postcommunist countries, women's issues were not being treated as a serious public policy concern. Think of the United States forty years ago, before the legal and social advances of second-wave feminism unraveled the fabric of gender relations. In that era before feminism took hold, when gender roles were assumed to be fixed and unchanging, few Americans wondered whether they had the option to change or to cast off their assigned role. So it was in Poland in 1990.

Although gender and women's studies had not developed in Poland when I began my field research in 1991, I was fortunate to meet Polish-born historian Bogna Lorence-Kot, who teaches in the San Francisco Bay Area.[21] She generously shared her then-unpublished research on Polish women's activism in nineteenth-century resistance movements. Her work and our 1991 conversations were paramount in shaping my ability to connect to and understand the complexities of gender roles in Poland. Gender studies scholarship did gradually develop in Poland, however, beginning in the early 1990s in Łódź, Warsaw, and Kraków, and I soon became part of and nourished by a multigenerational community of Polish feminist scholars. Their theoretical investigations into the culture's attitudes toward women greatly informed my own study of the Solidarity women and the national myths.

Gender scholarship focusing on the former Soviet Bloc region also evolved in the United States in the 1990s, but there have been relatively few studies of women, communism, and opposition as a triad.[22] Because Solidarity was regarded, first and foremost, as a trade union movement, these studies have mainly focused on working-class women or explore the construction of gender roles in a communist society with nationalist roots. Increasingly, however, new scholarship on the "Silences of Solidarity"—the title of a University of Michigan conference in September 2000—has delved into questions of gender, class, ethnicity, the various loci of dissent (urban areas, the provinces, the countryside), as well as grass roots opposition that was separate from Solidarity.

But while the field has opened up tremendously over the past fifteen years, during my first years of research, anyone who knew to listen for them would have been overwhelmed by "Solidarity's silences," especially regarding gender dynamics.

When I arrived in Warsaw, I learned that Westerners such as myself who came to Poland to do research or lend support in the aftermath of the 1989 political changeover were called "political tourists." Wherever a political tourist roamed, she was lucky if she had the support of a knowledgeable "political tour guide." A mutual acquaintance introduced me to Anka Grupińska upon my arrival in Warsaw.[23] We connected immediately, and she made a generous proposal: "I will lead you through Warsaw and lend you my eyes." With Anka as my guide, Solidarity women were willing to talk to me. Her name opened doors that might otherwise have remained shut to a Western feminist journalist.

In between interview sessions, Anka steered me through the city, revealing its historical dramas and secrets. She explained some of the postcommunist issues such as rising unemployment, ethnic conflict, and warring political factions, and she taught me how to navigate through the thoroughly dysfunctional bureaucracy. When I needed hard currency, Anka cautioned, "Never do business at a Polish bank," then escorted me to Victory Square to negotiate with moneychangers. When I needed to purchase train tickets, she led me through labyrinthine hallways to signless, dimly lit rooms, where tickets could be purchased without waiting in the chronically long lines at the train station. She taught me how to *załatwić*—the Polish word for "finagle," which applies to a customary mix of bartering, scrimping, saving, and sharing. It was the way people bypassed queues and shortages. Instead of waiting seven years for an apartment and five years for a car, friends, relatives, and acquaintances obtained such goods unofficially through loosely formed private networks or *środowisko* (milieu or social circle). This is a person's primary unit of social identification, a second family of sorts, based not on blood but on a mutual need to network. In a środowisko, people engage in załatwić. Later I would observe how these somewhat marginal, somewhat shadowy, thoroughly effective interactions imbued everyday life with the norms of an underground.

Anka also introduced me to contemporary writers and artists, to *bigos* and *shashlik,* and to Café Nowy Świat and the Wedel hot chocolate parlor. She drove her green Fiat Uno with missionary zeal. Her mission was to reclaim all the street names that the communists had changed. "It is my duty to ignore their fabrications," she declared. "I am familiar only with Warsaw's street names as they existed before the bloody communists took over."

Anka was especially well versed in the street names in what had been the Jewish ghetto. She showed me where Jewish resistance fighters had stored ammunitions in the old Brush Factory on Świrczynska Street. She identified the exact spot on the Umschlagplatz where Marek Edelman, the only then-surviving resistance leader, stood to observe the mass deportations of Jews to Treblinka. She pointed out the location of the ghetto wall where Teresa Prekerowa, a Catholic anti-Nazi activist, used to smuggle in food and smuggle out Jews. "After the two uprisings—the Ghetto Uprising in 1943 and the Warsaw Uprising in 1944—99 percent of the city ceased to exist," she told me. "Today, we call it 'the previous Warsaw'."

Although I am Jewish and Jewish themes have significantly influenced my sense of self and the world around me, it was questions of gender and power that were at the forefront of my consciousness. This was not the case for Anka, who had little interest in or awareness of her gender identity. However, the fact that I had studied Polish Jewish history and that Anka had toured the United States eased our moves across one another's cultural and psychological boundaries.

Most important, Anka helped me to develop my first set of interviews, offered to serve as my interpreter during my second visit (December 1990–January 1991), and arranged some of the interview appointments. I am eternally grateful for her enthusiastic assistance. "It's important to tell our stories before we're too old to appreciate them," she stressed. She believed the interviews would contribute missing pieces to the history of the democratic opposition, and she cared deeply about history, which is why she strongly advised me, "Just don't romanticize us. And please don't judge us. *See* us."

I've often been asked why, if the Solidarity women so fervently embraced anonymity, they agreed to be interviewed by me? I think it was because I first went to Poland at just the right time. June 1990 was the one-year anniversary of the new democracy, and people were still celebrating their victory. It was an exciting, spirited time. The impossible had been done. Borders had opened, life had opened, minds had opened, and women were available to tell their stories while their memories were still fresh. I was lucky. This opening narrowed when people began to confront the new demands on their lives that resulted from the political and economic reconstruction; but between 1990 and 1992 women sat with me for whole afternoons and evenings, drinking tea, smoking cigarettes, and discussing their lives and the communist norm.

I interviewed women of diverse ages and backgrounds: trade union organizers, bibuła editors, shipyard engineers, factory workers, medical doctors, nurses, academics and students, writers and artists, environmentalists, and peace activists. One woman introduced me to another, and that woman introduced me to her friends, her sisters and cousins, her mother and grandmother, until I had a list of names and addresses that covered the whole country. I traveled to several hubs of anticommunist activism—including Warsaw, Gdańsk, Łódź, Kraków, and Lublin—and interviewed many more women and men than I was able to include in this book. However, all of their stories lived in me as I wrote each chapter.

Some women I interviewed were eager to meet their first American and flattered to be interviewed. The key women players in the opposition, however, were accustomed to talking to Western journalists and writers like myself, although for most of them this was the first time they had been the subject rather than the interviewer or the media contact. Some of the women were quite pleased to have the opportunity to tell their own stories and enjoyed the thought of being profiled in the American press. Mostly writers and journalists themselves, they were familiar with and liked the American publications that reported Solidarity stories, and they probably thought that their stories, as filtered through me, would be added to the legend as already reported, would fill in the details in support of the main (male) story line. It was a story line they knew all too well because they had helped to script it.

I seriously doubt that these women realized at the time, for certainly I did not, that in retelling and reconstructing their narrative I would make them feel exposed and vulnerable, would put them in the risky position they had endeavored to avoid during communist times. Publication of my research, particularly in Poland, was going to make them visible, to "out" them, and it was not until later that we all wondered if that would bring negative consequences for them in their culture. But in 1990–92 such considerations were still in the future, and most of the women spoke openly and candidly. With little prodding from me, their words flowed. To my surprise, however, one activist later changed her mind about having her story published. In 2001, ten years after our first interview and three years after our final session, she told me she regretted having revealed herself. A union organizer, she was one of the few women to have criticized gender discrimination in the opposition. After much back-and-forth, we eventually agreed that she would be included as a nameless, faceless heroine. Her request and her unusual story exemplify the silenced plight of the anonymous heroine in Polish history. To underscore that gendered fate, I have given her the pseudonym Magdalena X.

Not everyone I asked agreed to speak to me. Some activists refused instantly when they heard that the subject of my research was women's opposition experiences. They suspected—correctly—that I must be a Western feminist because only a feminist would care to study women separately from men, and they didn't trust feminism or the implications of gender differences. Sometimes, a sensitive, persuasive interpreter would have to coax a person into being interviewed. Sometimes, an interview session would begin with the interviewee asking me to define feminism, and then a debate would ensue.

Mostly, these feminist-shy women wanted to know why I chose to study women's lives separately from men's lives, given that the communists had been equal opportunity oppressors. Oppression comes in many forms, I used to respond. I had not anticipated that my research topic would be considered novel in a country that had once had stronger equal rights laws than we have in the United States. It did not take me long to realize that what I was studying were the differences within a grass roots movement that had been based on solidarity and on postponing dealing with differences.

Most of my interviewees forthrightly declared that they were not feminists and had no intention of adopting another ideology when they had just discarded one. My point during such sometimes lengthy preinterview discussions was not to convert "nonbelievers" but to satisfy a mutual need to understand each other's thinking before we entered personal material. I have to admit, though, that I had not at all expected that in these conversations I would be asked to explain why I claim a feminist identity. Who was interviewing whom? I was also intrigued to realize that my interviewees were hungry for a feminist debate, if only to tell me what was wrong with feminism. Or perhaps it was also because our meeting provided a rare opportunity to entertain feminist notions.

"Communism did not solve the 'woman question,'" my interviewees told me again and again, and they wanted to figure out why. These conversations often helped to bridge uncomfortable assumptions about our very different experiences and perspectives. Thus, a breakdown of cold war divisions began in the living rooms and offices where we met and indulged a mutual curiosity that sometimes overcame preconceptions.

Whether conducted in English or in Polish with the aid of an interpreter, the interviews were, for me, an enthralling exercise in both seeing and listening. The interpreters—most of whom informed me that they were not feminists as soon as they learned of my research topic—listened with a fascination equal to my own as interviewees answered my questions about personal background, their family's position in the communist system, and how a woman awakened politically and became involved in the opposition. The interviews stirred in us a wide-eyed interest in the common facets of female experience in a communist system: the mass entry of women into the postwar labor force ("our forced emancipation"), the widespread use of abortion as contraception, the humiliating hospital conditions in which women gave birth, the utter sham of legal equality, and the exhausting "double burden" of domestic and workplace labor.

More often than not, women discussed the communist formula for women's liberation with bitter cynicism. I had thought, prior to coming to Central Europe, that state socialist systems had translated the principle of gender equality into respectable laws. I had thought that Eastern Bloc and Soviet women had already achieved, without a comparable struggle, the same rights and benefits that North American and Western European women had spent most of the twentieth century championing—equal employment laws; educational opportunities; child-care services; and progressive legislation on marriage, divorce, abortion, and maternal protection. Equal rights were incorporated into the constitution of postwar Poland in 1952. Birth control was free. Women were guaranteed one to three years of paid maternity leave for each child born and could return to their former workplaces if they so chose.

However, in the transition from theory to praxis, the socialist promise that women's participation in the paid labor force would win them their freedom had come to signify a grotesque propaganda lie. According to statistics, women generally worked four to six more hours per day than did men and earned 20 to 25 percent less. They also lagged behind in selection and promotion. No household could manage well on the salary of a single wage earner. Many women, like men, held down two jobs. This was especially the case for single mothers. While most women married young—the average age was twenty-three—one out of every two marriages ended in divorce before the women entered their thirties. With or without husbands, women were primarily responsible for maintaining the household and family life. Structures such as day-care centers, intended to support working mothers, were insufficiently managed, overcrowded, unwelcoming, and often far from home. Although more women than men earned advanced academic degrees, what this, sadly, produced was a highly qualified, underutilized labor reserve.

In Eastern and Central Europe, the use of women's labor power was driven by the need to rapidly industrialize the devastated post–World War II economies. The lofty ideals of equality and freedom were often obscured by the practical need to bring women into the labor force. Everyone had to work. Though there were advantages to the education and employment opportunities women enjoyed, these did not include any significant rearrangements of relations between the sexes. Men and women did not share power, as may have been envisioned by those who embraced the ideals. By naming capitalism as women's true enemy, the dominance of men over women in the socialist workplace and home could be over-looked. Men's role as fathers was not reimagined, and, consequently, women's role as their families' primary caretakers continued as if women were not also working full-time. Women's social position, the real litmus test for equality, remained bound to patriarchal norms.

That's why many women told me that "the law was reformed, but not the social reality." Matka Polka had been hoisted onto a tractor seat, her Soviet-red necktie flapping in the wind, so that she could help rebuild Poland's devastated postwar economy. This *super-kobieta* (superwoman) remained as self-sacrificing as her predecessors, scouring the city for food and standing in four-hour queues just to feed her family. Her labors were performed in the service of a higher good, and she accepted her unfair fate because she already knew the authorities would never allow women to improve their social reality.

Before I did research in Poland and other Central European countries, it was difficult to imagine a feminism that excluded women from actively defining their rights. The tragedy, I concluded from the interviews, was that gender equality under communism had become so closely, narrowly identified with a corrupt form of governance that women no longer trusted any feminist discourse, no matter what the origins. This led me to wonder the following: Would the association of feminism with communism jeopardize women's options in their evolving democracies? Would the citizens of new democracies eventually disentangle feminism from the communist experience?

The isolation wrought by censorship and propaganda had built walls not only between countries but within them as well. The interviews provided a rare opportunity for all present to hear and value women's honestly remembered lives, and I felt privileged to observe as women made connections between their own experiences and those of others. When an interpreter from Warsaw remarked, "We women have been similarly oppressed," she helped me to understand that the "woman question" had not been solved under communism, only profoundly silenced. Occasionally, an interpreter would become so engaged in an interview that she would forget my presence and would begin asking her own questions in

Polish, oblivious to my objections. "Please tell me what is being said," I recall asking during one meeting in Warsaw. "Shh, I will tell you later," the interpreter hushed me. After another interview, an interpreter said playfully, "You see? Polish women don't have to be feminists to be fascinating." I responded, "But the ability to value women's lives *is* a feminist sensibility." She pondered awhile before replying, "Perhaps I am a feminist."

When I asked some of my first interviewees who they thought were the most important women activists, the same four names always came up without hesitation: Helena Łuczywo, Barbara Labuda, Joanna Szczęsna, and Ewa Kulik. Each recognized that these women, and the others that some of them also named, had played vital roles in the democratic opposition. But when I then asked, "Are you saying that these women were leaders of Solidarity?" they responded either by negating my inference—"Don't exaggerate!"—or by saying that they were not certain.

Thus, a major focus of my book became to explore the meanings of statements such as "Women started the underground" and "Women pulled all the strings" and the implications of "Don't exaggerate!"

It's no exaggeration, however, to underscore that the *Tygodnik Mazowsze* editors had the unique capacity to institutionalize their endeavors, thus distinguishing their activism from other forms of Polish women's protest, forms that Barbara Jancar aptly labeled as symbolic, spontaneous, and unsustainable. In contrast, these pages depict a group of women whose development as agents of social change was continuous and built upon itself, located as it was in the media. They grew stronger in each successive chapter of opposition history, and so did the illegal press. But their influence expanded only up to a point and only as individual women whose central roles in the opposition were validated by the men who endorsed their specific roles. This is why in 1989 they were not publicly credited for their important contributions to the revolution's success. Without that credit, they were able to carry on in the realm of media but not in politics. And they were not allowed, and did not try, to make demands on behalf of women as a social group.

Then, suddenly, the final straw approached the camel's back. Instead of fully enfranchising Polish women, the new parliament proposed to introduce a ban on abortion in 1989. As nothing else did or perhaps could have done, this sparked the beginnings of a feminist movement in Poland, which fought an uphill battle to stop the draft legislation from being passed. But it was put into law in 1993, and over the next six years the defeated feminists had to regroup and develop a proactive strategy.

While this regrouping was under way, an article entitled the "The National Secret," which I had published in the United States, had been translated into Polish and appeared in *Pełnym Głosem,* a Kraków feminist journal, in 1994.[24] This article was read by feminists and taught in gender studies courses in Poland for several years but received no wider attention. And then, in June 1999, Warsaw feminist Agnieszka Graff cited it in an opinion piece she wrote, which was published in *Gazeta Wyborcza,* the Polish equivalent of the *New York Times* and the very newspaper the *Tygodnik Mazowsze* editors founded in 1989.

"Penn's article was shocking, yet Poland's national press was completely silent about it," Agnieszka wrote.[25] A foreigner had lifted the curtain on Polish women's hidden history, and the news set off an unprecedented controversy in the media, which continued for months and marked the first major public debate on women and political power in Poland's mainstream press. Moreover, it erupted during the country's celebrations of the revolution's tenth anniversary year.

Agnieszka Graff's article, sparked by my interviews with Solidarity women, called into public question the Solidarity legend as it had been received through the press. Suddenly, and for the first time, the revealed role of women mattered, and people were either excited or outraged. Without having intended it, it seemed as if my involvement in the Polish discourse on feminism, begun in my earliest interviews, was to be ongoing.

Back in 1991, perhaps anticipating that one day such a controversy might erupt, Barbara Labuda, a leading Solidarity organizer from Wrocław, asked me, "Isn't it too late to change the story that has already been presented to the world?" The answer is still not clear. But today democratic Poland has finally come to a point where it can claim its Founding Mothers—if it chooses to come to terms with the contributions made by its Solidarity heroines.

1. Women at the Gates
anna walentynowicz and the august 1980 strikes

The truism that "the past is prologue" asserted itself time and again in my research on women's involvement in Solidarity. It became clear to me that, before one could understand women's role in organizing the post–martial law underground, two formative earlier events—prologues to the underground—had to be deciphered. The first of these, the political fate of women workers in the 1980 nationwide strikes that birthed Solidarity, is investigated in this chapter. The second, the building of Solidarity's infrastructure immediately following those strikes and the roles that women were allotted in the movement during its brief legal life, is the focus of chapter 2.

Workers had been rebelling against the Polish workers' state since the mid-1950s. The key images of dissent, to quote historian Padraic Kenney, were of "men and boys throwing rocks at police, or being gunned down, or kneeling in prayer, women passing sandwiches to strikers over factory walls or sitting numbly on courthouse benches as their husbands are sent to prison."[1] Kenney stresses that such images reinforce the assumptions that women were not actively involved in opposition, usually stood on the margins, and, at best, performed supporting roles to their men.

Both the time-honored images and their accompanying assumptions reached their apogee in the famous summer strikes of 1980. But women were not just helpmates in 1980; they were fundamental to mobilizing Solidarity's successful grass roots popular movement. Then, at the moment of the nation's collective victory over one-party rule at the end of August 1980, they were sidelined by male trade union organizers. The women who had been crucial to the strike's success met a powerful rejection, both of themselves and of the new Solidarity movement's avowed democratic principles. That rejection, and the cultural history that drove it, helps explain many of the choices the Damska Grupa Operacyjna would later make during and after martial law.

The fate of Anna Walentynowicz, in 1980 a middle-aged crane operator at the Gdańsk shipyards, is particularly illustrative of how Solidarity treated women. Although Anna was as different as she could have been from the young Warsaw intellectuals who would eventually rescue Solidarity from martial law, her lesson was not lost on the women editors (or on other women throughout Poland).

Anna had been at the center of the events that birthed Solidarity, and along with Lech Wałęsa she virtually personified the 1980 Gdańsk strikes in the public eye. I met with her in Gdańsk in 2000 and was amazed to find that, well into her seventies, she had lost little of the pugnacious spunk that came through so clearly in the 1980 accounts of her role in the strike. An antiabortionist and devout Catholic, and certainly one of the least understood firebrands of the great August strikes, she is far from being a feminist—but she was and remains a fighter. "I will always fight," she declared during our meeting, her eyes gleaming with defiance and her arms crossed over her chest. We sat in her living room, a short distance from the shipyard, surrounded by portraits of John Paul II and icons of the Virgin Mary. Her long, pure-white hair was tied back at her nape, and, though diminutive, she looked muscular and compact, like a retired gymnast. She exuded strength, both inside and out. It is precisely this fighting spirit that elevates her above being merely a bitter victim of the gender and class bias that conspired to silence her and the other women who made Solidarity's victory possible.

Solidarity was born of strikes by shipyard, factory, and transportation workers that fanned out across the nation in July and August 1980 until an estimated one million workers had added their weight to the nonviolent protests and in a few short weeks turned them into the world's largest ever strike. The wave of strikes began with an unexpected increase in food prices, a move on the part of government that had triggered many previous strikes. But this time something unprecedented happened, and the protest was quickly transformed into an "all for one and one for all" solidarity strike.

The Inter-factory Strike Committee (MKS) at the Lenin Shipyard in Gdańsk became the organizing hub for almost all the strikes during what became known as "Polish August." Representing strikers nationwide, during the final, suspenseful weeks of the strikes, the MKS drafted twenty-one demands and then, in an unprecedented development, negotiated them face-to-face with Communist Party officials. The demands went far beyond the typical bread-and-butter trade union issues, and in the end the often rancorous talks between the rulers and the ruled produced a veritable human rights manifesto for communist Poland (if that is not an oxymoron).

The people of Poland had laid down their work tools and their differences in class, religion, and gender to achieve a landmark victory that was unmatched in Soviet Bloc history; as a result, on August 31, 1980, Solidarity—the name, the boisterous red logo, and the mass-based movement—was born. This set in motion a social revolution, which in nine years' time would help bring about the collapse of the Polish communist system and, by extension, of the entire Soviet Bloc.

In 1991 I visited Gdańsk, a blustery port city on the Baltic Sea, to talk with people about the contributions local women had made to the creation of the free trade union movement. "The catalyst for the August 1980 strikes was a woman," Małgorzata Tarasiewicz, a former Wolność i Pokój (WiP, or Freedom and Peace[2]) activist, stated categorically. Andrzej Gwiazda, one of the principal strike leaders, elaborated on this point by explaining to me that, in addition to one woman, Anna Walentynowicz, having catalyzed the strike, "Several women saved the strike at a pivotal moment." Their actions had made headline news back in 1980—not in the state-controlled press, of course, but certainly in the opposition press and in later reports by Western journalists and historians such as Neal Ascherson and Timothy Garton Ash.[3]

I would soon come to realize that the 1980 strikes marked one of the very few times in Polish opposition history when women and men openly shared the political stage. It was also one of the almost equally rare occasions when the media duly portrayed women as being essential at every level—from organizing the strikes and articulating the goal of social solidarity to drafting the demands and participating in the grueling negotiations. In previous protests, women, particularly working-class women, customarily played secondary roles as wives, girlfriends, sisters, and daughters—that is, they contributed as females, as private persons, but not as fellow workers or citizens. They were considered to be properly showing their support for the male strikers by standing *outside* the factory gates, not by crowding into the factory yard or barricading the gates.

During Polish August, however, women were characterized in the media and among co-workers as catalytic, pivotal, strategic, outspoken, magnetic, and persistent strikers *inside* the gates of the Lenin Shipyard. For seventeen glorious days, the spotlight shone on women, particularly those who served on or advised the MKS, whether they were addressing thousands of their fellow strikers, facing down government negotiators, or skillfully reporting on the strike's progress to the assembled foreign press corps. (Women's inside activism did not, however, deter hundreds of wives and girlfriends from dutifully pressing against the gates from the outside every day, in a vitally important show of support.)

The women-friendly environment inside the Lenin Shipyard can be attributed, in part, to the fact that the handful of women and men who organized the August strike and formed the MKS had already worked together as organizers for over two years. They attributed much of the strike's success to their preexisting bonds as fellow workers, longtime friends, siblings, and married or romantically involved couples. Even though the social cohesion that fueled the strike's eventual victory disintegrated rapidly after Solidarity became legal, during the strike, women were allowed to perform crucial roles and were appreciated for their contributions to a popular rebellion waged in the name of solidarity.

"We are all equal in the shipyard" became the broad and inclusive motto of the strikes. Differences were tolerated in order to present what was perceived to be a unified challenge to the state. An unusual tacit alliance made in the late 1970s among workers, intellectuals, and Catholic Church leaders enabled people to bridge political, intellectual, and class differences in 1980, at least temporarily. Slogans such as "We are all in this together" were deeply felt, and the word *we* applied to people of all ages and backgrounds who were involved in the strike—workers, priests, farmers, writers, students, and even women.

But although many women were involved in the 1980 strikes, some pivotally, only Anna Walentynowicz's name truly lived on, and it has done so in both fame and notoriety. At the time a fifty-one-year-old crane operator at the Lenin Shipyard, Anna was and remains associated with the rise of Solidarity more than anyone, save Lech Wałęsa, who played the leading man to her leading lady during the strike. Lech won the Nobel Peace Prize in 1983 and eventually was elected president of Poland. Anna briefly became a beloved national heroine but never rose to the political leadership that she secretly coveted. Instead, according to media and personal accounts, she metamorphosed into a cranky, moralizing, antagonistic pensioner who could not restrain her jealousy of Lech or her feeling that she had been abandoned by the workers to whom she had devoted herself. Indeed, she *had* been abandoned.

In her time, however, Anna was much lauded and embraced. For her crucial role in winning free trade unions from a communist regime, she became the distinguished guest of Pope John Paul II and global heads of state, the inspiring subject of films and theater, and Woman of the Year in the Netherlands. British journalist Neal Ascherson called her the "most powerful orator in the whole strike movement." In the eyes of British historian Timothy Garton Ash, she was "Mother Courage . . . the most popular member of the Free Trade Unions on the Coast."[4]

Within the Lenin Shipyard, admiration of Anna long predated the decisive strike. Indeed, her co-workers were so devoted to her that it was her unjust firing in the summer of 1980 that became the catalyst for the strike that touched off Polish August. Never before had a strike been called on such a simple, noneconomic premise—the plight of one feisty, forthright female worker.

Anna had lived alone in Gdańsk, in the same modest apartment where we were to meet in 2000, since she was widowed in 1971 after seven years of marriage. She was single when her only child, Janusz, was born in 1952, and the two of them lived for several years in a state institution. Though a devout Catholic, Anna had decided not to marry the child's father, about whom she commented with characteristic bluntness, "I won't tell you anything about my son's father because it's just not worth the effort." In 1964 she married a locksmith at the shipyard, Kazimierz, who adopted her son and took care of Anna during her near-fatal bout with cancer. The doctors had told her in 1964 that she had five years left to live, and when she proved them wrong and recovered, she felt her life had been spared so that she could accomplish something worthwhile. Early in 1971 Anna grew determined to fight the communist lie. With her husband recently dead of cancer and her son grown up, she actually felt she had less to fear now that she was alone.

The disastrous food price strikes of mid-December 1970 were the catalyst for Anna's decision. Workers on the Baltic coast had struck to protest an unexpected rise in food prices—imposed just before Christmas. At one point, demonstrators in Gdańsk raced to party headquarters to set it on fire, which reminded everyone of riots in the western city of Poznań in 1956, just as the Stalinists' grip on Poland was beginning to loosen. Angry Poznań workers had risen in protest against economic conditions, charged through the streets, and attacked the local party headquarters. They were gunned down by the police, who wounded an estimated nine hundred people and killed as many as seventy-five. In 1970 gunfire stopped the morning shift of workers at the shipyard in Gdynia, which neighbors Gdańsk. This incited strikes in other cities, and the military again retaliated, killing dozens of strikers.

Fearing an uncontrollable insurrection, the party deposed First Secretary Władysław Gomułka and replaced him with Edward Gierek, a former coal miner. Gierek flew to a shipyard site to talk, listen, argue, and negotiate with strikers. "I am only a worker like you," he postured humbly. "Will you help me?" "We'll help you," the workers shouted in response. By the end of January, what had begun with bloodshed ended in peaceful negotiations. But this mediation did not pacify Anna.

Much of the story of Anna's early years is typical of Poland's pre-war working-class population. Born in 1929 in the Wolyn region of southeast Poland, she was ten years old when Nazi Germany invaded Poland on September 1, 1939. World War II ripped apart the fabric of her family life and hurtled her, at a very young age, into a new and harsh world. She fell prey to a Nazi decree that halted the education of all Poles after the fourth grade, and she never returned to school. Her father was killed in the war effort, her brother was deported, and before the war's end her mother died of a heart attack. The orphaned Anna wandered north, working her way from village to village. She harvested, sold kitchen knives, and made whiskey. She lived with a family of farmers for several years, working like an indentured servant, until she could no longer bear the drudgery and ran away to the Baltic coast.

Anna's wartime experience of loss and relocation was shared by millions of Poles, who suffered not only under Nazi occupation but also from the Soviet Union's invasion of Poland's eastern boundaries sixteen days after the Germans stormed its western borders. The devastating impact of having been invaded twice at the start of World War II helps explain the impulses that drove Poland's wartime and postwar generations to fight so hard for freedom in the second half of the twentieth century—for, on the one hand, the Soviets rivaled the Nazis in their brutal military abuses and, on the other hand, while the Jews had been the primary targets on Hitler's death list, the Poles had been given the number two spot.

Through a series of decrees, the Nazis aimed to create a Poland made up solely of uneducated laborers (hence the law that stopped Anna's schooling), and they came close to succeeding in their ethnic cleansing program. Beginning in 1940, Heinrich Himmler, head of all German police forces, led a campaign to eliminate Polish teachers, artists, priests, and politicians and to move populations out of their native regions. After ridding the land of the racially inferior Poles, it was to provide *lebensraum* (living space) for the growing Aryan nation.

By the war's end in 1945, Poland was everywhere devastated. Sixty percent of the industrial base was demolished, as was every major city, save beautiful, medieval Kraków in southern Poland. About 12 percent of the country's Polish population—approximately five million people, three million of them Jews—had died or been killed. Mass graves stretched beneath miles of forest and meadows, inside and outside of the extermination camps. Much of the surviving population, like Anna, had been dislocated. Two million were deported to slave labor camps. As a result of relocation, border changes, or death, the country's other ethnic groups were also gone by 1945—the Germans were expelled, and the Lithuanians, Ukrainians, and Byelorussians were hurled into the Soviet orb. The prewar population of thirty-eight million had dwindled to twenty-four million. Instead of providing lebensraum, Poland survived Nazism as a barely livable space.

During the war, the Soviets were busy setting the stage for their postwar takeover. Afterward, they cruelly exploited the war's trauma by continuing to terrorize the population and lie about the wartime era. This helps explain why many people I interviewed hold the Soviets as accountable as the Nazis for the destruction of their country. Everyone who endured the twin evils of the Nazi and Soviet occupations was a survivor. Enmity toward the Soviets only intensified after the war, due in part to their extensive cover-up of their wartime misconduct, which started off with the signing of the secret Hitler-Stalin Pact just before the war on August 23, 1939. The USSR agreed to help Hitler dismantle Poland in return for being able to appropriate Poland's eastern territories and the Baltic states of Lithuania, Latvia, and Estonia, which Stalin wanted securely within his sphere. On September 17, 1939, Soviet Red Army troops crossed into Poland from the east, just sixteen days after Nazi Germany's invasion of Poland from the west, north, and south signaled the outbreak of World War II.

In 1940 the Soviets massacred and buried thousands of Polish army officers who had been interned in POW camps in the Katyn Forest near Smolensk, Russia. Stalin blamed the atrocity on Hitler's armies and vice versa. Soviets also forcibly deported an estimated two million Poles from eastern cities and towns to labor camps and prisons in desolate parts of the Soviet Union. By killing off its elites and uprooting whole communities, Stalin deliberately aimed to crush Poland's ability to restore its independence.

The most incriminating evidence of the Soviet's betrayal of Poland in the guise of being its liberator was the Red Army's blatant refusal to come to the aid of Polish resistance fighters during their 1944 Warsaw Uprising against the German military. The uprising lasted sixty-two days and received no assistance from the Red Army units camped just a mile from Warsaw's center. Nearly 160,000 Poles perished before the uprising ended. The Nazis rounded up and deported the survivors (only 162,000 of the city's prewar population of one million managed to survive World War II), then proceeded to bomb the city flat. When all but one-tenth of the buildings had been razed to the ground, the Red Army finally moved in from where it had been camped just across the river to chase out the Nazis and "liberate" a battered city that had been emptied of humanity.

Stalin then systematically eliminated all possible opposition to consolidating his conquest of Poland. In 1944 he had set up the Polish Committee of National Liberation, based in Moscow, as a rival to Poland's prewar leadership, which had been heading a government in exile in London since 1939. After Warsaw's "liberation," he moved the committee to eastern Poland and declared a provisional government,[5] which worked in coalition with the government in exile until 1947, when the communists seized complete control in a sweeping purge. The leaders and many members of Poland's political organizations were arrested, shuttled off to Moscow, or put on show trials at home and either executed or imprisoned.

The Poles use a special idiom to describe the communist distortions and outright lies—*białe plamy* (blank spots)—which refers to the ways in which the Soviets and the Polish Communist Party rewrote Polish history, erasing whole events and even legendary actors and epochs in an effort to reeducate public memory. Bolshevik fiction supplanted historical data, beginning with the most deceptive of the myths: *The Soviets liberated Poland from the Nazis.*

In addition to the postwar purges, there were also traumatic population transfers and border changes. At Stalin's command, Poland's borders were shifted: its eastern lands were folded into the USSR, and its western borders were pushed farther west, into defeated Germany. The redrawn borders uprooted many Poles and, along with the wartime deaths, wiped out Poland's identity as a multiethnic society with a richly diverse cultural heritage. In this, the Soviets had succeeded in manifesting one of Poland's greatest fears—cultural extinction. Poland had become a homoethnic society, and perhaps the only consolation was that, over subsequent decades, homogeneity would foster unity against the communists[6]—a unity based on the growing realization that the Soviet Red Army had driven out the Nazis in order to make their own predatory claims. The Soviet Union was Poland's captor, not its savior.

In 1950 a kindly man in Gdańsk suggested to Anna Walentynowicz that she apply for employment at the Lenin Shipyard. It would be a job with a future, she hoped, one where she could make something of herself. She was hired, and suddenly, after years of displacement and backbreaking work, she had a real job, wages, a home, and fellow workers. Thus, she did not, at first, see the new Polish government in a negative light. No longer treated like a peasant and indentured servant, she had been elevated to the highest status one could allegedly achieve in a communist system—she was a Worker. Anna took her new job as a welder very seriously because she felt that her labor ensured the safety of all who would board the ships. She was zealous in her allegiance to the communist work ethic—to sacrifice, to care for others, and to produce, produce, and produce.

Anna excelled in her new job. During 1950 and 1951, she felt hopeful and purposeful earning her first steady livelihood. Now she could care for herself and her infant son. She had bought into the era's propaganda posters of the happy, tractor-driving woman worker. Soon enough, the propaganda machine would discover her.

By the end of her first year, Anna was already officially recognized as a super-quota worker. In factory-sponsored competitions to produce the highest output, Anna had the highest score among all women welders—270 percent of the production norm. She got a medal, and management photographed her and the two runners-up, wearing overalls and goggles, for a display that was posted by the director's office. In 1951 Anna and other super-quota workers represented Poland at the annual Youth Festival and Congress of Trade Unions in Berlin.[7] To prepare for the international socialist event, the Polish participants were required to spend two weeks at a government-sponsored training camp learning how to march in step, to sing Soviet songs, to protect themselves from agents of imperialism, and to shun the temptation to remain in the West. At the festival, one or two members of the Polish contingent seemed to disappear each day, and the young delegates were told not to mention these occurrences when they returned home. The cover-up marked Anna's first contact with "living a lie," the first time her organization instructed her to deceive others, and it changed her life.[8]

Back at work in Gdańsk, Anna's eyes began to open. As a representative of the Women's League for her work collective, she met weekly with others to decide penalties and incentive awards. She noticed that at the meetings the men always spoke first, nominating their own people for premiums, so that when the women's turn came, the money had run out. Anna protested this unfair treatment. And not only were men earning larger bonuses than women, managers were filling their own pockets with some of the bonus money. The first time Anna saw her employer take a worker's money—"because he had dropped a lot of money playing the lottery"—she exposed the culprit publicly and demanded he return it. The following day the foreman informed her in a whisper, "Mrs. Anna, there was a phone call, you are asked to report to the office. If you should not come back, what about [your] child?"[9]

Most people who were called in for questioning stopped speaking out. Anna—brave, justified, but politically and strategically inexperienced—continued to expose wrongdoings. The time for organized collective action had not yet ripened, and Anna did not think to ask for her co-workers' support, but she certainly learned how to push the limits and get away with it. The authorities could demote her, isolate her, and threaten to fire her (and fire her they did—twice!), but she only grew bolder, louder, and more defiant. She had maybe seventeen thousand fellow workers as witnesses, and as they observed her repeated fist-shaking confrontations with management, they gradually awakened to their own passions.

Anna's and her fellow workers' awakenings were, in part, fostered by Poland's political climate at the time. For a short-lived period between the late 1950s and early 1960s, Polish society opened up. A relatively liberal atmosphere, a Soviet "thaw," had followed in the wake of Stalin's death in March 1953. By 1956 the entire Soviet orb had begun to spin on its axis. On February 25, Nikita Krushchev stood before the Soviet Party's Twentieth Congress and condemned Joseph Stalin and his reign of terror. The supposedly confidential speech exposing major episodes of Soviet tyranny was released to Warsaw Pact leaders and then circled the globe, without Krushchev's approval, setting off major shock waves.

The month after Krushchev's speech, First Secretary Bolesław Bierut of the Polish Communist Party died, and the two events sparked the unraveling of Stalinist rule in Poland. The Poznań rebellion that same year was the first such eruption in a satellite country, and it set off as many aftershocks as did Krushchev's revelations. The Polish Communist Party sought a new first secretary who would be able to calm the hot-tempered populace. It chose Władysław Gomułka, one of the few prewar communists to have survived Stalin's persecution twice—first during the purges of the 1930s and again in 1948, when Stalin had him imprisoned for espousing bold, though undeveloped, notions about a "Polish road to socialism." At that time, Gomułka had openly discouraged the collectivization of agriculture because he thought it would be nearly impossible to collectivize Poland's peasantry.

Released from prison after Stalin's death, Gomułka went from battered scapegoat to rising star in a frightening turnaround that was not uncommon among his political peers. Gomułka took office to face the formidable task of renewing popular faith in communism, which he did by promoting his Polish road to socialism. At first it seemed that Gomułka had ushered in a liberal era. For example, he tolerated the Catholic Church, making Poland the only Eastern Bloc country in which the Church was allowed a measure of autonomy. Clergy created a religious press in major cities, and the centuries-old Catholic University continued to educate students in the city of Lublin. Activist priests and their followers organized acts of charity, which encompassed activities that ranged from feeding the poor and preserving religious monuments to recording the government's human rights abuses against the

Catholic faithful and sheltering political fugitives. (Some of these activities did not necessarily have the backing of the Church hierarchy, which, as an institution, adopted a generally compromising and conciliatory stance toward the government.) Gomułka also dismissed Soviet officers from the Polish army, did away with collectivized agriculture, allowed workers to form their own councils, and loosened the state censor's grip on the press.

But the power of the Poznań revolt had emboldened neighboring Hungary, where student demonstrations in support of Polish resistance exploded into a national uprising, and Gomułka was soon to see the handwriting on the wall. On November 1, 1956, Hungarian premier Imre Nagy, an anti-Stalinist communist, declared Hungary's withdrawal from the Warsaw Pact. Three days later, the Soviet Union invaded Hungary, executed Nagy, and restored Stalinist rule. Gomułka quickly retracted his promise of a Polish road to socialism and resorted to old-style Soviet measures, particularly in curbing public expression.

Anna was undeterred by these political changes. She had an intuitive knack for organizing her fellow workers, and she continued to do so openly on the shipyard premises under the nose of her employers. "I knew that I could not conquer great wrongs myself, so I started with small things," she told the prominent Polish writer Hanna Krall in a 1981 interview.[10] Those modest acts included nurturing her co-workers with hot soup and milk at lunchtime and planting a flower garden to brighten the shipyard's lifeless grounds. Managers called her a show-off and accused her of needing attention, but her co-workers greatly appreciated her caring efforts to humanize the workplace and soon elevated her to symbolic status. She was the giving mother, they were her deserving family, and their employers were hard-nosed bullies who hammered away at their individual and collective goodness.

Anna's influence and popularity as well as her ability to rally her fellow workers and get them to stay cool and level-headed on the job so irritated and unsettled management that in May 1971 it began an intensified campaign of harassment against her. Anna had recently successfully dispersed a confrontation at the shipyard, on the heels of her employers' failed attempts to do so. Rather than ignore her or praise her for preventing a protest, management forbade employees to speak with her, restricted her to the locker room and her work station, and refused to allow her to share a restroom with the other women. The shipyard management could have used flattery and reward to set her apart from her co-workers and to rouse their doubts about her motivations. Instead, they made a victim of her, and her fellow workers' sympathy for her plight swelled when they learned of each new mistreatment—security guards once locked her in the locker room and another time jumped her at the main gate, snatched her identity pass, and dragged her to the guardhouse.

She continued to be a thorn in management's side, and the harassment campaign continued, more or less constantly, for more than ten years. Their frustrated attempts to restrain her proved no more successful than trying to sovietize Poland (a task Comrade Stalin famously compared to trying to saddle a cow) and eventually made a hero of Pani Ania—"Mrs. Annie," as her co-workers affectionately called her.

The Gdańsk party officials, too, clearly found Anna threatening and for the same reasons management opposed her: she had earned and held enormous persuasive power over her fellow workers. It is interesting that no other woman—whatever her class background—had been so scapegoated by party authorities as had Anna. It was a puzzling phenomenon, because only rarely were women singled out and persecuted independently from men in the 1970s and 1980s. Opposition editor Joanna Szczęsna once pointed out to me that "the police always treated women better than men, the educated better than the uneducated, and the known better than the unknown." With two out of three strikes against her, Anna's gender alone did not protect her.

The volatile interactions between Anna and her official nemeses can, in part, be explained by the fact that, in the wake of the 1970 protests and military violence, the times had become terribly unstable. The bloodshed that ended the 1970 strikes on the Baltic coast provided a chilling turning point for Anna and the other Gdańsk organizers. They would never forget the dozens of workers shot by the police and military—some right at their factory gates—no matter how thorough the party's efforts to erase the events from public memory. In fact, they considered it their duty to memorialize and avenge the killings, and eventually they learned to retaliate with forceful, though nonviolent, strike strategies.

After a student was murdered by secret police in Kraków in May 1977, Anna became one of the first workers in Gdańsk to search for nonviolent ways to funnel her rage into concrete, productive actions. Through the church she attended and from Radio Free Europe she learned about a group called the Workers' Defense Committee (KOR) and sought out its representatives in Gdańsk. She was put in touch with local KOR activists and soon became a core member of their group. Though largely made up of local intellectuals, the Gdańsk KOR included Lech Wałęsa, who had been fired from the Lenin Shipyard the previous year (for so-called unruly behavior) after one of his characteristically dynamic speeches.

KOR was founded by a group of courageous young Warsaw oppositionists, urban intellectuals who had been involved in the failed student uprisings of the 1960s.[11] These protests peaked in 1968 and were harshly suppressed; participants were imprisoned, expelled from university, and slandered in a nationwide anti-Semitic smear campaign. To their dismay, workers had rejected the students' appeals for support. Demoralized, the marginalized students observed the 1970 workers' strikes and, for a variety of reasons, decided not to join in. Those who still felt defeated by the outcome of their student protests feared the consequences of renewed involvement. Eventually, however, they regained their political direction and began to explore new ideas to educate and empower the workers and to forge alliances with them. They realized that the two main groups of dissent needed to work together.

The first significant opportunity to put the new ideas into action arose in June 1976, when strikes provoked by another increase in food prices broke out in the factory towns of Radom and Ursus. Rioters in both towns burnt down party headquarters. The government withdrew the price hikes but then cracked down on the population. Workers were imprisoned. This time, in contrast to 1970, the Warsaw intellectuals immediately responded by arranging for medical, legal, and social services to address the emergency needs of the arrested workers and their families. They also went one important step further when—led by Jacek Kuroń, Adam Michnik, and Jan Lityński—they took full advantage of the situation and formed KOR, making a historic move to unite their group of young intellectuals with workers against the state.

On September 23, 1976, fourteen persons signed their names to a declaration announcing to the nation and to the authorities that KOR had been created. When they published KOR's mission statement, the founding members, all based in Warsaw, signed both their names and home addresses. This defiant and courageous public declaration marked a new era in protest tactics, an era that would build unprecedented coalitions based on three key concepts: open dissent, nonviolent resistance, and the educating of workers to organize free trade unions.

KOR's founding membership was very small—only thirty-four people—and of those, only four were women. Its supporters, however, numbered in the thousands and included members of the Damska Grupa Operacyjna (DGO). KOR's primary goal was not only to assist workers and their families in legal and financial matters related to the strikes but also to educate workers about general employee rights and employment policies. In the first two years of its existence, KOR organized an underground press and illegally produced publications that specifically addressed workplace grievances and human rights violations.

While all this was going on, KOR's organizers continued to claim that it was a social, not a political, organization. But the government insisted it was political and reacted with arrests and expulsions of KOR activists, instigating a terror campaign reminiscent of the oppression of students and workers in 1968 and 1970 respectively. Nevertheless, the remarkable groundswell of protest continued and emboldened people to broaden the opposition's base of support in factories, parishes, and universities.

In May 1978 the KOR activists in Gdańsk founded a secret group, Free Trade Unions on the Coast, to support workers in the Baltic coast's "Tri-Cities"—Gdańsk, Gdynia, and Sopot. The Free Trade Unions leaders included Bogdan Borusewicz, the local KOR activist who was to draw up the original plans for the 1980 shipyard strike; ship engineers and seasoned dissidents Andrzej Gwiazda and Joanna Duda-Gwiazda; activist Bogdan Lis; shipyard nurse Alina Pieńkowska; Lech Wałęsa; and Anna Walentynowicz.

The Free Trade Unions group looked to KOR and its publications, *Biuletyn Informacyjny* (Information Bulletin) and *Robotnik* (Worker), for training in union organizing and workers' empowerment. The bibuła provided information on how to articulate and negotiate demands, to mobilize an occupation strike, and to carry out nonviolent tactics. It was in these publications as well that some of the DGO got their first publishing experiences.

KOR started *Biuletyn Informacyjny* in the autumn of 1976, and it became the country's first regular underground paper. It reported on legal and medical services that were available to persecuted workers and their families, and it recorded the authorities' human rights abuses. DGO member Joanna Szczęsna became one of the *Biuletyn*'s senior editors. "The goal of this bulletin is to break the state monopoly of information guarded by the existence of censorship in our country," its editors proclaimed. "The information published here serves the openness of public life and constitutes a chronicle of repression used against citizens and the national culture. The distribution of this bulletin is an active gesture in defense of human rights, and it exemplifies the use of these rights." Within a year, *Biuletyn* inspired both a working-class readership and a flourishing illegal press.

In 1977 Warsaw activist Helena Łuczywo cofounded and assumed the editorship of a second KOR publication, *Robotnik*. Published in Warsaw, this catalytic twelve-page workers' publication criticized factory conditions and promoted free trade unions among its working-class readers. Distributed at factory gates throughout the country, its circulation leapt from four thousand to twenty thousand copies per issue in the space of just one year. *Robotnik*'s success in helping KOR bridge the age-old gaps between workers and intellectuals was unprecedented in communist Poland.

By the summer of 1980, the Free Trade Unions on the Coast, drawing its power from its links to KOR as well as from its own resources, had become a stronghold of the burgeoning free trade union movement. They published the first Baltic workers' paper, the biweekly *Robotnik Wybrzeża* (Coastal Worker), which they distributed at churches and factories. Anna and Lech led discussions on strike strategies, including how to make demands for things such as wage increases, fewer workdays, and better safety conditions. And they all plotted how to turn into reality their dream of an independent trade union, the goal that topped their collective wish list.

The activists usually met with workers in Anna's home or the Gwiazdas' apartment to analyze the mistakes of past strikes and to draw lessons from them. For instance, December 1970 taught them not to take a strike into the streets because it gave the party an alleged reason to use tear gas and guns. Instead, they learned to plot occupation strikes and to organize strike committees, made up of trusted friends, that could not be easily infiltrated and divided. In addition, they realized that if their ultimate goal was to form free trade unions they would have to resist the temptation to settle for economic gains such as increased wages, price reductions, or the promise of more consumer goods. They would also have to reject the promise of greater autonomy within the existing official unions. They could only function outside of official structures.

Younger workers in particular proved to be a ready audience and large support base for the Free Trade Unions. At the end of the 1970s, one-third of Poland's work force was made up of men under the age of twenty-five. Bolder in their outlooks and better educated than their predecessors, they were able and eager to learn union organizing tactics. They felt that their future lay in the factories, and they wanted to reap the most benefit they could from the workplace. They did not want to follow in the footsteps of workers who had died or been wounded protesting price hikes or low wages. In fact, they did not want to die in battle at all. They were simply seeking a reasonable degree of autonomy and self-determination and no longer wanted to wait seven years to get an apartment or five years to buy an automobile. Fed up with Gierek's unfulfilled promises of affordable goods and decent wages, they continued their education in factory locker rooms and mess halls, where they exchanged copies of *Robotnik, Biuletyn Informacyjny,* and *Robotnik Wybrzeża* and absorbed the ideas those journals put forth in simple language. Many took KOR activist Jacek Kuroń's catchphrase to heart: "Don't burn down party headquarters. Form strike committees instead."

From a broad social perspective, the August 1980 workers' re-volt against the Polish workers' state can be seen as a logical extension of two developments: the society was getting organized and the state was growing increasingly inept.

Two major events paved the road to Polish August. In October 1978 Cardinal Karol Wojtyła, the archbishop of Kraków, became the first Pole to be elected to the papacy, and every Pole outside the party apparatus was absolutely ecstatic. Then, in June 1979, Pope John Paul II made a pilgrimage across Poland, and millions poured out to embrace him in Warsaw's Victory Square, on a meadow outside Kraków, and at the holy site of Jasna Góra in Częstochowa. Pope John Paul II's presence in Poland and his words of encouragement were like a revelation—the tides of Polish misfortune were shifting. "The future of Poland will depend on how many people are mature enough to be nonconformists," he intoned. And people responded, "We want God. We want God in the family circle, we want God in books, in schools, we want God in government orders."[12] It was a profound collective experience of solidarity, dignity, and national pride.

"It was as if the Pope's visit announced the birth of Solidarity one year later," reflected Irena Grudzińska-Gross in her book *The Art of Solidarity.*[13] It was as if people had suddenly come to see that "Poland was not a communist country, but a communist state," wrote Garton Ash.[14]

Looking at the strike from an intimate, more human perspective, however, it can also be seen as the logical extension of Anna Walentynowicz having been fired—again.

Before her final, 1980 firing, Anna had been instrumental in a series of protests that further fueled the shipyard management's antagonism toward her. On December 16 of each year in the late 1970s, she and Lech brought people together to honor the workers who had died in the 1970 food price strikes. In the unofficial ceremonies they held at the entrance to the Lenin Shipyard, participants lit candles on the spot where the first four workers had fallen, while Anna, holding rosary beads, led the group in prayers for free trade unions. After the December 1978 ceremony, Anna was arrested. The police tried to recruit her to become an informer in exchange for the promise of a better job and apartment and permission to travel abroad. When she refused, they threatened her, and she threatened them back. "Your days are numbered, and I couldn't care less" was what she told me she had growled at them.

The following December, many activists were arrested just prior to the anniversary. Nonetheless, an estimated five thousand people took part in the prayers, wreath laying, and singing of the national anthem. Many students from the nationalist group Young Poland were also among those who attended, and their presence is said to have helped heal the old wounds between students and workers left after the tragic 1968 and 1970 protests. During that somber 1979 ritual, Lech Wałęsa put forth a powerful vision of the future: let a monument be constructed on the shipyard grounds to commemorate the fallen workers. If necessary, he emphasized, the shipyard workers would build it themselves.

Clearly influenced by the pope's visit the previous summer, Wałęsa's speech was so compelling and prophetic that people continued to talk about it a decade later. "He had a way with words. [A]t the December Anniversary, the way he got them going—the crowd went wild!" shipyard worker Jerzy Borowczak recalled in a 2000 interview recorded by *Karta,* the Solidarity archives.[15] During the August 1980 strikes, Wałęsa's vision became a top priority in negotiations with party officials, and the monument was erected in time for the December 1980 commemoration.

But there was much to be endured before that 1980 anniversary came around, and Anna continued to be her bosses' favorite target. It seemed as if they spent their lunch breaks inventing ways to offend the essence of what workers like Anna represented: selflessness, communal ties, religious faith, and devotion to the pope (photos and posters of whom adorned the shipyard everywhere). Management particularly liked to torment Anna by pitting her basic entitlements against the needs of the work crews. On one occasion, they refused to issue Anna her vacation salary if the workers in her area didn't remove a poster of the pope that had been hanging in their mess hall since June 1979. The demand was humiliating, infuriating, scandalous, and sheer blackmail, and in a sense it forced Anna, an ordinary worker, into competition with the pope. It's hard to know who was more shocked—Anna or the management—when the poster actually was taken down.

Though Anna Walentynowicz possessed power, she was seen as

an idiosyncratic and isolated widow, and it was her vulnerability that eventually became a rallying point. But people also defended her because she was a little woman with a pugnacious vocabulary who fought back every time. The time was now ripe for the workers' devoted support of her to spark collective action.

At first it looked as if the August 1980 strike in Gdańsk was going to resemble its predecessors, consisting of protests against price rises and demands for salary increases. The Communist Party had just announced food price hikes—as usual, without warning—and this had spurred workers' protests in other parts of Poland. There were, however, several differences between 1970 and 1980. In 1970 the announcement had been broadcast two weeks before Christmas, as if it were not the most important holiday season of the year in a predominantly Roman Catholic country. In 1980 the new food policy was quietly introduced in July, during what the Poles call *sezon ogórkowy* (cucumber season), when most people were preparing for or had already left on vacation. In the summer, normal business routine slows dramatically as the cities empty of residents, who pack into their Polski Fiats and head for the mountains or lakeside retreats.

It was assumed that fewer troublemakers would be on hand during cucumber season to take issue with the price hike. However, First Secretary Gierek, eager to start his own vacation in early August, underestimated the public's reaction and miscalculated the resourcefulness of his opposition adversaries. Garton Ash, who reported from Gdańsk during Polish August, has noted that the country's plunging economy, while certainly a major cause of dissent, was by no means a sufficient or sole cause of the summer revolt. "The main causes were in the realm of consciousness. By 1980, a unique society, frustrated but united, faced a weak and divided power elite, which no longer had the means to win voluntary popular support, yet had not the will to command obedience through physical force. A shift of self-confidence had taken place from the power to the society."[16]

Hence, a lesson for Gierek: No matter the season, Polish workers were no longer going to put up with the government's manipulations. And so they rebelled, first in July in factories near Warsaw and then elsewhere, one after the other, week in and week out. The party had anticipated there would be some "work stoppages" (the communist term for strikes) and made quick concessions to each striking enterprise's economic demands—authorizing a 10 percent pay raise, for example. In so doing, the party aimed to isolate and to resolve each strike locally, thus preventing the striking factories from hooking up either regionally or nationally. The party thought this game plan would contain and quell dissent but had not considered that, even though the state controlled the media, news of each strike could spread swiftly across the country through the efforts of a handful of oppositionists. Gierek had forgotten to cut the telephone lines.

The telerevolution ignited. Because the phone lines still functioned, strikes erupted like brushfires. "It is hardly an exaggeration," Garton Ash reported, "to say that most of this information came from one telephone in one small Warsaw flat where Jacek Kuroń, assisted by a student of English from the Kraków-Student Solidarity group, kept a round-the-clock strike watch. From here, and from a score of other telephones, the latest news was assembled and passed on to KOR contacts all over Poland, to Western journalists, and to Western radio stations, Radio Free Europe and BBC, which broadcast it back to Poland in Polish. Thus, millions of workers were informed. . . . If Gierek had decided at the beginning of July to detain a few tens of activists, to cut a few hundred phone lines, and to control the international exchanges, the history of that summer might have been very different."[17]

The English-language student whom Garton Ash mentioned was none other than Ewa Kulik, and according to Ewa, Małgorzata Pawlicka was also managing the phones with her—they would soon emerge as two of the seven key women organizers of the Solidarity underground. In July 1980 the studious, no-nonsense, young women had only just begun to work with Kuroń and KOR. The lessons they learned that summer about how to generate information flow in support of a revolution would bear fruit for them and the movement sixteen months later and throughout the subsequent decade.

In early August 1980 everything came to a head. Anna Walentynowicz had begun collecting candle stubs from local cemeteries, which were the remains of candles that had been lit to honor the dead, to use to make new candles for the upcoming December ceremony. The police accused her of stealing the stubs, and on August 7, 1980, she was fired from her job.

With the advent of Anna's firing, members of the Free Trade Unions on the Coast and the Warsaw-based KOR quickly collaborated to bring Gdańsk into the growing number of strikes. They would call for Anna's reinstatement and make a few other—long overdue—demands, and in so doing, they would enlarge the aims of all the strikes. They based their organizing efforts on the assumption that Pani Ania's plight could mobilize thousands of workers on the Baltic coast: Her firing was unfair and inhumane. She was an older woman, all alone. The shipyard was all she had. People would not allow Anna to be sacrificed. And while striking to support one of the bravest workers they knew, they would show their own courage and call for the formation of free trade unions. These assumptions proved true.

Before sunrise on August 14, three young workers smuggled into the Lenin Shipyard leaflets and posters emblazoned with demands for Anna's reinstatement and a general 1,000-złoty pay raise. The young men marched through the yard distributing leaflets and yelling for others to join them in striking. A hundred or so workers left their work stations, gathered around the posters, and grabbed for the leaflets, which stated, in an open letter to the workers:

Anna Walentynowicz became an embarrassment because her example motivated others. She became an embarrassment because she stood up for others and was able to organize her coworkers. The authorities always try to isolate those who have leadership qualities. If we do not fight against this, then we will have no one who will stand up for us when they raise work quotas, when Health and Safety regulations are broken or when we are forced to work overtime. That is why we are appealing to you to come out in support of crane driver Anna Walentynowicz. If you don't, many of you may find yourselves in the same situation."[18]

The letter was signed by the founders of Free Trade Unions on the Coast and the editors of *Robotnik Wybrzeża,* Bogdan Borusewicz, Joanna Duda-Gwiazda, Andrzej Gwiazda, Jan Karandziej, Alina Pieńkowska, Maryla Plonska, and Lech Wałęsa—all members of Anna's activist cohort.

By about 6:30 in the morning, a large group had assembled inside one of the gates and begun to organize the strike. They were so fired up that they weren't going to wait for Lech Wałęsa, who had agreed to slip into the shipyard to help organize them but hadn't yet arrived. The workers' already short fuse had been lit, and the Lenin Shipyard ignited. Workers rushed to their strike posts. Factory gates clanked shut. The Polish national flag was soon seen fluttering atop the factory buildings.

From his home, Lech had heard the sirens signaling that the strike had begun, but by his own account he wasn't able to leave because the housework needed to be done—his wife, Danuta, was still weak after recently giving birth to their sixth child, a daughter. He took a tram to the shipyard, from which he had been barred since his 1976 firing, headed for a side street, and, without being seen, scaled the wall, or so the now disputed legend goes. He crept into the shipyard like a thief, he wrote in his autobiography, and felt as if he were "jumping head first into a great unknown."[19]

Before noon on the first day, Lech had formed a strike committee and ordered the director's chauffeur-driven limousine to bring Anna Walentynowicz to the shipyard. Then he and shipyard director Klemens Gniech went to a conference room and faced one another across a long table. Their negotiations were broadcast into the work yard for all to hear, as were all subsequent negotiations until the end of the strike. At this point, the strike committee's demands included the rehiring of Anna and Lech; a 2,000-złoty wage increase (double the original demand); protection for strikers against retaliation; and construction of the proposed monument. When Gniech agreed to build the memorial, the strike committee was emboldened to add a new demand—the establishment of a free trade union.

In the shops and homes surrounding the shipyard, workers and housewives hurriedly collected food for the strikers. They filled shopping bags, took up armloads of loaves of bread, and marched to the factory gates. Alina Pieńkowska, then a thirty-year-old union organizer who was to play a pivotal role in the strike, later recalled in an interview how she had raced through the neighborhood nearest the shipyard asking for food for the strikers. "Despite the fact that there were no well-off people living in the street, we quickly managed to collect several sacks of food. To us, this marked the first important show of support from the general public."[20]

The morning the strike broke out, Pani Ania was hiding from the security police at a neighbor's home, in case they would try to detain her from joining in the strike. She was shocked when she saw the director's limousine pull up just as she had been thinking that she needed to go to the shipyard before he tried to turn the workers against her by accusing her of abandoning them. She could imagine him saying to them, "There you are—you're striking on her behalf and she can't even be bothered to turn up."[21]

Anna reached the shipyard around noon. Several women holding flowers for her were waiting at the main gate to escort her inside, where cheering crowds helped her climb onto a steam shovel to say a few words. Anna looked out upon the enormous crowd, and it was "just like during the pope's visit," she told me, fervently waving her hands. "Above the crowd I saw the strike banner—*We demand: Rehire Walentynowicz!*" She stood high above thousands of people who had put down their tools to protest her firing and wept. Overcome with emotion, she couldn't later remember what she said to her audience other than "thank you." Afterward, she and Lech knelt together before a wooden cross that had been placed before one of the gates and led the strikers in prayer. Photographs of the two of them with their eyes closed and their arms folded on their chests captured an image that has become legend.

The function of memory, wrote political scientist Andrzej Tymowski, "especially when used to mobilize social action, is not the relating of dispassionate facts, but the presentation of a powerful, integrative image of a community with its own right to self-expression."[22] Anna's name inspired such unity.

Though originally it was her situation and not her initiative or organizing skills that launched the strikes, she also became a principal actor. As a member of the MKS, her organizing skills became evident. She plotted and strategized with other members of the MKS, organized demonstrations and daily negotiations with management, made speeches and spoke to the press, and aroused popular sentiment at key moments. For example, on the third day of the strike, one of the managers responsible for firing Anna spoke at length to the striking workers. He acknowledged their right to protest but also defended Party Chief Edward Gierek, "who is for us like the pope." Strangely, the workers applauded this man until Anna jumped to the podium shouting: "What are you doing? Do you know who this man is? He has persecuted me for years. He fired me two weeks ago." Her justified and timely outburst jolted the strikers back to their senses, and, suddenly enraged, they swarmed up to the podium, hurling insults at the fulsome manager.

Such breakdowns show how susceptible the workers remained to the communist voice of authority on which they had been socialized and, as well, to invocations of the pope's name, no matter who the messenger. Some might say that the incident demonstrated Anna's maternal moral authority, which vied with the communists' authority for the workers' attention. But it was Anna's fearlessness and honesty that people responded to. Her statements were, and remain, simple, logical, and passionate, and her timing during those suspenseful strike confrontations was usually impeccable.

"Anna became an icon, a woman fighter with steel nerves and courage, a heroic woman who generated respect," the Polish writer Izabela Filipiak told me during one of our talks in 2000. Although Izabela, who was born and raised in Gdańsk, was only nineteen in August 1980, her memory of the events remained clear because she had a front-row seat in that political theater. That summer after high school graduation she worked as a sales clerk in a small grocery store that stood directly behind the shipyard. Every day, Izabela walked to work past the shipyard gates, which were bedecked with flowers, photographs of Pope John Paul II, national flags, postcards, and banners proclaiming such declarations as "Victory only through solidarity and patience!" and "Justice and equality for all the nation!" "It was both exhilarating and frightening to witness," Izabela said, remembering the ocean of energy that had surged throughout the shipyard, unimpeded by police guns.

The commanding presence of Anna Walentynowicz, more than anyone or anything else, made the revolution come alive for Izabela. Anna raced from one end of the shipyard to the other to instruct and inform the strikers. She prayed with them daily and sang wartime resistance songs at night. The tiny activist carried herself, in Izabela's eyes, "like those larger than life heroines who dressed in armor, went off to battle, and made everybody obey and respect them." She was "Anna the Proletarian," which was, in fact, the title of a 1995 film documentary made about her life.

By Friday, August 15, the second day of the strike, fifty thousand workers from other local shipyards, factories, and transportation systems had weighed in with their support. The Paris Commune Shipyard in nearby Gdynia was the first to join the Lenin Shipyard. Then public transport workers in the Tri-City area also went on strike, and the Free Trade Unions on the Coast called for solidarity among all strikers to ensure that everyone would benefit, across the board, from the strike demands.

Husband and wife team Andrzej Gwiazda and Joanna Duda-Gwiazda both served on the pivotal MKS. In 1991 I met with them at their home in Sopot, a town neighboring Gdańsk. Beyond their sprawling cinder block apartment complex, much-traveled paths led to the sandy shores of the Baltic Sea. It seemed to me that the gods and goddesses of social change had made an apt choice when they tapped the wildly windy Baltic coast as the setting for revolution. The Gwiazdas' apartment was crowded with souvenirs from their travels in the days before the communists took away their passports, and they happily cleared a path to a sofa, where we sat and drank glasses of tea and discussed the August strikes.

Despite the massive show of support, the couple explained, the strike began to fall apart on day three, Saturday, August 16, when the strike committee agreed to the shipyard director's offer of a 1,500-złoty pay raise in exchange for calling the strike to a halt. This was a hefty offer, approximately one-third of the average monthly wage and high enough to seduce workers to end the strikes even if it meant forfeiting political demands such as free trade unions, amnesty for political prisoners, and access to free speech. The strike committee was divided. Should the Lenin Shipyard settle separately from the smaller plants and the transportation systems? Was it not wiser to remain in solidarity with them? Yes and no. The majority of the strike committee leadership—excluding a core group made up of Anna, Wałęsa, the Gwiazdas, and a handful of others—voted in favor of the wage increase, and Wałęsa reluctantly announced the strike's end. Some of those who opposed the settlement, including the Gwiazdas, immediately left the shipyard to publicize the decision and to encourage the other local strikes to continue.

Moving briskly, the director of the Lenin Shipyard appealed for everyone to vacate the premises by six o'clock that evening, and workers prepared to leave in anticipation of getting a Sunday break before returning to work on Monday. Back in Warsaw, the official communist news agency hurried to inform the foreign press that an agreement had been reached. According to the Gwiazdas, when news of the collapsed strike spread through the Tri-City area, delegates from the other strikes were incensed that the Lenin Shipyard had backed off so hastily.

During the couple's brief absence from the Lenin Shipyard, however, an extraordinary turnaround had occurred.

In the midst of the chaos of departing workers, Anna and shipyard nurse Alina Pieńkowska found each other and began discussing how to regroup their efforts. Anna said she felt responsible for all the other strikes that had come out in support of her and the Lenin Shipyard, and Alina, quick on her feet, suggested they try to rescue the situation by calling for a solidarity strike. They raced to the microphones, but they had already been shut off, and a taped announcement calling for all workers to clear the premises was being aired every fifteen minutes. The two women ran to the gates, climbed onto barrels, and beseeched the departing workers to stay put. "If you abandon now, we'll be lost!" The workers stopped. "Let us not sell out our colleagues for 1,500 złotys!" the women pleaded. "We must keep our strike going in solidarity with the other striking factories."

"I can remember the scene to this day: thousands of people on the bridge out of the shipyard," Alina recalled in her interview with *Karta* in honor of Solidarity's twentieth anniversary in 2000. (The interview was one of her last, for she died of cancer a year later.) "I persuaded the guards to close the gates and began to explain that the strike at the other gates had been extended, and I called on them to strike in solidarity with their colleagues. That worked—the crowd turned back from the gate. Of course, there were three gentlemen carrying briefcases who shouted: 'We're leaving!'—and they were quickly kicked out of the gate."[23]

In actions apparently independent of one another, two other women also stormed through the shipyard and practically barricaded gates with their bodies. Henryka Krzywonos, an organizer of the striking bus and tram workers, and Ewa Ossowska, a student activist with the nationalist, anti-Russian youth group Young Poland, both had the same impulse as Anna and Alina. "Buses can't face tanks," Henryka said, beseeching the homeward-bound men to remember the still striking transportation workers.

"Each of the women went to a different gate and stopped the workers from leaving the shipyard," Joanna Gwiazda recalled excitedly. "That is what they each thought should be done." It may seem remarkable that four women, two of whom acted spontaneously and independently, spoke in similar voices, but as Joanna explained it: "It is possible that their ideas were similar because they were all organizers, and two of them [Anna and Alina] had been involved in group discussions of the Free Trade Unions, where we had decided on these tactics long before the strike began."

Andrzej Gwiazda embellished on the gender dimension: "Just at this critical moment, each woman stood before the male workers, blocked them from leaving, and persuaded them to stay and close the gates. The women made strong, urgent pleas to 'not sell out our colleagues for 1,500 złotys.' At the time, 1,500 złotys was considered a lot of money. The men had to refuse the money being offered just to be in solidarity with their colleagues. This was hugely significant. If men had been in the position of those four women, they might not have been able to make such a dramatic impression in convincing people to stay. But these women showed themselves to be powerful. Men probably felt silly that they were meeker than the women who pleaded with them and blocked the gates. Men had given up too easily."

The women's intervention at that critical juncture revived the strike. They reaffirmed that the strike's main objective was not basic economic demands but *solidarity*. Their actions were so compelling that Lech Wałęsa was emboldened to make a formal call for a solidarity strike. Wałęsa, Anna Walentynowicz, and Ewa Ossowska all jumped onto an electric trolley and drove around the shipyard urging workers to stay. The three organizers looked "like a carnival float symbolizing The Struggle of the Workers Supported by Virtue and Youth," Garton Ash wrote in his book on the Solidarity revolution.[24]

At six o'clock that evening, several hundred workers remained in the shipyard—the strike had survived and the authorities did not try to break it up. Joanna and Andrzej explained that it was probably too risky for the party to order the use of force against the Gdańsk workers after the enduring trauma of 1970. It was likely that Gierek, who came to power in the aftermath of December 1970, did not want blood on his hands in 1980 or did not want to risk being ousted from power, as others had been after "work stoppage" crises. So Gierek ended up indirectly supporting a nonviolent revolution. He failed to stay in power, however, and was replaced in September by apparatchik Stanisław Kania, who was ousted in October 1981 and replaced by General Wojciech Jaruzelski, architect of the period of martial law.

By day four, Sunday, the Lenin Shipyard strike had resumed full force, marking what Garton Ash characterized as "a necessary catharsis, which purged the leadership of the timid and those interested in złotys."[25] The strike gained focus and got organized for the serious business of winning unprecedented gains. The MKS, with the invited participation of two representatives per striking industrial site (many of them younger workers in their twenties and thirties), set out to coordinate all the workers' demands and all the strikes that were taking place in the surrounding cities and towns. The MKS then proceeded to produce twenty-one consolidated demands, which included the formation of free trade unions; the right to strike; the right to free speech and publishing; and the restoration of the rights of political prisoners, expelled students, and strikers from 1970 and 1976. Then it established its main responsibilities: it would conduct negotiations with party officials, secure the demands before dissolving the strike, and organize free trade unions.

When the negotiations began, more strikes in solidarity with the twenty-one demands spread across the country. By the negotiations' midpoint, 200,000 more workers had put down their tools and organized strike committees and 260 intellectuals had signed a letter supporting the MKS. Needless to say, these actions led to demotions and leadership changes within the party's highest ranks.

On August 30, following a suspenseful week of negotiations, the party met all twenty-one demands. Against the backdrop of the rebellious sea, and with the salty scent of approaching storms filling the air, the Gdańsk Accords were signed on August 31. In an unprecedented move almost as historic as the emergence of Solidarity itself, the signing ceremony was aired on national television. By mid-September, Solidarity was legal, the Polish people grew to appreciate and then demand a freer press, and the telerevolution took a giant leap forward. Coordination of the movement's mass-based, nationwide actions would soon grow into a modern telecommunications network that informed the factories when to strike, the students when to stage sit-ins, and families when to protest food shortages.

"Solidarity was freedom, and freedom was like breathing again," Anna Walentynowicz recalled passionately. Always the caretaker, she had stayed behind at the shipyard on August 31 to straighten up the conference room and to collect, for safekeeping, some of the photos and postcards that had decorated the shipyard gates. Afterward, she celebrated the victory with some of her thousands of friends, but by then it was also clear to her that Lech Wałęsa had walked away with the leadership of Solidarity. She couldn't deny that he had played an awesome role during the negotiations, which earned him his new status as the voice and the face of Solidarity. She understood that, whereas she could incite people to action, his prodigious talent was in peacekeeping. (Whenever there were heated disagreements among the strikers, Lech was often able to calm everyone down just by singing the national anthem. Suddenly, people would be singing along, their voices drowning out the dissension.) But, she wondered, didn't Solidarity need more than one voice, more than one face?

Anna felt unfairly excluded and rejected—all, she said, because she was a woman. Not even Lech's sense of solidarity and loyalty had been able to bridge sexist attitudes, and I noted that when I asked Anna about the role she played after signing the Gdańsk Accords her tone of voice changed from excitement to bitterness.

Almost immediately after the first waves of euphoria had passed, Anna told me, she and other women began to disappear from center stage in the emerging political theater. Women's political marginalization is not unusual in the history of revolutions and their aftermaths. No one in Poland seems to have perceived it as an egregious contradiction or saw a causal relationship between it and Solidarity's capacity to remain true to its name. What was unusual was that female strike organizers had been able to play powerful roles at all.

The strike's victory had been an amazing achievement, but there was much that that summer's campaign for solidarity did not achieve: it did not consciously support women or strive to include women. And although their contributions to the world's largest strike were later woven into Solidarity's creation myth, the meaning of women's experiences and the limitations placed on their involvement were neither recognized nor explored—perhaps because there were soon so few women at the table who might have done such exploring.

Although she had been a member of the MKS Presidium and was one of only three women (the others were Alina Pieńkowska and Henryka Krzywonos) who signed the Gdańsk Accords, Anna was not invited onto the newly forming local, regional, or national boards. Those groups were created out of the various strike committees and had carried over most of their original—that is, male—members. Systemic gender discrimination precluded women's continued involvement and would continue to do so, unless you were the wife or girlfriend of an important organizer.

A year later, in preparation for the September 1981 National Solidarity Congress in Gdańsk, votes were taken to choose the Tri-City representatives, and again Anna was not nominated. According to political scientist Barbara Jancar in a 1985 study, there was some embarrassment that Anna's local chapter had failed to send her to the congress, and one delegate suggested she be given the right to vote anyway. But a proud and wounded Anna refused because she did not want to challenge a decision that had been made by majority vote in her local chapter. "A self-selected member of the free trade union movement, Ms. Walentynowicz played a significant role, but she failed to pass the test of free elections," wrote Jancar. "No similar incident is reported in the case of men."[26]

Anna's symbolic value to the workers' movement lived on, but though adored, she was not considered a serious player in the business of politics. She could draw forth powerful, emotional responses, but she could not claim a formal political role for herself; nor could she help other women to do so; nor did other women or men try to help her. Before the strike, the shipyard management had isolated her; now her fellow trade unionists had followed suit and raced off without her.

Sitting in Anna's sunny living room, where the entire Gdańsk opposition had once assembled, I asked her if she had wanted to be a leader. "At the beginning of the strike," she explained in a matter-of-fact tone, "a man came to pick me up and he said the workers wanted me to lead the strike. I said to him that I don't want to do it because if a woman becomes the head of a strike, it will diminish the seriousness of the event. If I had become head of the strike, people would have said, 'Woman, back to your pots.' And that is why Wałęsa took over the leadership. So, no, I didn't want to be a leader. For the goodness of the strike and Solidarity, I never wanted to do it, not even deep inside. I didn't see myself in that role. But now, from the perspective of today, I see that I had made a mistake. Because now, after twenty years, the meaning of the August events has been diminished. Nobody speaks about Solidarity in a good sense anymore."

Voting and elections belonged to men, as Barbara Jancar's study makes clear. But even before elections were held—and most were not held before the springtime—all decision making belonged to men, too. They staked their claims to the leadership structures immediately after the Gdańsk Accords were signed and went about setting up regional and national boards and scheduling elections. Solidarity's infrastructure grew out of the strike committees. Each locale's strike committee usually turned into a Solidarity committee, with its leadership based most commonly on self-selection, at least until elections could be arranged. Very few women were invited onto committees.

When he assumed his national leadership role, Lech Wałęsa pulled supportive young workers around him, but no one in his advisory circle was female. From his actions it was clear that Anna Walentynowicz, the movement's mother figure, was no longer of use to him. His wife could be found at home, where she belonged, with their growing family. The Black Madonna, Solidarity's icon of protection, could be found where she belonged, pinned to Wałęsa's jacket lapel for all to see. There was no longer room for a fiery, charismatic, aging, single woman in his domain. The results of the spring 1981 elections of delegates to attend the first National Solidarity Congress, to be held that September, show a dramatic underrepresentation of women. Only 69 of 881 elected national delegates were women—a figure that represented a mere 7 percent of the total. At the September congress, an even smaller number of female union officials were elected to join the National Commission. Of the 19 members on the Conciliation Commission, only 1 was female; of the 82 on the National Commission, only 1 was female; and the 21-member Auditing Commission had but 3 women.[27]

Most women were reluctant to trespass on the so-called male territory of politics. For example, Alina Pieńkowska—a key player in the strike, an MKS organizer, and a signatory of the Gdańsk Accords—was elected to the regional board for Gdańsk only by pure accident. She had refused to run for either the regional or the national delegation, but her name was mistakenly placed on the regional election list. She won in spite of herself and accepted the position. Had such an accident befallen Anna or other women, they, too, most likely would have overstepped rigid gender-role expectations to accept an official position in Solidarity.

In addition to gender-based factors, class also influenced women's ability to move into the political realm. The only woman from Gdańsk to actively run for the national and regional boards was ship engineer Joanna Duda-Gwiazda, the second woman member of the original MKS Presidium and the wife of a union leader. Both Gwiazdas lost at the national level but won regional seats. Joanna had the support of her husband and their network of friends, but her activist role was limited as well as strengthened by her marriage to Andrzej, who had an ongoing rivalry with Lech

Wałęsa. The two men competed against one another for regional and national leadership and disagreed bitterly on Solidarity's goals and policies. People in Gdańsk said that the growing hostility between the two men and their supporters was projected onto Joanna. Activists in Wałęsa's camp called her a witch, a woman who had hexed her husband and lured him away from peaceful interaction with Wałęsa. She had meddled in politics, and that was taboo.

In a 1984 interview in *Ms.* magazine, Anna Walentynowicz looked back on the events of 1980 and noted: "It's funny. I started Solidarity, but the winner was Leshek [Wałęsa's nickname]. It isn't right, but it's the situation we live in. The men are the public speakers; they have the authority and power. It's part of their makeup to feel they are first, and they don't want to share it."[28]

Ms. magazine's commentary likened Anna's situation to that of Rosa Parks, the U.S. civil rights activist, and drew parallels between the two of them from the perspective of the political silencing of women. Rosa Parks is known for having sparked the Montgomery, Alabama, bus boycott of the mid-1950s, which launched the civil rights movement and the political career of Reverend Martin Luther King Jr. Both Lech Wałęsa and Martin Luther King Jr. were awarded Nobel Peace Prizes, while the women credited with catalyzing the events that led to that prize faded into semioblivion and are remembered chiefly as symbols of their respective movements. In truth, both women were militant activists who, over many years, made serious contributions to their respective freedom struggles. But that's not how either has come to be remembered.

The Rosa Parks who refused to relinquish her bus seat to a white man is envisioned as a lonely old woman who, one day in 1955, was just too darn tired to obey the Jim Crow laws. But the woman the bus driver arrested was actually only forty-two years of age, and she had been energetically organizing antiracism groups for more than a decade. Hundreds of supporters stood outside the courthouse during Parks's five-minute trial, in which she was found guilty and fined ten dollars. After her release, at a celebration held at the church where Martin Luther King Jr. presided, Rosa Parks joined the black community's ministers on stage and received a standing ovation from the packed hall. But she was not invited to speak. Told that she had said enough, she sat silently on the stage while Reverend King spoke on her behalf.[29]

And that is how women are silenced within a single-issue movement that is bigger and more urgent than gender equality; that is how sex discrimination becomes an unacknowledged offense within a social change movement. For both Rosa Parks and Anna Walentynowicz, one stereotype was replaced by another when one form of oppression gave way to the next. Neither woman was old, helpless, or tired, but, nevertheless, it was her apparent vulnerability that was exploited as a call to social action. In similar ways, Rosa Parks, Anna, and other Gdańsk women were used for their functional and symbolic support of "the struggle" and then abandoned to the historians, who generally misinterpret them.

Certainly most commentators misinterpreted Anna's postvictory circumstances. "Call Walentynowicz the embittered other face of the European transformation that propelled [Adam] Michnik to prosperity and power," Roger Cohen wrote in the *New York Times* in 1999. "There are millions like her. Pensioners eking out a living on $200 a month."[30] What Cohen attributes to Anna's failure to keep up with societal changes, I see, rather, as society's failure to overcome gender discrimination. The inimitable Anna had so much going for her back in 1980—dedication, raw talent, and organizing savvy—and it seems to me that these demonstrated qualities would have been put to good use to benefit Solidarity. Her quick sidelining can only mean that Lech Wałęsa and other male organizers had all along regarded her as only a guest inside the gates, while she, after thirty years of defending workers' rights, had thought she was one of the hosts of the revolution.

Even while the shipyard strike was still in progress, there was visible evidence that Solidarity was not going to welcome Anna's or other women's formal participation. A slogan posted on one of the shipyard fences gave this warning: "Women, do not stand in our way—we are fighting for Poland." It was one of many such banners, many such statements, that were so much a part of Poland's freedom-fighting culture that they went unchallenged until the late 1990s, when Polish feminists began to make "lit-crit" mincemeat of them.

"Who is really speaking to whom in that slogan?" asks the

provocative Warsaw feminist Agnieszka Graff in a 1999 article. "WE refers not just to the shipyard workers, whose scared wives and mothers are trying to talk them out of striking. WE means all men, YOU means the women. OUR manhood is all the more obvious because the BATTLE is going on. A battle, as everybody must be aware, is the manly thing. Any attempt to intervene from YOUR, 'ol' women's' side will amount to STANDING IN OUR WAY. The slogan worked in two ways: it established the realm of political struggle as truly masculine and excluded women from the struggle."[31]

Graff clearly depicted the mind-set and the cultural norm that shaped the August 1980 strike. But in the almost total absence of a gender consciousness back in 1980, no one, including Anna Walentynowicz, challenged it.

Her name made history, but the value of Anna's contribution has been masked by the symbolic role she was assigned. Anna's plunge into obscurity is what she shares in common, very generally, with the Solidarity women who came after her—educated women two generations her junior whose lives and circumstances differed from hers in every way. Yet even though the positions of the '68ers within the opposition grew stronger over time and each woman gained increasing control over her role and her life, when the curtain rang down on their act, they were as forgotten as their predecessor. The difference between Anna and her successors is that Anna was pushed aside despite her loud objections; the '68ers, who called themselves Damska Grupa Operacyjna, accepted their dismissal and quietly moved on. In 1989, when the Polish Communist Party collapsed, most women who had been active in the 1980s Solidarity underground found themselves excluded from political life.

But during the sixteen months that Solidarity enjoyed legal status, the women '68ers actually surpassed the Gdańsk women in their ability to amass power and status. In those brief, heady months, they moved closer to the center of power than any woman or group of women had previously come. By the time martial law was declared, they hovered so close to the center that to me they appeared to *be* the center.

2. Solidarity's "Blank Spot"
the legal period and martial law

Women made up an estimated 50 percent of the membership of the now officially recognized Solidarity. Yet of these five million women, only a tiny handful of highly motivated self-starters actually became part of its political hierarchy or was able to participate in building its civic structures. During Solidarity's legal period, if a woman could manage the sexism—and most insisted they hadn't noticed it, given that nothing else was considered to be as oppressive as one-party rule—then Solidarity actually opened up new opportunities, primarily in education, the arts, trade unions, and the media. And women did not want to miss out on those opportunities, whatever ploy was necessary to get in. Some entered on the arm of an activist husband, others built on previous professional experience, while still others took advantage of university or community ties.

By and large, the Solidarity women who rose to positions of responsibility chose areas of activity where they wouldn't have to compete with men, where they could circumvent sexism, cope with it, tolerate it, and avoid it when possible. This may sound contradictory, but it's the very reason why sexism didn't bother them—because they had each individually figured out how to work around it and make it not matter. That's why most of the women I interviewed did not openly defy Polish cultural standards of proper female behavior. Instead, by being resourceful, cunning, and nonconfrontational, they found expedient ways to shape meaningful paths for themselves, paths that required dedication and self-sacrifice in order to attain decision-making status within their circumscribed sphere of influence.

With one single exception, the women I interviewed seem to have accepted the second-class role the Solidarity patriarchy imposed on them. The exception was Barbara Labuda, a politically ambitious intellectual who thought outside the Polish box. She surprised me when I interviewed her in 1991 by stating categorically, "Women did not have real equality under communism. And yes, the opposition treated women like inferior beings."

A member of the class of 1968, Barbara had had the unusual experience of receiving a feminist education while studying in Paris in the early 1970s, and she became the lone unapologetic feminist among her peers. It is interesting to note that, although she experienced sexism during her years of anticommunist activism, she said she was not persecuted for her feminist views or for her considerable political ambitions. Barbara's perspective, more than that of any other interviewee, helped me focus my research, for she was the only woman from the opposition elite who had discovered and embraced second-wave feminism. She shared a feminist language with me and was one of the rare women to offer me a gender analysis of the Polish opposition.

When I first contacted her in 1991, Barbara was a very busy legislator, and it took me six months to arrange an interview to record her experiences in Solidarity. A member of Parliament in 1991, Barbara represented the (then) reform-minded Democratic Union in the Lower Silesia region, of which Wrocław is the capital city. The fourth largest city in Poland, Wrocław had been a hotbed of dissent in the 1970s and 1980s, and Barbara had been a key organizer there. Her popularity led her to campaign for office in the first democratic elections in 1989. She was one of the handful of women who participated in the overthrow of the communist regime and then continued on in the partisan politics of the transition period. That was an incredible feat in a society that, from one system to the next, consistently obstructed women's participation in political and public life. But Barbara had defied the Communist Party and challenged male authority far more often than had her female colleagues, and she appeared to have found her place in the sun.

When we finally met, at Warsaw's Parliament Hotel, Barbara immediately took me in tow, and we hurried through the lobby in search of a private lounge. Much like the party machinery, the hotel's drab, communist-style decor had not yet been dismantled, and dark wood furniture, worn-out brown upholstery, and mustard-colored carpets went past in a blur as I chased after this obviously dynamic woman sporting short, copper-colored hair. As I strode briskly after her bright orange dress down long dark halls in our search, I imagined that Barbara must dedicate herself to all tasks with a similar electrifying urgency.

When one of the doors we opened finally revealed an empty room, we settled down for the interview, and the interpreter had to work diligently to keep pace. "Mine is a typical life story of an individual who tries to free herself in a society that was forcing people into their place," Barbara began. "I could tell you anecdotes all night long." I was willing to listen. We drank mineral water and summoned up a past that was further away in context than in time. She told me about her student activist days in the 1960s at the university in Poznań, when she first started to organize meetings and demonstrations and was introduced to police interrogations. She had participated in the nationwide university protests that erupted in March 1968. Like their counterparts in universities around the country, Poznań students uniformly demanded cultural freedom and the abolition of censorship. They had faced arrests, expulsions, an anti-Semitic backlash, and a wave of emigration. Barbara sadly watched many of her fellow students leave a terrorized Poland, and she joined them in 1970 in the wake of the government crackdown.

Barbara moved to France with her husband and infant son, feeling lucky to have escaped the political madness. In Paris her husband, Aleksander, taught Polish literature at the Sorbonne, and she studied political science, literature, and art history. It was then that she had her feminist awakening, she told me, noting that "there were many exceptional leftist women in Paris who could not stand being pushed aside by the men in the French Left." Barbara attended the consciousness-raising groups these women organized, and together they analyzed their professional aspirations, their personal relationships, and housework "in the spirit of feminism." Barbara recalled proudly that "even Simone de Beauvoir attended several meetings." French women were discussing the role of the social contract as a perpetrator of female oppression; they were confronting their men; and Barbara found this feminist education to be a life-changing experience.

When their fellowships were completed in 1974, Barbara and Aleksander returned to academic teaching positions in Wrocław, a major industrial and trade center boasting prestigious universities, and to new waves of strikes and government repression. It was a difficult adjustment, Barbara said, to have lived a headache-free, Western existence for five years and, upon returning home, to have her passport rescinded.

The August 1980 strikes that propelled Solidarity into being made it possible for the enterprising Barbara Labuda, who had helped organize local strikes earlier that summer, to assume a more central role in the Wrocław opposition. Because Poland's command economy rested on steel, coal, and cement, heavy industry had immense leverage in pressuring the government to concede the right to organize autonomous trade unions. With its large industrial base (steelworks, transportation, chemicals, food, and textiles) Wrocław played an influential role in the burgeoning trade union movement and quickly became one of Solidarity's strongest hubs—with Barbara Labuda as one of its movers and shakers.

Barbara spoke proudly of the city's rebel character and progressive tendencies, which even supported a politically ambitious woman like herself. The city's distinct flair for insubordination and solidarity during the communist era, she said, could be partly attributed to the events that took place there in the immediate postwar period. Like Poznań, Wrocław had been a German city until the end of World War II, and its postwar Polish residents found themselves filling an urban vacuum that the Soviets had created when they emptied the city of its German inhabitants and purged it of its German name, Breslau. The city's beautiful Gothic and baroque architecture notwithstanding, when its reluctant Polish population moved in, they brought their rage and bitterness toward communism with them. They also brought, Barbara added, a proclivity for experimentation on which political insurgency as well as cultural innovation thrived. "People were rebellious because they knew that the communist system was bad. Many people understood that, if there is going to be a protest, we will all protest. Even during the March '68 student demonstrations, workers brought us food and the taxi drivers refused to accept money from young people. By the time of martial law, a foundation for resistance already existed."

Shortly after the signing of the Gdańsk Accords in September 1980, Barbara began organizing and teaching classes for workers on the history of labor movements. "No one knew what real trade unions were," she emphasized. "Education started from point zero." She recruited colleagues from Wrocław University, where she taught French literature, to join her in providing workers with a civic education. Classes ranged from the history of democratic institutions and political systems to Polish history without the "blank spots," economics, literature, and the history of student movements. Teachers and students figured out together what to study. Mostly, Barbara stressed, what people were eager for was to expand their understanding of the world around them.

Barbara dedicated herself to winning the trust and cooperation of the workers in her training program. "The way you acted with workers was all-important," she stressed to me. She wanted to be accessible to them and to bridge the age-old gap between intellectuals and workers. She seemed to be building the education program before their eyes, wearing the whole gamut of hats from professor to administrator to typist to furniture mover in her bid to create a safe, congenial environment in which intellectuals, workers (both blue- and white-collar), and university students could all come together.

Solidarity thus became the true voice of the workers in a way that the Communist Party boasted of but never accomplished. Barbara was fortunate, she told me, that people desperately needed assistance, or they might not otherwise have given a woman such an influential role.

The classes became so popular that it seemed the buildings might crumble under their weight, for eight hundred or one thousand people would often besiege a room with seats for three hundred. Barbara, who had previously taught only at the university level, found this outpouring of enthusiasm and thirst for knowledge from adults of all ages exhilarating. She recalled that a new teacher once opened a class session by saying, "Please tell me what you know about Polish history, so that I can know what to teach you," only to hear the class shout in response, "We don't know anything! We don't know anything!"

After the signing of the Gdańsk Accords, such a release of energy was possible for the first time in decades, and it became palpable and infectious. In interviews with me and in published texts, men and women throughout Poland described the sensations of being liberated—they tasted freedom, they could breathe again, they relaxed and opened up, they felt at home in their country. People felt like they could say and do anything on the streets, in cafes and shops, in adult education classes, and before their employers. They could speak and publish their ideas, thoughts, and feelings.

Everyone attributed the newborn openness to Solidarity. By virtue of both its existence and their participation in its creation, people felt a sense of purpose, confidence, and legitimacy. By the simple act of telling the truth, Solidarity's moral authority towered above that of the communist state, which dealt in assertions, allegations, and accusations. A popular poster created in 1981 for Andrzej Wajda's acclaimed film *Man of Iron* shows a worker with his forehead encased by a giant metal nut, which is cracking: the free-thinking citizen breaks loose from the fetters of the state. *Renewal* was the catchword of the day.

Barbara called this period of experimentation and education the "enlightening of the people." "In my classes," she explained, "I listened to people describe their work experiences who had never before uttered words in public. Up until that time, their mouths had always been shut, just as they had been taught. Now they were learning to feel safe. It was breathtaking for them and for me. They were coming out of the dark of silence. People were no longer afraid."

Solidarity was all about voice. It was a time when voice was being regained and the "blank spots" filled in. "Storytelling exploded on an unheard-of scale," recalled Maria Janion, one of the country's most eminent public intellectuals. "The missing parts of history's puzzles were uncovered and put back in place. Magazines were full of interviews then, and everybody was eager to read their revelations. What fascinated me at the time was to notice the variety of tones and the passion with which people described their experiences. Concealed, forgotten, fossilized experiences all came to life."[1]

The sixteen months before martial law was imposed was a time of unprecedented freedom and, Barbara said, one of the most exciting times in her life. The union training center she organized became a model for thirty-six such workers' universities, called *wszechnica,* which sprouted across the country. While Solidarity was legal, the workers' wszechnicas were extremely popular because they satisfied a pervasive desire for education, communication, and interaction among social groups and because they linked the present day to a precommunist, prewar cultural practice.

Wszechnica is a historical term that invokes national pride and literally means "comprehensive educational facility." The original model, established during the interwar Polish republic (1914–18), provided university-level humanities and science courses for adults and inspired later variations. Long before Barbara founded the Solidarity era's first workers' school, wszechnicas had became associated with another type of Polish learning—clandestine study groups called "Flying Universities," which were created as part of the anti-Nazi cultural resistance to teach banned subjects such as Polish language and history. Comparable secret fora were organized by communist-era oppositionists in the 1970s and during martial law as well. In postcommunist times, university tutorials that are taught informally (without credit) with the aim of deepening students' knowledge of specific topics are still sometimes called *wszechnica.*

Barbara's innovation proved a huge success, and her initiative made it into the historical record—not, however, under her name. Instead, she told me, the encyclopedic *Who's Who in Solidarity* credited the well-known Warsaw organizer Henryk Wujec with her creation. "Wujec was inaccurately identified as the founder of the first workers' university. He personally apologized to me for the error, but the publisher never corrected the mistake. The actions done by women," she noted bitterly, "are often credited to men."

Barbara later told the *OŚKA Biuletyn,* a Warsaw feminist quarterly, "I think a great number of people in the opposition noticed the unfair treatment of women, but it didn't disturb them. Often my awareness was triggered by a trifle. For example, at a meeting, a man would ask the women to serve the coffee, tea and biscuits, while turning to the other men to engage in a creative discussion. I was bothered by the way women allowed others to treat them as inferiors. They had become so accustomed to that treatment that they took it for granted."[2] She tried unsuccessfully to appeal to her friends, but they were cold to the idea and "reacted negatively in all settings, whether social, private or professional. In the 1970s, universities were oases of democracy, at least of a limited kind. We were able to elect our own representatives to the university authorities. Men mostly occupied the managerial posts. Women did not want to run in an election because they considered themselves unsuitable. In everyday life, it was necessary to constantly persuade and prevent against discriminatory behavior."[3]

Like Barbara Labuda, when I began my research I was bothered when I learned that people committed to the democratic opposition showed little or no concern for women's rights. I had thought that, in a society based on the communist premise of women's legal equality, women's rights, much like workers' rights, would have been a part of the opposition's daily vocabulary and would have been reflected in its democratic values and objectives. Moreover, communism had abused its promise of gender equality just as it had exploited the notion of a workers' state. If women hadn't been aware of both these abuses, why, I wondered, had they worked so hard to support Solidarity and to dismantle a system that had guaranteed them more legal rights and social welfare benefits than Western women have ever possessed?

I had also assumed, when starting out, that the breakdown of the Eastern Bloc was, to a certain extent, a measure of communism's failure to fully emancipate women. And, indeed, that was true. But I hadn't realized that women—not only in Poland but throughout the Eastern Bloc—would reject not only communism but emancipation as well and would throw out the baby with the bath water. It took me time to understand what Polish feminist theorist Agnieszka Graff later discussed with me, explaining that "one of the key elements of the ethos of the anticommunist opposition is the belief that women ought not to mix up with politics and that serious treatment of their problems is harmful to democracy."

Certainly neither Solidarity nor the Gdańsk Accords promised women either liberation or equality in exchange for their support. Solidarity affirmed the traditional virtues of a woman's domestic role and defined her fundamental needs as shorter shopping queues, more consumer products, and a lighter double load of compensated and domestic labor. Women's interests beyond their domestic care-taking duties were neglected or, at most, subsumed into the trade union's broader demands for labor rights—shorter work days and workweeks, better wages, the right to strike, and so forth. Gender inequalities in the workplace—such as unequal pay scales, glass ceilings, and gender-segregated jobs—were, however, not considered part of the labor rights package.

"The male-dominated hierarchy of Solidarity was markedly unsympathetic to any demands for women's human rights beyond such traditional women's issues as protection of maternity," U.S. law professor Isabel Marcus emphasized in conversation with me. The Gdańsk Accords, she pointed out, focused on women in their roles as mothers and heads of their families but failed to recognize their right to build their identities as citizens and workers. Only three of the twenty-one demands the accords granted were directly related to women. One demand was for an increase in the number of placements in day-care centers and preschools for the children of working mothers; a second called for introducing a three-year paid maternity leave; and the third aimed to reduce the retirement age for women from age fifty-five to fifty and for men from age sixty to fifty-five. None of these three agreements was fulfilled prior to the imposition of martial law, though that was not a gender-specific affront. The party delayed or reneged on the majority of its accord commitments.

Why did so few activist women even think to challenge the gender inequalities they encountered inside and outside the movement? Why did they show no active interest in or desire for organizing around women's issues such as safeguarding equal rights—working toward the improvement of social, medical, and legal services—or raising public awareness around sex discrimination or violence against women?

In 1980 (and, as it turned out, well beyond), if thoughts of feminist advocacy arose at all, bringing them up was considered premature. There were limits to what a communist-bred mind could imagine, and gender constituted one of those massive mental blocks. Rather than grapple with what might prove to be an iceberg of a problem, it was easier to rationalize that feminism's time hadn't yet come and to insist that treating it seriously was a luxury the opposition could little afford under an authoritarian system. At least, that's what women told me that they had told themselves.

Many women from Barbara's generation of '68ers were actually sympathetic to feminist issues, but they chose to keep a distance from them because no conceptual or organizational space yet existed in which to explore women's interests. Joanna Szczęsna explained it to me this way back in 1991: "There are three reasons why, in Poland, the women's movement did not exist for many years. First, Polish society is very traditional. Paradoxically, it gave women a special position, for better and worse. Better because Polish women were very important in their homes and as the supporters of their men's careers. Secondly, the most outstanding and active women were absorbed by the opposition movement. The freedom-of-all issue was our top priority. It was not time to consider the specific interests of women or of others. And third, I think that most women were so busy in their daily lives that it was impossible to get interested in feminism or any other movement. You have to have free time to get involved in a movement. Communist life was so terrible, especially for Polish women, who had to stand in long lines and so forth."

"Women's rights were a back-burner issue. They were not a priority for the opposition," Wanda Nowicka, now the director of Warsaw's equivalent of Planned Parenthood, told me in 1998. "Many of us believed that we were fully equal, even though we were not. But believe me, we had many of the appearances of equality, particularly in comparison with women in the West. We often saw ourselves not only in a good position but sometimes in a better position than Western women. While women in the West fought for the right to work, we already had that right. At least 40 percent of Polish women worked professionally. Western women had to struggle for prestigious careers such as doctors, judges, and professors, which we could occupy with relative ease. We were not aware of the discriminatory mechanisms, which surely existed. What mattered to us was the belief that if you wanted to achieve something, you could do it. My mother had been a respected judge. Many of our mothers were professionals. For us, it was obvious and natural. Believe me, many professional women did not think we should be envious of you American women. What we envied was your economic wealth and freedom. But it had little to do with gender roles. Still, I cannot say I was not a feminist during the communist times. I think I was always a feminist by nature. It was obvious to me. But I only became actively interested in 1989, when democracy came. If I had been made aware of a sexist problem in earlier years, I would not have thought it was a priority. I believed that freedom and independence came first, and then other things like women's rights."

Communist propaganda specifically set out to make a mockery of Western feminism, and it succeeded—even among worldly intellectuals such as Anna Bojarska, a well-known novelist and '68er, whose frequently banned literary works were usually produced illegally or abroad. Bojarska was interviewed by the *Women's Review of Books* in 1990: "What did we know about Western feminists? To take one example—that they burnt bras—bras that were not available in Polish stores, and if they were, they were not the right color, style, and quality, not to mention size. Day to day existence has been such a struggle, that the problems [of feminists] seemed so silly to us. We would love to have those problems! . . . In the seventies and eighties, feminism did not exist in Poland. . . . It's just that we are always behind. Chalk it up to our 'civilization gap,' to our political circumstances—that is, communism."[4]

Anna Bojarska had been misled, as I too had been, to believe that independent feminist endeavors, outside of state control, simply did not exist during communist times in Poland. Actually, they did, but they were so marginal that few people were aware of their presence. In part, this was because feminism was not identified with Solidarity. When, for example, I asked Anka Grupińska back in 1990 whether there were feminists among the Solidarity women whom I should interview, she shrugged off the question: "If there were feminists, they had nothing to do with Solidarity." By this, Anka meant not that feminists shunned Solidarity, although I later learned that some did, but that Solidarity had no room for feminists. Solidarity's message and mission were so overpowering that, if something wasn't identified with its robust red banner, then for all intents and purposes it didn't exist.

In truth, feminists did have "something" to do with Solidarity in 1980, for one of Poland's first feminist groups, modest in numbers though it was, came together in *opposition* to the opposition and as a reaction to the failure of the Gdańsk Accords to safeguard women's rights and interests. While feminism did not truly take root until after the fall of communism and only began to flower in the mid-1990s, as I shall explore in later chapters, it was not *strictly* a postcommunist phenomenon. However, that fact is little known either inside or outside Poland. Small numbers of women first began organizing, almost invisibly, in the late 1970s. Just as KOR's human rights thinking was shaped by Western ideas, so too did Polish feminists find inspiration in Western feminist literature, which was smuggled into the country from wherever a student, professor, or daughter of a Polish diplomat might have discovered it—the United States, France, Britain, Germany. From that point on, feminism very slowly developed a quiet, modest life of its own, usually on campuses and independent from and in opposition to both communism and Solidarity.

Warsaw University women had begun to meet and discuss feminist ideas in the late 1970s, and their discussions gained momentum as they reacted to the Gdańsk Accords. British researcher Anna Reading reported that by the autumn of 1980 "a group of women at Warsaw University became disillusioned with the sexism of Solidarity and the restrictive content of university courses. The women began their own consciousness-raising groups, held lectures and debates on women's issues and delivered leaflets round factories and schools. A key figure was Renata Siemieńska, a sociologist at Warsaw University . . . who since the late seventies has offered a seminar on feminism."[5]

The group members made a point of educating themselves, but

they did not directly challenge Solidarity or publish their criticisms in any of that period's new independent media. While some feminist consciousness-raising activities were feasible in 1980, the time for confrontational feminism would not arrive for another nine years. No one wanted to risk being expelled from the university by party officials, especially given that the women had no reason to expect that Solidarity would defend their freedom of feminist expression. When martial law was imposed, the Warsaw group lost members as people retreated out of fear and harder times. The few who remained active turned to organizing nonthreatening cultural activities by or about women. Because the group kept very quiet about its activities until the mid-1980s, other campuses never got wind of it.

It wasn't only that people believed that feminism was insignificant or a luxury or a frivolous Western phenomenon. It wasn't only that feminism was perceived as a manifestation of deceitful party rhetoric or was an idea whose time had not yet come. It was also that these notions were supported by a strong, underlying, unspoken cultural message: feminism's time should never come. Most Polish women accepted their society's continued, unacknowledged silence around gender issues.

Novelist Izabela Filipiak, who began her studies at Gdańsk University just as Solidarity was legalized, described feminism to me as a veritable taboo. "I didn't know what a feminist was in 1980. I don't remember ever hearing the term. But I knew very well that taking care of any kind of women's causes was something horrible, something that one should not do. It could ruin you. It was forbidden. It was so much forbidden that no one should waste their time discussing it. This wasn't the result of communism. This was patriarchy."

In analyzing the Gdańsk Accords as they relate to women, several scholars have noted how thoroughly they reflect the patriarchy. While the three proposed policies mentioned previously did address the real needs of working mothers, they also "helped maintain them in traditionally subordinate positions, reinforcing the image of women as secondary wage earners focused on the family and the home." This was the conclusion of Ewa Hauser, Barbara Heyns, and Jane Mansbridge in a 1993 article on the Solidarity heritage.[6] U.S. scholar Barbara Jancar found evidence supportive of these conclusions in Paragraph 6, Article 4, of the statutes, which "gives as a union objective 'the strengthening of the family as well as family life.' . . . The statutes suggest that the Polish worker is not concerned with women's problems in and of themselves, but with their impact on family life. . . . The larger issues of social reform and human rights took precedence over special interest demands. Women's concerns were integrated into general issues and seen as basic components of the social problem."[7]

In a statement that perfectly illustrates the opposition's failure to understand or to seriously address gender issues, a Solidarity activist told U.S. journalist Lawrence Weschler in 1981 that "Western reporters misunderstood Solidarity's line on women's issues. You were misled by our call for 'a return to the traditional role for women' into imagining that Solidarity was somehow hopelessly sexist. By insisting on family values, Solidarity was trying to correct the outrageous exploitation of women."[8]

Women were, indeed, exploited. They were poorly compensated in their jobs, and the wage inequities between the sexes never improved. But Solidarity's proposal to improve the conditions of family life not only didn't solve the problem of "outrageous exploitation," it flat-out ignored it. It also neglected the realities of working women who did not have children or who were not living for their families alone. It simply shifted the emphasis from the communist ideal, which emphasized women's role in the labor force, to the patriarchal ideal of women's role in their families. Solidarity might more effectively have addressed the issue of women's exploitation by challenging the party to adhere to its promises of adequate childcare, parental leave, and equality in employment and social security benefits.

The value placed on family life also obscured the problematic power dynamics that existed between men and women in the home. It would have been too much at that time to broach gender-sensitive subjects such as domestic violence, rape, or the unavailability of contraception and the use of abortion as a form of birth control. These were considered matters of private life, and because the state notoriously invaded people's privacy, the opposition shied away from appearing to do so.

In Poland from the postwar years into the early 1990s, notions of gender equality had become so closely identified with communism that by 1980 the two terms were virtually interchangeable. The party was viewed as the source of a "forced emancipation" that had produced an exhausting daily routine for women and drove a psychic wedge between men and women. Because feminism was blamed for the double burden that fell upon women's shoulders, women's liberation was not viewed with favor.

"We always talked about equal rights, but equality was really meant to pressure women to work," Anna Walentynowicz told me. "In reality, women got lesser pay and had to work a second shift. That's why we used to say: 'We have too much equality!'" When women said this, Anna commented, it was usually with bitter cynicism. Apparently, the party's perversion of basically sound principles had poisoned the ideals themselves, and the opposition was reluctant to appropriate even a perfectly good ideal if the party had abused it. Instead, the opposition negated the ideal and countered with tradition—often with outdated traditions such as the notion that women's proper place was in the home.

Legal scholar Małgorzata Fuszara, who analyzed the catastrophic abortion ban legislation in the early 1990s and later cofounded the Gender Studies Program at Warsaw University, told me she had not really thought about women's rights during the communist era, although she had been an advocate both of human rights and of Solidarity. "I became interested in feminism when the abortion ban proposal was first introduced in 1989. Before then, I never thought I would be involved in feminist topics. Like many women in this part of Europe, we rejected the Communist Party's emphasis on equality as being an artificial claim in the law and all official declarations. On the one hand, it was artificial because we were not equal. On the other hand, we felt that we should not be treated as a special part of society. We belonged to society as a whole. I used to feel nervous when the first secretary and other party leaders would begin their speeches: 'Citizens, women, and young people . . .' They represented women as a special group separate from citizens. It was a complicated problem."

It was a complicated problem because real equality should not have engendered a special position for women that was separate from men. Yet, paradoxically, in Polish culture the traditional image of womanhood, Matka Polka, portrays women as special. Matka Polka occupied an elevated position in the private sphere, and it was said that "woman" was treated with greater respect in Poland than in other cultures (particularly in Russian culture). Thus, according to the national tradition (which, to my ears, sounded similar to the party's claim that communism respected women better than did other political cultures), the fact that women held a special role ruled out any serious consideration of real conditions of inequality. Another traditional belief complemented the notion of women's specialness—women were thought to have a heightened capacity for personal sacrifice in the name of the collective good. Liberally espoused by both the communists and the opposition, this notion fed a credo that asserted that problems affecting the society as a whole should take precedence over women's specific needs.

Thus, as was also the case elsewhere in the Eastern Bloc, the democratic opposition in Poland never considered women's rights within its human rights framework. Nor did it examine sex role differences or inequalities within its own activist milieu. When the oppositionists reproduced the language of the traditional human rights corpus, it was, perhaps unwittingly, always with male referents, reflecting the belief that citizenship and the public sphere were male while home and domestic duty, the private sphere, were female.

The looming presence of the Communist Party also contributed to the fact that the opposition's conceptual framework did not differentiate the human rights of women or, for that matter, of ethnic groups or economic classes either. The framework lacked specificity, and no one questioned it because, again, everyone was oppressed under communism. Among oppositionists, "us versus them" was enough to justify the need for societywide reforms in a seemingly homogeneous nation. The only recognized and validated identity was that of the worker. There was virtually no understanding that women's rights deserved a legitimate position in the larger quest for freedom and justice. "In Solidarity . . . the political struggle pitted a unitarily conceived 'state' against an equally undifferentiated 'society,' leaving little space conceptually or organizationally for a specifically feminist consciousness or voice," Hauser, Heyns, and Mansbridge observed.[9] In other words, the consciousness needed to address the "them within us" had not yet developed.

The historic silence around feminism wove a shroud of confusion that would not easily unravel. Its warp and weft were evident in a conversation I had in 1990 with a Solidarity activist, who, years later, asked to remain unnamed because she was embarrassed to have made the statement. She was clearly offended by the then-newly proposed law that would ban abortion, which was being hotly debated at that time. "If you are against the abortion ban," I asked her, "does that mean you are a feminist?" She responded: "Until this moment, I had never thought about abortion as being associated with feminism and the rights of women. I thought about the abortion ban as an idiotic social phenomenon because its effects will be harmful to women and to the whole society—to men and children, too. Maybe it is a phenomenon that should be connected with all of society, not only part of it. Since feminism is only about part of society, we are not interested in it. We are interested in issues that are understood as the whole of society. And if feminism is not just about women, then I still do not like the name 'feminism.' I do not like to hear about women's rights. I prefer to hear about human rights."

Despite their exceptionally activist lives, when first interviewed for this book, most of the female oppositionists—with the aforementioned exception of Barbara Labuda—believed, like their sisters around the country, that communism had given women "too much equality." They did not think that women's rights should be made a priority of the prodemocracy movement.

A discussion of sex roles was—and remained until the 1990s—completely absent from progressive dialogues in Poland, where even the language itself was not constructed to embrace certain Western ideas such as "the personal is political." This key feminist notion, which was radical when first uttered in the United States in 1968, quickly became a catchphrase of Western women's movements, and it opened up discussion on the political dimensions of private life. For example, how did power relations shape marriage, the organization of family life, and child rearing? In Western society social roles and behavior inside the family had previously been treated as private matters, which were not worthy of analysis, were not to be discussed at home, aired publicly, or framed in legal terms. Private life belonged to a "zone of silence," until feminists cracked the ice.

No matter how widely accepted the notion that "the personal is political" became in the West, however, it lost any meaning in a communist context, where people jealously protected their personal lives from political—that is, government—scrutiny. Anything that was identified with politics was considered an invasion of individual privacy, and that key difference in social experience and perspective helped me understand why Barbara Labuda's feminist views had attracted few sympathizers back in Wrocław in the 1970s and 1980s. Not even her female friends cared to analyze gender roles. Barbara's powerful political awakening in France had set her apart from her contemporaries, who were back home living out the social drama of the "Polish context."

"During Solidarity's legal period, I was the only female political adviser on a national scale, but I also took the time to arrange administrative details and other logistical things," Barbara told me. "Women took the time for what I considered to be the real work, that is, directly helping people. These kinds of labor divisions foreshadowed the distribution of power after martial law was repealed."

Barbara and Aleksander, an activist and professor like his wife, were elected to the regional Solidarity board, and he served on its presidium. The couple had a liberated marriage, Barbara told me with some pride, shaped by their Paris experience. By liberated, she meant that husband and wife shared domestic and parenting duties while both maintained intensely busy work routines. This was considered extremely unconventional for the times in what Barbara emphatically characterized as "parochial, patriarchal Poland."

Though, with exceptions like the Labudas, Polish gender roles remained tradition-bound, Solidarity nevertheless bred a subversive unconventionality that rattled the authoritarian status quo. It did this by encouraging people to express themselves freely and to pursue civic activities of their own invention. The sixteen legal months were heady, exciting times in Poland, and Barbara told me she usually slept no more than three hours a night, what with managing the union training center, teaching at the university, writing a doctoral dissertation, and raising their ten-year-old son, Mateusz.

"I have wonderful memories despite the fact that I was permanently tired," she said, trying to recall how she managed everything without collapsing from exhaustion. "Until my work in Parliament began, I used to think that if a person has the engine, she can go on for a long time," Barbara explained. "As a parliamentarian, I depend on adrenaline. There is no police, no fear. I've always worked a lot with little sleep, but without the fear, paradoxically, it is harder to stay awake."

Barbara was not the first woman to tell me about her sleepless yet tireless days and the sense of urgency that had driven her efforts to build Solidarity. I was coming to realize that sleeping habits figured prominently in many activists' recollections. Bringing democracy to Poland had not been a nine-to-five job.

During Solidarity's legal period, the government with which the union had to deal proved mutable, and no one could predict how relations between it and Solidarity would unfold. Lech Wałęsa continually reminded both sides to keep talking "as Poles to Poles," just as they had done during the excruciating seven days of negotiations at the Lenin Shipyard. To the principle of nonviolence, developed by KOR in the late 1970s, Solidarity added the notion of a "self-limiting revolution"—evolutionary social change, cooperation with the state, and civic action with built-in restraints.

The Solidarity era began with a government shake-up when First Secretary Gierek was forced to step down in the first week of September and was replaced by Stanisław Kania. Kania—a former head, at different times, of the army and the secret police—was closely associated with General Wojciech Jaruzelski, who at that time was the defense minister. In February Jaruzelski would be appointed prime minister and would hold both ministerial posts. As the legal period went on, Jaruzelski's power increased, and he devoted himself to plotting Solidarity's downfall. Before Solidarity was one month old, its members celebrated a noteworthy concession: the government agreed to permit a national radio broadcast of Sunday Mass, the first since World War II. Other exceptional agreements made over the next year included a formal apology by Warsaw University to the victims of the 1968 anti-Semitic purges; the city of Radom's agreement to provide monetary compensation to the workers injured in the 1976 protests; and, most historic of all, the November 10 registration of the "independent, self-governing trade union Solidarity." Of course, Solidarity's gains were not all a result of civilized talks. Now ten million strong, the union often needed to flaunt its weight in order to gain the party's attention, and strikes and sit-ins were felt to be necessary to winning hard-core demands such as the removal of regional and local party leaders or the right to establish independent campus groups. For its part, the government continually provoked the new union, igniting disturbances around the country that ranged from threats of strikes to full-blown workers' protests and student sit-ins to belligerent name calling and combustible ill-will. Among the government's first egregious offenses, which began surfacing as early as October 1980, was neglecting to pay the wage increases it had agreed to during the summer strikes. The party also put off registering Solidarity. The union warned that a general strike would be called if registration wasn't completed by November 12, and the government finally complied—two days before the deadline.

Other conflicts soon arose. For example, farmers demanded the creation of an agricultural union, and Rural Solidarity was registered in February 1981 after farmers staged a month-long sit-in. Another heated, month-long clash ensued over the institutionalization of a five-day, forty-hour workweek, to which the government finally agreed—after Solidarity instructed its membership not to work on Saturdays. But few of these concessions were ever implemented.

For all their provocative actions, however, Solidarity members never resorted to the violence of guns or bombs. Perhaps one of their most "violent" acts was to deface a Soviet war memorial in the city of Lublin, and on Wałęsa's orders local Solidarity members cleaned up the site. The government, however, did use violence. One of the bloodiest incidents started on March 19, 1981, when police quashed a sit-in by Rural Solidarity in the city of Bydgoszcz in northern Poland in which dozens were hurt and three people were hospitalized, including a well-known activist named Jan Rulewski. Solidarity demanded that the perpetrators of what came to be known as the "Bydgoszcz crisis" be punished and called for a nationwide strike.

On March 27, the movement held a four-hour warning strike and threatened to escalate to a general strike on March 31 if the government did not respond. It was the largest strike in communism's history. U.S. journalist Tina Rosenberg reported that "Solidarity had the power to bring Poland to a halt. But whether to use that power was another matter."[10] The government made what appeared to the ever-vigilant Soviets to be shocking concessions by agreeing to compensate workers for their strike hours and to replace the Bydgoszcz region's provincial governor, deputy governor, and party head. These settlements did not satisfy the radical unionists led by Rulewski and Andrzej Gwiazda, however, who believed that the time was ripe to overthrow the government. They accused their high-level opponents—Wałęsa, Michnik, and Kuroń, among others—of undermining Solidarity's power by being too moderate.

Acutely aware that Soviet troops were already pushing toward Warsaw, Wałęsa headed into negotiations with Deputy Prime Minister Mieczysław Rakowski under massive pressure from the radicals to push the limits and from his KOR advisers to go for moderation. In the final hour, the Solidarity leader and the party official struck a compromise and the strike was called off. This provoked a furious outcry within Solidarity that focused on the lack of democratic process involved in agreeing to the compromise. Outraged activists also denounced the compromise itself for failing to demand that the police be held accountable for the violence.

The Bydgoszcz crisis marked the beginning of serious rifts within Solidarity. In the union's failure to escalate the strike, its weakness had been utterly revealed. And, equally serious, in the wake of the crises, the party began to draw up lists of activist troublemakers who should be targeted in the event of martial law.

The summer and fall of 1981 were characterized by mounting economic crises and food protests. The economy definitely worsened during the sixteen months of Solidarity's social initiatives. The soaring debt to the West hit twenty-three billion dollars in 1981, and people had not anticipated setbacks such as new shortages of raw materials and consumer goods, longer queues, and the unavailability of "guaranteed" rations. The failing economy provoked rabid bouts of finger pointing. Trade union leaders challenged the party for its long-term neglect of deep-seated problems, and the government blamed the economic crisis on Solidarity and its incessant strikes. The government also regularly demonized so-called extremist, urban-based, KOR intellectuals (such as Michnik and Kuroń) and stressed that the workers were being poorly advised by them. This was ironic, given that the more radical workers accused the same intellectuals of being excessively moderate.

Adding to the confusion, Church leaders usually weighed in on the side of the party's allegations against the intellectuals. Even though the pope spoke frequently of Poland's moral right to independence, the Polish Church often sided with the government in urging an end to labor unrest. In the eyes of the Catholic hierarchs, too much democracy was not necessarily desirable. "The Church insisted that Solidarity's mission should be the moral and spiritual transformation of the nation rather than reform of its political system," wrote Polish-born news commentator Jarosław Anders.[11] These allegations against KOR drove wedges into Solidarity, weakening ties between workers and intellectuals and between Solidarity and the Church. People began losing confidence in Solidarity.

Following that summer of economic crises and food protests, Solidarity convened its first annual congress in September 1981. The Soviets declared it "an anti-socialist and anti-Soviet orgy." Wałęsa was elected chairman of the union with just 55 percent of the vote, defeating Jan Rulewski of Bydgoszcz, Andrzej Gwiazda of Gdańsk, and Marian Jurczyk of Szczecin.

On October 18, 1981, at the very moment Poland seemed to be coming apart at the seams, the Central Committee removed First Secretary Stanisław Kania from his post and replaced him with Jaruzelski, who, at that point, held the posts of first secretary, prime minister, commander in chief, general of the army, chairman of the National Defense Council, and minister of defense, giving him unprecedented power. Appointing an army officer rather than a politician to that post was an unprecedented step on the part of the Central Committee. Jaruzelski brought a general's authority to political office. The rumble of social unrest continued to grow, the economy continued to plunge, there were shortages of everything, and the queues for the limited goods were insufferable.

In his second week in office, Jaruzelski began making clandestine plans for implementing martial law, including staging war games with mock army raids and the mass internment of six thousand "activists." Based on this covert exercise, he concluded that his martial law plans should be shrouded in secrecy until a surprise assault could be made successfully, preferably on a Saturday night in order to minimize the opposition's ability to mobilize strikes and protests.[12]

In a major show of force, less than two months after Jaruzelski's appointment, the government ordered police to quash an occupation strike at a firefighters academy in Warsaw. The violence of that action shocked the country, and it also employed a tactic that was a precursor of worse things to come—Solidarity's telex and telephone lines in the nation's capital were cut off.

Despite the weakening of Solidarity's popular base of support, due in part to ongoing infighting and in part to its failure to carry through with strikes that would have forced the government to negotiate, and despite the rumors of impending military intervention and martial law, Solidarity continued to believe the party was bluffing. By December, however, Jaruzelski's war plans were in place.

Solidarity's National Commission assembled in Gdańsk on the weekend of December 12 (the start of the tenth anniversary commemoration of the victims of the 1970 protests) and voted for a December 17 national day of protest against the state-sanctioned violence against the firefighters. In its most radical move to date, the commission also voted to hold a February referendum to ask its membership whether it would give a vote of confidence to General Jaruzelski and whether it would support the establishment of a temporary government and free elections.

Later that same day all communications lines in Gdańsk were cut.

Barbara and Aleksander Labuda had made arrangements to connect with Władysław Frasyniuk, Wrocław's representative at the Gdańsk meeting, to get reports on the Saturday session, which they knew would be long, tiring, and filled with conflict. They tried time and again to phone Frasyniuk from their Warsaw home. Despite the fact that telephone service was never reliable in communist times, the Labudas suspected trouble, especially since news had been circulating earlier in the day that army troops were moving through the country.

"The first night of martial law was one of the worst nights of my life," Barbara said, shuddering at the memory. Loud banging startled the couple just before midnight, and four armed soldiers barged into the apartment yelling orders. One jumped out onto their balcony, another blocked the front door, and a third shouted, "We have to take your husband."

When Barbara demanded to know what was going on and whether they had a warrant, the police aimed their pistols at Aleksander and ordered him to freeze. Aleksander packed a suitcase, even though the police said he would not need it, and was then handcuffed and taken away. "We are only carrying out orders," one of the officers actually said apologetically to Barbara as he exited. "Only later on, did I understand what he meant," she told me. Barbara immediately telephoned an attorney who represented Solidarity. "My husband's been arrested," she managed to say before the line went dead, as if the wires had been cut. She quietly arranged to have a neighbor stay with her son and then hurried off to warn people in Wrocław.

Police with patrol dogs were marching in the streets, which were lined with army cars. Barbara drove cautiously through the city, stopping to search for friends. She realized later that she had been very lucky because "each time I arrived at a friend's home, it was just after the police had left"—few of the incursions had been as civilized as the raid on her apartment. It was mainly her male colleagues, it seemed, who were being arrested.

Driving stealthily, Barbara passed not far from Solidarity headquarters and saw everyone who ventured toward the building be arrested on the spot. Turning around she drove through the downtown district, noting that special riot units, called ZOMO, were escorting trams and buses back to their depot. Looking up, she saw a red and white flag on the bus depot. "We activists used to tell each other that if ever there was martial law, we would hang red and white flags from our windows, the Polish national flag. And so

I knew—it was martial law." It was around three o'clock in the morning.

"When martial law was declared, at least 10,000 cars with armed men stopped in front of as many houses and apartments to take their inhabitants away," émigré activist Irena Grudzińska-Gross later reported.[13] Police crowbars cracked open the doors of almost everyone who was considered an organizer of people, including at the factory level. The homes had been marked in advance, and the raids were strategically planned and executed. An estimated ten thousand people were arrested in the first few days—approximately nine thousand men and one thousand women—including the majority of Solidarity's male-dominated leadership, most of whom had been staying at the same hotel in Gdańsk that weekend, making them easy prey. Army troops simply surrounded the building and took them en masse. The apprehended men—including longtime activists and spokespersons Bronisław Geremek, Andrzej Gwiazda, Jacek Kuroń, Adam Michnik, Karol Modzelewski, Janusz Onyszkiewicz, and Henryk Wujec—were all transferred to detention camps.

Lech Wałęsa was arrested in his Gdańsk home and then flown to Warsaw early Sunday morning, where he was placed under house arrest in a suburban villa. Throughout his internment, the government pressed Wałęsa to collaborate and made offers of a conditional release, all of which he rejected. Amazingly, he did manage to smuggle out messages calling for nonviolent resistance, which circulated throughout Warsaw. But Wałęsa's capture was symbolically also the movement's capture, and the massive roundups left Solidarity a rudderless ship and created an alarming vacuum in opposition authority.

On a special 6:00 AM radio broadcast the Sunday after the arrests, General Wojciech Jaruzelski declared: "Citizens and Lady Citizens of the Polish People's Republic! I turn to you as a soldier and chief of government! Our country is on the edge of an abyss. Achievements of many generations, raised from the ashes, are now collapsing into ruin. State structures are no longer functioning. New blows are struck each day to our flickering economy. Living conditions are burdening people more and more."[14]

"Few Poles would have disagreed with General Jaruzelski's description of the late 1981 climate," Barbara Labuda acknowledged. Change had indeed come to mean breakdown, and the situation had become alternately exhilarating and terrifying. The state no longer controlled all forms of public life. That was the exciting component of having won an autonomous social movement. But Solidarity's very existence also exposed a fundamental incompatibility between government and society in communist Poland, as Irena Grudzińska-Gross explains in *The Art of Solidarity,* her 1985 book on the graphic images that the movement generated before and during martial law. "The two protagonists of Polish social life speak different languages and share no common ground," Grudzińska-Gross writes. "The government uses and advocates violence, while the society is profoundly pacifist. The government is atheistic, while the society is deeply religious. The government is pro-Russian, while the society is strongly nationalistic. The government is communist, while the society believes in democracy. The government is anti-Western, while the society worships the West, and the United States especially. Moreover, the society is devoted to the Romantic cult of freedom, believing in human rights and national independence as giving birth to and nourishing each other. The Polish situation, then, is inherently, structurally flawed, and only external force can keep it in place. Such a situation is extremely dangerous for all of us."[15]

Actually, a martial law plan had already been in development years before the idea of a free trade union movement called Solidarity had crystallized. According to Tina Rosenberg, the government, first under Party Chief Władysław Gomułka and then under his successor, Edward Gierek, had been plotting to wage an internal war since the 1970 Gdańsk riots. This plan had been pulled from the files and revised in response to the 1976 workers' rebellions in Radom and Ursus. During the August 1980 strikes and into the following autumn, a more detailed game plan emerged, which called for an army raid on the Lenin Shipyard in Gdańsk, militarization of all communications structures, and the closing off of roads out of the Baltic seaport towns.[16] A list of the most dangerous opposition leaders was appended to the plan. By the close of 1980 the entire scheme had been presented to the Polish government and then sent on to Moscow. After the Bydgoszcz riots in March 1981, the list of insurgents had lengthened and the government's preparations for a future crackdown became more serious.

During the fifteen months the Soviets were pressing for martial law, Jaruzelski had stalled. He gave the Soviets two main reasons for doing so. First, he surmised that the Polish army was not yet psychologically prepared to fight Polish workers. Remembering that many soldiers had refused to shoot at their fellow Poles during the 1970s workers' uprisings, the prime minister did not think he could count on his army's allegiance. In keeping with a time-honored code of honor, Poles do no (or did not) fight one another. Jaruzelski's second reason for stalling was that he wanted to wait until Solidarity weakened. With Solidarity's popularity far greater than that of the party at the time, there was no telling where a soldier would place his loyalty when put to the test.

Jaruzelski's reasons had unnerved the skeptical Soviets, not because they sounded logical but because they sounded like excuses. The Soviets believed that Jaruzelski and the Polish Communist Party were neither capable of nor willing to bring down Solidarity and had already become the pawns of the grass roots movement. The USSR cut back its economic provisions to Poland, putting the country in danger of starvation, according to Tina Rosenberg.[17] And it threatened to invade Poland itself, positioning troops at the Polish border four times during Solidarity's short life as a legal entity.

Would the USSR have invaded, or was it a bluff to push Jaruzelski into action? Was martial law actually the lesser evil? Those important questions are still being asked. Though they didn't want to lose Poland—their bridge to the West and their largest satellite country—the Soviets were actually reluctant to invade. They couldn't afford Western political and economic sanctions. Nor did they have enough troops, given the situation in Afghanistan. The times and circumstances were very different from those in which the Soviet Union had invaded Hungary (in 1956) and Czechoslovakia (in 1968), whose rebellions had come from within their party's top tiers. In Poland, the reforms were being advanced from an organized population ten million strong.

A few days before he finally struck, on that perfectly positioned Saturday night, Jaruzelski had beseeched Moscow to assist him with troops, should backup be needed. But after breathing down Jaruzelski's neck for more than a year, they refused to intervene, fearing Western sanctions.

General Jaruzelski did not, it turned out, need the USSR's help. When he ordered martial law he placed the government under the control of a twenty-one-man Military Council for National Salvation (WRON). Army generals and commissars took over the ministries and most of the large state-owned enterprises. "These measures will be temporary. There will be no turning back from socialism," the general stated in his 6:00 AM address.[18] This warning, in and of itself, would have remained just dull rhetoric if it had not been backed up by the ominous presence of guns and tanks, by isolating communications shutdowns, and by the menacing shadow of the Soviet Union. Almost twenty-three minutes long, Jaruzelski's address was repeated on radio and television every hour well into the afternoon. Between the broadcasts, stations aired Chopin and patriotic songs. Jaruzelski concluded by echoing the end of Poland's national anthem—"Poland is not yet lost as long as we yet live."

WRON immediately issued twenty martial law decrees that seemed to appear almost instantly on lampposts and buildings in every city and town across Poland. The twenty decrees swiftly wiped out the twenty-one demands that had created Solidarity. Civil rights were suspended; the frontiers were closed; travel and communications between cities were prohibited; all public gatherings as well as the distribution of printed material and printing equipment were banned; a 10:00 PM to 6:00 AM curfew was imposed; mail and telephone were censored; all schools except for nursery schools were closed indefinitely; and the armed forces were authorized to use "coercion to restore calm, law, and order."

"The Polish term is *stan wojenny*," Barbara explained to me. "It means 'state of war.'" People called it "Jaruzelski's war," implying that he had waged war against his own country.

Having witnessed some of martial law's first casualties on the streets of Wrocław that first day, Barbara realized it would not be safe to remain in her home. It was still not yet dawn, and Jaruzelski's first broadcast had not yet been made when she returned home to pack before finding shelter elsewhere. A sudden banging on her door interrupted her packing; Barbara froze, thinking the police had come back, and did not dare answer. "I worried that they could hear my heart pounding hysterically," she confessed. Finally she heard the intruder's footsteps fade away. Half an hour passed when she again heard a knock, clearly not the authorities' banging, and recognized a friend's voice whispering, "Basia, Basia, it's me." Assuming that both of the Labudas had been arrested, the friend had come to retrieve their son, Mateusz (Basia).

Barbara went into hiding that first Sunday. A week later, when she realized that she might be there indefinitely, she arranged for her son to move to the home of her apolitical in-laws in another town. She chose not to send Mateusz to her own parents' home because hers was an "activist family" involved in the opposition.

"The nation woke up that Sunday morning (those who had slept) to a different world," Irena Grudzińska-Gross wrote in 1985. "Wherever one looked there were tanks, soldiers with machine guns directed at passersby, road blocks, and long military convoys moving in all directions. The General was talking about a 'state of war,' an incomprehensible but threatening neologism; TV announcers suddenly appeared in military uniform. Curfew, searches, mass arrests, shootings of strikers—it all meant WAR. . . . The roadblocks, tanks and regulations had a practical side, like the immediate interruption of communication, the isolation of various centers, and the arrests. . . . But they were also made conspicuous just to instill fear— a practical but measurable result."[19]

In an upsurge of national rage, factory and university strikes broke out across the country on Monday, day two of martial law. In fact, the mobilization of strike committees had begun spontaneously on day one, with the organizers acting independently because they could not contact one another, given the communications blackout.

In cities and towns throughout the country, protest flyers calling for occupation strikes were mass-produced on duplicating machines and distributed to local populations. Strike organizers at the Ursus tractor factory near Warsaw, for example, declared: "Members of Solidarity! Compatriots! The purpose of this attack is to liquidate our union. It means that a state of emergency has been declared in violation of the Constitution of the PRL [Polish People's Republic]. We must respond—in accordance with our statutes—with an immediate nationwide general strike."[20]

Appeals rang out from the shipyards in the Tri-Cities of Gdańsk, Gydnia, and Sopot; from the steelworks in Nowa Huta near Kraków; from the shipyards in Szczecin; from the coal mines in Silesia; from the munitions factory in Radom near Warsaw; and from university campuses in Poznań, Kraków, Warsaw, Wrocław, Lublin, and Łódź.

People massed together instinctively, as they had done during the summer-long strikes of 1980. The people had shared a collective experience of freedom and mass action, and it remained alive during the initial days of martial law. The outraged nation looked like it was not going to back down, even though the battle seemed hopeless from the start as an unarmed, leaderless, nonviolent resistance tried to face off a modern police state.

Events unfolded in Wrocław much as they did elsewhere. Barbara recalled that she went to the university, where her colleagues who had not been arrested had organized a strike committee and were preparing leaflets for distribution. She asked how she might help and was told, "You must join [Władysław] Frasyniuk. He was not arrested in Gdańsk and has returned to Wrocław. You two must organize everything else."

Like Zbigniew Bujak, the Warsaw regional leader, and Bogdan Lis in Gdańsk, Frasyniuk had narrowly escaped arrest that first night. The twenty-seven-year-old former truck driver and mechanic, who oversaw his region's one million union members, had left Gdańsk immediately after the meeting adjourned. He and his delegation heard the news about martial law on the train ride home. A conductor helped them jump off the train shortly before its arrival in Wrocław, where police were waiting to arrest them.

Heading to the bus depot to search for Frasyniuk, Barbara saw riot troops empty Solidarity's regional headquarters of its entire contents—files, papers, telephones, typewriters, and furniture. "Within twenty-four hours, we lost our access to the world," she sighed. And by December 17, the military had quashed all the strike efforts in the Wrocław region. "Tanks surrounded the factories, entered through the main gates, followed by the ZOMO. They handcuffed everyone in sight. They went from one factory to another, repeating the pacification. I watched it all. None of our strike efforts succeeded."

In less than one week, the military crushed all impromptu rebellions throughout the country, one after the other, and arrested thousands more activists, eventually totaling an estimated fifteen thousand. General Jaruzelski had effectively wiped out the Solidarity leadership and shattered all communication links. Paralysis threatened to overcome the nation.

On December 20 Barbara, Frasyniuk, and others in Wrocław decided to organize an underground. "Everything had to start from ground zero," she emphasized. "In Wrocław, the greatest numbers of people out of the whole country were arrested, around two thousand right away. These included many of our regional leaders as well as activists from the factories and the universities. We had organized a strong opposition to martial law, but they had executed an even stronger repression."

The initial mass arrests were vital to the party's success because they effectively decapitated Solidarity, a political force made up of national, regional, and local policy-making committees. "The key to the arrests became obvious after a few days: these were the people who would be able to function in a conspiracy," wrote Warsaw sociologist Jadwiga Staniszkis. They included "[t]he leaders of the August 1980 strikes; printers of bibuła papers before and after August 1980; regional activists with high prestige and good contacts among workers; and people who were the objects of resentment by the party and internal security apparatuses in the late 1970s."[21]

The government attempted to provoke distrust among Solidarity members by exacerbating a class division between the intellectuals and the workers and, in so doing, hoped to further delegitimize the already weakened movement. The arrested leaders, who were internationally known, were interned in more comfortable quarters than were the striking workers who had been hauled away from factory sites that first week. The workers were given harsh prison sentences, which they served in unheated cells. Thousands more workers were fired from their jobs for their participation in the occupation strikes. Still others faced the threat of unemployment if they refused to resign from Solidarity and to sign the government's loyalty oath, which stated: "I will cease all activities harmful to the state." Absurd words, considering that all such activities were already forbidden and virtually impossible to pursue.

"The existence of Solidarity, of an independent union, is incompatible with keeping so many union people in jail as political prisoners," stated Warsaw activist Ewa Milewicz, who had reported on the Lenin Shipyard strike for *Robotnik* back in August 1980. "If they remain in prison and something called Solidarity continues to exist, people will reject it as a changeling—a government union. Those who belong to it will be ostracized as having betrayed their own people."[22]

The simultaneous coordination of strikes and other forms of protest that had been a cornerstone of Solidarity's success was now impossible. With travel prohibited, mass transportation restricted, and the border blockaded, local populations were almost completely isolated from one another. What Timothy Garton Ash had cleverly dubbed Solidarity's "telerevolution" was destroyed. Night and day, the population was left in the dark, unable to communicate, to learn what had happened, to decide what to do. "If Martians had landed on earth, people could not have been more disoriented," Milewicz stressed in an interview published in the United States in 1982.[23]

Lawrence Weschler framed the debacle this way: "Solidarity was a movement that lived by breathing the openness it exhaled. Jaruzelski's brilliant insight was that the way to extinguish the movement was not so much by attacking it directly as by smothering the openness it lived on. For months, everyone had known everything. Now, suddenly, no one seemed to know anything.... It comes down to something as clichéd as this: Information is light. It was precisely the sudden lack of information that rendered everything so stark.... No wonder that after a few days of resistance, they seemed to crater."[24]

With no leaders, no communication, and no networks left, the telerevolution lay in shambles, its printing presses smashed, its papers burned to warm the soldiers who now occupied the streets. Were alternative strategies even feasible, or was it wisest to admit defeat?

The obvious answer was to form an underground.

Various Western journalists have profiled some of the Solidarity activists who assumed public responsibility for the underground. Lawrence Weschler said of them that the political courage they exhibited is rarely witnessed among so many individuals from one generation. The profiles were of the male representatives of the National Commission who had eluded arrest and gone into hiding to regroup and to try to save the trade union movement from total demise: Zbigniew Bujak and Wiktor Kulerski of Warsaw, Władysław Frasyniuk of Wrocław, Władysław Hardek of Kraków, and Bogdan Lis of Gdańsk.

But if these men were in hiding, who was hiding them? If information had to be gathered and disseminated, who figured among Solidarity's top news producers and purveyors? If the task was to reunite activists, who had created Solidarity's databases of national contacts? According to Barbara Labuda, the kinds of knowledge and expertise that the political emergency demanded were all stored in the minds of women, in particular a core group of media-savvy conspirators who lived in Warsaw. Some of these highly sophisticated activists were even the friends and informants of those Western reporters who so carefully profiled the men.

"You've come to learn about Solidarity women, so I will tell you the truth, but who will care to publish it? Everyone in Poland knows that women started the 1980s underground, but no one bothers to talk about it," Barbara stated, sitting back in her chair to observe my reactions as she disclosed the story behind the headlines.

"Three of us took charge. I headed the Wrocław region with Władysław Frasyniuk, who was a national trade union leader and one of the few influential men to escape arrest. In Warsaw, Helena Łuczywo and Ewa Kulik organized the underground's national headquarters, together with Zbigniew Bujak, a trade union leader like Frasyniuk. Helena was a brilliant organizer. Under her direction, six women published a weekly newspaper called *Tygodnik Mazowsze* that served as Solidarity's voice."

In addition to Helena and Ewa, Barbara named Joanna Szczęsna, Anna Dodziuk, Anna Bikont, Zofia Bydlińska, and Małgorzata Pawlicka. They became the editors, reporters, and publishers of Solidarity's independent press, the movement's communications strategists, who knew how to find out what was going on amid the chaos of dispersion and how to reconnect people and networks. Men were nominally in charge of the underground, Barbara asserted, but "behind the image of our male working-class champions, like Władysław Frasyniuk and Zbigniew Bujak, stood women, who did the conceptual and organizational work. Men didn't have the skills to manage the underground. Women were the brainpower, but we were discreet because we had to protect our own identities from the authorities. Otherwise, they would figure out the puzzle—that women were the *real* organizers." I listened, amazed, as Barbara described a political drama she characterized as Poland's "national secret," something everyone knew, but apparently not consciously, and so it could be forgotten or overlooked.

At the end of our 1991 interview, I asked Barbara why she had waited so long to tell her version of the story. "I asked the other women to come forth with me immediately after the government changed hands [in 1989]," she said, "but they refused. Either they were too busy, or they thought they'd be mocked, or they didn't see the purpose it would serve."

3. Dark Circles
building the solidarity underground

.

Today, Helena Łuczywo is one of the wealthiest and most powerful people in Poland. She heads the newspaper, radio, television, and Internet empire that grew from the seed of *Gazeta Wyborcza* (Election Gazette), the first independent national news daily in postcommunist Europe. Founded in 1989 by Helena and fellow champions of democracy, *Gazeta Wyborcza* emerged from that year's Round Table negotiations between the Communist Party and Solidarity, which decided the terms for the political change-over. During those pivotal debates, the communist government agreed to set partially free elections for June 1989 and to allow the democratic opposition to publish its own newspaper; that was the moment when Helena decided to produce *Gazeta Wyborcza,* which retained its name beyond 1989 to commemorate that historic election.

Using antediluvian printing presses and lead type, she played midwife to a newspaper that enjoyed meteoric success and soon installed state-of-the-art equipment, employed more than twenty-four hundred people nationwide, and was selling half a million copies per day. When Agora, the paper's parent company, went public in 1998, some twelve hundred of its employees, including the cafeteria staff, were made rich overnight.

Helena Łuczywo began the business education that made possible her key role in those record-breaking achievements twenty years earlier in Poland's political underground, where the management of a free press, not a free market, monopolized her energies. When martial law was declared in December 1981 and Solidarity was instantly stripped of its legal status, thirty-five-year-old Helena dove into hiding and began to spearhead an ambitious conspiracy to rescue the crippled trade union movement. By imprisoning its leaders and outlawing its publications, the party intended for Solidarity to slip into silenced obscurity. Helena had other plans. She orchestrated a wide range of clandestine activities, including the production of the weekly illegal newspaper *Tygodnik Mazowsze* (Regional Weekly), intended for nationwide distribution. This mammoth enterprise was carried out in people's homes, in basements and attics, in churches, and in cars—in other words, Helena and her compatriots pulled it off without the use of real offices. Ironically, the military intervention proved to be a fertile training ground for a CEO-in-the-making.

I first met Helena at *Gazeta Wyborcza*'s original headquarters on Warsaw's Ilwicka Street in December 1990, nine years after the declaration of martial law and almost eighteen months into the new democracy. Housed in a former nursery school, complete with sandbox and swings in a back courtyard, these offices seemed symbolically in tune with Poland's then-fledgling political reality. The building bustled with buoyant energy as twenty- and thirty-something young men and women raced neck and neck through the narrow hallways, in and out of offices, their arms cradling papers. I wondered whether Helena enjoyed operating a newspaper out of an office building after the exciting sprawl of the officeless underground.

Boxing gloves hung on one wall of Helena's modest cubicle, passed on to her by Adam Michnik, her famous opposition colleague and *Gazeta*'s editor in chief. I asked if the gloves had been put out to pasture after a battle gloriously won. Had she needed them in the transition from one-party rule? Helena laughed heartily and poured us cups of coffee. I appreciated the way she relaxed in her chair, as if there was no need to rush our meeting. Today, her jam-packed schedule might rule out such a slow-paced, in-depth interview, though even back in 1990, she showed little interest in being the subject of a profile and especially was not keen to discuss her personal life.

"We don't divulge the details of our personal lives the way Americans do," she said matter-of-factly. I took her point, but then she dutifully addressed some of those intimate matters, because, after all, she is a media professional and understood the task at hand. Still, she has never liked the limelight and prefers to play behind the scenes—like a corporate executive, like a woman who knows how to hold power in a man's world, like someone raised in an authoritarian society, where public glory can quickly turn into public condemnation. Helena proved to be complex and controversial and a woman for whom democratic values remain dear, but these impressions didn't emerge from one meeting alone.

What I did notice at that first interview was how skillfully she fielded my questions and without wasting words answered only the ones that were specific to either her activist experience or her knowledge of the broader political context. As I listened to her describe how the underground came together, peppering the facts with her analysis, that strange abstraction called "the underground" began to make sense to me.

"I was totally surprised by martial law," she told me. "I'm very optimistic by nature. Somehow, even though some people had said something terrible was going to happen—the police were everywhere, the troops were forming, and things like that—still, when it really happened, I was surprised. On the very first night I naively believed that it all might end soon. We used to say at the time: 'The winter is yours, the spring will be ours.' But even though I was convinced in the first days that martial law was not going to last, I and others immediately began to set up an information network."

As she understood it, the response to the political crisis that confronted her and thirty-eight million other Poles in December 1981 called for reorganizing Solidarity's nationwide network of contacts, fixing its headquarters in Warsaw, and putting in place a game plan to distribute information quickly. "The most important goal was to collect and report reliable information to people about the events that followed December 13," said Helena, who had been directing the independent Solidarity Press Agency, known as

AS, when General Jaruzelski seized the country's communication systems.

Her answer was to found and publish *Tygodnik Mazowsze,* the weekly paper that became Solidarity's new voice and remained so until the victory over communism in 1989. Designed to keep the nation both informed and hopeful in the face of its humiliating loss of freedom, the four-pager was launched in those early, severely restrictive days when official permission was necessary even to buy typewriter ribbon and typing paper.

"The goal was simple—to 'preserve Solidarity using every constructive means possible,'" she told me. For Helena and others, those means included accepting tough personal sacrifices. Forced to give up all traces of a normal life once she went underground, Helena placed her eight-year-old daughter, Łucja, in the care of grandparents. She also separated from her activist husband, Witold, in order to lessen the risk of either one of them getting caught by the police. Eventually, the couple divorced because, as Helena observed, "While strong marriages usually held together in the underground, if they were already weak, the pressures of an underground existence exacerbated the weaknesses."

But while the loss of "normal" life was an inevitable consequence, the underground also gave individuals like Helena a unique arena in which to show their stuff. As *New Yorker* writer Lawrence Weschler observed after reporting from Warsaw under martial law, "Just as it was probably inevitable that the regime was never going to be able to capture every single one of its opponents straight off that [first] night, so it was also highly likely that several among those whom the regime failed to capture would prove themselves activists of exceptional sophistication, intelligence, and daring."[1]

Although even before December 13, 1981, Helena was gaining a reputation in opposition circles as a brilliant editor and organizer, taking charge of the martial law crisis was not a foreseeable next step in her opposition career. In October, just two months before martial law began, she told American National Public Radio: "The first part of the Revolution has been completed—the abandonment of the old system. We are in the middle of the Revolution and what we must do now is create the new system. We hope for a parliamentary democracy, modeled on the West, plus the statutes of Finland, geopolitical and military dependence on the USSR, and a large rein of internal independence."[2]

Her statement implies that she and others took precautions not to provoke the Soviets, who had been threatening to invade Poland. At the same time, like Helena, most of the key organizers were less fearful of their own government, thinking that their mighty Solidarity could only become stronger now that it was legal. They were so busy building the movement that few came up for air long enough to consider seriously that Jaruzelski might successfully immobilize them. Oppositionists had, to be sure, anticipated some kind of government intervention and to that end had hidden money, typewriters, paper, and printing presses, just as had their predecessors under earlier regimes. Some people had also planned where to hide themselves and how to find one another in the event of a crackdown. They identified homes and individuals that would be "safe," that the secret police were likely to pass over.

What people had failed to consider was that Solidarity's entire leadership might be jailed in one fell swoop overnight and that they would need to assign fill-ins to quickly step up to bat. Even if they had discussed such options, it's doubtful, due to sexism in the ranks, that Helena would have been nominated to be the acting director and supervisor of damage control. Giving a woman the leadership reins would have been considered veritable suicide for Solidarity, I was told, because the weaker sex is, well, weaker, and thus activists would suspect that a communist plot was afoot. It was lunacy to expect that a woman, who was counted upon to play a supporting role to men in the male-dominated Solidarity hierarchy, could be a stabilizing force and could inspire confidence when the whole trade union movement was in shambles. Only other women were able to cast rigid stereotypes aside and recognize the true value of Helena's potential and, later, of her achievements. Among themselves and in our interview sessions, women activists praised her prodigious managerial talents and dubbed her the "mastermind of the conspiracy."

In fact, whenever I asked women to describe their efforts to oppose martial law—What did you do? Who guided you? How did you find shelter?—they usually responded, "Helena Łuczywo told us what to do." According to women of all ages and backgrounds, Helena was the chief organizer, the person to whom every activist was accountable after martial law was imposed. "Helena decided everything. She understood what was needed," women told me. "Helena had all the answers and was always ready to act."

It was only by chance that Helena became involved in the opposition. Her rite of passage happened in 1976, much later than for most of her generation's rebels. An economist and linguist by training and married to an engineer, until the mid-1970s she led a rather ordinary life, working at a bank, teaching English as a second language, and raising a toddler.

Then, in the summer of 1976, Jacek Kuroń, already a legendary oppositionist, contacted her with a request. Would she serve as an interpreter for a Swedish television crew that had come to Poland to interview workers striking to protest food price hikes in Radom and Ursus, two factory towns on Warsaw's outskirts? The protests turned violent, as had happened during the 1970 factory strikes, but this time the government quickly withdrew the price hikes and then cracked down, persecuting and imprisoning workers and putting the urban-based KOR intellectuals who supported them under surveillance.

Helena had kept a safe distance from KOR until Kuroń made his request. Sensing that it meant trouble, she did not want to arouse police suspicion, did not want to give up her stable life, and did not want to risk her family's safety. Nevertheless, she said yes, and listening to the Swedes' interviews with the mistreated Ursus workers sparked her political awakening. In 1976 the opposition was like a spirited stallion galloping into uncharted territory. She leaped on, took full control of the reins, and never looked back.

In the late 1970s Helena went on to work for the underground press, where she learned the publishing trade, bibuła style. Though she began by typing manuscripts, she quickly rose in her chosen new world and in 1977 cofounded and edited *Robotnik,* the galvanizing workers' publication that advocated for free trade unions. "We wanted to start free trade unions in Poland. We were sure that if the workers did not get organized, if Polish society did not get organized, we would never achieve anything. The whole country would be run as it had been—based on lies, inefficiency and oppression," Helena explained.[3] In his autobiography, *A Way of Hope,* Lech Wałęsa recalled *Robotnik*'s role in the August 1980 strikes: "The entire shipyard had been in a ferment from the moment the gates opened that summer morning because of an editorial in *Robotnik* listing our demands."[4]

An indication of Helena's growing importance was the secret police's close scrutiny of her life. They raided her apartment more than twenty-five times in the late 1970s, threatened to remove her daughter from kindergarten and primary school, and got her fired from a teaching position.

Then came Solidarity's 1980 victory. "We worked for free trade unions, but we never expected such a success," Helena said. With *Robotnik*'s mandate delivered and Solidarity made legal, Helena teamed up with several friends to create and direct the Agencja Prasowa "Solidarność" (Solidarity Press Agency), the only media outlet to disseminate uncensored news to the growing independent press in Poland. The press agency, usually referred to simply as AS, was Helena's brainchild, people told me, a news service that aimed to improve the circulation of information through Solidarity's regional unions. While the government continued to control all preexisting newspapers, radio, and television, it had conceded to Solidarity the right to create alternative media that would represent the various regional unions.

Officially launched in January 1981, AS was the only independent press agency in Poland and reported on Solidarity's ongoing negotiations with the government, as well as publishing the trade unions' official declarations, resolutions, and demands. Its editors aimed to make AS an information clearinghouse for the trade union movement by facilitating the exchange of news reports and orienting journalists to current issues. The editors solicited journalists from the independent press to catalog all the Solidarity papers and bulletins in their regions and to send the information for publication in AS. It also listed international press sources and subject indices. The bulletin was "of outstanding journalistic quality," wrote émigré activist Irena Grudzińska-Gross, and its editors were "real information age heroes (or rather heroines, since the majority of them were women)."[5]

Everyone seemed to agree that AS was a crazy enterprise because the 150-page weekly digest was launched even before its editors had acquired telexes, telephones, or a full staff. Though it did have an office, AS shared many characteristics with Helena's 1980s underground activity—a knack for piecemeal production, for example. The resourcefulness and improvisation required to get AS up and running even before all the parts were in place represented precisely the kind of know-how, or will, that a political emergency like martial law would later demand.

AS was widely used by media sources throughout the country, and even by the government, because it provided a dependable news service at a time when many inexperienced people were beginning new media ventures. (There had been few opportunities to produce real news prior to Solidarity's legalization.) What Helena lacked in equipment she made up for with the staff she hired. The members of her editorial team had gotten their publishing experience in the 1970s samizdat press, just as she had, and together they ran a tight ship. While other publications started and folded within Solidarity's short legal life, before the events of December 13, AS was on the road to building an information infrastructure for the emerging civil society.

AS also was one of the few organizations to document the history of Solidarity's legal period. The news that its staff collected, ordered, and disseminated—news of Solidarity's cultural, civic, political, and economic inroads—established a historical record. That record also included a rudimentary database of regional and nationwide contacts, the vital resources and networks that later enabled the underground to reassemble Solidarity's information systems during martial law. AS had addresses, and those proved to be a precious commodity during the communications blackout that began in December 1981.

Agnieszka Maciejowska worked as a journalist in a newspaper office next door to AS and used to run into its editors in the hallways. (After martial law, she went to work for *Tygodnik Mazowsze*.) She told me she had viewed the group as a whole and each member individually as hard working and remarkably professional, especially given that none had ever received formal training. The no-nonsense confidence that impressed Agnieszka also impressed others with whom I spoke, and they were widely admired for their stamina and singular focus. They even garnered admiration for their harried appearance.

"We used to call them the 'Dark Circles,' because they worked day and night, they never slept, and all had dark circles under their eyes," Agnieszka recalled when I interviewed her in Warsaw in December 1990. "At first we thought the shadows under their eyes was a fashion trend, an intentional application of eye makeup." But it was the mark of fatigue and adrenaline, a visual reminder of the massive energies required to build a grass roots movement. Their literal dark circles added to the mystery and magnetism these women exuded while they were shaping a "dark circle" of conspiracy to overthrow the communist system.

Working "24-7" in their race against the party's politically inevitable backlash, the AS staff never stopped to think about the fact that nearly all of them were female. Organizing a women-dominated press had not been a conscious aim on the part of Helena or her staff. I was told it was more a matter of happenstance, of people choosing to team up because they were friends, enjoyed working together, and hoped for a meaningful exchange of knowledge and skills. Nonetheless, Helena's initiative in creating AS marked one of the few efforts by a woman to enter Poland's male-dominated field of opposition journalism and to draw other women into that sphere.

At midnight on December 13, Helena was working in the Solidarity office on Mokotowska Street when ZOMO broke down the doors and began making some of the first arrests. Helena was one of the lucky few who escaped. But without access to her office and its vital contents, and given that nearly all the opposition men were, or soon would be, either imprisoned or in hiding, she realized that it was crucial that she pull together her AS colleagues, *if* she could locate them.

Helena put out the word, and by Tuesday afternoon, December 15, seven women in hiding made their way to a clandestine meeting with the help of trusted friends, who had walked from house to house during those first three days of martial law to seek them out and to deliver the messages. Telephone service had already been cut off and would remain off for a month. Transportation had been temporarily shut down, public gatherings were banned, and a nighttime curfew was in place. The only means of communication left was to carry messages on foot across a city the size of Boston.

At the specified time each woman trudged through subfreezing temperatures to an apartment in Żolibórz, a northern district of Warsaw, to begin plotting to save Solidarity. Each knew without a doubt that they would fight back. Solidarity was their dream come true, their life's work and mission. It was only later that they realized they had formed the only all-women cabal in Poland to make a counterstrike against martial law. The seven conspirators were Helena Łuczywo, Joanna Szczęsna, Ewa Kulik, Anna Dodziuk, Zofia Bydlińska, Małgorzata Pawlicka, and Anna Bikont.

Helena Łuczywo, age thirty-five, was married and had one daughter (soon to be in the care of Helena's parents). She was the initiator and driving force behind the team of seven women activists that would soon name their group Damska Grupa Operacyjna, "Ladies' Operational Unit," or DGO for short.

Joanna Szczęsna, age thirty-three, was single and the mother of a two-year-old son. She was Helena's right-hand woman and co-pilot at AS. Joanna, like Helena, had become a respected bibuła editor in the late 1970s, and when the two women teamed up during Solidarity's legal phase to produce AS, it proved to be a great meeting of the minds. The friends enjoyed a dynamic work relationship wherein Helena's communications and managerial skills readily complemented Joanna's editorial and narrative flair. Their combined talents were going to be put to their fiercest test under martial law. Joanna's mother, who lived in Łódź, took care of Joanna's toddler son in order to support her daughter's ongoing activism. Fair, extremely thin, and usually quite reserved, Joanna had what could be called a "spy mentality," and she liked to be invisible. She also was a good storyteller and had a wry sense of humor; the younger women in the DGO looked up to her. She admired Virginia Woolf and the films of Wim Wenders and Jim Jarmusch and, I think, would have fit easily into the bohemian milieu of New York's East Village.

Ewa Kulik, age twenty-two, was single and childless but seriously involved with her activist boyfriend. A self-declared "rookie in the anticommunist opposition," Ewa was a tall, slim blond with elegant cheekbones, whose focused, edgy fearlessness belied her youth. Yet she also exuded a confidence and competence that, in 1981, might also have been seen as the arrogance of youth—if so, the arrogance was merited, for Ewa was soon to excel in a position of enormous trust and responsibility. Her political activism had begun in 1977 when a fellow student at the esteemed Jagiellonian University in Kraków was senselessly killed during a clash with police. She went on to help found an autonomous student union and to become a distributor of KOR literature. During the August 1980 strikes, she and Małgorzata Pawlicka worked the telephones in Jacek Kuroń's Warsaw apartment, providing regular updates to the Western press about the suspenseful negotiations under way in Gdańsk. Ewa had only recently arrived in Warsaw to take a job editing Solidarity's regional newspaper, *Niepodległość* (Independence).

Anna Dodziuk, age thirty-five, was divorced (but would soon marry her activist fiancé while he was in prison) and the mother of an eight-year-old daughter with Down's syndrome. Dark-haired, dark-eyed Anna lived in Mokotów, a southern district of Warsaw, with her father and a nanny, who helped raise the child. A longtime activist, she had worked four jobs during Solidarity's legal phase—as a therapist in a family research and counseling center (a rare profession in a communist society that did not encourage attention to the individual or to nurturing relationships); as a student of sociology and ethnography; as a parent; and, every night, as the editor of the AS bulletin. Eventually, she left the therapy clinic in order to do her job at AS. The caring "den mother" of the DGO, Anna told me, "I do things because of ideas and because of friends." It was her friendship with Helena and Joanna that took her to AS and from there to the meeting on December 15.

Zofia Bydlińska was in her early thirties and a single mother of a grammar school–age son. Zofia lived with her mother, who helped care for the child while Zofia edited opposition literature for several Solidarity publishers. Keen and forthright, Zofia had helped organize the NOWA publishing house, and she exuded an intense and focused energy that, together with her practical mindedness, made her an invaluable manager.

Małgorzata Pawlicka, age thirty, was single and lived with her family. Małgorzata had begun her opposition career doing layouts for *Robotnik* and helping Ewa update the Western press about the August 1980 strikes. It was said that she and Ewa spent twenty-four hours by the phone, that they ate and slept by the phone. When martial law was declared, she was working as a reporter for AS. Chic and beautiful, according to her friends' accounts, with almond-shaped eyes and cheekbones even more pronounced than Ewa's, she was the fashion plate among the DGO, whose clothes were usually nondescript, at best. (Małgorzata later rejected her friends' tales of her fancy wardrobe as "pure legend!": "No one had money or luxury items like designer clothes. This was communism and we were all poor.") Smart, quiet Małgorzata proved to be a workhorse in the underground, a woman who knew what the job was and was there to get it done.

Anna Bikont, age twenty-three, was single and doing graduate studies at Warsaw University. Anna was at the DGO's initial meeting by virtue of having run into Helena on the street. She knew Helena from her work operating offset presses for bibuła production. Proud of the fact that her press job was not considered conventional women's work, Anna, like Ewa, had been awakened to political activism after the 1977 death of the Kraków student. The least experienced of the seven, with her bright eyes and wide smile she seemed the antithesis to Ewa's intense drive and appeared to me more typical of their age group. Eager, responsive, and diligent, Anna was not a leader but an indispensable supporter.

Zofia was the first to articulate for me a sentiment the others also eventually expressed: "It was natural for us to come together. We all worked for the Solidarity press, and we weren't arrested. It was simple—the movement had to be recaptured." She spoke matter-of-factly, as if their collective response had represented perfectly ordinary behavior. "Someone had to act. We had the know-how. Why not us?"

"For most of us, organizing the underground was a continuation of our opposition work prior to Solidarity," was the way Ewa put it. "What we had to do now was not totally new to us since we had already had the experience of activism in the 1970s. We weren't going to just pick up something else. It was not in keeping with our characters. Martial law did not dispirit us. It made us angry, and when women are angry, we get something done."

Most of the key women organizers of the Solidarity underground had been born in the mid- to late 1940s and belonged to Poland's sixties generation—the '68ers. Their coming of age within the context and against the backdrop of a communist state had played a formative role in making a free press and a telerevolution possible. Despite their often considerable differences in background, temperament, skills, and even motivation, they held several things in common. They grew up in educated households. They experienced the class purges and anti-Semitic outbursts of the first decades of communist rule. For most, their political development began during high school, where they joined informal student groups that explored how their Soviet-style system could be reformed from within. And, somewhat later, they shared the shock of realizing that the all-knowing party was a pathological liar—thus corroding any hope they may have had of liberalizing the system from within. Then they attended university and found themselves facing expulsion and jail sentences, and later criminal records and employment restrictions, for organizing student rallies and speaking out against censorship. Each of the women told me, in her own way, that she considered herself lucky to have begun relying on her own free will and wits before a fully developed adult life had been carved out for her, knowing that it would have been hard to walk away from professional and family duties.

In the broadest terms, Poland's '68ers followed a course parallel to that of the sixties generation in the West, displaying an impressive capacity to think outside society's boxes and to utterly disrupt the status quo. Both groups shared a coming of age in an industrialized country under rigid cold war divisions. Both groups shed their political illusions, found their rage, and endured the ensuing psychic implosion. Both groups searched for identity and community and rejected "the system." And both made history. Even though East-West exchanges were few and far between, that "sixties" spirit—the consciousness, the critique, the impact, and the aura—transcended borders.

But despite their similarities, there were fundamental differences between the West's sixties and Poland's. Perhaps the most striking difference was that, while the West had causes, Poland had a single, overriding Cause. Various movements—for example, civil rights, women's rights, counterculture, and antiwar—were the galvanizing forces behind America's social upheavals. But as political columnist Teresa Bogucka underscored to me, for Poland's "Class of '68," as their younger admirers called them, "our protests were all about freedom." Freedom, plain and simple, was not a noun but a verb, an action, a process, perhaps even a meditation, and it became deeply internalized. None of the women I interviewed took its meaning for granted.

"If the truth be told, Polish people struggled for heavier issues than did Westerners," Wanda Nowicka told me in 1999, on the revolution's ten-year anniversary. Now a leading women's rights advocate in Warsaw, Nowicka described herself as having been a devoted but not very active Solidarity member. Poland was not the United States, she reminded me. "We were a relatively poor society, most people had more than one job, and none of us had civil liberties. We fought for individual freedom and for independence from a totalitarian regime. Of course, we strove for economic rights and human rights, too. But the stakes were much higher than in a democracy like the United States, where justice is not an abstraction."

In every action taken during those formative years—whether it was marching in a mass protest, praying in an activist parish, signing one's name to a petition, or simply learning the names of political prisoners from an illegal newspaper—each of the women I interviewed said she felt her consciousness grow. It is telling that several emphasized that their political development was directly related to their capacity to free themselves from fear. "You cannot understand this kind of fear if you have not lived in an authoritarian system," Poznań Solidarity activist Anka Grupińska told me. "It's different from the fear you create for yourself. Somewhere very deep inside, everybody in Poland lived with this fear because, on any given day, you could be arrested. On any given day, you could go to prison. I have claustrophobia. I couldn't imagine myself being locked up in a jail cell, but I knew that if I were going to be imprisoned, I would have to overcome my claustrophobia. Now

I cannot imagine going back to being in such a psychically dangerous situation. But at the time, I was prepared for anything."

The other side of fear, the women learned, is freedom; and when they defined pivotal moments in their personal evolution into opposition activists, they talked of "stepping over to the other side."

It took strength of character, courage, and intelligence for these disenfranchised young women and their male counterparts to stand up to an oppressive state, to refuse to be its object of manipulation. Each of the women I interviewed stressed, often repeatedly, that none of them could have marched forward without the support of family, friends, and the opposition community they helped build in the 1970s. For many of them, the seeds of that community were planted during high school, when they forged lifelong political, as well as personal, bonds with like-minded classmates they met—depending on family background—in communist youth organizations, in religious youth groups, or at school. "We were fifteen years old when we began deciding how to improve society," Irena Grudzińska-Gross told me with the passion of someone about to recount the tale of a magnificent and formative journey.

For much of Solidarity's core group, the quest for a better society began very early when compared to the first postwar generation of American youth. In Poland, high school was the cradle of an intense political activism that did not begin until college for their contemporaries in the United States. In part, I think this can be attributed to the fact that young Poles were instilled with a profound sense of social responsibility to their country, for they were born into the newly founded Polish People's Republic in the desolate aftermath of Hitler's war and were raised with the somber knowledge of what their homeland had just suffered. But while several of the women I interviewed spoke of the burden they carried as postwar children raised in the wake of such profoundly traumatic events, it became clear from my earliest talks with former '68ers that they were not all rocketed into the opposition from the same launching pad. I interviewed a wide range of women, not just the future DGO, and found that all starting points—homes that were anticommunist, apathetic, devoutly communist, or devoutly Catholic—could lead to underground activism during martial law.

Artist Monika Krajewska, who grew up in a household best described as discreetly anticommunist, discussed with me the overbearing influence of politics on her generation's mind-set, beginning in childhood. The only '68er I interviewed who had written down her memories of those formative years, Monika described her generation's early awareness of communism's restraints. In the "world of totalitarian communism, where children played around monuments they had not yet learned to despise, ideology penetrated everybody's private life, including a child's life," she wrote in a paper she delivered at a 1990 conference on "the transition." "One could accept or reject the system but not ignore it. In fact, what I remember best from my childhood, from my early contacts with the world, are just those small acts of rejection that my parents, hardly in a rebellious mood after surviving the Nazi occupation, dared to undertake, such as listening to Radio Free Europe." "From my first days at school," Monika wrote, "I knew I was not supposed to say anything about Radio Free Europe as well as many other things to my friends and teachers. . . . As a ten-year-old I knew exactly what I was supposed to tell strangers and what not to say, but I do not remember my parents ever explaining it to me. Ever since, I have continued to acquire the skills that formed the second set of natural reflexes on this side of the Iron Curtain: how to control and censor oneself on the phone, in conversations and letters."[6]

Given the various patterns to self-censorship that young people from all walks of life had to develop, it didn't surprise me when Poznań Solidarity activist Anka Grupińska—whose parents passively opposed communism—said emphatically, "Opposition meant, first and foremost, finding one's self and then learning the history we were denied in the classroom."

The '68ers I interviewed who grew up in communist households—among them Irena Grudzińska-Gross, Helena Łuczywo, and Anna Dodziuk—described their common paths to dissent differently from the women whose home environments had not been sympathetic to communism. These three future underground publishers had not planned to rebel against the system or against their parents, who were high-ranking party bureaucrats working in the nation's capital. As part of a privileged class in an allegedly classless society, Helena, Irena, and Anna Dodziuk were members of what was then called the "red bourgeoisie."

"We belonged to a communist elite, which allowed us to feel protected and secure in our thinking," Irena told me. "We were reformers, not opposers. We were leftist." From Anna Dodziuk's perspective, "We were conditioned to be 'true believers.' We were idealistic youth, raised on utopian notions of the collective good." Their parents, they were given to understand, were transforming Poland from a semifeudal economy with a largely illiterate populace into a modern, industrial, literate nation—rebuilding the country literally from the ground up. They believed that communism had all the answers, and in their eyes it was the only path forward.

Helena was the daughter of Jewish-born parents who fled to the Soviet Union during World War II and returned to Poland after the communists came to power. Her father held a top post in the government's propaganda department. Before the war broke out, Helena's mother had studied law, but in Russia she earned a second degree in engineering, which she put to work in an auto factory after returning to Warsaw. She was an ambitious woman, and she raised a daughter who also single-mindedly pursued her own ambitions.

Anna Dodziuk's family background was similar to Helena's in that her Jewish-born parents held important positions in the communist system. Her father, a party member since 1925, became a deputy in the foreign trade ministry in the postwar government. Her mother worked as a librarian for the Central Committee until she died of cancer when Anna was nine years old. Like Helena, Anna was raised to think of herself as Polish and atheist—but not Jewish. People of "Jewish origin," as it is commonly said in Poland, rarely lived as a "Jew by choice" following the Holocaust. Few survivors chose to live as Jews or to educate their children in Jewish religious or secular traditions. It was not uncommon for Poles to hide or to keep silent about their Jewish identities for decades after the war because terror and anti-Semitism persisted under communist rule. In fact, it wasn't until the years after 1989 that many Poles began to learn that they were of "Jewish origin" and that their relatives had been slaughtered in Nazi death camps.

Growing up in a communist household, however, made one's

Jewishness especially "not important." It was part of the past, and only the future mattered in the postwar years. Anna Dodziuk recalled that in her family political events and social goals were always more important than personal life. The fulfillment of a higher good was a destiny that she and others accepted until their high school years, when groups of friends began to gather to explore the implications of their sociopolitical inheritance. "We grew critical of Stalinism but remained committed to communism," Anna recalled. "Like our parents, we students believed that the worst years, the initial postwar years, had ended. Our parents had sacrificed material and spiritual needs in the name of the future. By the 1960s, when we looked ahead into the future, we thought that 'true socialism' could unfold and that basic freedoms would be restored."

Beginning in 1956, however, with the crushing of the Hungarian revolution and reimposition of repressive measures, Poland's postwar generation began to question how their parents could continue to hold a stake in communist ideals, given the dictatorial practices to which they were suddenly witness. In the wake of events in Hungary, First Secretary Władysław Gomułka of the Communist Party withdrew his promise of finding a "Polish road to socialism"; intensified censorship; and cracked down on party revisionists, Catholic Church leaders, and workers. The late 1950s and early 1960s were horrifying and exciting times in which to be growing up with a desire to serve a greater cause.

For Anna Dodziuk and her friends, everything in those years, from their conversations to their social cliques, revolved around politics. "Politics was a means of finding ourselves, of defining who we were and what we would do with our lives," she explained. Young people discovered intellectual strength in numbers and joined together to push aside the party's smoke screen of deadening propaganda to try to uncover the truths buried beneath it.

Anna and Irena, who were in school together in Warsaw, both drew inspiration from their brilliant, audacious school friend Adam Michnik, who began his long career as the think-and-do guru of intellectual oppositionists in high school. In 1961, before Michnik was expelled from high school at age fourteen (after delivering a lecture on school reform, note the latter word), he started a political club that was alternately called the Seekers of

Contradictions and the Crooked Circle Club. It offered even a Polish schoolgirl, socialized to be timid and to not compete with boys, opportunities to hone her debating skills.

By 1964 small signs of resistance were visible. That year, Anna and her friends marveled at the bravery of a group of prominent writers who sent a formal, signed letter to the prime minister demanding "a change in Polish cultural policies in the spirit of rights guaranteed by the Constitution." Anna described waiting for the retaliatory other shoe to drop, but it didn't drop, and they weren't reproved. However, the following year, two Warsaw University graduate students, Jacek Kuroń and Karol Modzelewski, were punished for exercising freedom of speech in their "Open Letter to the Party," in which they renounced the ideals that had brought Gomułka to power. The letter also called for the creation of pluralistic workers' parties, the purpose of which would be to empower the new class of workers created by postwar industrialization. Empowerment of the workers was advanced as the best way to fortify the workers' state.[7] The authors, then in their late twenties, were each given three-and-a-half-year prison terms, and Kuroń was thrown out of the Communist Party. Michnik was also arrested—for helping to pen the letter.

Anna and her circle of friends, who soon earned the nickname "The Revisionist Toddlers," were inspired by the fearless actions of these older students, who remained their mentors even while in prison. The young people didn't mind the nickname, and it didn't stop them from considering the challenge Kuroń and Modzelewski had set: to think about how to liberate the working class from the communist state. "We thought in terms of socialism, and we came to realize that, according to Marxist analysis, the working class was oppressed, just as Marx had written. However, ironically, the workers were oppressed by the Communist Party. We decided that the best solution would be to increase the participation of the workers in the party. The way to do that would be to establish workers' parties. We thought, that way, with the workers' involvement, the system would automatically change."

The meetings Anna attended in the 1960s—part debate club, part book group—were typical of the social activities for young adults reared in a socialist tradition. Together, friends went to theater performances, listened to jazz, and debated the prevailing "isms" of their times. All in Anna's group were exceedingly precocious and read avidly—political theory by Marx, Engels, and Weber and poetry and literature by beloved Polish writers such as Adam Mickiewicz, Czesław Miłosz, and Wisława Szymborska. If they hadn't later been branded as social pariahs and political outlaws, they might all have become humanities professors.

The social aspects of those high school gatherings were as important as their intellectual content. "In part, I became an activist out of a desire to be in contact with my friends, to be a part of a community, and to establish a sense of permanence in my life," Anna recalled. "Looking back, I see the various ways we came together as preparation for later activism." She joined a group of socially conscious students in pursuit of community, meaning, and romance. In part, love inspired her politicization, which was not unusual. Tinged with excitement and hope in otherwise hermetic surroundings, the meetings offered a lively, romantic haven for nonconformist young men and women, many of whom met a future spouse or partner there.

By American standards at the time, these were virtuous, serious youth. No frat houses, beer brawls, or cruises in Dad's Cadillac. No hippies, no yippies, no "happenings." No student protests— yet. No rage—yet. Instead of taking illicit drugs, books were their drug of choice, especially the *prohibita,* books that the state had censored.

Far from wishing to rebel against their parents, however, these young people still hoped to make their parents' ideals worth believing in. Poet Ewa Lipska, herself born in 1945, illuminated the earnest mission of the '68ers in her poem "We."

We—the postwar generation . . .
Analyze every earthquake in detail . . .
Suffering from insomnia, moth-like.
Called up to concentrate.

Like Anna Dodziuk, Irena Grudzińska-Gross relished the sense of community that her group of school friends provided, and she, also like Anna, met her future husband among them. (Unlike her friends in the future underground, however, Irena was to write of Poland's martial law years from outside its heavily patrolled borders.) Passionate about the ideas that fueled their high school debates, Irena actively shaped the group's articulation of its positions. "The political element was a basic ingredient of our friendships, but it was not declared as 'politics,'" Irena explained. "We did not define our interests as political. This was a strategic form of self-defense to distinguish ourselves from the communist notion of making politics, which was a kind of nineteenth-century Hegelian caricature of men sitting in a central office pronouncing the fate of the world. For our group, politics was viewed as hierarchical, as above us, as separate from us. We would say that we don't do politics. Instead, we would say that we defend students' rights, we seek to improve society. Our work was both a self-defense and a rejection of politics."

Irena helped me understand the carefully calculated language that she and her friends used to distinguish their conversations about politics from the state's political rhetoric. "The communist system was a trap because of the way that the party defined politics," she told me. "The one-party government produced a certain image of politics and of opposition. According to the Communist Party, opposition could never be successful. In the 1950s and early 1960s, people who tried to create undergrounds were defeated. An organized opposition was a straight road to prison because the police would always be stronger, or so the party led us to believe. We did not want to repeat these failures. So our group looked for a way to organize and voice our ideas that was visible and public, that could come out in the streets rather than function underground. By 1968 we had not developed this notion in a profound way, but we had an instinct that this was the way to go. Being part of a communist elite, we felt that it was our right and obligation to go forward and say what we thought about the party because we felt responsible for what was going wrong. It became our duty to step forward and speak openly."

Irena continued, "I participated in many negotiations with various official school bodies, which accused us of overstepping our privileges and threatened to close down our club. At the time I did something, which, in retrospect, was a terrible mistake. The authorities requested that we prepare a list of our group's members, which I did. Later, in 1968, the students named on that list were interrogated, and I felt horrible. But I had not foreseen that such an event might happen. I was too innocent and had no sense of conspiracy back then."

The strong Catholic tradition of passive resistance was another path to activism for some members of the Class of '68. Magdalena X, the one female activist who asked to remain anonymous, told me that was the route she had taken. "I missed the experience of being indoctrinated with communism, which meant that my childhood growing up in a close-knit Catholic neighborhood was unique, almost idyllic," she told me when we met at her home in the summer of 1991. "My mother used to tell me, when I was a child, that Poland was occupied by a foreign country. Conspiracy is in my blood. When the government enforced martial law, I knew what to do, like second nature. My mother had taught me." Magdalena's mother was among the many Catholic victims of arrest and imprisonment during the Stalinist late 1940s and early 1950s. Magdalena recalled: "In my childhood, my mother would tell me: 'When I was in jail, my cell floor was inches deep in water. The heaters never worked and rarely did a cot have a blanket.' My mother advised me: 'If ever you are arrested, be sure to take your galoshes and warm underwear, and if there is time, grab a piece of bread.' This was the image of arrests and imprisonment, which I had inherited from my mother."

From a family of Catholic intelligentsia that had defended its right to religious expression even during the Stalinist years, Magdalena X grew up in a major city in an insular Catholic neighborhood that organized its own cultural centers, recreation clubs, social services, and parochial schools, which the whole community safeguarded against the communists' repression. Through the local church, Magdalena's mother and other women arranged charity and defense funds for arrested neighbors and collected statistics on human rights violations. Later, during the 1970s and 1980s, they also secretly distributed such information to the opposition press.

Unlike her Solidarity counterparts who came from communist

households and rejected the party in their high school or university years, Magdalena was raised on a tradition of passive resistance. "We learned about history by reading the [World War II–era] tombstones. It was a form of resistance to the system. We rarely did anything in blatant opposition . . . while people like Adam Michnik and Jan Lityński were already trying to change lives by the time they were in secondary school. Those who were leftists made many mistakes, but without them we never would have been able to achieve anything. Some people envied us for never voting or partaking in anything communist, but if you must know the truth, I felt like I didn't have a conscious choice. It was automatic for me not to participate. Resistance had been predetermined by my parents." Like so many young people, however, Magdalena dreamed of a more active struggle. "I wanted to break out of my parents' community and make my own decisions. I wanted to educate and organize workers."

Magdalena realized in her teen years that she had a passion for activism that following in the family tradition might not be able to satisfy. She had "clean hands," as she put it, and wanted to get them dirty, to understand the system from within in order to change it. Her contemporaries who were raised in communist households shared a similar inclination, and although they could not have articulated the feeling at the time, they too were moving beyond the traditions of their parents. They too wanted to get some dirt beneath their nails.

In its search for ways to repair the communist system, Poland's sixties generation mirrored its contemporaries in other Eastern Bloc countries. Reform was the watchword of the day, and the overriding question was how to liberalize the Soviet-style systems from within and to gain autonomy from the monolith that was the USSR. Unfortunately for the reform-minded idealists, the bubble that had been dangerously stretched in 1956 finally burst in 1968. It broke in Poland, in Czechoslovakia, and throughout the Eastern Bloc.

Societywide reforms had finally begun to take hold in Czechoslovakia, the last Stalinist stronghold. Bold demands for the restoration of the rule of law, the abolition of censorship, the opening up the educational system, and the rehabilitation of political prisoners spurred a change in the government leadership. Revisionist Alexander Dubček replaced Antonin Novotny in January 1968. Dubček led high-ranking party officials in a reform campaign, and the nation mobilized quickly and brilliantly to exorcise its rigid Stalinist norms. This movement was called Prague Spring—"socialism with a human face."

In Poland, students appealed optimistically to the Polish Communist Party to emulate the Czechoslovakian government's example, but they were bucking a counter-trend that had recently developed. In January 1968 the government had banned a Warsaw theater production of *Dziady* (known in the English-speaking world as *Forefather's Eve*) by Adam Mickiewicz, Poland's great nineteenth-century national poet and writer. Although Mickiewicz's writings often reflected his lifelong struggle to free Poland from Russia, *Dziady* had nevertheless passed official inspection, so enthusiastic audiences at the sold-out Teatr Narodowy (National Theater) felt free to cheer all the analogies they could find between the play's antitsarist message and their contemporary situation. For example, each time one of the characters, a Russian officer, declaimed, "No wonder they damn us here, because for one hundred years Moscow has sent only the worst scoundrels to Poland," the audiences practically brought down the house.

When party authorities abruptly closed the show, it marked the first time Mickiewicz had been banned since tsarist authorities did so when the playwright was still alive. Outraged students at Warsaw University protested the twentieth-century ban, beginning with a demonstration on January 30. Thereafter students and professors collected three thousand signatures on a petition that was delivered to the Sejm, the Polish parliament, on February 16. Campus expulsions followed: the Ministry of Culture expelled Adam Michnik and Henryk Szlajfer from Warsaw University on March 4.

Then students organized a second demonstration. On March 8 five thousand students poured onto the main yard of Warsaw University shouting, "Poland is waiting for her Dubček!" They demanded the reopening of *Dziady* and the readmission of the two expelled students. The government's retaliation was swift and harsh and spurred two weeks of spontaneous student demonstrations, campus sit-ins, and petitions in other major cities, including Wrocław, Łódź, and Kraków. As the protests spread, the lists of demands grew to include freedom of expression and autonomy for student organizations.

March 1968 saw the most massive tide of unrest in Poland since 1956, when factory workers had taken to the streets to protest work conditions. But the 1968 instigators were students, not workers, and the government was able to disable them with university expulsions, beatings, arrests, and a relentless media assault that was part of a vicious anti-Semitic campaign.

The media accused the student protesters of plotting a Zionist conspiracy, which, allegedly, they were concealing behind "typical" radical student demands for free speech and a free press. The stunned protesters were helpless in the face of the media's aggressive denunciation of all student leaders as noncommunists, "agents of international imperialism," and "Zionist lackeys."

Anti-Semitism had been growing within the party ever since Moscow and the Warsaw Pact denounced Israel during the 1967 Six-Day War. Then, however, Jews had been exploited in internal power plays within the Communist Party. Now, anti-Semitism was turned outward, and students were not the sole victims. All Jewish citizens were purged from the labor force in universities, ministries, the media, and hospitals. Office managers nationwide were mandated to compile lists of Jewish employees and then to fire them. Some of the people targeted did not even know they were Jewish. Families such as Helena's and Anna Dodziuk's, whose Jewish identity was known to them but was considered unimportant, were shocked to find that, in the eyes of the state, a Jew was a Jew, however he or she self-identified. Between 1968 and 1969, thousands of people lost their jobs and many more emigrated. Exact figures are difficult to gauge, but over a three-year period—from 1968 through 1971—Poland's Jewish population of forty thousand dwindled to somewhere around ten thousand. Those who remained, noted Timothy Garton Ash, were "marked for life."[8]

Anna Dodziuk's father had always thought that communism would protect him, his family, and other Jewish Poles from racism, as it had during World War II. Instead, "in 1968 he was forced to 'retire' from his job," Anna told me. He had been rejected by the ideal to which he had devoted his entire life. "The anti-Semitic purge was the last straw for him," she sighed. He took to following his daughter and her twin brother around the apartment, pleading with them to leave Poland before it was too late. Her brother went first to Italy and then to the United States, but Poland was Anna's home. She stayed and became increasingly involved with her fellow student activists. "I was too connected here," she told me.

Outside the universities, there was no active support for the demonstrators. Although some people had hoped the workers would also take action, the students remained isolated. The government leaders had accurately gauged the industrial workers' reluctance to support a protest "instigated by Jews." The anti-Semitic campaign successfully discredited the student movement and confined dissent to the campuses. Without a broader base than just the university, the demonstrators faced a brutal showdown in which dozens of students were arrested and locked behind prison bars.

The events of 1968 broke apart the student movement, and it was years before the participants could digest what had happened and could use the experience to regroup in continued opposition to the regime.

When I sought a perspective on the events of 1968 from a vantage point outside the Crooked Circle Club, women from the DGO referred me to Teresa Bogucka, one of the many '68ers who ended up in the underground and who later joined the staff at *Gazeta Wyborcza*. Teresa and three other women (Irena Grudzińska-Gross, Irena Lasota, and Barbara Toruńczyk) had played a leading role in organizing the student demonstrations at Warsaw University, and she had arrived at her activism by following yet another of the many possible paths.

Teresa was raised in a household of Catholic intellectuals, but, unlike Magdalena's family, hers was not part of an organized religious community. Teresa's parents were artists and art critics, and although politics was an unavoidable topic under a regime that censored all forms of expression, it was art that defined the family's passions. In high school and university, Teresa became involved in a mostly Catholic (that is, noncommunist) student group that was already more skeptical about communism than were the revisionists who made up Anna's milieu. By the early 1970s, however, after surviving the party's repression of their student protests, the two groups joined together.

I met with Teresa in the summer of 1991 in her Warsaw apartment, which like many writers' havens was intensely alive with strewn papers and books, a demanding cat, and overflowing ashtrays. At the time, she was writing a weekly political column for *Gazeta Wyborcza,* and her recollections of 1968 were serious, bitter, and tinged with a columnist's sharp wit. "We tried to break through the government's hypocrisy. When I read the newspaper reports on our demonstrations—which accused us of complaining about everything—I remember that I agreed with how they presented us because we had complained about everything, from price raises to the Warsaw Pact."

She discussed the decision to protest, the strategies they planned, and the shock of their quick and total defeat. The government's use of anti-Semitism was the most painful offense, she said. "We were horrified at how easily the government could tamper with the whole society and undermine students," she explained. "Before the purge began, I had never thought about anti-Semitism or about the backgrounds of my friends. Suddenly I was forced to see that Poland has a history of anti-Semitism that could be used at any time to quell opposition."

Teresa's reflections, especially since they came from a non-Jewish participant in the student protest, shed light on an important juncture in the lives of the first postwar generation. The communist state had always downplayed social, cultural, and class differences. Its propaganda alleged that all citizens were workers helping to build the utopian state. However, in 1968 differentiation in the form of anti-Semitism suddenly threatened to divide Christian and Jewish Poles. For people who had lived through World War II, the 1968 assault was an emotionally charged conflation of past and present, for they saw a new generation forced to make distinctions among their friends, just as their parents and grandparents might have had to do during the war. For students like Teresa, reared on both Catholicism and the communist myth of a classless, raceless society, being forced into awareness of any identity differences felt like an act of betrayal.

Many very concrete betrayals also occurred at this time, for the police pressured students hard to inform on one another. The year 1968 marked the postwar generation's first experience of police harassment and interrogation. It was a tactic during interrogations for the interrogator to slander the Jewish students to their Christian counterparts, such as Teresa, then to pressure the latter to collude. "People were intimidated into betraying their friends. Anti-Semitism was one of a variety of mechanisms that the interrogators employed to break us. Fear was the basic method used to trap us—fear about our families and fear about the future. None of us knew how to defend ourselves," Teresa explained. "The lid on a Pandora's box flew open. We were so confused. Our emotions were being pulled in all directions."

When organizing the protests, the students had not anticipated either the range of official reaction or the trauma the demonstrators would suffer as a result. "Like children, we learned what happens when you play with matches," Teresa sighed. Not understanding the implications of the government's assault until long after their defeat, the protesters eventually suffered a cruel awakening: the enemy was no longer the Soviet Union; the enemy lurked in their own history, in the government, and even in themselves. And from this realization, activist students drew the conclusion that social change would never be carried out from the top down.

"The only consolation for us was all the student support around the country," Teresa said, explaining why she went on to help organize subsequent rallies to protest the mass arrests. She was apprehended by police and spent over five months in Mokotów Prison in Warsaw, where she shared a cell with three women who had committed petty thefts. "It seemed that dark ages had descended," Teresa recalled. "The repression made Poland prior to 1968 look like a free country. We were so naive and guilt-ridden, believing that we had turned Poland into a different country. We all lost friends and neighbors, who left the country either because they were Jewish or students or both."

Though prison conditions were bearable and she was not physically abused, "the worst thing was feeling humiliated," Teresa said, and the greatest humiliation was the daily interrogation. "Interrogators tried to make us reveal bad things about our friends.

Eventually, the inquisitors trapped me with a simple trick. At night, in my cell, I could hear somebody sending Morse code. I thought friends were passing me information. The message said that Jacek Kuroń and Karol Modzelewski, two leaders of the student demonstrations, had been sentenced for espionage. Espionage was punishable by death. In a last-minute effort to save the two men, the message urged: 'Everyone should talk.' So I talked. I said we weren't involved in espionage. I said we were merely holding study groups. Later, when I was released and discovered the truth about the Morse code message—that neither man was accused of espionage, that I had been deceived—I broke down. I was depressed for months afterward and afraid to act."

DGO stalwart Joanna Szczęsna also took part in the 1968 university demonstrations, though she did so in Łódź, a city just south of Warsaw. When the student protest in Łódź collapsed, as it had everywhere else, Joanna was glad to have survived unscathed, but she was frustrated. Wanting to do more, she joined a clandestine anticommunist group, even though she did not feel much affinity with its members. In 1970 she was arrested in a raid targeting that group and given a one-year jail sentence. "At that time the system did not separate out political prisoners. I had a criminal sentence so I was treated like an ordinary criminal and put in a cell with other ordinary criminals. Fortunately, I found common language with the young girls who shared the cell with me. They were seventeen or eighteen years old. Every evening I would tell them stories, and I never, before or after, had such a faithful audience. My situation was relatively good. My mother is a special person. She believed that if I was in trouble, she should help me. She wrote letters to me every day and sent me packages and money. It was not paradise, of course. I had constant nightmares in which I never finished my studies, I was rejected from society, and my life was over. It was not, after all, 1980, the time of Solidarity."

Describing the evolution of protest movements during the 1970s, Joanna divided events into what she called the "first" and "second" times. These early demonstrations were "the first time" that her generation staged public protests and the first time that, individually and collectively, they confronted the state's aggression. It was the first time that they were arrested, imprisoned, interrogated, and utterly humiliated. It was the first time that they watched friends emigrate and contemplated leaving the country. It was the first time that they feared for their lives.

The vitally important support networks that the opposition later organized did not yet exist in the late 1960s and early 1970s. Standing alone as an individual confronting the authoritarian maze was a terrifying experience for those inexperienced men and women, still in their late teens and early twenties. I was struck by the fact that each woman I interviewed about those times spoke of her feelings of profound shame for her vulnerability and inexperience and for the havoc her actions had caused in society at large. Each of them said she eventually reached a point where she no longer trusted herself. "We were paralyzed" is how Teresa put it.

"I couldn't stand it any longer, so I left the country," Irena Grudzińska-Gross recalled, speaking of the outcome of her involvement in the 1968 demonstrations. "I didn't have the imagination to foresee that things might get better. I was in terrible shape. It took me years to understand that 1968 marked the beginning of communism's defeat. The Communist Party had committed a veritable suicide, but at the time we students thought the suicide had been ours."

As a result of her instrumental role as one of the organizers of the Warsaw University demonstration, Irena was arrested and both her parents were fired from their jobs. Her mother, a medical school professor, was accused of being unable to raise her daughter properly. Such a woman should not be allowed to poison the minds of other students, she was told at the time of her dismissal. "Both of my parents were anguished by the consequences. They had been working for the Communist Party all their lives, and then it turned against their child."

Irena spent seven months in prison before standing trial with thirteen others, including Teresa Bogucka, who were accused of being student leaders. She told me that one of her worst moments in prison came when she realized, in late August 1968, that Czechoslovakia had been invaded by Soviet and Warsaw Pact armies and that Prague Spring was no more. "A police interrogator called for me very early one morning, before normal hours for interrogation. The interrogator showed me a newspaper, which said the Polish army had been 'invited' to Czechoslovakia, when, in fact, Poland and the Soviet Union had invaded. I thought the end of the Czech experiment was the beginning of war. The interrogator made a speech that we should be grateful that the Communist Party stopped us before the same thing would have happened in Poland. It was nonsense, but I felt guilty."

By the time Irena finally stood trial, the political furor had, fortunately, died down, and she received a lenient sentence and, later, an amnesty. However, "that did not mean that I was able to get a job or return to the university," she pointed out. "Life remained very difficult, so I decided to emigrate."

In October 1969 Irena and her boyfriend emigrated to Italy, where they married and resumed their graduate studies. Her family remained in Poland. She wrote in a 1999 essay that appeared in *Media Studies Journal:* "We were all members of the defeated group of what would now be called 'pro-democracy students.' Most of us were 'lucky' enough to be of Jewish origin and therefore able to emigrate: the Polish government hoped that Poland would have a better future without our 'foreign element.' We left behind friends and relatives to whom we wanted to be of use."[9]

"I missed Poland very much," Irena confessed to me with a sigh, as if, having decided to leave, she should have put it all behind her. "In 1971 I received a ten-day visa to visit. Immediately after my arrival, I was surrounded by the police, who followed me everywhere I went. At the time there was not yet an opposition, so I had no way to feel safe or protected. When I applied to have my visa extended, I was interrogated." When she refused to inform on her friends, her visa was canceled immediately.

Back in Rome, she received an application for a fellowship to Columbia University, which friends had sent her, and applied for a visa to the United States. At the American Embassy, her interviewer was openly hostile. "You see, it was the early 1970s," she reminded me, "and the interviewer saw me as a sentenced student leader from the university movement. 'So, they are fishing for troublemakers all around the world,' he said to me. When I looked at him, I saw a policeman. By that time, I could recognize a policeman anywhere in the world. I assumed I would not get an American visa. But in fact, they did give it to me. There was no legal reason not to give it to me. I was a political prisoner; I was not a member of the Communist Party. But it took them so long to give it to me that I decided to stay in Italy." Eventually, however, she was awarded another fellowship to Columbia University, where she earned a doctorate in 1976.

When we first met in Warsaw in 1991, I had no idea that Irena had emigrated permanently in 1969 and was then in Poland only to visit. People spoke of her as if she had always lived among them. In spirit, she had. In a later conversation, Irena described her émigré existence as living in two places at the same time. Writing of her émigré perspective on events in Poland from abroad, Irena wrote in 1999, "We [émigrés] were convinced that everything that was important was happening in Poland. It was there that people risked their freedom, coped with political changes and provoked them. We in exile were listening attentively, trying to understand, to help if we could. The best we were able to do was to tear the veil of anonymity that covered our friends in Poland and that made them vulnerable to persecution. This was a difficult task, especially in the 70s. The term 'dissident' did not yet exist, and President [Jimmy] Carter had not yet enshrined human rights as a principle of American foreign policy."[10]

"A certain life ended in '68," Irena stressed to me. "The medium of opposition as we knew it was destroyed by the police and by emigration. Those people who remained were isolated, at least in the beginning." In the aftermath of the expulsions and prison terms, the marginalized former students questioned their identity, social role, and future. Would their personal interests and convictions always collide with an intrusive government? Would fear compromise their dreams of freedom and justice? How could they ever fall in love, raise children, or pursue a career when the government could so easily destroy them? This entanglement of the self and the state was an absolutely integral part of the postwar generation's evolution into anticommunist activists.

For many young women and men, having a prison record meant losing their rights to education and employment. "When I was released, I faced a paradoxical situation," Joanna explained to me. "According to Polish law, I had a criminal record. I also had a duty to have a job after my prison term. But nobody wanted to hire me." After six months at a boring, low-wage job, Joanna went to Lublin, where she was accepted at Catholic University, the only private university in the Eastern Bloc. "Only Catholic University admitted students who had been sentenced after the March events as regular students and not as night students," she told me. "I met people who had also been expelled in '68 from Poznań, Warsaw, and Kraków."

In the early 1970s, expelled students from the Warsaw circles to which Anna and Teresa belonged began to meet again in one another's homes. "We'd come together at parties, not really to dance and drink but to talk and talk," Anna Dodziuk recalled. They helped one another reconcile the past trauma and reassess the system that had become, in their eyes, unreformable. Analyzing the past, these friends worked together to identify the common elements in their stories: their naïveté, their fear of violence, the penalties suffered by their families and themselves, and the government's viciousness. They discussed how they might have acted otherwise, how they might act in a future situation. They invented self-defense tactics to use at interrogations and in prison. They forgave one another and eventually forgave themselves for their ignorance, for the betrayals, for the failed nerves.

Without their supportive circle of friends, each of these students might have remained isolated and burdened with irresolution. Instead, as many told me, they helped one another adjust to the government's restraints on their education and employment. Each also told me she eventually stopped caring about the stigmas she carried. Once they had hoped that the system might rid itself of its authoritarian evils, but now these former students were being cleansed of illusion. The stronger their friendships grew, the less each needed the approval of the state. They were drifting away from the lives they had always thought they would lead in communist Poland, unsure of where they might land, but at least they were moving together. Anna described the change to me in words that reflected the sentiments of other women I interviewed: "Freedom was stirring within and among us."

From their new position of relative safety, the young intellectuals delved in to explore more deeply the nature of repression and resistance. They discussed the necessity of nonviolence and the power of truth, transparency, and autonomy to challenge the state. Adam Michnik advanced the notion that dissent among social groups was an evolutionary process and that Poland needed an opposition movement. The aim of such a movement was not to overthrow the dictatorial government but to find a "sphere of possible compromise." Rather than telling the government how to reform itself, as students had attempted to do in 1968, in the 1970s they explored ways to unite and to create support systems for themselves outside of state control. Sources of power lay elsewhere than in the government. Power was defined as a social relationship among groups. The workers, the clergy, and the intelligentsia were identified as the three core groups to defend the nation's independence.[11]

Thus, the seeds of KOR were planted in November 1975, when, in the first organized political effort since 1968, fifty-nine individuals, most of them writers and scholars, signed a letter to the government demanding an expansion of basic freedoms. That letter was oppositionists' first organized political effort since 1968, and it spurred reprisals. Each of the petitioners was subjected to a house search and forty-eight-hour detention. Then in June 1976 the oppositionists in Warsaw immediately responded to the strikes in Radom and Ursus by arranging to provide medical, legal, and social services, and KOR was formed. When KOR indirectly spurred Helena Łuczywo's belated entry into the opposition, new opportunities opened for other women activists, who soon coalesced around her.

For several of the women I interviewed, the period spanning the mid- to late 1970s represented a turning point in their development as activists. Joanna also spoke for others when she described the process that led her to openly identify with the opposition and recalled the moment of reckoning and action that signified "the second time" for publicly defying the party state and for braving the repercussions.

Joanna moved to Warsaw in 1975 after finishing her studies in Lublin. Stigmatized as she was by a police record, her opposition curriculum vitae, if such a document had existed, would have read: "Education: Expelled; Employment: Blacklisted." When she arrived, she noted that "the situation was very different from Lublin and Łódź. An opposition society existed, made up of maybe five hundred to one thousand people. There was a support group. I made new connections." She befriended Jacek and Grażyna Kuroń, who organized many KOR activities from their apartment, and became coeditor of KOR's *Biuletyn Informacyjny* (Information Bulletin).

Joanna kept that editorial position a secret, however, because she did not want to risk losing the salaried job she had found as a radio programmer. In those times, she reminded me, the police were turning Warsaw inside out in their hunt for "deviants." "[T]he air was always thick with house searches, detentions, and arrests," she wrote in a memoir entitled "In St. Martin's Church," which was published in the illegal literary journal *Zapis* (Record) in 1977. [12]

During Joanna's first year at the *Biuletyn,* she avoided signing her name to the masthead, although even this precautionary measure did not assuage her fears. Fear itself was like a prison, she wrote. "It is probably self-centered to consider one's own fear an extremity, but this was what hurt the most."[13] During those times, Joanna shared many characteristics with her women friends in the opposition. She lived with a sense of urgency. She lived on the move, always planning for the moment of her arrest. She was prepared to call out Jacek Kuroń's phone number to passersby and yell to them to notify him or his wife if she was apprehended. "I do not like theatrics in public," she stressed, "but it would be worse to be detained with no one noticing or taking interest."[14]

In 1977 the Warsaw police arrested one of Joanna's coeditors at the *Biuletyn,* Seweryn Blumsztajn, whose name, unlike hers, always appeared on the masthead. Blumsztajn's arrest occurred in the wake of nationwide factory and campus unrest, which had first erupted in 1976, a year of brutal showdowns between government troops and factory workers. Then, in early 1977, a student organizer, Stanisław Pyjas, was killed in a university demonstration in Kraków in support of workers' rights, and his death precipitated the activism of a whole new generation of students, including Ewa Kulik, Anna Bikont, and Anka Grupińska. Shortly after the authorities cracked down on KOR, arresting several members and collaborators, Joanna joined others in her office in signing a petition to protest the wave of injustices. She was immediately fired from her job at the radio station.

At the time of Blumsztajn's arrest, Joanna worried that the disastrous events of 1968 were being repeated. "I keep asking myself: Ten are arrested already, will that be all? Will my turn come?"[15] While many of her friends were being interrogated and detained, Joanna hid or moved around the city, unable to keep still, unable to flee. She sublet flats or slept on sofas in the homes of fellow activists. She recalled that it eventually got to a point where pieces of her wardrobe were dispersed throughout the city.

"I pick the homes I stay in with care. They have to be close enough to what is going on for me to be able to catch the news, and distant enough for me not to fall right into a house search," she wrote in her memoir. As much as possible, she tried to be invisible. "They will get me if they are to get me, but I do not want to make it easier for them."[16]

Ignoring the advice of even her closest friends to consider leaving Warsaw, she remained there. "I scan the street in a flutter to check if I am being followed. I scan the surroundings of my friends' homes to check if there is a guard. This is a different kind of me, unacceptable. There is no room left here for decision, for choice. . . . I had become incapacitated."[17]

She felt guilty that others, especially her coeditor, were behind bars while she remained free. "[T]he arrest of Seweryn Blumsztajn infuriated me the most. . . . After all, he had been doing exactly the same things I was doing. We edited the same Bulletin together. . . . I look at his pregnant wife, and I am ashamed to live in a country where one cannot even count on the blows being justly distributed."[18]

Joanna considered her friend's fate not in terms of his maleness or Jewishness but in terms of his visibility. In her eyes, her own invisibility separated her from Blumsztajn and from true dissent, and the awareness of her fear and powerlessness filled her with rage. She decided to join a hunger strike being organized at St. Martin's Church to protest the mass arrests, including Blumsztajn's. "To a certain extent, fear had brought me to the hunger strike. Fear of arrest, but also of myself who, seeing evil, would be capable of saying: 'Excuse me, but this does not concern me.'"[19]

Joining the hunger strike was the most reasonable thing to do, Joanna concluded. "When I have already lost my home and job and have nothing else to lose but my freedom, which is in the balance anyway, I see everything from a peculiar vantage point. What is reasonable and what is madness?"[20]

Joanna actually found the week of fasting and resting rejuvenating. One evening, while listening to Radio Free Europe at the church, she heard her name announced on a list of participants in the hunger strike, and she realized that she was no longer afraid. Now she was visible. She existed in the world. Joanna's decision to begin signing her name to the *Biuletyn* masthead marked her next step as a challenger of authority.

In the interviews I conducted, other women expressed sentiments similar to those that Joanna analyzed in her memoir. Anna Dodziuk told me that, as her fears diminished, so did the government's control of her: "If you believed the government could harm you, then it could do so. But once you realized that the party wouldn't kill you, that opposition was not the same as war, that the world was watching, that the party primarily aimed to intimidate and inconvenience activists, then your own stakes in the game changed."

Poznań activist Anka Grupińska said, "When you do what you want and not what you're expected to do, the real confrontation between you and the government comes out in the open. In that confrontation, every time a person steps over fear, it seems that the system's stronghold loosens another notch." Anka took her first giant step over fear in reaction to the 1977 police killing of the Kraków student. "The student's death marked the first act of violence against *my* generation," she stressed. "The murder became the most important political event for me. His death said to me not that I could have been the student, but, rather, it signaled to me that the lie had gone too far. I had reached my limit."

Helena added these thoughts when I told her what the other women had said: "You don't want to fear the system, and you learn not to fear it by directly facing the obstacles the government places in front of you. Then it is a matter of time before everything weakens and you begin to feel free. You realize the system can't hurt you. This is the opposition's meaning. We didn't want to be afraid anymore."

In a pre–martial law interview, Helena described the "luxury" of being "out" as an oppositionist. "Between 1976 and 1980, we were subject to petty harassment, repression, and censorship. Fortunately, Poland is not the USSR, so we were not sent to labor camps. Nor were we imprisoned for a long time, due to strong leaflet campaigns and Church reaction against the state. This may sound paradoxical, but people in the opposition were in a better situation than those who had to hide their feelings, who had to lie to keep their jobs and who lived in this schizophrenia—all the time saying one thing at home and another thing at work. Our situation was even luxurious because we could say what we wanted. We were on the other side."[21]

"The underground varied in character depending on the region. Warsaw was very feminine. Women started the central structure of the underground there," Ewa Kulik told me. "I remember the first meeting; it was a meeting of women. We invented the whole idea of how to organize an underground, how to build it and how to run it. The center was built by women. Not the factory committees, which were organized afterward and run by men, but the center, which was built around the women from the independent press."

When the seven women huddled together in that Warsaw living room on the third day of martial law, the prevailing attitude was "let's get down to business." They talked in low voices over glasses of hot tea, ashtrays always close at hand, the window curtains drawn. Their war room needed to be guarded, so a friend stood watch, looking and listening for the police. Although none of those present could later recall for me the agenda or the flow of discussion, I imagine that the meeting was called to order with a round of crackerjack storytelling about how each had managed to elude arrest.

Ewa had just graduated from Jagiellonian University the previous summer and had moved to Warsaw to work for Solidarity. Though all citizens were legally required to register their place of residence, Ewa hadn't yet done so in Warsaw by the ill-fated Saturday night when her supper was violently interrupted. She had been sharing a convivial late-night meal with her activist boyfriend, Konrad Bieliński, and his grandmother shortly before the midnight raids began. "We got a call that the telexes were not working in the Warsaw office of Solidarity. Then somebody rang the doorbell and knocked on a window. It was the police! I said in a brave voice: 'I am not going to open the door at this late hour.' They broke down the door with crowbars. A group of men wearing camouflage uniforms barged in and grabbed Konrad. One raised a club over his head and yelled, 'Martial law! We are taking you to the internment camp. We are taking you to Białołeka.' I was sure that Białołeka was somewhere in Belarus. I thought they were the Red Army and that they were taking Konrad to the Soviet Union! They checked my ID. I was not on their lists. They only took Konrad away. Fifteen minutes after they left the flat, I left. I spread the word that the Soviets had taken Konrad to an internment camp in *Belarus.*" A relative newcomer to the big city, Ewa only later learned that Białołeka was a prison outside Warsaw.

It was bitterly cold that December, the wind so inhibiting that it seemed to conspire with the government's freeze on all activity. Ewa wondered whether she should go home or into hiding. "I had no imagination for martial law, no previous experience. It was abstract," Ewa recalled. "Then I saw the tanks. Then I saw the ZOMO. They looked like warriors from the Middle Ages. Then I saw the soldiers. It was a very cold winter. The soldiers stood around boxes of fire to warm themselves. No people were in the streets. No trams, no buses, no street lights after curfew, petro shortages. It looked like war."

In contrast to Ewa, Joanna Szczęsna had already survived more than ten years of confrontations with the state and was able to envision martial law in vivid detail, in road-rage red, in fact. The weekend that martial law was declared, Joanna, whose daunting surname means "lucky," had been working for a West German correspondent at his country home. When she returned to Warsaw on Sunday, she found that her front door had already been pried open and her flat raided. Her two-year-old son had spent the weekend with her mother, who lived in Łódź, about a two hours' drive south of Warsaw. Of the three single mothers in the group that Helena had convened, Joanna was the only one whose own mother was arrested and interned that Sunday. She had not been as lucky as her daughter had or as their surname implied. Joanna's brother and sister-in-law immediately stepped in to take care of her son until other arrangements could be made.

Joanna told me that when she heard martial law had been declared, her first thought, defiant and ironic, was: "I suppose that means I don't have to go to work today. I will catch up on sleep instead." Joanna, like the other Dark Circles women, had slept very little in the previous sixteen months. For example, while traveling to, covering, and then writing about an extremely long Solidarity meeting in Bydgoszcz during the March 1981 crisis there, Joanna had set a personal record of working sixty hours without sleep. She was eventually to surpass it, but that story comes later. Suffice it to say here that Joanna, like Barbara Labuda and others, included information on her sleeping patterns whenever she recalled her political activism.

Like Joanna, longtime activist Anna Dodziuk had already survived two decades of repression and resistance. She had just put the fifty-ninth issue of the AS digest and then herself to bed on the night of December 12 when knocking at her front door awoke her at two o'clock in the morning. A friend wanted to use Anna's telephone because her own phone was not working and the woman's daughter was missing. "I was so sleepy," Anna confessed, "that I told her my phone was disconnected, too. I had no idea whether this was true, but I was too tired to think clearly and suggested to her that she try using a telephone at the main post office." Anna went back to bed for not more than another two hours when another friend came, not to use the phone but to whisk her away. "Brace yourself," this man told her. "Collect your things." She quickly packed a suitcase with clothing and books. "We compared what we each had packed. He had prepared for a strike, and I prepared for prison." She slept through the first day of martial law, "happy for the opportunity."

Anna Bikont's first reaction to the crackdown was to wonder whether she had forgotten to pay her telephone bill because her phone line was dead. She had slept through Saturday night and learned about martial law on Sunday morning from one of the hourly radio broadcasts of General Jaruzelski's proclamation.

Immediately, she went to a friend's home to hide, only to find the door unlocked, the apartment empty, and a note saying the friend had gone to Anna's home. Next, Anna set out to search for her good friend Zbigniew Bujak, the head of Warsaw Solidarity. Instead she bumped into Helena Łuczywo on the street, and the next day they began the search for Joanna and their other colleagues.

Even before December 13, Helena had developed a reputation as one of the movement's smoothest escape artists. Some people insisted that she possessed special intuitive powers—"an internal radar system"—that warned her of approaching danger. Helena's actions on the first night of martial law only lent "proof" to the assertion. Just as ZOMO, the special military troops, began splintering the front door of the Warsaw Solidarity office with crowbars, Helena and her husband slipped out the back and raced off into the night. The police waited for the couple in their apartment for several consecutive days, but, familiar as they were with surveillance, Helena and her husband never appeared. Too busy to be bothered by her pursuers, Helena was already scheming how to recover Solidarity's losses—in outright defiance of the law.

By the end of day two, Helena and Anna Bikont had made contact with Ewa and with Zofia Bydlińska. Unlike most of the others, Zofia had not been sought out by the police. She always preferred to keep a low profile because, though her commitment to dissent was strong, her family's nerves were weak and she was usually careful not to cause them unnecessary worry or danger. However, the police did catch up with her by the end of December and took her to headquarters for questioning. They demanded that she sign a loyalty oath vowing not to work for Solidarity. She refused to sign and expected to be arrested, she told me. But they released her.

On Tuesday, Joanna, Anna Dodziuk, and Małgorzata Pawlicka joined up with the others, after receiving hand-delivered messages from mutual friends. Małgorzata had spent the first two days in Mostowski Palace, the Warsaw Police Department. She was surprised to have been apprehended because, on the one hand, she considered herself a marginal player in the opposition and thus not very threatening. However, she did work for AS, which magnified her importance in the eyes of the state. Through her, the police might be able to find others in her crowd of troublemakers. When they searched her home, they found no incriminating leads, neither address books nor recipes for explosives, but by detaining her they must have felt they could at least break a cog in the gears of dissent as represented by AS. On the other hand, she reasoned, some arrests seemed randomly made to intensify the confusion and fear. What's more, some of the early releases were also randomly made, including lucky Małgorzata.

Let go on Tuesday, Małgorzata managed to show up in time for the DGO's inaugural meeting—a meeting that might be viewed as ongoing for the next seven years.

In my interviews with them years later, I found that each woman's memory of that historic meeting was consistent with the others, such that I was able to piece together the plan of action they made there. To them, the goals were self-evident: to demand an end to martial law, the release of all political prisoners, and the restoration of Solidarity's legal status. They understood that these demands would require negotiations with the government and that the government could only be pressured into negotiations by a strong opposition. The toppled trade union movement would need to jump back onto its feet, reassert its voice, and demonstrate mass-based support. It was too soon to tell whether that would be feasible.

The group turned their thoughts to the membership, the people, the "society," as oppositionists used to say to accentuate the differences between the people and the authoritarian "state"—otherwise defined as "Them" versus "Us." They needed to devise a way to convince the society that the state had not destroyed the entire movement. How could they instill confidence in Solidarity's capacity to survive martial law and regain its legal social structure? They knew the government would try to intimidate and brainwash the population into believing that the odds of that happening were insurmountable. Somehow, the vision, the memory, the reality of that lived experience called Solidarity had to withstand the government's violent measures to obliterate it.

The women decided that, for the time being, the movement should not try to resurrect the former Solidarity structures, such as the political committees that had operated nationally, regionally, and locally. In order to circumvent the repression, the movement needed to reinvent itself and to create a new kind of social structure. It should become decentralized because hierarchies would be nearly impossible to manage under the circumstances and also because adopting a different way of doing things would help throw the seemingly all-knowing government off their trail.

The downsizing and streamlined activities they envisioned would allow for the lateral exchange of information, in contrast to the hierarchical chain of command that had previously characterized the movement. The women believed that the spreading of information would soon become more important (and was less dangerous) than, for example, organizing union meetings in factories. "Information is light," they wanted to remind the nation.

The seven conspirators wisely surmised that, to a certain extent, their response to martial law must closely resemble a return to pre-Solidarity days. In that era, from the mid-1970s to August 1980, the opposition had operated in the shadow of state supremacy. All activist efforts had been conspiratorial in nature. Workers and intellectuals joined forces covertly, assembled in clandestine meetings, and illegally published an uncensored press. The secret police were constantly breathing down their necks, searching their homes, planting bugs, making arrests and interrogations, and suppressing student and worker protests. Precisely because many activists had already endured and overcome comparable repression in the 1970s, the women concluded that post–martial law Solidarity could adapt that experience to the new crisis—having come through that tunnel before, people could do so again. Thus, they came to their decision: Solidarity will carry out its purpose and activities underground.

Underground, yes, but not anonymously.

They all voted against anonymity. The underground needed known leaders, signed declarations, and well-circulated publications. Otherwise, anyone, including the government, would be able to claim credit for their efforts. An identifiable underground could not be infiltrated or undermined as easily as one that was nameless and faceless. Only these women would be nameless, had to be nameless, or otherwise the scheme would not hold together.

A to-do list was started: *Find the men. Hide them and hide our-*

selves. Make contact inside the prisons and internment camps. (The prison walls proved to be incredibly porous.) *Inform the membership about Solidarity's strategic resistance. Reassure the population that the movement's strength is unconquerable.* "In the very beginning, we all handled nine or ten tasks at once because so many things had to be put in place simultaneously—the apartments where we could live in hiding and do our work, the information to collect and disseminate, and so forth," Ewa recalled.

Among the first tasks was to find any Warsaw Solidarity leaders who had escaped arrest. The women developed an elaborate plan to hide and disguise whomever they found, to publicize that they were safe and living underground, and to arrange secret meetings between them, trade union representatives, and local advisers.

Always concealing their own identities, the women also began publishing a newsletter called *Solidarity Information Bulletin* twice a week. This precursor to *Tygodnik Mazowsze* contained news reports, information on arrests and prisons, and words of guidance aimed at broadcasting across the nation the message that Solidarity was alive and well and would never surrender. According to the practical-minded Zofia, "The most important part of our plan was to gather and distribute information: Who was arrested? Where were they imprisoned? What could be done? People needed to know what to expect."

Their plan reflected the women's shared understanding of the crisis at hand. With the trade union movement splintered, information channels needed to be rebuilt and people reunited. The women were ready to step into the leadership vacuum in order to organize others, but they recognized that without the men they would not have a legitimate movement. "Women could not sign anything because no one knew our names, or if they did, no one associated us with political decision making," said activist Barbara Labuda, confirming what Helena and company also explained to me. "If four women called for a strike, people would have thought it was a provocation."

Salvaging the inspiring image of working-class heroes leading society to freedom was also an instrumental piece of their strategic plan. The male leaders not already in prison were extremely vulnerable to arrest, however, and they, not the women, were the objects of ongoing police searches. They could not risk the exposure of organizing the massive outreach that the situation demanded and would not be able to maintain their leadership roles without the women's initiative and support. The seven women agreed that the men needed to be protected, disguised, concealed, fed, and housed—which sounded both perfectly logical and wildly ambitious. How would they carry it out? How would they gain people's cooperation amid the pandemonium of surveillance and diffusion?

The situation called for a tactic of mutual reliance. The women decided that the names of the male leaders in hiding and in prison must be used to represent the underground, just as they had represented legal Solidarity. Ewa explained the delicacy of the situation to me: "It was important not to step on anyone's toes. We tried to make it very clear that the women who had not been arrested were filling in temporarily, until the men were released or safely hidden. 'They are the real leaders,' we used to say."

Sitting at Ewa's kitchen table one June evening in 1992, I watched her smoke and prepare sandwiches as she recalled how she helped locate two male Solidarity leaders who had successfully evaded the police. Finding the men had been one of her first assignments, and it "was not easy to find fugitives in a population of thirty-eight million people."

This was my first meeting with Ewa, one of the few Solidarity organizers who spent almost the entire 1980s living an underground existence. From the age of twenty-two to twenty-nine, her sense of community, social responsibility, and authority developed underground. Among the women in her group, she was the only one whose romantic relationship survived the strain of underground existence.

Ewa grew up very quickly, she told me. Coming of age in the underground set her apart from most of her contemporaries, who were attending university, getting married, and planning families and careers. In spite of her youth, Ewa played an instrumental role in keeping Solidarity alive, and she displayed the same steely intensity that seemed to characterize all the female insurgents who steered the Warsaw underground. "We all possess an 'activity impulse,'" she told me. "None of us mopes about our problems. We get up and tackle them."

During week one, while they were in the midst of resolving the first of many unusual newspaper production hassles, Ewa and the other women learned that Zbigniew Bujak, the chairman of Warsaw Solidarity, and Wiktor Kulerski, its deputy chairman and director of Warsaw region educational and cultural programs, had not been arrested. Then, just before Christmas, the women heard that the two were in hiding near Warsaw. Immediately after Christmas, Ewa set out to find them.

She found Kulerski first, then Bujak. Both had been hiding in homes in Ursus. "Bujak was as important to the underground as Lech Wałęsa had been to the factory strikes that produced Solidarity. Even Wałęsa used to say that one day Bujak would succeed him," Ewa told me. Bujak was to become a key figure in the underground. According to Solidarity organizer Barbara Labuda, his vital role would not have been possible without the women's efforts to protect and bolster him.

It was either by sheer accident or by good karma, or both, that Bujak had eluded Jaruzelski's troops as they stormed through Gdańsk on December 13. The twenty-seven-year-old working-class hero had been attending Solidarity's National Commission meeting and had left on Saturday night, planning to take a 3:00 AM train home to Warsaw, together with his friend Zbigniew Janas, union chair for the Ursus tractor factory. Totally unaware of the raids, the two men enjoyed a late-night meal, then made their way on foot to the train station. They could not help but notice the swarms of police cars that surrounded a nearby hotel, and they went to investigate. An administrative assistant for Solidarity answered their energetic knocking on the locked hotel doors and gave a hushed warning to run away immediately; the police had already arrested many of the other Solidarity delegates and were now searching their hotel rooms. The men decided to split up, and each found a hideout in or near Gdańsk. After a week, Bujak, disguised as a railway man, stole back to Warsaw on a train headed south. From there he went into hiding in Ursus, a nearby factory town.

Kulerski had spent Saturday, December 12, working at the Warsaw Solidarity headquarters and waiting for Bujak to call in from the Gdańsk meeting. By ten o'clock that evening, he decided to leave the office, even though Bujak still had not called. On his way to his home in a wooded Warsaw suburb, he called the Solidarity office for an update and learned that the telexes had just been mysteriously cut off. It was not a mystery to Kulerski, who had learned much from hearing about his father's experiences in the anti-Nazi underground. Unlike most of his colleagues, including Bujak, Kulerski had anticipated government intervention and now realized that the showdown had come. He hurried home to bid farewell to his wife, packed some belongings, and left. When the police arrived soon thereafter and awakened his wife, who had gone back to sleep, she could honestly say she had no clue as to her husband's whereabouts.

The police scoured the area surrounding Kulerski's home for days on end, unable to trap their prey. They apparently did not speculate that he might be in hiding elsewhere or that their efforts had been made futile by the twenty-two-year-old female who soon located the fugitive. Occasionally, word of mouth travels faster than police cars. Or maybe it boiled down to the fact that an entrenched authoritarian bureaucracy and its reprobate police forces are no match for the "activity impulse" of freedom fighters.

In finding Kulerski and Bujak, Ewa also discovered that she had a hidden talent for detective work. Someone in the courier network the women had set up had suggested that a priest in Ursus—an activist, like many church officials—might know where the men were hiding. It was purely a hunch, but Ewa acted on it and wrote first one and then a second letter for the trusted courier to hand-deliver to the priest. Receiving no response to either, she made a deduction: "The fact that he took the letters made me think he knew where they were. Otherwise, he would have returned the letters with a message that he could not help me. No word whatsoever meant he must have known something."

Guessing that the priest needed to meet her personally, she visited him in Ursus and introduced herself. "Bujak and Kulerski will know for certain that this message is from me," she told him and handed over another letter to be delivered to the two men. The letter contained code words and phrases, which she knew the men would recognize and trust.

On her next visit the following week, Kulerski was waiting for her in the church. "What do you need?" he asked. "We need you," Ewa replied. "Everything else has already been organized. You cannot remain outside of Warsaw. People need to know that you are free and supporting them. We've arranged a pickup, hiding places, and false identification cards. We will take care of you and Bujak in Warsaw. Right now, we need a statement from you, and we will publish it."

In less than two weeks, Ewa had made initial contacts with several more Solidarity men and was arranging their hideouts and typesetting their speeches for publication. By New Year's Eve, she and the six other women had completed preparations for the men to return to Warsaw to head the underground. To bring Bujak and Kulerski back from Ursus, Ewa and a friend, Magdalena Korotinska, took the bus there, dressed in peasant attire. They met the two men in an open field near the Ursus chapel and paired up like couples from the countryside; each couple took a separate bus back to Warsaw, where the men were housed in separate apartments. Ewa had already started her duties as head of the underground's Organizational Bureau, which consisted of a single typewriter and, later, two large suitcases—one to store paper files and the second to conceal the typewriter. From now on, these two men would represent the bureau and she would manage it.

Ewa returned to Warsaw triumphant. "Because Bujak was the second most popular leader, the fact that he had not been caught was extremely important for people psychologically. He was our living symbol. We needed to keep him with us in the underground for as long as possible." Jaruzelski held Wałęsa, who refused to cooperate, and the Warsaw underground claimed Bujak.

A month later, the women launched *Tygodnik Mazowsze,* with the statements of the Solidarity men prominently featured on its inaugural front page.

4. Floating Offices
publishing the underground newspaper

"*Tygodnik Mazowsze* was a sign of stability in otherwise chaotic times. Without it, the underground could not have existed and would never have lasted so long," Irena Grudzińska-Gross told me. "It was the most visible manifestation of Solidarity's presence." Anna Bikont characterized its impact even more forcefully: "By the end of our work for *Tygodnik Mazowsze* [in 1989], we were the most modern newspaper in Eastern Europe, even though we were an underground paper. I don't mean that we were just the most important of underground newspapers, but of all newspapers in the Eastern Bloc."

"I would even risk the assertion that the history of the beginnings of the Warsaw underground is the history of the underground press," Zbigniew Bujak declared in a 1984 interview, published in Poland while he was still in hiding. "By this, I don't mean that there weren't independent groups of activists from the very outbreak of the 'war,' but simply that until they had a network of distributors in the factories, they were nothing more than groups of activists. Only when the networks began to function and could be used to solicit answers to questions or to send out instructions was it possible to begin organizing enterprises on a broad scale. We were told by many people that it was when we finally began publishing a weekly that many other organizational details improved, including the payment of union dues and the creation of several factory papers."[1]

How, during an era of repression, was *Tygodnik Mazowsze* able to move from its birth at a clandestine meeting in mid-December 1981 into a position of such power and influence?

The newspaper's first edition appeared on February 11, 1982, and "against incredible odds, it appeared weekly from the beginning of martial law until the end of communist rule," Irena reported. "The illegal circulation of up to eighty thousand copies of each issue was," she emphasized, "an enormous undertaking." *Tygodnik Mazowsze* had by far the largest circulation of all the underground newspapers and, according to all accounts, was the most important and popular among them. Thousands of hands created each issue, with typewriters, public telephones, hand-delivered messages, and private apartments replacing the computers, office phones, telexes, and office space that had been confiscated in police raids.

Twenty-two pages of conventional type were squeezed into four legal-size pages. Dense and portable, like the underground itself, *Tygodnik Mazowsze* offered Poles a concrete example of what uncensored news looked like. It was a reminder of democracy's voice, a reminder that "the future [is] already inside us," as people used to assert in defiance of the military coup.

To mass-produce the weekly paper required the skilled and volunteer labor of thousands of conscientious risk takers—from reporters and editors to forgers and makeup artists. By 1984 several hundred people had become full-time conspirators, while some ten thousand people in the Warsaw area alone worked in various underground enterprises, from printing to distribution. More than one hundred thousand people did limited tasks, such as offering their homes and delivering messages. In addition, each week hundreds of thousands of people read the newspaper and shared it with friends, co-workers, and family members, such that reading the paper became as much a collective activity as publishing it.

Like most Poles who had watched the labor movement grow into an entity powerful enough to challenge the authoritarian regime, Helena Łuczywo and company were keenly aware that it was the people—individuals with a common goal—who had given

Solidarity its life. They built their plans on the shared certainty that the people would also ensure Solidarity's survival. And they were right. I was struck by the fact that each of the paper's seven founders emphasized to me how very many people were to be congratulated and thanked for their contribution to *Tygodnik Mazowsze*.

As Helena saw it, the process of producing the newspaper was as important as the product itself. It was an organizing tool. "You have to have tasks to perform to keep people working together and organized. The most popular form of keeping people together was publishing magazines—printing and distributing them," she told me in our first interview. "In the Polish underground in general, the first sign of a group's existence was usually the publication of a leaflet or newsletter. But whether a publication was done above-ground or underground, it required the cooperation of thousands of people. That is why we arranged to produce and distribute *Tygodnik Mazowsze*. We wanted to get people involved in concrete actions that would offer them a sense of purpose and hope. By helping us publish the newspaper on a day-to-day basis, people felt like they were still building Solidarity. The movement remained alive and tangible, even though all of our activities had to be carried out in secrecy, even though people risked arrest, even though the work conditions were constantly changing."

There had to be a method behind the apparent madness of the women's decision to publish the underground weekly. To build an information network—primitive, covert, low-tech—the organizers needed living quarters, workspaces, printing equipment, and transportation. They needed names and addresses, false identification cards, and lots of cold cash. Also high on their list were costumes, cosmetics, and props to build a wardrobe of disguises. In the two months between the December meeting and the publication of the first issue, the stage was set for a great conspiracy, and the players got into their roles—trying on uniforms, glasses, hair tint, whatever they imagined a given situation might demand. For their part, Bujak and Kulerski stayed sequestered in their hideouts during the first month, letting their beards grow and waiting for their false ID papers. Helena and company, too, usually remained indoors during the first four weeks, although they sometimes ventured out after sunset to do business and reconnaissance.

The Warsaw Underground Headquarters, as the women christened their entire operation, consisted of three main divisions: a publishing section (responsible for the newspaper, books, and other publications); a general operations division; and, for lack of a better term, a bodyguard department, which arranged the protection of the male leaders in hiding. This enterprise operated as the representative of the regional leadership body that had survived Solidarity's legal period. National Commission delegates Zbigniew Bujak, Wiktor Kulerski, and Zbigniew Janas acted as the main spokespersons, and from prison Adam Michnik and Jacek Kuroń contributed advice on its goals and direction. Other underground groups and publications either were part of this network or worked autonomously and sometimes in opposition to its goals. People clashed over whether the underground should be centralized and whether aggressive actions against the state, such as factory strikes and street demonstrations, should be mobilized. The male and female organizers responsible for the Warsaw Underground Headquarters endorsed the often unpopular positions of decentralization and of clandestine rather than confrontational protest.

Warsaw was one among various regional operations that reorganized after December 13. The others were also based in major cities—Gdańsk, Kraków, Wrocław, and Lublin. Due to the prohibitions on communication and travel, each region took on the weighty task of independent reorganization. Given that they did not succeed in making contact with one another until late January, it is noteworthy that their concerns, goals, and activities were generally in synch in the weeks before they reconnected. Each region independently called for a stop to martial law, the legalization of Solidarity, and the release of the internees. While these were clearly logical demands, the shared perspective nonetheless attests to the level of effective coordination and communication that had been achieved during the legal phase. Each region also scrambled to find factory representatives, volunteers, housing, money, and equipment.

There were interesting regional differences as well because the regroupings were made in accordance both with who was available to step into leadership and with the traits and conditions that had characterized a given region's legal structure prior to martial law. Gdańsk, Wrocław, and Kraków, which represented many more factories than did Warsaw, organized their priorities and activities around those factories, whereas Warsaw created its nucleus around *Tygodnik Mazowsze,* which became central to the needs of the other regions. Warsaw also was both the most efficiently managed region and the one region that continually pressed for maintaining a decentralized structure to the underground.

And Warsaw alone stood out as being uniquely feminine, as Ewa pointed out. This was remarkable, given that Solidarity was male-identified to an extreme. There were a few instances where individual women performed important roles alongside a region's male leadership, as Barbara Labuda did in Wrocław, but the group activism of the Warsaw women was truly unique. It probably would not have been possible for women elsewhere to assume a position comparable to that of the Warsaw group—Gdańsk and Szczecin were workers' hubs and much more "macho" (to quote Ewa), and Kraków and Lublin were Catholic and very conservative. However, women organizers active in those and other cities recognized the prominence of the Warsaw group and attributed much significance to the national role it played. For example, Magdalena stressed in conversation with me that the "real national coordination came out of *Tygodnik Mazowsze.* Whenever we wanted something like contacts or money, we always went to Helena, Joanna, and Anna D. If not for them, Solidarity would not have survived through all the hardest years. Their goal was much more than to be an editorial board of a weekly. It was the center of all contacts for the nation. Because they worked closely with Bujak, all went smoothly in Warsaw, but it was really thanks to them."

In the regrouping of the Warsaw region, Ewa Kulik became Helena's second in command, responsible for ordering the parts and assembling the engine of the complex network that Helena mapped out. Ewa's official title was chief of the organizational bureau of the Warsaw region, which meant, she told me with a laugh, that she accepted responsibility "for the jobs that no one else wanted to do." She took charge of hard-core logistics such as recruiting thousands of volunteers and makings lists of their names and addresses. She approached factory workers to request addresses of people willing to make newspaper deliveries to the factories. Using her lists, she organized and directed networks of printers, couriers, and distributors, who were assigned to carry out specific duties in each subdivision. The couriers passed messages between individuals and groups in Warsaw, as well as between cities, and were assigned to work either under Ewa, for the men in hiding, or for the *Tygodnik Mazowsze* staff. Messages were dropped off in private mailboxes, slipped under doors, tucked beneath towel dispensers in public restrooms, exchanged in airports, or simply hand-delivered. People did a lot of walking. Ewa told me she never walked so much in her life as during martial law, and when the government finally reopened public transportation, it became a cause for celebration.

The distribution chain was composed of up to three hundred apartments used for storage, drop-off, and pickup, and thousands of volunteers made it possible to transport the newspapers and other publications all around the country. "It is so much easier to distribute when you know where you are sending things to," Ewa recalled, smiling. Once they began asking, she told me, "everybody began sending us addresses. Whomever we met—a friend, relative, someone's fiancé—we collected their addresses. After a while, we organized the apartment lists by city district. We'd wait until a district was organized before making use of the apartments. Once an apartment network was set up and merely needed to be maintained, I'd turn it over to another activist, so that I could concentrate on other activities."

Those other activities included setting up what Ewa called a "central post office," a safe apartment where people could bring her messages. She'd either answer them herself or redirect the messages to the appropriate people at *Tygodnik Mazowsze,* the printing houses, or the various union cells in or near Warsaw. It took her long hours to read and reroute the sea of messages and packages that were delivered each week.

The underground activities were well subsidized. The regional underground unions charged their members nominal dues, the paper sold for a "symbolic price" (1.5 złotys) outside of Warsaw, and donations came in from readers.[2] However, the most substantial funds came primarily from Western support and from

Solidarity's bank accounts in the various regions, from which, in response to rumors of the impending military coup, funds had been removed before the accounts were frozen. Eighty million złotys were thus rescued from Solidarity bank accounts in Wrocław about a week before the coup. The government retaliated by accusing regional Solidarity treasurers of stealing money from the people, and in Wrocław, the treasurer, Josef Pinior, was imprisoned for embezzlement.

Raising funds became a regular activity of every underground enterprise in order to cover the costs of equipment and labor. The newspaper staff and the network employed many people who had been fired from their official jobs, and activists such as Helena, Joanna, and Ewa, who lived and worked full-time in the underground, were able to earn real wages. "People [in the underground] had purpose and money, the means to support themselves and their families," Ewa noted.

Although for security reasons the DGO worked out of makeshift offices, which they put together and dismantled almost weekly, they managed to maintain a regular production schedule, and each woman assumed specific roles and responsibilities. Had they published a masthead, Helena would have been listed as publisher and editor in chief, for she shaped the newspaper's policies and its relationship with regional leaders. She was the brains behind the development of the paper's format, content, and tactical use as the opposition's main voice. Anna Dodziuk acted as managing editor, Anna Bikont and Zofia were senior editors, and Małgorzata worked as staff reporter. Joanna was the paper's logistics coordinator and also acted as the equivalent of associate editor. (Because Ewa did not help to produce the paper, she would not have been listed on this hypothetical masthead—though all her activities were carried out in close coordination with *Tygodnik Mazowsze*.)

These editorial positions were never strictly defined or adhered to because there were too many shifting variables to take into account—for example, raids, arrests, and equipment breakdowns. Staff functions often overlapped or were interchangeable. Flexibility was paramount. The DGO were the grand dames of damage control—a team of chameleons fanning out across the city, adopting whatever guise a given situation demanded. Not just reporters and editors, they were also detectives, hunters, barterers, fire chiefs, realtors—and magicians.

Though the paper did not have a masthead, the Solidarity logo was always stamped on the top of page 1, with Lech Wałęsa's famous words quoted underneath: "Solidarity will not be divided or destroyed." The tiny print on the four thin pages of each issue was produced on offset machines. Last used in the 1970s by bibuła publishers such as NOWA and Krąg, the offset presses had wisely been stored whenever new ones were purchased, in anticipation of a future showdown between the government and the opposition. By early 1982 they had been taken out of storage and reassembled in seven houses across Warsaw. (The organizers chose houses, rather than apartments, in order to conceal the presses' thunderous noise.) Each weekly printing of *Tygodnik Mazowsze* was divided among the seven locations, in case one or more of them was discovered and the equipment seized. Subdividing the printing meant that, while a police raid might slow down production and reduce the total number of copies published, it could not—and never did—totally stop the paper's regular appearance.

"It was done very primitively, by hand," Helena explained, pointing out that they adopted not just the presses but many of the production techniques used in the 1970s. Paper and equipment were smuggled off the black market. Chemists who supported the opposition manufactured the ink. (One recipe called for laundry soap, and some people said that they could identify the publication date of a journal or book simply by smelling it.) "You had twenty kinds of print shops, twenty kinds of printing methods, different kinds of typesets and duplicating machines," Helena elaborated. "The newspaper was done on silk screens, too, and then each of them produced from a few hundred to a few thousand copies. Our weekly circulation ranged from forty thousand to eighty thousand. The copies printed would be transported to several apartments, where they would be divided into packages of five hundred, one hundred, fifty, twenty, ten, and sent to other apartments. Each week this work gave lots of people something to do. They would collect and carry, then someone else would do something, and then the money would go the other way around. This is how we preserved the ties between people."

Anna Bikont recalled her daily routine: "In the morning, I used to make contacts with informers and couriers from different regions. All of these people were also in hiding. We had a rule that if someone was hiding, he could only meet with other people who were in hiding; he could not meet with people who were not hiding. We wanted to maintain communications at the same level for everyone. In the beginning we copied all the information by typing it ourselves. Later, we organized groups of typists and printers. It became a large organization which needed good management."

Distribution was the most dangerous phase of both newspaper production and network operations because that work proceeded in the open. Stacks of publications or supplies traveled in car trunks, in shopping bags, or in the suitcases of Westerners returning to their countries. "It was a challenge to persuade people to distribute," said Ewa. "First of all, no one had this kind of experience. It also was difficult to find people from the factories to distribute inside the factories because they were afraid of getting caught. This was understandable because the factories were usually the final destination, and therefore, were the easiest places for infiltration, for informers to do their work."

Despite the dangers, there were ample willing volunteers, and the newspaper was distributed to readers faithfully every Monday. Although the women had no fixed offices they did have a fixed schedule. Monday was for editorial meetings. Typing, final edits, and layout were done Tuesday through Thursday. The paper went off to the printers on Friday, and between Friday and Sunday, the staff oversaw print production and distribution. "Lots of work and little sleep," Anna Dodziuk recalled.

Whenever possible, they relaxed on Sunday. That's when Joanna said she would kick off her shoes and unwind, sort of. Joanna worked on all aspects of the paper's production and did extensive networking as well, making contact with international supporters and feeding news to the foreign press such as the *New York Times,* Agence France Presse, Radio Free Europe, and the BBC. "She was the most mobile of our group," according to Anna Dodziuk. Indeed, Joanna had to be nimble, like a spymaster; she had a wide-ranging stable of people she "handled," and those connections had to be carefully maintained. It was said that she knew the location of almost every public phone booth in Warsaw. "There was no real break between my work and my life because on my day off, my favorite pastime was to read the underground press," Joanna confessed. "On Sunday afternoons, I would sit down with a large stack of newspapers and read through them all."

And when the weekend was over, the women went back to their "not really an office" for the Monday editorial meeting and very real and serious discussions: What is the underground's purpose? Should it endorse an armed or a nonviolent resistance? Should it call for strikes on the First of May or candlelighting on December 13?

It was Helena who orchestrated the network of what she dubbed "Floating Offices"—the locations from which the newspaper and underground were run. With so many people getting involved in illegal organizing, she anticipated that the risk of betrayal and infiltration would be enormous and ongoing. She conceived the Floating Offices as a safeguard.

"We arranged a complex schedule for newspaper production and for people in hiding," she explained. "People and plans altered as frequently as did the beds in which activists slept. Every two weeks we switched the apartments where we lived, and every four weeks we changed the apartments where we edited the newspaper. We thought it was the safest way. After a few months, we'd come back to the first places. Had the plan operated smoothly, it would have been fantastic. But it didn't always work. There was, for instance, a relatively high turnover of couriers and distributors throughout the country. Some people would get arrested or scared, and you couldn't always go back to the same apartment, or you were given the wrong address. We were constantly looking for new apartments and new people. Otherwise we couldn't operate. We maintained these arrangements until 1989. We changed all the locations for all the things we did because we thought it was the safest way. If you were caught, you went to prison. So, of course, we never used real offices."

The underground's apartments often housed as many as six people at one time, and the unusual arrangements gave rise to the moniker "Styrofoam Generation," because activists in hiding often slept on foam mattresses (a symbol of alternative lifestyles in the United States as well). During the first weeks of martial law, organizers lived in the same apartments where they worked in order to minimize the chance of getting caught. They rotated among one hundred apartments located in Ursynów, a southern suburb known as the "Bedrooms of Warsaw." Many professionals in their thirties lived there, including Joanna prior to martial law. After going into hiding, she returned to Ursynów to connect with residents and to organize their apartments into the underground's first main base of support.

As apartments in the suburbs were usually larger than those in Warsaw proper, it was possible for the women editors to both work and sleep in Ursynów. According to Ewa, "Only a handful of the apartments that we used came from the workers' circles because workers usually had more children and less space for our activities." As more apartments were added to the network and as the underground's workload diversified, the network of hiding places was separated into apartments for sleeping quarters, for editorial offices, and for mail drops; and after public transportation resumed, the network expanded to encompass more than the one district.

These Floating Offices—elaborate and durable, yet ephemeral—held together a quixotic and collapsible social movement. "We had to set down some rules of conspiracy and coordination for all the activities," Helena explained. The general rules seemed to boil down to the old cliché "Here today, gone tomorrow." People were constantly on the move. Wherever they assembled, they arrived with alibis and aliases. They traveled light, taking only what they could easily carry. When editing the newspaper, they had to be able to conceal all evidence of their labor at a moment's notice. In the event of a police raid, they could clear out of an apartment in a flash. The minute a hideout was exposed, it reverted permanently to being a family's home.

Only on rare occasions were the women caught with their guard down. For example, in the early spring of 1983, the Security Service discovered one of the newspaper's distribution centers. This caused a three-week interruption in production and was followed by a reduction in circulation until the distribution network could be reconstructed.[3] According to Anna Dodziuk, "It satisfied the secret police to know that a bust would cause us a major setback. I think it caused them greater satisfaction to laugh at us than to kill us." On two occasions, the Security Service published counterfeit editions of the paper, although neither attempt was successful because people noticed that the type was different from the paper's normal print and that the language was terribly rhetorical.[4] "The government never imagined that we would be able to overcome their tactics to stop us," Anna Dodziuk emphasized.

Every imaginable precaution was taken to ensure that participants in the underground were not caught or otherwise endangered. Indeed, the need for security led Ewa to discover that she had a penchant for paranoid fantasies and a keen ability to invent security measures. For example, knowing that the secret police's records on oppositionists included detailed descriptions of oppositionists' physical appearance and usual attire, Ewa and others eluded the police—and occasionally fooled each other—by wearing unlikely outfits, including the uniform of the secret police. Ewa recalled being approached on a Warsaw street corner by a dour plainclothesman with the "stupid mustache" that all secret police sported. Fearing arrest, she was completely surprised when he proved to be the person she had arranged to meet—Gdańsk trade union organizer Bogdan Lis.

"Step by step, the whole network developed according to security needs," Ewa emphasized. "Security was the most important aim, the most important aspect." It was also Ewa's responsibility to ensure the safety of the many volunteers who worked for the network. "Because people were usually frightened, I would do the most dangerous work while helping the others to relax. I'd tell stories and jokes to show people that I was not afraid, even when I was frightened." She explained, "It was my duty to avoid danger at all costs. My most unpleasant job was to reject a person's offer to help us or to turn down the use of someone's apartment if I suspected it was being watched. I never sent another person, not even the couriers, into a situation where there was reason to suspect danger. Instead, I would go."

Among Ewa's most important tasks was the responsibility for protecting the male Solidarity leaders, acting as their handler and arranging all of their affairs, including meetings, correspondence, and hiding places. She was personally responsible for Bujak and Kulerski, while other union leaders were assigned teams of people who protected them and managed their daily routines. "I also was very protective of Bujak. Many people wanted to meet with him. But I couldn't allow it, if a person didn't know how to move around in public without being followed. Otherwise, Bujak might get caught. Unfortunately, I disappointed many people, who misinterpreted my decisions to mean that I didn't like them or didn't want to work with them. It often turned out to be thankless work."

Other than among the management and political leadership, there was virtually no sharing of information within a given team or among the teams of couriers, handlers, printers, distributors, and so forth. "The less you know, the better for you," people used to say. Every activist was responsible only for his or her specific task, whether it was printing papers, passing a message to Bujak, typing articles, lending an apartment, or delivering newspapers to a factory. No one was asked to multitask, and no one was given more information than was necessary for them to carry out the expected task, not even the names of the people within their own teams. Everyone used pseudonyms, including Ewa and the *Tygodnik Mazowsze* editors. "Let's not get caught!" was a slogan of the day.

Joanna Szczęsna, who together with Helena oversaw the publishing of the newspaper, described the editors' basic formula of conspiracy: "Commit nothing to paper and develop a second set of eyes at the back of your head." She took the motto seriously and learned all phases of the newspaper's production literally by heart. It was her duty to memorize the kinds of information that are normally stored in rolodexes, file cabinets, and computer databases.

Each *Tygodnik Mazowsze* editor realized that, in the event of her arrest, knowledge of her sphere of work would be lost because the bulk of information was stored in her head. The editorial team resolved this problem by assigning to Helena and Joanna understudies who would memorize the same material their bosses had internalized. Joanna described the understudies' duties in her unpublished article "Women in the Opposition."

Tygodnik Mazowsze was a great institution working under extremely difficult circumstances. Each of us, the women who worked for it, had not only to edit texts and write articles, but also to deal with numerous organizational matters, without which the paper would not exist. For example, at different times I was responsible for international contacts, for print production materials that were smuggled from abroad, for updating the foreign press on the situation in Poland, and for contacts with the imprisoned leaders. If ever I were caught, my friends at *TM* would have to do my job. (Keep in mind that everything was done in conspiracy and so, I had to know everything by heart—all names, addresses, and telephone numbers.) My "understudy" had to memorize all of my underground contacts to be able to pass this information on to my colleagues. She also had to know where I hid the Union's money, how I smuggled letters to Solidarity representatives in Western Europe, and so on.[5]

In the Polish underground, subterfuge became a necessary and studied art form, Joanna explained during one of our first meetings in the spring of 1991. One important source of information was an illegally circulated manual called *Mały Konspiracja* (The Small Conspirator), which instructed activists on the ABCs of opposition work, from how to organize underground groups to how to behave if arrested or interrogated. It provided guidelines for preparing false identification cards, airing radio bulletins, and smuggling information. Readers were advised to hide address books and typewriters, to limit telephone calls to sixty seconds or less, and to learn how to detect plainclothesmen. Such bibuła put into print what the DGO could not.

Taking their cues from history, what little the underground women did write down they always destroyed, so that the police wouldn't find incriminating information scrawled on paper—an address, a name, a date and time. British historian Timothy Garton Ash recalled meeting with some of the women in the 1980s. "They scribbled their messages on scraps of paper," he wrote. "Then they burned the scraps in a candle flame while chattering loudly about something else, for the benefit of hidden police microphones."[6] Information was literally light. Nothing could be carved in stone.

On the one hand, this practice was problematic. Because most evidence was erased or turned to ash, there were few records, apart from the newspaper itself, of the women's activities, making documenting their experiences in the underground a difficult task. On the other hand, that the underground was self-erasing conveyed a powerful message: The disappearing act was a perpetual feature of its existence. It would vanish permanently only when it could take the communist system with it. "Here today, gone tomorrow" thus held fast as the underground's mission statement as well—that is, "Communism here today, gone tomorrow" or "Winter yours, spring ours."

In Poland the making of a *podziemie* (underground) has been a revered protest tradition since the nineteenth-century uprisings against tsarist rule. Americans march on Washington, and Poles build undergrounds. To invoke the spirit of a heroic underground heritage, Helena and company only had to look back some forty-two years to September 1939, when Nazi Germany's invasion of Poland triggered the start of World War II and Polish political leaders fled to London to set up a government in exile. Thousands of citizens went into hiding in Poland's cities, towns, and forests to create an anti-Nazi underground resistance movement. And although its numbers were not as colossal as those of the 1980s underground, its mission, Helena emphasized to me, was certainly a thousandfold more dangerous.

Some of those resistance fighters lived to celebrate Solidarity and then eventually to counsel Helena and her colleagues on how to build an underground. Although it soon became clear that certain World War II tactics were not applicable to the needs of the 1980s, a sense of historical continuity nonetheless helped to mitigate the desperate paralysis that sank in after martial law was imposed. "Solidarity always tried to find a historical tradition for all its actions," Irena wrote. "[It] was the movement's idea of legitimacy."[7] Eventually, people were able to say to themselves and to one another, "If our country could survive Adolf Hitler, we can survive General Wojciech Jaruzelski." However, that sentiment evolved only gradually.

The first violent days of Jaruzelski's war were so frightening and disorienting that people were reminded more of the nightmare of the German occupation than of the Polish tradition of courageous resistance. Because World War II marked the most recent in a long history of subjugations and military occupations, even Poles born after Hitler's war were raised on images and family stories of those hellish six years. Remembering the Nazis was an almost reflexive response when people heard the wailing sirens, the thunder of gunshots, and the shouts and screams from homes being raided and then when, peering through their window curtains, they saw tanks rolling down desolate streets, militiamen stationed at street corners, and friends and relatives being taken away. "World War II and the occupation were a severe trauma," Irena wrote. With martial law, "people all over Poland reached for the same historical analogy."[8]

"The WRON," she continued, "like the Nazis, instituted a very harsh censorship, forbade any display of patriotic or political convictions, closed theaters and movies, monopolized the means of communication, and controlled all art production. Solidarity had to retreat from the streets and go underground."[9] But the nature of its underground resistance needed to be defined, and it was initially difficult to gauge the options through the haze of tear gas. In addition, the historical parallels that martial law evoked had quickly sparked a wide range of emotions and reactions that made it hard to mobilize people. Ewa told me that most people were fearful, or at least apprehensive, and had to be persuaded to help the organizers, though some, the enraged aggressors in the mix, wanted to mount an armed resistance. The DGO, on the other hand, opted to wage a cultural resistance because it both reinforced Solidarity's emphasis on nonviolence and mirrored the community-oriented component of the World War II legacy.

During the war, Poles fought the Nazis on two battlegrounds— the underground state was militant and armed; the underground society was cultural and pacifist. The underground state, in response to the Nazi takeover of the Polish government, aimed to recreate the deposed state complete with its government and military, and it set about to do so beginning in late 1939. First from France and then from Britain, the government in exile cooperated with the Allies, appealed for worldwide support of the Polish war effort, and prepared for its return to Poland at the war's end. The military branch of the government in exile, the Polish Home Army, was poorly equipped and often stationed in forests, from which it made futile, surprise attacks on the German troops. However, military victory was not the underground state's main goal, as Irena pointed out. "In fact, the overwhelming military superiority of the Germans caused the underground's leadership to turn its attention to society, its organization, and its moral, financial and medical well-being."[10]

The underground society fostered a cultural resistance to Nazi rule, the primary purpose of which was to encourage cooperation, unity and hope. A web of coordinated activities, from study groups and art exhibits to music and theater performances, was conducted in secret; medical aid and food supplies were collected for the families of political prisoners; and, of course, an illegal press reported news of the war effort to the general population. "That was the model Solidarity was to follow," Irena wrote. "Besides, Solidarity was not a state but a mass movement within a state, and it continued to exist and to grow stronger. Hence the only way in which Solidarity could defend and recreate itself was by defending and recreating society. The anti-Nazi underground's tradition was most useful in all this . . . [by giving] Solidarity a vocabulary, models of behavior, political methods of fighting the enemy, jokes and satire, and even songs. . . . [T]he entire country now made active use of its accumulated knowledge of civic and anti-Nazi resistance."[11]

Irena, who left Poland in 1969, belonged to the groups of émigré activists who collaborated with the democratic opposition from the United States, France, Britain, the Netherlands, and elsewhere. Such groups formed a community in exile—multigenerational and transnational—that became a vital outpost of concrete assistance and long-term support for Poland's democratic opposition. Like Irena, the intellectuals among them also published, and émigré journals such as *Aneks* (Annex)—which was cofounded by Irena, edited in France, and printed in Britain—became valuable forums in which Western readers could become acquainted, in translation, with Polish voices from behind the Iron Curtain. "We wanted to add to what we had left behind in Poland," Irena wrote.[12]

Irena became an activist émigré in 1970, when Amnesty International contacted her, as it had others in her position, on behalf of Polish dissidents. "After I emigrated, I provided protection to my friends through Amnesty International and Western newspapers and journalists," she told me. "My function, for which I felt very responsible, was that people on the front line of political struggle in Poland needed support from the outside. Obscurity could destroy people living in an authoritarian system. I always stayed intensely in touch with people and events in Poland, from exchanging letters to sending forbidden books, and later on, equipment and money for underground activity."

In her book, *The Art of Solidarity,* Irena introduced English speakers to Solidarity's vibrant struggle, both legal and illegal, and drew historical parallels with the anti-Nazi resistance. She focused in particular on Solidarity's verbal and visual outputs—its posters, graffiti, slogans, buttons, and media—which had roots in or coincidental resemblances to various wartime traditions. For example, it was quickly realized that the acronym for the Military Council for National Salvation, WRON, was one letter short of the word *wrona* (crow), which had been used as slang for the Nazi eagle during World War II. In the 1980s, the image of a crow, intermingled with the acronym WRON, was used and abused repeatedly in political art. The Solidarity underground also borrowed code words from the period of anti-Nazi conspiracy. Along with bibuła, code words like *kocioł* (cauldron) came into use. To signify that an apartment was surrounded by police, potted plants (in "cauldrons") were placed in apartment windows to warn activists not to enter the building.[13]

"When you grow up in Poland," Helena explained, "you see lots of movies about the Nazi occupation, you read lots of books, and you somehow know how the resistance worked—probably not all the details, but you know the basics. Poles have a great sense of history. Poles feel history. We know lots of things, as if we had sucked them with our mothers' milk. It is the same way a Pole knows about the Nazi occupation. Even if you do not have all the facts, you know what it looked like, more or less, and you have a sense of the resistance movement."

Helena pointed out to me, however, that while the arts and the media—such as graffiti, slogans, bibuła, and secret code words—were replicable forms of resistance, most of the organizing tactics that had been used against the Nazi occupiers did not offer Solidarity an effective modus operandi. She recounted that in the first days of martial law, for example, DGO talked to former organizers of the anti-Nazi resistance to learn their conspiratorial methods and tried to organize the Solidarity network on a principle known as "fives," which had been used during the war. "The idea is that you have five people who have five people and then another five people. Each group of five is in touch with another group of five. Not a complex idea, but the idea was that people would be responsible for collecting information in various domains—in universities, factories and other regions, and so on."

Regrettably, Helena recalled, the principle of fives kept collapsing on itself because of too many unpredictable variables. In fact, most of the anti-Nazi resistance tactics that she learned sounded better than they worked in practice and didn't adequately match 1980s political reality. It was more effective, Helena realized, for Solidarity organizers to trust their own instincts in this new showdown, whose players and rules differed dramatically from the World War II experience. It took time, however, for the organizers to realize that General Jaruzelski's repression was not going to recapitulate the Nazi's bloody and deadly occupation.

Helena discussed with me how her awareness of the differences evolved, beginning with her realization that it was utterly mistaken to compare Jaruzelski's prison wardens with the Nazis. Though Jaruzelski held the entire nation under house arrest, the Polish Communist Party, unlike the Third Reich, was not waging an imperialist world war and was not committing genocide. Indeed, Jaruzelski had dared to claim that he was "preventing a war" because the enforcement of martial law kept the Soviets from intervening. That is how he had justified the military coup. It is supremely ironic that the general alleged that martial law was protecting Poland's trade union movement both from an external threat like the Soviet Union and from an internal threat that he insisted was of Solidarity's own making.

Communists like Jaruzelski needed to invent enemies, Irena stressed in her book. "One might argue that the Communist system structurally needs both internal and external enemies; after all, its ethos is class warfare, not class compromise." The imposition of martial law gave an incontrovertible signal that Jaruzelski never intended to compromise. He justified his every move and wreaked havoc with his country's vulnerabilities, even exploiting the trauma of World War II to terrorize people who might have otherwise mobilized against him. "The analogy between this 'state of war' and the German occupation was . . . , paradoxically, encouraged by the government itself," Irena wrote. "Playing on Polish anti-German feelings and fears, [communist] propaganda made the war seem ever-present and the Germans always at the Polish door, ready to invade."[14]

Helena and company recognized that the Polish government and the looming Soviet shadow were the immediate, direct danger and that measuring all political perils by the yardstick of the Nazi occupation was a red herring. They made a conscious effort to use their newspaper to change the public perspective and to divert the cultural conversation to the present.

"We saw that an underground in the period of martial law would have to be different from the resistance to the Nazis for two main reasons," Helena said. "First of all, we did not have to risk shootings or torture. We were not facing extermination camps and death. We were not trying to drive out a foreign occupier. We were all Poles. So the risks we faced under martial law were much different. The threat was not that you would get caught and tortured. The threat was that you'd get arrested and during your time in prison the government would succeed in its efforts to pacify people. The government intervention was called 'normalization.' The most serious threat was that Solidarity would dissolve into this normalcy."

It was the combination of the Communist Party's pacification campaign and its military might—an insidious "good cop/bad cop" formula—that threatened to extinguish Solidarity. First use force, wound your victims, and afterward dispense the salves free of charge, compliments of the workers' state. Or first seduce the people with offers of salary raises and the promise of more consumer goods, then beat them up if they don't cooperate in denouncing Solidarity.

This was an internal war, and the Communist Party understood its targets exceptionally well precisely because it, too, was Polish. Both sides spoke the same language, they lived in the same neighborhoods, and sometimes their children attended the same schools.

There were even "intermarriages" between the children of party elites and oppositionists. Tina Rosenberg interviewed Jaruzelski's daughter Monika, a rebellious high school senior in 1981 who left her parents' home and moved in with her boyfriend, a radical leader of the student Solidarity group. "After the declaration of martial law, she occasionally used her chauffeur-driven car to transport clandestine Solidarity activists from one hiding place to another."[15]

There was a hazardous side to this intimacy between foes, as Helena and company were well aware. The Solidarity underground was extremely vulnerable to the secret police's potential to penetrate its networks. For example, the party and police informers infiltrated the factories with relative ease. The DGO recognized that the opposition's skills were going to be tested beyond their previous experiences.

"Once the military blocked all the strike efforts that followed the declaration of martial law, people stopped protesting. They lost confidence in Solidarity," said Helena. "They believed that they could no longer win more than they had already gained during the movement's legal period. They were afraid. We worried that no one would care about Solidarity anymore. Consequently, the goal of the underground was not to fight the regime but to restore Solidarity's legitimacy and credibility among its members. These two essential differences from the Nazi occupation also make for totally different ways of thinking and behavior."

That understanding is what gave rise to Helena's seminal image of Floating Offices, which were actually the reinvention of another old Polish protest tradition. Helena spoke to me in English (she had trained as a linguist and taught English prior to her opposition involvement), and in our conversations she used the English words "Floating Offices." It wasn't until later that I learned (via Ewa, also a linguist and translator) the clever cultural meaning underlying the phrase in Polish, *Latająyca Redakcja*. Literally translated as "Flying Offices," the Polish phrase makes clear reference to the historic model for Helena's idea, the *Latająyca Uniwersytety*, or "Flying Universities." These originated in the nineteenth century, when tsarist occupiers tried to Russify their new colony by outlawing the Polish language, culture, religion, and history. Poles responded by taking their national identity, religion, and cultural heritage underground, setting up secret study groups to educate children and adults in all things Polish. Designed to preserve the cultural heritage, such Latąjyca Uniwersytety were revived during the Nazi occupation and then throughout the communist era in order to teach forbidden subjects such as psychology, history, literature, Catholicism, and Judaism.

Helena drew from the spirit of this model to fashion a contemporary parallel. The Floating Office became a metaphor, a concrete reality, and an organizing principle by which to guide the management of the underground network.

From the start, *Tygodnik Mazowsze* provided a vital forum in which the Solidarity leadership could air its strategy sessions and solicit responses from its members. The population needed to come together to think, as they had when Solidarity was legal. By focusing on the here and now and not on the past, the newspaper encouraged readers to assess issues of real consequence such as the truly crucial early questions related to structuring the underground: Would the underground be hierarchical and structured or decentralized and informal? Would the emphasis be political or cultural? "Many people debated the subject. It was a very important discussion because it directed the course of the underground," Zofia told me.

The newspaper's premier issue, dated February 11, 1982, published an interview with Zbigniew Bujak and Wiktor Kulerski that steered the debate on structure. It was a debate that was to continue until the regional representatives convened for the first time in April to concretize their position.

> *Editor:* How do you evaluate the present situation? What are Solidarity's chances?
>
> *Bujak:* It's still too early to assess our options in a way that would clearly spell out what we should be doing. We do not know whether it will be several years or only several months before we can call an action to force concessions from the Military Council for National Salvation [WRON].

Editor: Can we hope to force the government to return Solidarity to us in a form we can live with, and how would this be possible?

Kulerski: Any concessions the government might be prepared to make depend entirely on the activism of the community. That's why it is necessary to begin to build a second union structure immediately: to create its basic units, to organize the flow of information and unofficial publications, and to improve communications generally. This is the most effective kind of pressure. The state would find it far more advantageous to officially accept a limited range of free movement for Solidarity rather than to allow the rise of a shadow structure that has nothing to lose.

Editor: You speak as though we should settle in for a long march. . . . Isn't there a need for large-scale, dramatic actions, which would increase our bargaining power with WRON?

Kulerski: Spectacular actions, calculated for effect, have much less meaning today than does day-to-day resistance in our communities. This lets the authorities know that society must be taken seriously because we are still capable of collective action.[16]

The underground organizers settled in for the "long march," working with what they commonly referred to in the newspaper as an "alternative society" or "social solidarity." According to Irena, "The program that emerged spontaneously after the coup is one of social solidarity . . . , [d]ecentralized civic initiatives . . . , [t]he collection and dissemination of information necessary to break the isolation, to counter the government's efforts to disrupt group ties."[17] It was "solidarity," uncapitalized.

As Anna Dodziuk pointed out and the others confirmed, "The party could slow down the leadership of Solidarity, it could delegalize the movement, but it could not stop the kind of organizing that had begun on the grass roots level. It is so clear that, through Solidarity, society had organized itself very quickly between 1980 to 1981. We used a formula then that was useful under martial law: 'Every day works for us.' If the party had given us an additional six months, it would have been impossible for them to stop us so easily. In some ways, in fact, it was too late anyway because the society was already organized."

It was true, as Anna stated, that Jaruzelski couldn't stop them, could hardly keep track of the rotating locations of their resistance. The oppositionists wondered what the general could really see behind his trademark pair of dark, round glasses. He had taken to wearing dark glasses in the 1940s, after his unprotected eyes were almost blinded by the blazing sunlight he endured while toiling in Soviet labor camps during World War II. As his power over the country swelled, his opaque and impenetrable glasses became a metaphor for the dark times he brought upon Poland. Apparently unaware of any dark circles save the two through which he saw the world, Jaruzelski completely failed to notice the women activists of the DGO.

Today, the 290 issues of *Tygodnik Mazowsze* preserve the history of the 1980s opposition and provide the most comprehensive journalistic record of the Polish communist system in that decade. In the course of its seven-year history as the country's most widely circulated independent press, *Tygodnik Mazowsze* reported and editorialized on every major event: the mass demonstrations on the second-year anniversary of the Gdańsk Accords on August 31, 1982; the delegalization of Solidarity on October 8, 1982; the suspension of martial law on December 31, 1982; the refusal in April 1983 by Marek Edelman, the revered Warsaw Jewish ghetto resistance fighter, to participate in the regime's commemoration of the anniversary of the Warsaw Ghetto Uprising; the pope's visit in June 1983 and the termination of martial law a month later; Lech Wałęsa's Nobel Peace Prize in October 1983; the 1984 and 1986 amnesties; the September 1986 founding of the Temporary Solidarity Council; in 1987 the nationwide masses and demonstrations, the pope's third pilgrimage to Poland, and the formation of Solidarity's National Executive Committee; the student demonstrations and the new waves of strikes in the spring and summer of 1988; and, finally, the Round Table negotiations in April 1989.

"*Tygodnik Mazowsze* was no doubt an ambitious project, and very ambitious people managed it," Anna Dodziuk told me. "We

were ambitious in terms of the outcomes of our efforts—circulation, distribution, and content. But *Tygodnik Mazowsze* was not
the *New York Times*," she wryly noted. "The newspaper's main
purpose was to remind the population that a unified voice of opposition continued to exist." It is worth noting that, despite the fact
that the staff rarely slept, there was a notable lack of spelling and
other typographical errors in all 290 issues—not a claim the *New
York Times* can make. The editors were also meticulous in their
fact checking. In 1984 *Poland Watch*—the U.S. journal that reported on and supported Solidarity from its Washington, D.C.,
base—noted that, "so far, very few factual errors have appeared in
the paper."[18]

A typical issue contained news reports, editorials, briefings on
local and regional Solidarity events, and the occasional opinion
poll. It also published columns by well-known writers and activists;
profiles of Solidarity leaders; and resources for students, workers,
and the families of political prisoners. It was the weekly from which
the provincial and factory bulletins reprinted the national regional
and local news that *Tygodnik Mazowsze* covered, even seemingly
minor events such as a student protest at a secondary school or an
individual's refusal to do military service. Articles, written mainly
by the editors and their collaborators, were punchy, forthright,
and informative. The staff also collected information from underground news agencies such as Niezależna Agencja Informacyjna
(NAI) and Informacja Solidarności (IS) as well as from factory and
regional bulletins. A high-priority aim was to inform people of their
rights, and the newspaper reported on incidents of censorship and
on government rulings. "Other objectives were of lesser importance," Helena told me. "For example, the objective of promoting
political strategy. Overall, there were not many decisions to
make—a few in the beginning and then at certain points later on—
but for the most part, very little changed from day to day, until
much later."

Both within and outside *Tygodnik Mazowsze,* opinions about
the newspaper's role and significance varied—sometimes widely.
Poland Watch underscored in a 1984 article that "[t]he concern for
accuracy and the paper's commitment to document the repressive
measures of the authorities makes the paper one of the most valu-

able sources of information on the current situation in Poland."[19] Helena, however, viewed the paper's worth primarily as a "practical organizing tool. It was not strategic in a political sense. It couldn't report real news because it was a weekly paper. It provided information, not really news. Yes, it was opinion making, but we didn't publish very outspoken editorials because that was not the paper's purpose. Its purpose was, as the most important publication of the underground press, to keep Solidarity alive."

For émigré activists like Irena, *Tygodnik Mazowsze* was a vital lifeline. In her view, it did, indeed, report real news of Poland and the opposition, news that she couldn't find elsewhere. Irena noted in a 1999 essay in *Media Studies Journal* that, even though the paper lacked space, it "always put all the news in a most succinct form. People used to joke that a telephone pole is a tree cut down and edited by *Tygodnik Mazowsze*. You can see today the same sparse style on the front page of the biggest Polish newspaper, *Gazeta Wyborcza*."[20]

Irena's copy of the newspaper was airmailed to her New Haven, Connecticut, home by her brother, then one of *Tygodnik Mazowsze*'s clandestine distributors. The paper arrived each week, she wrote, "with better regularity than other publications. My brother . . . would fold every new issue, put it in an envelope and send it to my address—always inserting a different last name (he fished for them in American movies and English novels, sometimes addressing me as Jayne Mansfield or Charlotte Bronte). We believed, probably rightly, that it was my name that was 'arrested' and not my address. In the second half of the '80s, I became very dependent on that 'subscription,' as were the readers who shared the copy that I received."[21]

Although Helena downplayed the significance of the newspaper's contents when she spoke to me, Joanna, like *Poland Watch*, held that the newspaper was an instrumental record of government repression and popular resistance. "It recorded Solidarity's illegal existence and chronicled the repression. Each victim's name was published. This was important to us and to our readers because the Communist Party had tens of thousands of anonymous victims. Our task was to make sure the arrests would not be forgotten or continued. We published the list in every issue, along with articles about political subjects, underground culture, opposition in the Soviet Bloc, and so forth. It was a normal newspaper."

In a way, Joanna's choice of terms was quite accurate. The newspaper was indeed "normal" in the sense that it adhered to the fundamental principles of journalism: it told the truth, served as a watchdog over political power, and remained loyal first and foremost to its readers, the citizens of Poland. However, because it functioned as Solidarity's voice, the newspaper was hardly independent from institutions.

One of *Tygodnik Mazowsze*'s major successes was in disrupting the government's pervasive control of the media. "The breaking of the government monopoly on information was and is one of the main goals of the opposition. So far, its success is astonishing," Irena reported in 1985. Quoting figures collected from inside Poland in June 1983, she cited the proliferation in Warsaw alone of 162 underground periodicals and eighteen book publishing houses. At least seven hundred publications, ranging from a few hundred to thousands of copies each, had appeared in 1982.[22]

New Yorker correspondent Lawrence Weschler wrote from Poland during martial law, observing that where Solidarity "proved effective in the months since the coup is in establishing networks of support and communication. . . . This sort of loose network may someday prove important to mass mobilization. . . . Most visible . . . evidence of underground activity can be found in the extent of clandestine printing."[23] In fact, as Irena pointed out, newspapers like *Tygodnik Mazowsze* were called "the ultimate weapon against social control. No foreman can persecute Solidarity activists unnoticed, no arrest is ignored, few Solidarity initiatives remain unknown. The press is truly the life stream of social resistance."[24]

Often people published bibuła to declare the existence of their group or of themselves; it was vital to have a voice in the underground, just as it had been before martial law. The proliferation of "paper munitions," as these local or modest publishing efforts were called, signified one of the ways that people reinforced Solidarity's continuity. But *Tygodnik Mazowsze*'s purpose went far beyond these aims to anchor the norms of a free press in Polish society during inhospitable and unfree times.

According to a *Poland Watch* report in 1984, one of the main debates between the editors and the readers centered on *Tygodnik Mazowsze*'s information policy—in particular, on its regular reporting of human rights violations. "*Tygodnik Mazowsze* provides extensive reports about police repression, particularly in the provinces. A number of critics have charged that this endless chronicle of repression and harassment makes the paper monotonous and uninteresting. The debate became public this spring [1984] when *Tygodnik Mazowsze* published a letter from a group of readers complaining of the monotony of the paper. The editors argued, in reply, that all instances of repression, particularly against people whose names are otherwise unknown to the public, must be recorded somewhere. Only in publicizing the ordeal of such people could one hope to protect them against further repression."[25]

By insisting on naming the names of the otherwise anonymous victims of government repression, *Tygodnik Mazowsze* encouraged the monitoring of human rights abuses in Poland. The paper's information policy created both a record and a resource, which Solidarity support committees in Western cities such as London, Belgium, and New York could retrieve and disseminate in their efforts to rally international aid.

Inside Poland, people like Wanda Nowicka—who considered herself an "average reader" and "ordinary member of Solidarity"—found that reading *Tygodnik Mazowsze* made it possible to distinguish between real news and propaganda. "It was very special to read the lists of people who were being jailed, to see how much Solidarity cared about individuals, about every individual who was taken away, who was kept in jail," reflected Wanda, who today directs the Federation for Women and Family Planning in Warsaw. A warm and thoughtful woman, in her early forties when we spoke in 1998, she seemed to savor the memory of being able to read the pages of a paper so crammed with news.

Sitting in her office in residential northern Warsaw, Wanda told me how the paper had enriched her daily life. "Solidarity was so unique. By the middle of 1981, people knew that the government was going to stop it. We could feel it. Even so, martial law was a big shock. No one wanted to say good-bye to our Solidarity identity. So the underground press sustained us. One, the newspaper placed value on individuals, on personal lives and matters such as listing the internments; and two, it presented a completely different, honest analysis of the political and economic situation, which you could never find in the official press.

"Being able to read real news was an eye-opening experience," Wanda explained. "It always raised my inner awareness about the actual ways that the society was disempowered. It was completely amazing. Even our intellectuals continued to learn by reading the news. Just by reading the news, you learned that you were manipulated by propaganda. You knew this already in a general way—you could smell it!—but the translation of this awareness into concrete issues was a different story. Reading the newspaper was like taking a practical course in politics and history."

Dominika Suwik, two generations younger than Wanda, drew a similar conclusion in a study of the newspaper she wrote in 2000 while at Warsaw University: "If the official line was to erase an event from the collective memory, people could be sure that *TM* would not allow it. At the same time, the newspaper avoided the ridiculous pathos often found in contemporary reports of the underground, the strikes, etc. It even made fun of the martyrological way of writing and talking about Poland's history, calling it 'the combatants' way.' The events were reported very soberly, and if a dramatic flare embellished reports of strikes, for example, it was by recording the words of ordinary people, who were directly quoted at length. This is a powerful device, which appeals to both well-educated and uneducated readers. *TM* occupied a real place in people's consciousness; it was among the people, not somewhere outside or above."[26]

But while the paper itself could be "among the people," the women of the DGO quite literally could not. Not only did they put in seven days a week in their Floating Offices, but they did so in an unsafe environment where extreme caution was mandatory. I could not help but be curious as to how this affected both their personal lives and their ability to work effectively, especially given the many years they lived under such extraordinary stress.

"Did you expect to get arrested?" I asked Anna Dodziuk.

"I was careful to avoid it. I never telephoned colleagues whose phone lines were tapped, and I didn't sign my name to petitions. I also knew that they could not arrest everybody. There were enough tanks to scare people—two on every corner in the beginning—but there was a shortage of people in the security service, which meant they could not follow us all the time. Besides, I was too busy to be scared. I felt I had to act. Neither I nor my friends had a choice. To live in those times, you had to be able to look at yourself when you got up in the morning. Whether you were a woman or a man, you had to look at yourself in the mirror without feeling sick. The only way to survive was to do something in the underground."

"Were you able to detect police surveillance?" I asked Helena.

"I never noticed the police because I am near-sighted. I cannot recognize faces easily. My assumption was that I should not even try to look out for the plainclothes police, and I gave this advice to others. 'Don't try to notice. If they deploy lots of people in cars, you may not be able to notice. You have to assume that you are always being followed and that you are not able to notice. Your precautions must be such that you are able to disappear out of the blue.'"

"Were you afraid of getting caught?" I asked Zofia during an interview that was constantly interrupted by *Gazeta Wyborcza* staff asking her questions. The way she sat at the edge of her seat, ready to respond to the next production question or crisis, served in its own way as an answer to my question. I gathered that there had been little time to fear getting caught.

"If you think about something constantly, it will surely happen," she replied. "I was frightened if I thought that we might get caught. We did not because we were very sensitive and cautious to the possibility of infiltration at any time. Mostly, I felt free. It was a relief for me to work on *Tygodnik Mazowsze*. I realized that all my life I wanted an end to the hypocrisy. Working on the newspaper was useful work. I had a lot of friends who, at that time, had their ordinary work, where they had terrible managers and labor conditions. They were depressed. They didn't have anything to do with the opposition directly except for being sympathetic. But when they lent their flats to the opposition, this contribution gave them a sense of purpose."

"Were you ever scared?" I asked Joanna.

"It was mixed. The dictatorship was not very forceful. Of

course, there were hardships and some deaths. But I was a woman, educated, and a well-known oppositionist, which meant that the police would treat me better than others who were male or uneducated or not known. I also knew that my behavior would be rewarded and supported by society and friends. I did not feel alone. Most importantly, I had no doubt that I was right."

"What did you learn from your involvement in the underground?" I asked Ewa.

"I learned to be tolerant and compassionate," she responded after a few moments, smiling pensively. "I learned that everything does not depend on me, that the circumstances we faced were beyond the control of any one individual. I learned what can happen when people mobilize in pursuit of a common purpose."

"Do you know that you are called the 'unsung heroine of the underground press,' that people say you're an organizational genius?" I asked Helena.

"I thought organizational skills were a natural way of thinking and that everyone thought this way, that is, to set up an organization," she replied. "It is probably a quality that I have, which I did not realize at the time."

5. Wild Card
the female stereotype as camouflage

Did the gender of the original *Tygodnik Mazowsze* team have a meaningful impact on the success of its mission, or was the fact that women founded and ran the newspaper merely coincidental to the powerful role the newspaper performed as Solidarity's voice? This question, though little discussed in opposition circles or by analysts prior to Solidarity's 1989 victory, is pivotal to an understanding of why the underground succeeded.

By the mid- to late 1990s, researchers of Poland's trade union movement began to perceive gender as a core determinant of the opposition's wins. In a seminal essay entitled "The Gender of Resistance in Communist Poland," historian Padraic Kenney emphasizes that, in a homoethnic society such as postwar, communist Poland, allegedly atheist and classless, "the greatest . . . division was that of gender."[1] Looking beyond the conventional notion that women were simply supporting their men's struggle against the male-dominated state, Kenney stresses that "women were not simply 'also' there."[2] They carried out their resistance differently and separately from men and, at times, proved more effective.

Solidarity was disadvantaged, Kenney observes, because both it and the party were playing on the same masculine field. Locked in combat, the party and the union nonetheless shared similar masculine assumptions, values, and language about power, politics, private-public spheres, and women. Then he posed an extremely provocative question: "[S]ince in effect workers and the Party grounded their discourse in the same location, the factory, conflict was rendered most difficult—and, what is more important, more easily diffused. But what about an opposition that used an entirely different set of assumptions and demands: could such opposition prove more threatening to the state?"[3]

Although Kenney noted my research on the *Tygodnik Mazowsze* women, he took stock of this particular group's contributions only in passing. A closer look at the Warsaw women who produced *Tygodnik Mazowsze* provides an unexpected answer to Kenney's question. While a great deal of their success underground was due to their skills as communicators and organizers, these formidable women also discovered early on that they had a wild card up their collective sleeve, and they used it to immense advantage. The wild card was the fact that they, and nearly everyone who supported their operations, were women. Their femaleness (but not feminism) combined in a variety of ways with ingrained Polish gender roles and knee-jerk sexism to support "an opposition that used an entirely different set of assumptions." Opposition women found themselves on a playing field where the enemy team was so invested in maleness—its own and Solidarity's—that it actually could not see the large, well-organized group of nameless, faceless women working, literally, on the home front to destroy it.

It was a combination of male cultural blindness and the Warsaw women's fanatic attention to secrecy and security that kept most DGO members and supporters out of prison. The *Tygodnik Mazowsze* editors went to extreme lengths to hide their identities, even quickly dropping the playful name they had chosen for themselves. Damska Grupa Operacyjna was meant to poke fun at the secret police, whose special undercover operatives, created especially for the martial law period, were called "Grupa Operacyjna." The female conspirators used the acronym DGO several times to sign off on the rare memos they sent but ceased using it—indeed, they also stopped sending memos—when they realized it could be deciphered to implicate "women." They continued to use DGO among themselves, however, as a symbol of their women-run enterprise, one of the underground's best-kept secrets.

After that initial potential slipup, the editors kept their identities so well hidden that the police never did suspect who was in charge of *Tygodnik Mazowsze*. As deputy editor Joanna Szczęsna was clearly proud to tell me, "They refused to believe that we were the editors, even though they heard about us over the years. Instead they accused various men in hiding such as Janusz Onyszkiewicz and Konrad Bieliński of being its editors and continuously searched for them." Summing up the government's mind-set, Joanna stressed that "The military government did not take us seriously. They underestimated women. This proved advantageous for us."[4]

"The police probably thought of me as an ordinary housewife," said Anna Dodziuk, whose stockpile of illegal newspapers, harbored underneath her refrigerator, was never discovered during police raids. "And I decided, yes, let them think so! It will be safer that way."

It did not take women long to realize that they could exploit to their advantage men's deeply ingrained perspective on sex roles. They proceeded to camouflage themselves and their work behind a range of female stereotypes, as well as behind and under household appliances and other domestic objects. "A pile of diapers was the proverbial hiding place for illegal literature," Warsaw artist Monika Krajewska wrote in an unpublished 1990 essay.[5] She and others commonly concealed papers and equipment in laundry chutes, ovens, washing machines, and inside as well as underneath refrigerators.

Feminized spaces—the rooms, nooks, and crannies that typified women's domesticity—were consciously chosen for stashing illicit materials, as it was accurately surmised that the police would not think to search the pantry, laundry corner, or a child's bedroom. The smallest products of conspiracy, such as letters and political buttons, found storage in pickling jars, flowerpots, and cosmetics containers. That the very household objects and domestic spaces that epitomized the apolitical life a woman was assumed to lead came to serve such dual purposes was, in its way, emblematic of the double lives that women led underground.

Eventually, the female stereotype was consciously exploited in more complex ways—all in the service of bringing democracy to Poland. Because Polish culture is extremely patriarchal, women are strongly associated with private life, not with the political or public sphere, and are assumed to be apolitical. It is telling that women's culturally assigned place at the margins of political and civic life was neither questioned nor vanquished by the Solidarity women who exploited it and stepped outside it. Women and men alike explained this mind-set to me by saying that women did not have the time to take on additional responsibilities outside of their homes and families. Over the years, I heard a litany of reasons that "excused" women from equal representation or participation in the democratic opposition: "It was not a question that women were treated by men as inferior, but they just had no time for such work." "It is typical of Polish society that matters of the nation belong to men and matters of the family belong to women." "Biological and cultural reasons explain why it is not natural for women to care about politics." "Maybe there was discrimination, but I did not see it. Women just gave up [politics] by themselves." "Women are not ambitious." Given this almost universal perspective, it is no surprise that during martial law, women's presence in a public space automatically tempered the state's perception of whether political subversion might be afoot. Militia posted on a street corner did not suspect that a woman carrying shopping bags was anything other than a shopper. But a man carrying a knapsack or shopping bag looked armed and dangerous, and he could expect to be searched on the spot.

"Police were simply less suspicious of women," emphasized Barbara Labuda of Wrocław, whose experiences matched those of many of her Warsaw counterparts. It is not surprising that it was Barbara, the most feminist among the underground women, who pointed out to me that in the minds of the secret police a woman's presence tended to conjure images of Matka Polka and home-cooked meals. Though the Warsaw organizers did not necessarily share her analysis, all agreed with her that it was simply safer for women than for men to engage in conspiratorial activities.

Knowing, or intuiting, that the presence of a woman depoliticized given situations, the underground organizers selected women to be escorts as well as couriers. Since security concerns

Helena Łuczywo, Warsaw, 1981   Courtesy KARTA Center

Małgorzata Pawlicka and Helena Łuczywo reporting on the
Solidarity National Congress, Gdańsk, September 1981

Ewa Kulik and Konrad Bieliński in 1990

Ewa Kulik and Irena Lasota at the
Solidarity National Congress, 1989

Małgorzata Pawlicka,
Warsaw, 1980

Joanna Szczęsna *(second from
left)* with group at party, Warsaw,
1981 Photograph by Tomasz Abramowicz,
courtesy KARTA Center

Anna Bikont *(at right)*, Warsaw, 1990

Anna Dodziuk, Warsaw, 1982

a Dodziuk *(seated at left)* at a party in
saw, mid-1980s

Barbara Labuda at Solidarity rally,
Wrocław, 1981   Courtesy KARTA Center

Barbara Labuda as member of
the Polish cabinet, 2003

Tanks line Zbąszyń Street in Warsaw
during martial law, December 13,
1981   Photograph by Jacek Zolnierkiewicz,
courtesy KARTA Center

Collage of *bibuła* (underground
newspapers)   Photograph by Czarek Wierzbicki

An office raided during martial law,
Warsaw, December 1981   Courtesy
KARTA Center

Unidentified underground press operation, Warsaw, mid-1980s
Courtesy KARTA Center

Women at the gates of the Lenin
Shipyard, Gdańsk, during the August
1980 strike   Photograph by Bogusław
Nieznalski, courtesy KARTA Center

The Lenin Shipyard at the moment of
the strikers' victory, Gdańsk, August
1980   Photograph by Witold Górka, courtesy
KARTA Center

Anna Walentynowicz during the Gdańsk shipyard strikes,
August 1980   Photograph by Stanisław Markowski

Walentynowicz in her
ment, Gdańsk, September
Photograph by Shana Penn

Irena Grudzińska-Gross, Warsaw, 1990

Anka Grupińska, Rafał Grupiński, and the American
reporter Robert Kirkland *(foreground)* at the Committee
in Support of Solidarity, New York, 1986

Małgorzata Tarasiewicz reporting on a hunger strike in Gdańsk, 1988

demanded that a male leader never travel unescorted to meetings, it was believed that he would be more inconspicuous if his bodyguard were female. The two could stroll romantically hand in hand—to a secret trade union meeting.

The usually casually attired DGO often donned ultrafeminine disguises in the name of the cause of freedom. Outfitted in fancy silks and high heels and wearing makeup, the newspaper editors often masqueraded as, well, as women, fashionable beyond recognition. "Elderly" and "pregnant" women also succeeded in duping the police. "Women from my newspaper staff were expectant mothers several times in the course of our eight years' existence," Joanna Szczęsna recalled, smiling. Special pockets, sewn at navel level onto the inside of loose garments, were made to hold newspapers, leaflets, and books. "Police did not conduct body searches of women," Joanna explained with another mischievous grin. "The trick worked best in wintertime. In spring or summer, a gust of wind could ruffle light-weight clothing and reveal the true shape of a woman's body."

Joanna seemed to particularly admire the older women who had worked as couriers under the unsuspecting eyes of the police. By the time of martial law, many of them were already fearless old hands at conspiracy, having run messages in the anti-Nazi resistance—a fact that the police apparently failed to recall or consider. Well past retirement age (fifty-five for women, which was five years earlier than for men), these women felt they had little to risk since their children were already grown and out of the house. Their modest bravery and wartime experiences inspired confidence in younger activists, including Joanna: "They looked very innocent in their hats and thick glasses, supported by their walking sticks. On several occasions, one of them had difficulty finding the place of a secret meeting and had to ask a policeman to help her locate a given address."[6] In keeping with Polish custom, plainclothesmen dutifully offered the fragile-looking couriers their seats on trams and buses, or so the anecdotes went.

There was a flip side to this conscious manufacturing of an image of passive femininity, and it too could hoodwink or disorient the police. By virtue of their maternal authority, women were able, at times, to pacify the enemy verbally. Just as feminine pleas could coax reticent volunteers to lend their apartments or to run messages, womanly appeals to members of the male militia could have the power to tone down a potentially violent scenario. For example, when ZOMO stormed into Barbara Labuda's apartment at midnight on December 13, yelling orders at her and her husband, Aleksander, she used the tone of her voice to advantage. Despite the fact that the soldiers held her husband at gunpoint, she snapped at them: "A child is sleeping. Lower your voices!" They did.

Though a woman could intervene when it was probably best that a man do little or nothing, Barbara's defusing of that situation did not keep Aleksander from being handcuffed and taken away. Unharmed and free, she went into hiding in the large industrial city of Wrocław. After December 13 she played a role comparable to that of Helena and Ewa in Warsaw, working closely with trade unionist Władysław Frasyniuk and several other men to organize the Wrocław region's underground. Her role differed from that of her Warsaw friends in that she was not part of a female team. The lone woman in her leadership circle, she was largely responsible, in the eyes of the Warsaw women, for building the Wrocław underground into the strongest of the regional groups. Not known to be bashful, Barbara confirmed this to me.

Not only were women unlikely to arouse the authorities' suspicions in the first place, even when they were suspected of wrongdoing, but women were treated more leniently than men. According to Joanna, who consistently pointed out gender differences to me, "Fewer women than men were regularly surveilled or arrested, and when they were imprisoned, their sentences were relatively short, usually under one year; men in contrast received multiyear terms." After the first few months of martial law, women realized that they were not being terribly harassed. By July 1982, all interned women had been released from the camps, and from then on, women were arrested only sporadically and at random. It soon became clear that the military crackdown would not be brutal and that the secret police were not concerned with women.

Its own culturally ingrained sexism proved to be the Communist Party's disabling blind spot. The men in charge, General Jaruzelski chief among them, looked at women and saw Matka Polka, completely overlooking Polish women's historic capacity for conspiracy. Had they recognized women's prowess, the party, the army, and the secret police might have thoroughly defeated the democratic opposition. While they might have been more vigilant a decade or more earlier, by 1981 the party had weakened to a point where cultural sexist biases had come to overrule political communist ideals; and that paradox escaped few of the key women organizers with whom I spoke.

Several factors reinforced the party's blind spot and contributed to the women's ability to continue their activism. Three of these could be characterized as tactical decisions. First, the party simply wasn't prepared to defend itself against people who were empowered by a nineteenth-century romantic notion of Poland's imagined (and potentially attainable) nationhood, an ideal the party did not believe in and thus, apparently, had not factored into its planning. Second, the full-scale repression that would have been necessary to stop the activist women would have spurred global consternation and thereby jeopardize the Western monies the Polish government desperately needed. The United States, for example, had imposed sanctions immediately upon Jaruzelski's declaration of martial law.

The third and perhaps most devastating tactical error was that Jaruzelski repeated the blunder his predecessor, Gierek, made during the August 1980 strike. He seriously misjudged the power of the opposition press and communications networks to stir up dissent. True, Jaruzelski had ordered blackouts, shutdowns, and curfews, all of which immediately paralyzed the opposition. But, as Joanna pointed out, he failed to capture and immobilize the very people—the women—who had built some of the opposition's strongest media and communications systems.

The party's inattention to women as an opposition force can also be laid, in part, at the feet of its own internal confusion, which by 1981 was almost as endemic as its ambivalence and corruption. No one belonged to the party because they embraced its ideals. People held onto their membership cards because of the attendant perks—the summer dacha, spacious apartment, and imported caviar. This exchange of material goods for loyalty oaths had begun during Gierek's rule as a way to amass supporters in the midst of mounting economic and political crises.

Such sad signs of human corruptibility were only one end of the Polish spectrum, however. At the other end was the surge of idealism and optimism that Solidarity had revived in people's hearts and minds—so infectious that even communists surprised the country by signing up for membership and joining strikes. One-third of the Communist Party's three million members had joined Solidarity by early 1981, as had 40,000 of the 150,000 officers in the police force. It was even said that a member of the Politburo paid Solidarity membership dues. It was not easy to define a Polish communist during the final decade of one-party rule.

Things had changed since the harsh Stalinist days when a traitor was a traitor, regardless of gender. Even just ten years prior to martial law, "real" communists would have meted out equal abuse to women and men alike, as happened during the 1968 university demonstrations, when male and female students suffered comparable repercussions. But by 1981 communism's "true believers" and their lofty ideals, such as gender equality, were gone, though martial law made it clear that Might still made Right. Yet even that bottom line had narrowed in scope and conviction when compared to previous decades.

The Polish Communist Party had to contend with internal contradictions and external pressures both inside and outside the Soviet orb, which probably shaped much of its character, including its eventual unwillingness to impose a Stalinist model of martial law. It used to be said in Poland that Polish communists were Poles who, metaphorically speaking, had had their Polishness erased. They had strayed from the nationalist path to salvation and allowed themselves to be swayed by foreign, antireligious, internationalist forces. They had been Sovietized—a horrifying sign to most Poles that the Russians had partially succeeded in their two-century-long attempt to Russify Poland by force. There was never a strong homegrown Communist Party in Poland, as there had been in prewar Czechoslovakia, Germany, or even the United States of the 1930s. Nationalist aspirations and the age-old enmity toward Russia both had consistently served to weaken communism's hegemony in Poland. Russia had historically been considered uncivilized and culturally inferior, though physically and politically more powerful. And the clearest evidence of Russian power and primitiveness,

Poles alleged, was its barbaric violations of women. Russians were said to treat women like beasts of burden and sex slaves, forcing even their own women to do physically demanding labor and military service. In addition, before World War II, Poland was largely agrarian, illiterate, and politically conservative. It lacked the welcoming conditions for a modern, industrial, centralized state, which is why Polish communist sympathizers looked eastward to their all-powerful neighbor, the USSR, which opened its doors and beckoned them in. Before and during World War II, Polish communists got their training in the Soviet Union and then returned to Poland at the war's end to install communist authority. All were regarded with venom by their fellow Poles, who saw them as Soviet henchmen doing Moscow's dirty work of wiping out Polishness— if not physically, then spiritually and culturally.

In the wake of World War II, the communist agenda became absolute heresy to the Polish sensibility, though not to the man who would usher in martial law in 1981. General Jaruzelski was not politically naive, but he was caught up in a concatenation of events and biases that caused him to make decisive tactical errors. His complex and contradictory biography shows a Pole who embraced communism during World War II, but his profile as such departs from type. To begin with, he didn't come from a Jewish or communist household, as did many of the Polish men and women who fled the Nazi invasion to live out the war in the Soviet Union. In puzzling contrast, Jaruzelski came from a landed estate in eastern Poland and was raised on family legends about his grandfather's bravery during the 1863 uprising against the Russians and subsequent exile to Siberia.

The general's wealthy, Catholic, nationalist family, which had taught him to abhor the Bolsheviks, was swept up in the wartime deportations to Soviet work camps. At seventeen years of age, Jaruzelski was toiling in southern Siberia close to the Mongolian border, a victim of Stalin prior to his conversion to true believerdom. In her fascinating study of Jaruzelski, U.S. journalist Tina Rosenberg concludes that his transformation in early manhood into a Red Army recruit came about both as a result of and in spite of the persecution he suffered during his three and a half years of forced labor in the USSR.[7]

Leaving his mother and sister behind (his father had died of dysentery in Siberia), Jaruzelski joined a Polish unit of the Red Army in 1943, and a year later, in August 1944, he was part of the Red Army troops that were camped out on the banks of Poland's Vistula River, within easy viewing distance of the Warsaw Uprising, for sixty-three days. After the Polish Home Army hopelessly lost their battle to defend Warsaw against the Nazis, the Red Army units, and Jaruzelski, waited for the Nazi troops to exit, then marched in to stake Stalin's claim.

In seeking to explain his Stalinism to Tina Rosenberg, Jaruzelski cited communism's promise of social justice. "We needed more justice in Poland," he said. "The West, with its colonial wars, racism, Mafia, and economic disparities, was not a model."[8] To an extent she believed him, knowing that, within the context of his generation, communist ideals rang pure and true.

But what Jaruzelski was most drawn to, Rosenberg concludes, was the Soviet Union's absolute, unlimited power, the kind of power that could protect backward, feudal, and now devastated Poland from another Western incursion.[9] In short, the Soviet Union was where the power lay, and Jaruzelski wanted to be with the power.

Given who he was and how he got there, it was outlandish to even suggest to Jaruzelski that women might thwart, might outmaneuver, his martial law plans. His problem was Leonid Brezhnev. It was Lech Wałęsa. And it was the haunting specter of Stalinism. Helena Łuczywo was not the problem. Women did not have power.

And so it is unsurprising that the general and his party made their decisions as if women did not have decades of opposition experience, had neither organized trade unions nor produced and distributed bibuła to factories, coal mines, and shipyards. It was both ingrained and convenient for the party to assume that, under the restraints of martial law, women either would be preoccupied with managing their households in the absence of their incarcerated husbands or could be easily pacified by additional consumer goods.

This latter assumption seems to me a profound indication of the disconnect between officialdom and women's everyday life. It was put into practice during the two weeks between the first night of martial law and Christmas Day, when the shops were suddenly filled with food and other supplies. The ploy was intended to mollify women, who had endured increasingly long shopping queues that autumn, and was bolstered by two prevailing cultural assumptions—that women were disinclined to have anything to do with politics and that they would protest hardship and injustice only if at their wit's end.

What's puzzling is why the party did not comprehend that women *were* at their wit's end and that, whether their grievances were consumer driven or politically motivated, they had ample reasons to actively oppose communism. Their deep and chronic problems were unlikely to be altered by the sudden or sporadic appearance of a few more consumer goods. A concerned and weary Warsaw housewife drew this picture of her daily life in a 1981 National Public Radio broadcast: "I stand in a queue, and if there is not a line, I do not go in because I know it means there is nothing in the shop to buy. Often I just stand there without knowing what is being sold until I get inside. I buy whatever there is to be had. I stand in queues several times a day for up to four hours. My two-year-old child has to stand with me. The shop is full of other women with their children running around, crying, fighting, eating. This upsets me the most. It's our biggest problem. We are now bringing up our children in the shops."[10] Women's anger was not solely motivated by consumer shortages and economic want; like men, they were also incensed by the government's injustices and human rights violations, and they said so. "I wasn't fighting for freedom and democracy per se because these were abstract concepts. However, I was fighting to protect my friends from the authorities," said Holocaust researcher Anka Grupińska of her activist days in Poznań during the late 1970s and the 1980s. "My main motivation was to free friends from prison and to avoid prison. I also wanted the freedom to get a passport and travel whenever and wherever I wanted to go. I wanted the ability to act in the open, not undercover anymore, but legally. I wanted us all to be able to live openly, publicly."

Women's anger was also fueled by the history, of which they were well aware, of Russian savagery against the Poles—the most recent example of which occurred during World War II. The Soviets understood, far better than the Poles, that a woman's role within her family and community was to sustain social ties *and* to fan the flames of dissent. Hence, during the war hundreds of thousands of Polish women were separated from their husbands or fathers, imprisoned, or coerced to do heavy labor or care for deported children in Soviet work camps and settlements. *Exile and Identity,* by Stanford University historian Katherine Jolluck, is the first comprehensive study of Polish women's deportation experience,[11] and she documents their lives under the constant threat of sexual violence, regular, invasive body searches, beatings, and rape. The gross indignities imposed on them extended to their living conditions (a paucity of food, clothing, shelter, and medical treatment, together with uncontrollable disease and filth) and their forced labor at futile and dangerous tasks. Immediately after a summer 1941 amnesty liberated the deportees, the Polish government in exile recorded testimonies of some two thousand of these women, documenting torture and terror that rivaled the Nazis' tyranny.

The atrocities were solemnly invoked, as were other wartime memories, forty years later during martial law. For just as Polish communists could be understood to represent the despised Russian enemy, the Solidarity women who exploited the female stereotype can be seen as symbolically avenging their foremothers' submissions to their Russian oppressors. If, as Irena Grudzińska-Gross has written, a Polish woman's identity was "linked to the integrity of her body, the site of her Polishness," then if she could be physically and emotionally broken down—like the World War II deportees—she stopped being a Polish woman.[12] On the other hand, a woman who retained control over her body, as the Solidarity women did during martial law, was able, in her own mind at least, to restore dignity to both womanhood and the nation; she redeemed history. For the women who used the female stereotype to fight martial law, their bodies became a symbolic battleground on which to drive out the foreign virus of Soviet communism.

Not only did the culture's assumption that women were unlikely or less likely to protest run counter to logic and to communism's feminist rhetoric, it also seemed to me to contradict the mythos of female heroism that is ingrained in every Pole. There are nine-teenth- and twentieth-century nationalist tributes in nearly every genre to the brave Polish women who fought in resistance move-ments whenever their men were imprisoned, deported, or exiled. Every "real Pole"[13] is supposed to know about women's resistance against Nazi Germany and Tsarist Russia—as Helena said, the his-tory of Polish freedom struggles is as deeply encoded as if "we had been fed this knowledge with our mothers' milk."

It may be, however, that Jaruzelski's soldiers had lost the cul-tural awareness of this source of national pride. Before martial law was imposed, the army and police underwent a long period of "training" so they could be trusted to take up arms against their fellow Poles. To transcend their hatred of communism and other "things Russian," the party fed them a steady diet of distorted his-tory that may have fostered their ubiquitous cultural amnesia.

The Communist Party's sexist blunders may have reinforced women's ability to remain invisible, but, regardless, women were well aware that it was not their manipulation of gender stereotypes but their concrete skills that were most integral to the demands of the underground. During the first year of martial law, Solidarity made several attempts to bring its factory cells together around a unified strategy and to mobilize mass actions such as strikes. By the end of that year the government had released Lech Wałęsa from house arrest and had suspended martial law (in name only), while simultaneously incorporating its chief features into the civil code. These and other strategic victories for Jaruzelski helped make it clear to Helena and company that Solidarity's prowess as a fighting engine and as the people's negotiator with the state had been utterly emasculated.

Shortly after martial law was imposed, Solidarity began playing a strategic game with the government and lost. It is important to understand this episode because, in part, its (negative) example structured what the opposition women did. A review of the first year's events illustrates how a series of defeats turned the under-ground away from its original game plan and toward an increasing dependence on organizing styles and locations of resistance that were specific to women.

Begun at the outset of martial law, reliance on women did not really solidify until the end of 1982. In the first half of that year the Solidarity underground had achieved several important gains that fostered hope. The men and women not in jail had gotten the presses up and running, they had made contacts with one another around the country, and they formed the Temporary Coordinating Committee (Tymczasowa Komisja Krajowa, or TKK). Made up of Solidarity delegates who had eluded arrest, the TKK was a temporary decision-making body that was to represent the National Commission until Solidarity's legal status got reinstated.

Ewa described to me how the TKK was formed. In February 1982 the Warsaw team (made up of Bujak and Kulerski, Ewa, and the *Tygodnik Mazowsze* editors and their various advisers) decided to try to make contact with the other regions. At the behest of Bujak and Kulerski, Ewa directed her corps of messengers to make contact, via hand-delivered letters and word of mouth, with regional groups in major Solidarity cities to bring all the regional representatives together in April to create the TKK.

"Of course, we worried about doing this," Ewa acknowledged, "because it meant we were all going to be together in one place, and so we feared getting caught because that is how it happened in Gdańsk at the start of martial law. Nonetheless, we went ahead and organized the meeting here in Warsaw. All of us worked on the preparations. The *Tygodnik Mazowsze* editors found a house for the meeting. Organizers from the various regions brought people to Warsaw, and I arranged for them to stay at separate addresses. From those addresses, each person was taken by a courier to meet one or more of us who made up a close circle of people. Then we each escorted a regional representative to the house."

Representatives in attendance at the inaugural meeting on April 22, 1982, included Bogdan Lis of Gdańsk, Zbigniew Bujak of Warsaw, Władysław Hardek of Kraków, and Władysław Fraysniuk of Wrocław. Attendees also included Anna Bikont, Joanna Szczęsna, Helena Łuczywo, Barbara Labuda, and Ewa Kulik. Together, Ewa reported, they "discussed what to do. Helena, the *Tygodnik Mazowsze* staff, Barbara Labuda, and I worked as editors and drafted the program text. The men were thinking, the women were formulating. We women also said what we thought, of course. Generally, there was always a consensus among us." The group spent the first day debating the merits of calling a general strike. Gdańsk was always in support of a general strike, Ewa stressed, but the Warsaw contingent supported general ongoing resistance and did not want to organize a general strike, mainly because they did not think people would participate. "We had lost every strike effort in December, and it seemed too soon to try again; plus we were not equipped."

Tygodnik Mazowsze had already published extensive debates on whether an "instant change" strategy or a "long march" strategy should guide the underground's activities, and these were picked up by the TKK and continued throughout the year. Advocates of the "long march" strategy, who were based predominantly in Warsaw, foresaw that the constant challenge to the underground would be, to quote movement theorist Adam Michnik, the "conflict between the attempt to maintain a mass base for the movement and the need for the underground union's cadre structure to function effectively."[14]

In letters that were smuggled out of Białołeka prison and published in *Tygodnik Mazowsze,* Michnik made eloquent arguments in support of his position: "It is not widespread terrorism that Poland needs today. It is widespread underground activity that will reconstruct society, spreading throughout towns and villages, factories and research institutions, universities and high schools. Underground Solidarity has to encompass all this. The institutional form of this movement should be left."[15]

The proponents of the "instant change" strategy, based mainly in Gdańsk and Wrocław, called for the underground to organize a nationwide general strike that would force the government to compromise with Solidarity before the state could activate its normalization policies. The challenge of this proposition was that, were the underground to call such a strike, it had to succeed in its first attempt; there would be no second chance and no crying wolf. Michnik put it this way: "[O]nly a spectacular defeat of WRON's pacification plans can restore to the agenda the possibility of a genuine compromise between the authorities and the people. Otherwise, the authorities will not budge an inch."[16]

The TKK debated the issue at its inaugural meeting until all finally agreed that a general strike should be used strategically and that the group would wait for a timely moment before calling for one. The question would finally be settled later in the year, though unfortunately by default, after consecutive defeats made the "long march" scenario a veritably foregone conclusion.

At the April meeting, the group also discussed setting up a foreign bureau in a city in either Western Europe or the United States. Warsaw opposed the idea. "We believed that the most dangerous spot in our whole organization would be the point where we had contact with the West," the hypervigilant Ewa reported. "We didn't need to get technical support from Westerners because we already had our technicians abroad, who were sending us equipment. Every region had someone who worked for them from abroad. We thought it was best to remain decentralized, including, if not especially, at the international level."

But Bogdan Lis of Gdańsk argued for Western representation, and Wrocław backed him up. Barbara Labuda told me that Wrocław was eager to make contact with foreign media, politicians, writers, and so forth because they wanted to rally the support. "Our idea was to go to the foreign embassies to build an organization in the West," she told me by telephone not long after I had met with Ewa to discuss the TKK. When the group took a vote—and it should be noted that the women voted too—the majority favored the creation of a Western base. Barbara was happy that her side won the decision. "It was a historic meeting," she concluded emphatically.

The TKK also agreed to call for a boycott of the government's annual commemoration of International Labor Day on May 1 and to call for a mass demonstration on August 31, the second anniversary of Solidarity's birth. But the most important outcome of the April meeting, in Ewa's opinion, was the decision to present Solidarity members with a vision of the underground as an alternative society that would carry out specific activities on a regular basis. For example, the TKK would call for commemorating the thirteenth of each month by having sympathizers place lighted candles in their windows. "The candlelighting was meant to symbolize that we are not giving up, we are aiming to negotiate with the Communist Party on a new agreement for the legalization of Solidarity," Ewa said.

The TKK-organized actions began on International Labor Day with the first mass demonstration to take place in Poland since December 1981. It overwhelmed the nation's capital. Two days later, rallies in Wrocław, Gdańsk, and other cities celebrated the patriotic anniversary of the signing of the 1791 constitution by raising the prohibited red and white national flag. Facing down ZOMO, the crowds shouted, "Gestapo, Gestapo!" and "We want Lech, not Wojciech!" The authorities detained several thousand people during that week and imposed a temporary telephone blackout in Warsaw and Gdańsk. On the five-month anniversary of martial law on May 13, university-based demonstrations erupted nationwide, leading to the arrest and internment of several prominent deans and professors.

On July 21 Jaruzelski announced the release of thousands of internees, including the one thousand or so women who had been interned in December, and Ewa recalled that Solidarity's immediate future was looking promising. Even the cancellation of Pope John Paul II's summer 1982 visit to Poland was not met with despair. At that time, the Polish Church was headed by Primate Józef Glemp, who continues to officiate in 2005. Taking his instruction from the Vatican, during martial law Glemp regularly cautioned Solidarity to resist the temptation to stage public protests, and he admonished the Church's more radical priests not to support civil disobedience openly in their sermons and publications. Although it was a crime to harbor political fugitives, the primate's warnings did not stop many local church leaders from finding ways to assist the underground.

The relationship of the Church leadership to the party government was always complex. Jarosław Anders writes in *Foreign Policy* that it was complicated by the Catholic hierarchy's protective, pragmatic self-interests on the one hand and its symbolic role as a bastion of national resistance on the other. After martial law, the local churches created a "wide support network for political prisoners, unemployed activists, and even underground Solidarity leaders. At the same time, however, the church almost certainly participated in secret negotiations with the regime."[17]

On August 31, the second anniversary of the Gdańsk Accords, the year's largest demonstrations broke out across the country, and they ended in violence and a series of shocking blows to the movement. ZOMO responded to the demonstrators with firearms. Seven deaths were reported in *Tygodnik Mazowsze,* and more than four thousand protesters were detained.

On September 3 the government accused several former KOR leaders of responsibility for the August 31 protests and charged them with conspiracy to overthrow the state. Things got worse during what came to be known as Black October. On the fifth of that month, Władysław Frasyniuk and Barbara Labuda were arrested in Wrocław while on their way to a meeting. Frasyniuk's replacement, Piotr Bednarz, would himself be arrested by the end of the month.

On October 8 the Polish parliament officially delegalized Solidarity. In response, the TKK called for a four-hour strike on November 10, the second anniversary of Solidarity's registration. But workers in Gdańsk did not want to wait a month before venting their rage, and spontaneous strikes erupted in the shipyards there on October 11, with workers demanding the release of Lech Wałęsa and the relegalization of the trade union movement. Before the rest of the nation had time to react to events in Gdańsk, the government had already imposed a communications blackout on that city, isolated it completely, and militarized the Lenin Shipyard.

A week later, on October 20, the TKK called for an eight-hour strike to be held on November 10 and for continual actions throughout December. The protests were to culminate in a general strike the following spring and a total boycott of the new government-sponsored unions, whose formation had begun earlier that year as part of the process of institutionalizing normalization. In a declaration published in *Tygodnik Mazowsze,* the TKK stated: "Dissolving all the trade unions . . . is an acknowledgment of WRON's failure. They did not succeed in breaking the trade union movement. The Sejm . . . dared, against the will of its electorate, to de-legalize the trade unions, which are comprised of 90 percent of all adult citizens in Poland. . . . Solidarity may only be dissolved when thus decided by its members. Our Union still exists, and will still work for the Independent Polish Republic. . . . Solidarity calls all Union members, all workers, all trade unions to boycott the false unions."[18]

But the November 10 strike failed to materialize. On October

21, shortly after the TKK strike announcement had been published, Lech Wałęsa was released from house arrest. The government had finally concluded that Solidarity's inimitable leader caused more trouble locked away than he would if he walked free. A few days later, Władysław Frasyniuk and Barbara Labuda went on trial; Frasyniuk received a six-year sentence and Barbara a one-year term. At the end of November, a humiliated TKK retracted its call for December actions. On the eve of martial law's one-year anniversary, Jaruzelski indicated that he would suspend martial law by the year's end. Then, two days before Christmas, the remaining internees were released. Finally, on the last day of December, the regime did indeed suspend martial law—while simultaneously incorporating its main features into the civil code.

By this point, Helena and company well understood that the unprecedented social movement represented by the underground would have to gear up for the long march after all, just as Wiktor Kulerski had forecast in *Tygodnik Mazowsze*'s inaugural cover story ten months earlier. People remained hopeful, and there was no chance the underground was going to give up, but exactly what they might accomplish was at that point an unanswerable question.

"During my visit to Warsaw last October [1982]," Lawrence Weschler wrote, "one of the most frequent bits of graffiti I saw was a simple logo—CDN. In Polish, CDN stands for *Ciąg Dalszy Nastąpi* and means 'to be continued.' . . . The Western press has a tendency to focus on news stories during climactic developments and to fade out during the interim—the long, slow periods when revolutions gestate—so that we may expect Poland to be receding, further and further, into the back pages of our news journals during the months ahead. We should not, however, be misled. The saga of Poland is definitely CDN."[19]

On May 26, 1983, Bujak published a statement in *Tygodnik Mazowsze* that formally signaled the end of one opposition chapter, characterized by strikes and other forms of mass mobilizations, and the rise of a new phase of "long march" activism. "It was precisely November 10 that became a turning point for the Union. It became clear that the idea of organizing a general strike could not succeed. People realized that in our situation, it was a daydream to attempt to build a structure that could initiate and conduct such a strike. Those who are active today have a better sense of reality. They have matured. Working with them is much easier and more effective. There are fewer conflicts now. Major portions of the underground have remained hidden for over a year and a half. This is important in and of itself. Now everybody who wants to be active and cannot do it aboveground has the possibility of hiding, and he knows it can be done and knows how to do it. This fact now hangs over the authorities."[20]

The underground spoke often of its hope of sustaining some form of continuity with Solidarity as it had existed prior to martial law—for example, by putting forth known trade union leaders such as Bujak and calling for peaceful protests. But in reality, the underground's loosely formed infrastructure marked a radical departure from the political operations and formal hierarchies that had been built during Solidarity's pre–December 13 days. The movement's key centers of power when it was legal—the factories, coal mines, and shipyards and the decision-making committees—lost their predominance after organizers realized that negotiations with the government and spontaneous actions like workers' strikes could not build sufficient support. As a result, the male-dominated formal structures that had been created during the legal phase devolved into a reliance on informal social networks, such as the Floating Offices that the *Tygodnik Mazowsze* editors coordinated. Men and their power sites now had to share the opposition stage with women and *their* power bases—the home as publishing house, the home as post office, and the home as safe house.

It may be helpful, at this point, to clarify the nature of "home" and of private and public activity in a totalitarian system, as it differs from the situation in a democratic society, where the dichotomies and contradictions are more clearly drawn, though no easier to reform.

Tactics employed against Poles by the Russians after World War II indicate that the latter understood, apparently better than did the Jaruzelski regime, a crucial national dynamic: the Polish home (particularly bourgeois, nationalist, Catholic homes) was the traditional breeding ground for resistance. In a significant, though little known, wartime chapter beginning in 1940, the Soviet Union deported an estimated two million Polish men, women, and children from the newly occupied communities in eastern Poland to labor camps and prisons in isolated outposts of the USSR. The Soviets used this forced exile to crush the Polish resistance they knew would be forthcoming if the communities remained intact.

The way that a society separates its private and public spheres influences how gender difference is perceived within that society, and although no one society fits neatly into an "either/or" situation, certain general characteristics have held over time. Historically, the public sphere has been dominated by men, while women have been identified with the home. Although the home has been conceptualized as an apolitical sphere outside the public realm, it nonetheless has always been shaped by political realities. To ignore the impact on gender relations of how power dynamics are played out privately as well as publicly perpetuates women's subordination to men and restrains their entry into public life.

In Poland and other Eastern European countries, both men and women participate in the public sphere insofar as both have worked for wages since the end of World War II and the creation of the Eastern Bloc. But even though both men and women contributed to their country's economic life after the war, if one were not part of the state machinery, one had no power in the public sphere. Those who held dissenting views could only express them privately, which diminished the public spheres of debate, art, and commerce. Male privilege in public life was limited to members of the party elite, and people resented the way communism disempowered men by excluding or restraining the traditional male role in public and political life. Only certain men could have power; most were treated like women—as was often bitterly explained to me in interview sessions.

The much narrowed public sphere did, however, include women as workers. And although women's special burden under communism was to assume a double responsibility as worker and mother/housewife, by taking advantage of unprecedented postwar education and employment opportunities, they were able to advance beyond the social positions of their mothers and grandmothers. This had not been possible previously and was not the case in the West in the aftermath of World War II. Thus, men's mobility in the public sphere was suppressed while women were allowed to enter on narrowly defined terms, which were neither better than nor equal to men's downgraded social position.

The particular restraints on male and female roles in a communist society produced new tensions between the sexes. It appeared that women had gained power while men had lost power. This distorted view was sometimes turned against women to allege that they benefited from communism while watching, unsympathetically, as their men became emasculated under a system that espoused women's liberation rhetoric. Solidarity women, guided by their awareness of this antiwoman sentiment and truly empathetic to men's loss of masculinity, opted to bolster their men and their community. That is partially why they believed it was premature to entertain feminist ideas, which would only introduce more gender differences, more tensions, more questioning of power distribution between the sexes.

Another dimension of how an authoritarian system produces tensions between the sexes as it shapes public and private realms can be seen inside the home. Under communism women still dominated the organization of space in the home, but they had to share that space with activities that, in the West, more often occur in public arenas. Opposition organizers gathered in living rooms and kitchens, where they produced illegal literature, performed readings of their works, and studied censored scholarship. Men usually dominated such meetings, while women served the men and cleaned up afterward. Conventional inequalities between the sexes persisted.

The actual amount of space in a home could also complicate relations among family members. Because housing shortages were chronic, newlyweds commonly moved in with one spouse's parents. When a marriage ended in divorce, the ex-spouses often continued to live together. Apartments were small and often included children and grandparents. The overlapping roles and generations rubbed against one another as people struggled with a secular and tyrannical state; intellectual and material impoverishment; and, in Poland, a Catholic religious tradition.

Given these constraints inside and outside the private sphere, thousands of women nonetheless decided to clear space in their already crowded lives and apartments to make room for the new opposition—the one that was wielding "an entirely different set of assumptions and demands" and was suddenly, by default, in charge.

The reason women could so effectively use "feminized spaces" to hide contraband was because their homes had become a primary locus of resistance and the chief breeding ground for civil society. While it is true that the 1970s opposition had also functioned illegally in people's homes, the scale of the 1980s underground was much greater because people were bringing what remained of a mass-based, structured, social movement into their living space. That shift alone, after enjoying sixteen months of freedom and a dynamic public life, created an instant increase in the quantity and quality of women's participation because, according to Polish tradition, women rule their homes. The lending of apartments to the opposition, for example, became largely women's prerogative and responsibility, as Joanna stressed when she wrote: "It was always a woman, it seems, who was responsible for the decision, very crucial to our newspaper, of whether to let us use her family house or apartment for our work—for printing, editing, meetings, storing things. Decisions were obviously made by the whole family, but a woman's voice was always the most important. We never used anybody's apartment without the knowledge of the hostess."[21]

The host, on the other hand, was occasionally left in the dark, especially if a woman thought her husband might object to sheltering activists. On one occasion, the wife of a member of WRON lent the *Tygodnik Mazowsze* editors the basement of her four-story home—she told her husband that a group of psychoanalysts would be using it. "She was," Joanna recounted, "a cheerful, overweight woman who used to say, 'Had the police caught you, our house would be the best place for it. They would probably kick my husband out of the Party, and I would at last have a chance to slim down on a jail diet!'"[22]

Under authoritarian rule, the home had become a sanctuary, where people could freely speak their mind, do as they pleased, manage small, private enterprises—and plot the revolution. However, in the case of the 1980s underground, two new phenomena are worth noting. First, women not only opened their homes to civic activities, but they also became more actively involved than they had been in earlier periods. No longer simply serving tea and cakes, they were conspiring with other women at their living room meetings. Second, because the home became widely used to shelter people, the housing networks fostered social interaction, grass roots outreach, and education. They created a lively, widespread community made up of uncommon social arrangements.

The underground's infrastructure thus became dependent on women, and by meeting the demand for private space, women's activism broke with cultural assumptions about their so-called proper place. Although greater value was always assigned to male protest, and men's resistance efforts remained indispensable, the decentralized formations that emerged to replace Solidarity's top-down organization afforded women an unanticipated advantage: they were able to enter wider spheres of activity and influence, and the scale was unprecedented. For example, Helena and company sought out areas of work, such as the media, where they had already established their reputations, and they rose to decision-making authority over thousands of people. They and others were able to do so because, according to Joanna, the male leaders backed them up. Women could take on work that needed to be done but that men didn't want to do. Polish women, as Joanna more than once made a point of emphasizing, do not compete with men.

When I first met Joanna at New York's Algonquin Hotel in April 1991, she told me about her life and the opposition community with a storyteller's flair and presented me with a copy of her recently completed essay, "Women in the Opposition." The only member of the DGO to have put her experiences in writing, Joanna had prepared her eight-page essay in English for a talk she presented at an American university in 1990. Regrettably, it remains unpublished. An informative mix of journalism, sociology, and history, it opens with an interesting qualifier: "The problems of the women's liberation movement have never been of much concern to me and if I did give it any thought, I saw myself as a rabbit being experimented upon. Thus, I will talk only about matters that I personally witnessed. I shall not attempt to make any generalizations nor to present the problem globally."[23]

In a counterintuitive way, this disclaimer, like the rest of the essay, shows Joanna's sensitivity to gender distinctions. I see it as a caution to the American audience not to mistake her for a feminist, for it often happened in American academic circles in the early 1990s that former dissidents were treated like radical royalty and female former dissidents like radical feminist royalty. Feminism went with radicalism at that time in this country, but not yet in Poland. It would not be until 1999 that Joanna would identify herself as "feminist from time to time." But Joanna's fellowship years at Stanford and Princeton Universities attuned her to the realities of gender dynamics, and that is reflected in her essay. Her thoughts helped orient me to some of the complexities of female identity and experience in the Solidarity underground.

Joanna was the first person to tell me that the party's leaders had overlooked women's activism. It was also she who perceived that activist women used their invisibility to coordinate underground activities and to bypass arrest. And she saw that women had been assigned lesser roles by virtue of their gender—roles that she and other women had agreed to occupy. But though she understood some of the root causes for the opposition's division of labor by sex role—only men officially held political power, for example—she never went so far as to say, in bold, Barbara Labuda-like terms, that sexism colored the gender dynamics within Solidarity. What she would allow is the following, as recorded in her essay.

If one compared the number of women who were active in the underground and the number of women who made their careers there, the latter would seem extremely minimal. Even though a large number of women, after having worked for the opposition for many years, are as competent as men to perform certain tasks and to take certain, often prestigious positions, there are comparatively few who do so. Why is that?

First, I think, women themselves do not compete with men. They will not rival them for important positions and achieve success only when they are beyond competition, when they are unquestionably the best, when there are no men who could compete with them. If there are men who could compete with them, then the man wins, even though he might be equally, not better, qualified to perform a given task. Secondly, the structures of the underground were less formal. . . . This is the reason that women occupied important positions according to their qualifications, talents and levels of involvement in the underground, but not in the official structures.[24]

Historian Barbara Jancar's research findings reinforce Joanna's observations: "Women appear more marginal to the organizational structure of opposition, with visibility in leadership depending on male endorsement. Where structures and organizations are not primary issues, women show ability both individually and on a mass basis to profit from an unstructured situation."[25]

The underground was regarded as relatively unstructured, when compared to Solidarity in its legal phase, but, in fact, it was structured by women. With manly tests of power and politics now on hold (no strikes, street protests, elections, or negotiations), the underground arena was less desirable to men. The door could be opened to women.

For the first time, women's activism can be seen as undeniably central, not at all marginal, to the opposition's strategies, structures, and activities. Structurally, women's participation in the underground differed in significant ways from their activism in earlier decades. Large numbers of women got involved; their activities were well planned and spontaneous; they took instruction from other women; and the structures under which they participated, though informal and illegal, were organized.

As a result of their efforts to recruit volunteers to perform the "feminized tasks" the underground relied on—such as delivering messages, typing, distributing materials, escorting people, and lending apartments—Helena and company were able to organize a network of women activists that was indicative of these new structures. Though the majority of the women were retired or single, they otherwise spanned an enormous range of society. While sympathizers who had families hesitated to jeopardize their children or spouses, Joanna points out in her essay that some of the most unlikely among them volunteered their services. "A mother of four, whose husband was in prison and who did not have much time, became an understudy; she had to have a good memory and provide absolute guarantee that she would not be arrested. . . . A physically paralyzed girl kept track of what was said on the police radio station; she was happy that, having to stay at home all day, she could do something for the underground. . . . The youngest, 14 years old, carried illegal publications in her schoolbag. The eldest courier was almost 80-years-old, which made it possible for her to pretend to be deaf and to not answer questions during police interrogations."[26]

It was not the DGO's conscious aim to create a women's network. However, given first that Polish women did not compete with men and second that they definitely wanted to participate in the opposition, the women in the network were predisposed to take their cues from Helena and her team of full-time professional activists, whose guidance they trusted. Hence, women were attracted to those areas of activism where seasoned female organizers had already prepared a work space and invited their involvement.

When Solidarity moved indoors, when its men came home to roost indefinitely during that first year of martial law, politics came home to women by coming to women's homes. A woman could no longer say she did not have the time or wasn't biologically inclined to get involved in politics. She recognized that she and her home were needed. The women in their private spaces were on familiar ground, a known playing field—but they were going to use it in a brand-new way. The adage "If you can't bring Mohammed to the mountain, bring the mountain to Mohammed" springs to mind. And, to mix religious allusions, what Polish women brought down from the mountain was the defeat of the Communist Party.

6. A Third Space
mutual dependencies and cooperation

"Somebody was to be in hiding at our place, and we were quite terrified. Even more than getting in trouble, we were afraid of a total stranger staying in our tiny apartment for an extended period of time. Ewa Kulik came, and we immediately felt that it was not the first time she had lived with strangers. She behaved as if she had left us a moment before and simply came back home. She didn't ask about anything. She found the salt and the frying pan straight away. She never made us feel uneasy. . . . She didn't boast about what she did; she didn't talk about it at all. We only saw that she slept little, worked a lot, locked herself in her room, and tapped on her typewriter."[1]

Thus began an anonymous tribute to Ewa Kulik published in August 1986 in *Tygodnik Mazowsze,* part of a regular "Prisoner of the Month" feature highlighting jailed activists. Ewa and her boyfriend, Konrad Bieliński, had been arrested by police in April 1986. They barged into their apartment in the middle of the night, dragged her out of bed, and pulled Konrad away from the computer. Ewa was released in a general amnesty the following autumn.

I came upon the portrait of Ewa only by chance while scouring the 290 issues of *Tygodnik Mazowsze,* which, though run by women, seldom reported on women's interests or profiled, even anonymously, the individual women who contributed to the "conspiracy." The unique tribute was written by one of Ewa's volunteers, a *bezmienne bohaterka* (anonymous heroine) who clearly had thought a lot about the young fugitive she harbored.

One day, when it seemed that there was some danger, she packed up and was gone in three minutes—although she had been living at our place for several weeks and had many things to take with her. . . . For a long time she didn't come. I even wanted to ask friends about her, but I didn't really know whom I should ask. And then suddenly she appeared—in a brand new version. She often changed her hairdo, hair color, clothes—I think it was kind of fun for her. Her looks were in total contradiction to what we would expect to find in a conspirator or someone chased and hiding in random places: she wore hats, turbans and toques, she had wonderful stylish sweaters, which she knitted herself. At the same time she had no expectations whatsoever about how she lived and ate. She was faultless in her difficult role of a person in hiding. . . .

I never heard her complain, not even that she was tired, or that she was wasting her best years. One could feel that her situation was her choice and not an unfortunate plight. . . . I believe that women play a huge part in conspiracy, doing all the dirty work, but it is mainly men who are spoken about.[2]

Ewa and the *Tygodnik Mazowsze* women did not seek or get praise and public recognition for their work in the underground. And yet, the special magnetism the underground held for them lay in the fact that it allowed them more power and social responsibility than any of them had ever known.

The underground was not quite private space and not quite public space. It was a third space, part workaday world and part war zone, where social expectations unraveled and where this team of women called the shots every day, on their terms, in their domain—at least to the extent possible in an authoritarian system with strong patriarchal roots. The underground fostered a free space for women that transcended everyday reality and social roles. It marked a departure from the double burdens of labor and domestic duties and an experience of autonomy and activism separate from men. Just look at Ewa Kulik, who, for most of her twenties, held one of the most exciting jobs in all of communist Poland—a job without a clear future, perhaps, but with tremendous responsibilities.

"It was a *podziemie kobiet* [an 'underground of women'],"
Maria Janion, Poland's preeminent intellectual, told me. She had coined this phrase in an effort to describe to me "the presence of some other, literally underground, female reality enclosed in the already well-known picture of the underground."

The underground became the border zone between the private and the public, between the past and the future, between tradition and democracy. It was that in-between space where boundaries blur, roles and rules relax, and change takes place. The more I became aware of this border zone of experimentation and alternatives, the more important the question of gender dynamics and identity became to me. I was curious to know the following: How did men and women relate on a daily basis? How did they perceive one another's role and value? What was new, different, uncomfortable, or life changing? What transpired underground that didn't happen in normal life? On the one hand, women's activism was regarded by men and most women as necessary but not politically significant, since politics was perceived as a male field of action. On the other hand, anonymity and women's alleged political indifference gave them an unusual advantage to transform their society and to grow individually beyond the cultural norm. How did they manage their lives, and what was important to them singly and as a group?

All of the women of the DGO said they coped with the extraordinary demands and stresses of underground life by relying on one another like sisters, like the dearest of friends. Their support of each other helped make victory possible. Men and women relied on one another in unprecedented ways as well, and the sharing of power between them is a vital part of the story of how the underground was sustained. The housing networks that the women coordinated also fostered new relationships as people moved in and out of the Floating Offices and rotated their living quarters. These mutual dependencies and cooperation—particularly between the sexes in the leadership circles and among the wider rings of friends, acquaintances, and strangers that bolstered the underground's day-to-day activities—contributed significantly to their collective victory.

The opposition was creating community. No longer seeking out dialogue with the government, people were now talking to each other; moving in and out of one another's homes; cooking, cleaning, and reading together; sharing space; and simply being human together. By making use of unusual social arrangements, such as the Floating Offices, men and women were becoming, in the simplest terms, responsible citizens to one another. And an important part of that responsibility, which women emphasized in their interviews, were the special (and fun) bonds that they formed.

"It was a great adventure in friendship," Anna Bikont told me. "We spent more than ten hours each day working and talking. We were some of the hardest working people in the underground. The most exciting thing for me was the long conversations we carried on late into the night. Everything was an adventure. We usually had to share a room because our hosts could only give us one room and usually only one bed. After three months, I exploded and said that I will never sleep in the middle again!"

Helena said she imagined that the "friendships among the women in the underground might be similar to those shared by men in a war. If you live through very challenging extremes, your relationships with other people become much closer. Everything you experience is more dramatic. You meet with people more than normally, and what you share with them is more important. As a result, the friendships and other relationships you have are, generally speaking, much richer and more meaningful to you. This I can say most certainly. It's much more than what you can have, let's say, working in a bank."

The women worked together in close proximity, sharing housing, meals, and confidences and worries about their children, their romances, and pending marital separations. They grew intimate and tolerant of one another's needs. "We supported each other," Joanna emphasized. Just as, historically, wars have increased women's opportunities to participate in public and economic life while men were away doing battle, in 1980s Poland, with the Solidarity men "away," women were left to sustain the community.

And, like men going off to war, when Solidarity women went underground, they were forced to uproot themselves from their peacetime responsibilities. They set aside their family duties, entered the world of political subversion, fabricated an intricate secret code, and concealed themselves within its web. Ewa Kulik adopted mainly male pseudonyms, such as Patryck, Karol, and Eryk. Barbara Labuda often alternated between Bella and Kinga. Helena and Joanna shared a few aliases, a favorite being *robaczek świętojański* (lightning bug).

As proud as each woman told me she was to have broken the government's monopoly control of information and its freeze on civic life, their daily life in the underground could be as exhausting and uncomfortable (though not as dangerous) as life in a foxhole. Maria Janion told me of a visit Helena made to her Warsaw apartment during martial law: "Helena was hiding and came to see me on some business. She said, 'It is so hard to hide. I wish I could just sit down and read a book, be home.' She envied me that I could sit in my own home, although I had had my own share of unpleasant adventures with the authorities. I saw her as a great figure. A woman fighter who sacrificed a lot."

As late-twentieth-century women, Helena and company juggled more than their share of responsibilities, which were both typical (family, lovers, job) and atypical (their hosts and hostesses in hiding, the national network, a self-limiting revolution). Of the women in the Warsaw group, only Zofia and Anna Dodziuk were not in hiding and lived in their own homes. Helena, Joanna, Anna Bikont, and Małgorzata oftentimes lived together in hiding, and Ewa first hid alone and later was joined by her boyfriend.

None of the DGO ever totally abandoned their aboveground lives. Rather, they led double lives, attempting to coordinate the secret network and to maintain their relationships with lovers and children. "I didn't have a husband or children at that time, so my personal situation was not dramatic," Anna Bikont explained. "It was more difficult for Joanna and Helena because they both had small children. However, if they had been caught and jailed when, in the beginning, the police had searched for both of them, they would have been separated from their children anyway."

Some of the time, Helena hid with her activist husband, Witold, and her daughter, Łucja. Nine years old at the outset of martial law, Łucja eventually went to live with her grandparents, and Helena and Witold visited her on weekends. Other times they made careful arrangements with friends to bring her to a park or playground, where they could spend all too brief hours together. By 1988 Helena and her husband had separated, and they later divorced.

"There is no recipe for having a happy child," Joanna, a single mother, concluded while describing her efforts to juggle motherhood and revolution. Her son, born in 1979, lived with her brother and sister-in-law between the start of martial law and July 1982; thereafter he lived either with Joanna or her mother. Joanna's relationship with her mother, who fully supported her daughter's political work, reinforced the whole family's ability to withstand her long absences. "Leading an unpredictable lifestyle as I did and keeping my maternal responsibilities together was difficult. It is hard to say whether I have done a good or a bad job as a mother. Children are just as likely to be happy or unhappy regardless."

Anna Dodziuk and Zofia also were single mothers at the time. A nanny helped Anna with childcare duties so that Anna could work her two jobs—as a psychotherapist and as a newspaper editor. Anna's demanding family life included raising a daughter with Down's syndrome, who required two weeks of medical treatment in Germany each year and daily special attention. Although Zofia did not live in hiding, she worked full-time on the newspaper staff, which meant that she was often pulled away from home for days at a time. She relied on her mother for help with raising her son, who was seven years old at the start of martial law. "I lived with my mother. She and my son knew about my activities. My involvement frightened my mother, and she transmitted her fears to my son. I became concerned that, if ever I got arrested, my mother might not be the proper person to take care of my son because she might only escalate his fear."

"Once I was taken by the police from my house," Zofia continued. "They wrongly suspected me of an activity, so they didn't detain me for long. In the meantime, a friend stepped in, took charge of my son, and brought him to his father, who lived outside Warsaw. So nothing bad happened to my son in that instance. It was actually a good experience because from that moment onward, he knew he could always count on my man friend. He had somebody to whom he could turn when he was worried. He knew what I did, and he knew I could get caught. But now he felt supported. By the time of the Round Table talks, my son was proud of me because I could finally reveal what I had been doing."

"Dr. Spock does not teach parents how to raise children and conduct conspiratorial activities under the same roof," activist Monika Krajewska emphasized in an unpublished essay she shared with me. "Politics and children were rarely discussed together."[3] But for Monika, the mother of two young boys when I interviewed her in 1990, the two subjects were inseparable. An artist who lives in Warsaw with her husband, Stanisław, and their family, she belongs to Poland's sixties generation. When she and her activist friends started raising families in the 1970s and 1980s, they had to figure out how best to protect their children. Would it be better to hide their political activities from their children or to disclose them? Monika did the latter, and during martial law she and her husband held illegal seminars in their home as part of the Flying University. Looking back on that era from the vantage point of 1990, she wrote:

> When women involved in the opposition became mothers, they faced the difficult dilemma of whether to withdraw from the movement or expose their children to a constant sense of insecurity. The possibility of arrest and imprisonment was always present in the minds of the parents, a potential threat that was added to the usual list of parental worries.
>
> One of our friends, an active distributor of Solidarity bulletins illegal under martial law, told a typical story. He was given a manuscript, which he folded and put into his bag. His four-year-old son looked at him with horror and pointed to his father's sleeve: "Papa, you must put it THERE!" In such moments, it deeply mattered whether anyone had witnessed the scene. But who would scold a child for that?
>
> Over the past decade, I watched my friends' efforts to bring up normal children in an abnormal situation of political repressions, or more mildly, while living a double truth. The results were often funny. Little Hania [a friend's daughter] sat quietly

for an hour going through books, page by page. She had once witnessed a police search in her home. Less funny were the threats of harming children, which the police used to weaken the parents' spirits.

Most anecdotes about children's behavior circulated in the hardest times—the time of martial law in 1982. It was then that a little boy told his parents: "Back at the kindergarten we told Miss Kasia that our generation is lost for the Commies."[4]

Stories about precocious children provided heartening respites from the pressures of conspiracy. And so did love. "We couldn't function without love," Barbara declared proudly. Lovers needed to be masters of flexibility in order to adapt to years of transitory sleeping quarters. Nonetheless, they carried on, despite the dearth of privacy and the scarcity of space and time. Ewa spoke to me at length about the array of fluctuating circumstances she and Konrad weathered in order to be together. After a while, she said, nothing they had to cope with took them by surprise—except for the police, who eventually caught up with them. Ewa lived in hiding from December 1981 to May 1986. During the first year she lived alone and moved from apartment to apartment frequently, but that changed.

My husband, Konrad, was my boyfriend at that time. He escaped from internment in December '82. He pretended he was sick and was taken to a hospital to be examined. After the examination, he slipped out of the hospital, while the secret police waited for him in the lobby.

From that moment, we began to live together. Living together in the underground made us closer. It was also stressful. That is why after the underground we did not want to marry. We wanted to know whether it was love or a need to be together. There was an enormous need to be with someone, to be close, to not have to pretend that you are not afraid. Love was an outlet from all the stresses.

Together, we lived with several families. After some time, we got an empty apartment. We lived like squatters for a few months. An elderly woman had died and her grandson gave us the keys to her apartment. We lived there until the administration got interested in what had happened to the apartment.

Then we rented an apartment from people who did not know who we were. We pretended to be a young couple—I was writing a master's thesis and Konrad was teaching at the university. The arrangements went through the channels of people who had emigrated. It was the best place for us to live because no one would get in trouble or arrested if we got caught.

The last apartment we rented belonged to people who knew who we were. They sympathized with our work and they also needed money. We were desperate for a place to live. Each year it got harder and harder to get an apartment. The police were active, and people got caught. We used the last apartment for almost a year. It was against all security rules, but we had no choice. We were caught there and arrested. The couple was arrested, too, leaving two small children with their invalid grandmother.

There was a dark side to underground existence. Several women from outside the close-knit *Tygodnik Mazowsze* circle—from what I call the second tier and below—spoke with bitterness about the isolation and uncertainty they felt and the dichotomies and contradictions they faced. Anka Grupińska of Poznań, for one, described the mixed feelings she had about her activist commitment and the hardships of its day-to-day life-style. She mourned the loss of a normal life with its promises of family, career, and material comforts. On the one hand, she told me, "I think the underground was a waste of time. Nothing was heroic under communism. On the other hand, my sense of honesty wouldn't let me do anything else. All of my friends were in prison either in May or in June. If they were not imprisoned in June, they could be arrested the next month. If my husband was not in prison this week, he could be in prison next week. I didn't feel like a heroine in the Warsaw Uprising. I felt it was my bloody duty that I hated and had to do. It was a waste, but on the other hand, I felt like I couldn't avoid it. It consumed my family life, my privacy, my passions, my career. All I had left were underground papers."

Anka, born in 1956, had been involved in the Poznań student opposition in the late 1970s, and she celebrated the creation of

Solidarity in 1980 but did not feel motivated to help build its legal structures. In fact, she took the occasion to withdraw from activism in September 1980. "It wasn't my time for involvement," she stressed in our 1991 interview in Warsaw. She wanted to focus on her private life instead. She and her husband, Rafał, had just bought a house with a loan from her father, and she was pregnant. "I remember thinking, 'After two years of being married, we're going to have a family life. A house and a baby.'" She also wanted to complete her last year of studies in contemporary American literature and poetry, and she graduated from Poznań University in 1981. Regrettably, for Anka, her period of what she called "nonpolitical thinking" was short-lived, and she found herself returning to opposition activism much sooner than anticipated.

Anka took a job teaching high school English language courses that September. Rafał was teaching fine arts and Polish literature in another high school. Both were happily involved in their new home and her pregnancy, Anka recalled wistfully, until October. "I lost the baby. And soon after that, martial law came. That marked the end of my family life, which never had enough time to develop." Almost immediately after martial law was imposed, school officials told Anka that she had a "bad influence on students" and was not a good teacher. By June she had been fired from her teaching position. "They didn't let me be an adult for very long," she said, the residual anger still discernable in her voice.

Anka resumed her political involvement and found that "It was 1976 all over again—fighting against lies and fighting against everything that was evil. However, this time, it was a different equation. I was no longer a student and the formula was tougher. Now there were soldiers, policemen, detention centers, and jail sentences."

She recalled a visit with friends from Frankfurt during the martial law period. "At that time I looked very masculine. I behaved like a tough boy. When my friends visited, and some of them were women, they felt uncomfortable with me. They felt guilty about using perfume, wearing makeup, things like that. If somebody had given me perfume at that time, I would have been offended. The world I lived in was so basic that no opulence was desired. Nothing. Not even colors. I never wore bright colors. Yellows, pastels—

impossible! I wore gray, black, dark brown. When I saw a person wearing pink, I treated such a person, although not consciously, like a superficial idiot without any depth inside her or him."

"Years later I met a friend in the Frankfurt airport," Anka explained. "We hadn't seen each other for three years. I was wearing a pink sweater. We went to the duty-free shop and I bought a bottle of perfume. She looked at me and said: 'I am so happy that you know a woman can buy perfume for herself.' We started talking, and it was quite clear that she had worried that I had turned into Rosa Luxembourg."

Anka reflected, "When I think about it today, it's frightening. I would never, ever want to repeat that experience, even though it was honest. In that sense, the underground was great because everybody was courageous. There was solidarity among us. Still, I was never able to breathe freely."

Anka introduced me to her friend Agnieszka Maciejowska, the woman who was to tell me that the *Tygodnik Mazowsze* editors were known as the Dark Circles. A Warsaw activist, Agnieszka was newly out of graduate school with a philosophy degree in hand when she went into hiding for seven years and found that martial law had postponed her professional aspirations, apparently indefinitely. She turned from lofty discourses on Kant and Heidegger to lowlier logistical pursuits—such as finding people, funds, and equipment. She knew the former AS editors because they had all worked in the same office building prior to the military coup. After December 13 she made contact with Helena and got her first assignment—working for Ewa in the Bureau for Interregional Contacts to organize the couriers who were sent to towns outside of Warsaw. Agnieszka soon headed the bureau herself and then moved on to work for the Myśl publishing house, where she directed a unit that serviced the printing needs of illegal presses throughout the country. Agnieszka explained her involvement in the following manner.

It could be said that I was a full-time underground employee. Work was my private life. After some time, I felt discouraged because I was always in hiding and the work became mundane and routine.

My personal life was confined to writing letters, visiting prisoners, and talking to lawyers. Only rarely could I spend time with my boyfriend, Tadek, who was in prison three separate times, for a total of two and a half years. Even after he was released, I didn't have much time to be with him because I was working for the Warsaw underground five days a week and only returned on the weekends to Tadek and our flat in the suburbs. I remember I would bring him presents from Warsaw, and he would laugh, saying that I behaved as if he were still in prison and I was bringing him presents there. It was impossible to behave differently. Other friends of mine were in prison, too. It was not enough that he was out because others remained in jail. That knowledge hung over us. Still, I didn't have the feeling that I sacrificed my private life to a political situation because the opposition was my personal choice. I invested my emotions in it, and especially the feeling that I was setting my private records straight with the authorities. Politics affected me personally. What I did was not a sacrifice but my private interest. . . .

Those times gave me the feeling that I was needed—meaning that I, the person that I am, with all of my positive and negative sides, was needed. . . . The kind of friendships one developed in the times of "real socialism" were special, emotional ties that were appropriate for the underground. During those times, loyalty was very important—the feeling of living and being among people who were real friends, who would never reveal my name, even if they were beaten by the police. I once sent a messenger with Bujak's letter to Frasyniuk. The messenger was caught by police and severely beaten. The police wanted him to identify the person who had given him the letter. He refused, and spent a lot of time in prison. There is no way I can compensate for what happened to him. They don't beat people any longer. I can't compensate in the same way for what he did for me.

Five to seven years is an incredibly long time to live in hiding, to be the houseguest of strangers, to chase down increasingly scarce sublets year after year, to agonize over your separation from lovers and families, and to rely on relatives and friends to help raise your children. Every participant in the underground was cognizant of the demands, the hazards, the gamble, and the long-term investment they were making in a distant democratic future that *might* be had in their lifetime, that *might* be possible if the rest of the population did not forget about Solidarity.

I found no single, overarching motivation that moved women to become part of the underground and endure its outlandish inconveniences and impositions. Some, like Barbara Labuda, got involved for political reasons or, like ambivalent Anka Grupińska, were driven by a sense of moral responsibility. Others, like Monika Krajewska, rallied to the aid of a relative or friend, or, like Agnieszka Maciejowska, they were simply tired of "living the lie" and wanted to "set their personal records straight." Some activists dropped out during the underground phase, either because they were burnt out or because the new battlefield was too dangerous. Others stepped in the moment the stakes suddenly escalated, even though they had only passively supported legal Solidarity.

And many who were totally new to activism also jumped in, having been so horrified by the military coup that it "pushed them into our arms," as Wrocław organizer Władysław Frasyniuk put it.[5] These were people who felt compelled to act, to do something, anything, even if the activity had to be fairly risk-free. As Zofia Bydlińska recalled, "I had a lot of friends who at that time had their ordinary work, where they faced terrible managers and conditions. They were depressed. They didn't have anything to do with the opposition directly except for being sympathetic. But they lent their flats to the underground, and this contribution gave them a sense of purpose."

"[T]here is no social group or institution that did not produce any new activists after December 13," Frasyniuk told the editors of *Konspira,* a collection of interviews with members of the TKK that was published in Poland in 1984.[6] One of those social groups was women, and the TKK was well aware of their participation, their members having worked very closely with women and having depended on them—even during the *Konspira* interview sessions. But *Konspira* reveals scant information on women's contributions. One reason is that the women were extremely protective of their anonymity, and the interviews were surreptitiously collected during the dangerous early years of martial law, between 1982 and 1984. Ever-cautious Ewa Kulik said that the making of those interviews had been controversial from the outset because, as she explained, "I thought the meetings themselves and the information that was recorded would endanger us!" Apparently, even in 1992 the project still infuriated her. Despite her disapproval, Ewa had monitored the interviews with Bujak, and Barbara had done the same when Frasyniuk was interviewed. Not only did Ewa think the men should not have granted the interviews, she certainly didn't want the women's names exposed or any clues to their identities revealed. I had to read very carefully to find signs of their presence.

"If you were to base your knowledge about the underground on the TKK documents or regional structures, you would probably come to the conclusion that it is something like a monastic order. There is not one woman among the signatories of declarations, communiqués, and appeals," note the *Konspira* editors in introducing the subject of women's involvement. "But the participation of women is significant, and . . . women may be more eager to take up activity than men."[7]

Adding to this *Konspira* discussion, Frasyniuk noted, "They don't regard their activities as being prestigious, they want nothing for themselves, they aren't nosy. In Wrocław, it's almost always women—often single, living alone—who provide apartments for underground activists. Men, on the other hand, do this unwillingly. Even in families, women are more active and usually take the initiative. . . . It doesn't matter whether a woman is a professor or a cleaning lady, she runs around like a messenger providing food or tea and doesn't ask questions. And she knows what she's risking. Anonymous heroines, that's what I'd call them."[8]

Among key Solidarity figures like Frasyniuk, women were acknowledged as useful in fulfilling not leadership roles but the virtuous, necessary support roles of manager, administrative assistant, and housekeeper. Frasyniuk shows his appreciation of such labor, and by calling women anonymous heroines, he accentuates their selflessness and willingness to do the ordinary tasks that needed to be done. Women didn't demand ego strokes, as he indicates men would have done, nor did they make wish lists of desired paybacks. Such observations primarily reinforce the Matka Polka stereotype and conventional gender roles rather than honestly depict the contributions of women activists.

According to my interviews, however, women did have idealistic expectations. Women believed they were making an investment, like men, in freedom, democracy, and citizenship. Women acted not as anonymous heroines but as responsible citizens. And they acted "as if" they were free and equal, just as the opposition had encouraged Poles to envision themselves.

It's clear from another *Konspira* interview that some Solidarity men would find such assertions preposterous and instead would prove themselves to be as misguided as the Communist Party in underestimating women's capacity for revolution. Gdańsk activist Bogdan Borusewicz, who helped lead the August 1980 shipyard strike, married Alina Pieńkowska, the Lenin Shipyard nurse who helped save that strike from falling apart, while he was in hiding during the 1980s. But it doesn't seem likely that the strong, outspoken woman was sitting in on the *Konspira* interview session when Borusewicz pointed to the inherently weak, unstable character of female activists: "Women in the underground are more amenable and less demanding than men. They don't have great personal ambitions, and they don't have to be part of the center. They're willing to clean up after the printers or deliver letters. Men, however, are against using women. Traditional views have an influence here, but also the fear that women are weaker and less stable. These fears are justified, however, because women are rarely so strong as to not spill everything during interrogation. Naturally, if they go underground not because of their principles but because of their husbands or boyfriends, they don't break, since this would endanger their loved ones. In general, anyone—male or female—who doesn't have a rational basis for his or her activities sooner or later breaks down."[9]

Clearly, during the underground years, gender relations were regarded in conventional terms, and gender-assigned roles determined the division of labor in the underground. Women were assumed to be supporting men, and men, of course, assumed the dominant role. But there was also an unprecedented level of mutual reliance between men and women, and the conventional notion of what constituted proper interaction neither reflected nor hindered the development of a fascinating dynamic. Independently of one another, both Ewa and Barbara told me about this dynamic, in which, over the course of time, traditional gender roles seemed to reverse between the male political leaders and the female organizational leaders.

"Women were more mobile than men," Ewa pointed out to me when we shared sandwiches and tea in her kitchen. They were able to move about in public unfettered, precisely because they were *not* the sought-after TKK. This "mobile factor," as Ewa dubbed it, reinforced the indispensability of women's participation, a vital contribution to which the *Konspira* editors merely alluded. Men's movements, in contrast, were proscribed. Their contact with the world outside their hideouts was mediated by the women who served as their bureau administrators, couriers, and escorts.

Barbara Labuda was aware of the gender dynamics at play, and she described the situation as "paradoxical," emphasizing that "Frasyniuk saw me as his assistant, and I saw him as mine!" Ewa too was aware of the paradox and pointed out the restrictions she placed on Bujak's daily routine: "As head of the regional underground bureau, I regulated almost all of Bujak's activities. I decided who met with him, where he hid, and when his wife could visit him. I felt terrible for him, especially because, in the underground, I was in the better position. I lived with my boyfriend. I traveled around the region to meet with union representatives, printers, and illegal publishers. I coordinated three hundred apartments in Warsaw and managed hundreds of people. Compared to me, Bujak was isolated. He only saw his wife three times a year, and then only briefly. He must have felt, at times, like a token symbol."

I discovered from reading *Konspira* how painfully slow, trying, and depressing endless days spent in hiding could be for men. Gdańsk organizer Eugeniusz Szumiejko wrote of how he coped with the separation from his family: "I've developed a special self-defense mechanism: weeks and months go by, and I don't think about my family. I do this because the days when I long for them are very painful. . . . [E]veryone with a family has to keep in mind the question: how much for himself, and how much for the country?"[10]

Visible and vocal but effectively immobile and trapped by circumstance inside flats they could not call home, the male leadership paid a high price in order to preserve popular confidence in Solidarity's political foundation. Frasyniuk spoke of this frankly in his *Konspira* interview. "Being in hiding does not always mean attending continuous meetings or organizing something. Sometimes there are lifeless hours between one contact and another, or empty weeks after a big roundup. Once we sat depressed for two weeks, eating rice and macaroni because there was nothing else in the house. If you sit for twenty-four hours like a stump, and only one contact comes to see you daily, then you practically stop thinking. That is, you only think about organizing conspiratorial activity. You become extremely one-sided. People discuss things in order to revise their own opinions, and loneliness makes this impossible. It increases egocentrism, for instance: I have a toothache or headache, and no one is here, they've forgotten about me, they don't care. This creates a negative attitude toward one's surroundings."[11]

Such living conditions, while stressful, also influenced people's everyday experiences in humanizing ways. Men and women in hiding agreed to the uncommon circumstance of living with strangers, and ordinary people accepted the unusual opportunity to open up their homes to political fugitives and conspiratorial activities. It became clear during many of my interview sessions that the unconventional living arrangements had spawned—for male and female guests as well as for their hosts—new awarenesses about the individual, the self, and community. The concerns and vulnerabilities that hosts revealed in the privacy of their homes deepened the resident activists' connection to and understanding of their fellow citizens—"These are the people whom I was elected to represent." "These are the people with whom I am building a new society." The activists also gave the people who housed them an intimate view of public figures—"Ah, so the charismatic leader is a human being just like me." "Aha, if she can dedicate her life to political resistance, then so can I."

As Ewa recalled it, "If I lived with people in their apartment, I spent time making contact with them. I could not just treat them as a means to an end. I learned that, in order to function together in their homes, it helped if I showed people that we did not have to be afraid of anything. I spent time talking with them about their problems, their jobs, and their children. We became friends."

Bujak and Kulerski often roomed together and grew accustomed to one another's personal habits, developing an intimacy similar to the one women reported and interacting, in their own ways, with their hosts. Bujak, for example, wrote: "Wiktor Kulerski and I once stayed with a divorcee who had two children. . . . Wiktor helped this woman so much—jumped to help her and kissed her hand—that, how shall I say, she began to look at him seriously. One more week and she wouldn't have wanted to live without him. As it was, she already had tears in her eyes. So I said, 'Wiktor, let's get out of here because once she falls into this, it'll be very bad.' This finally got him moving. He hadn't noticed anything himself. But to this day, he likes to wash the dishes."[12]

Ewa was particularly sensitive to the feelings of the male leaders whose identities and whereabouts she guarded. "The men had to accept that we women were in charge. This was problematic." On the one hand, she believed that the men respected her and the other women. On the other hand, the authority that women held to direct networks and to arrange men's schedules produced friction that remained largely unaddressed. "The necessity of remaining invisible made men uncomfortable," Ewa explained. "They had a visible role, but their activities had to be carefully monitored. Men like to be in the spotlight. They loathed living like dependent women, imprisoned inside an apartment." Ewa acknowledged these tensions but did not know how to resolve them. "It was a delicate situation, and I worried that the men would subconsciously grow to resent me."

Gossip permeates even the best-intentioned social circles, and "poisonous gossip" that spread among the activists exacerbated the differences in men's and women's circumstances. The underground channeled information, and that included rumors about betrayals, infidelities, and the like. "People made snide, sometimes very damaging, remarks about the dependent work relationships between women and men," Ewa recalled. "Some people said that Bujak and I were lovers, which greatly upset his wife until we cleared up the matter when we finally met. They also called Bujak a puppet in my hands and referred to him as 'Ewa Bujak.' I felt awful when I heard that. In Polish society, especially in the workers' circles, it is the worst humiliation to say that a man is in a woman's hands. It means that he has no will of his own. Bujak didn't have to prove himself. He really was in control. But I felt that in order to stop the stupid and vicious rumors, I had to find somebody else to substitute for me in the meetings with the underground activists. I constantly looked for a male activist to do the job. I only succeeded when my boyfriend, Konrad, and Henryk Wujec came out of prison. Zbyszek [Zbigniew Bujak] never showed that he took all the gossip to heart. We remained friends. However, I could feel how free and happy he felt that he did not have to follow my lead after we were released from jail in September 1986." Ewa never broached the subject of their work relationship with Bujak because, she said, "I didn't want to hurt his pride."

Despite such difficulties, Ewa felt that the era of unorthodox accommodations marked a special and very valuable moment in time. "One could think that being in the underground meant being cut off from ordinary life. How untrue. It was only in the underground that I became very close to people, who were helping us, and to their private lives. It was five years of my life. I would never have had such close relations outside the underground. I met so many wonderful people. I never regretted it."

When they named her "Prisoner of the Month" in August 1986, the *Tygodnik Mazowsze* editors also published a tribute to Ewa by Jan Lityński. Unlike the *Konspira* interviews, with their generic allusions to women, this tribute evokes a Solidarity woman as seen by a fellow Warsaw activist—a man who acknowledged her as a peer.

Everything Ewa does is done seriously, very skillfully and effectively to the end. This applies to how she handles organizational matters and interpersonal cooperation both. Obviously, a person with Ewa's character must have been controversial. In fact she did raise much controversy—she didn't avoid conflicts. But I never noticed in her a willingness to force her own opinion at any cost. All quarrels and disagreements concerned the work, the activity.

Despite all her enthusiasm and commitment, Ewa was capable of showing self-control, or perhaps I should even call it a slight irony toward herself and her surroundings. Thanks to that distance, she never crossed the thin line dividing a deep, authentic commitment from fanaticism.

I only know her initial period of activity in the underground from the others' stories. But I do know how much Zbyszek Bujak and Wiktor Kulerski owe to her. It is no exaggeration to say that it was much to her credit that Zbyszek had not been caught for so many years.

When I went into hiding myself, at the very start I became aware that without her, our functioning would be much worse. Ewa took care of many unprepossessing, arduous, tiresome matters, so that we—who gave our names—and she—who remained in the shade—complemented each other. At the same time, she knew how to create an atmosphere in which work became fun. She introduced an element of easiness. Although our situation was so abnormal and the stress was overwhelming, Ewa could always laugh.[13]

Many ambiguities colored sex roles, and the perception thereof, as they were played out in the underground, where men felt constrained and women experienced boundlessness. Rigid sex stereotypes loosened their grip. Mutual dependencies developed between the male leaders and the female advisors who served as their invisible deputies and protectors. Men relied crucially, directly, and indisputably on their female counterparts more than at any other time in the opposition's history—or perhaps more than they had ever previously realized or accepted. The unprecedented level of interdependence between, for example, Władysław Frasyniuk and Barbara Labuda in Wrocław or between Zbigniew Bujak and Ewa Kulik and the *Tygodnik Mazowsze* editors in Warsaw forged a lateral exchange of cooperation, influence, and power.

The underground was good for women, and women were good for the underground. While those men who had not been imprisoned hid at "home," utterly depending on women but maintaining formal leadership, women organizers grew extremely independent—so independent that they surpassed the cultural norm.

7. Patient Revolution
women and leadership

The key to the underground's ability to keep motoring along for seven long years, according to Helena Łuczywo, was to be found in the very nature of women's leadership style. The underground's everyday reality, for the most part, was uneventful, and Helena made a point of stressing that it "was actually very boring." She recognized, however, that its durability and longevity made room for the new groups, ideas, and protests that emerged in the late 1980s and helped Solidarity bring about the unexpected change-over of 1989.

But in the years leading up to 1989, the task of blowing fresh energy into Solidarity week in and week out seemed to Helena to be necessary, noble, and quite possibly fruitless. "No one believed that Poland would escape communism. It was the system. You could read and dream about Poland becoming independent, but the system seemed very stable. We didn't know how to rid ourselves of communism without a major war. We thought communism would go on forever. It's clear the necessary changes didn't happen overnight. Looking back, we made a patient revolution, the kind that women are best suited to manage."

Helena's image of a "patient revolution" resonated with the opposition's guiding concept of a "self-limiting revolution"—peaceful civic actions with built-in restraints—that Solidarity had adopted. But Helena added a new dimension to the Gandhian concept of nonviolent resistance—women's (allegedly) patient touch and an abiding faith in women's eventual success. But why would Helena feel that women rather than men were best suited to manage a patient revolution?

Though men had invented the notion of the self-limiting revolution, throughout the months of Solidarity's legal existence, they had increasingly failed to adhere to their platform of dignified coexistence. As much as they claimed to be creating a peaceful civic sphere and not challenging the government's power, they were actually doing both. In particular, they made overt threats against the state, their behavior grew more pugnacious rather than more peaceful, and in the process they lost sight of their self-imposed limits.

When the male leaders diverged from the movement's original premise, the membership lost confidence in them. Muscle-flexing civic action is risky business when one's nemesis is an authoritarian regime, and even if the leadership had behaved faultlessly during the legal period, Solidarity's very existence would inevitably have become intolerable to the communist government. The union was powerful, and it made unacceptable demands—from worker-controlled factories to free elections and referendums.

While incarcerated under martial law, Adam Michnik wrote continuously and prolifically (and patiently) from Białołeka prison, and in a piece written in the spring of 1982 he reflected on why Solidarity's practices had diverged from the original platform. "The mighty and spontaneous social movement . . . did not possess a clear vision of specific goals or a well-defined concept of coexistence with the communist regime. It allowed itself to be provoked into fights over minor issues, into inessential conflicts; it was often disorderly and incompetent; it lacked familiarity with its enemy and the enemy's methods. Solidarity knew how to strike but not how to be patient; it knew how to attack head-on but not how to retreat; it had general ideas but no program for short-term actions."[1] Solidarity was young and feeling its oats, and it charged ahead as far as it could before the inevitable happened.

The self-limiting revolution was brought to a halt by what journalist Lawrence Weschler referred to as Jaruzelski's "self-limiting counter-revolution." On the one hand, the general had implemented the strongest repressive measures in the history of communist Poland and in so doing had put an abrupt, traumatic end to the population's most liberating experience in fifty years. On the other hand, as Joanna Szczęsna stressed, after the initial months, the dictatorship's crackdown was relatively mild when compared to the crushing of Czechoslovakia's Prague Spring in 1968 or of Hungary's 1956 uprising.

The military intervention in Poland established riot units rather than death squads, internment camps instead of gulags, and curfews instead of gallows; and, briefly, it offered more abundant consumer goods as a pacifier. Jaruzelski's unwillingness to alienate Western aid providers, combined with the fact that he didn't have the personnel to mount a full-scale oppression, also worked as built-in restraints. The greatest damage the general could do after overwhelming Solidarity militarily was to normalize certain martial law policies such as the delegalization of the trade union movement, imposition of state-controlled unions, refusal to negotiate with Solidarity, and mandatory loyalty oaths.

Joanna Szczęsna told me that she and her cohorts believed Solidarity would eventually regain legitimacy, "though no one could guess how much or when. At the top of my list, I thought we would return to a seventies form of tolerance. A coexistence between opposition and communism. A nonaggression pact. But we never anticipated the collapse of communism!" Jaruzelski's military coup had been such a devastating success that the history and mind-set of the times, and of the general behind the dark glasses, made it impossible to think that the Communist Party could be overthrown.

"Martial law showed who was in control. Its purpose was to frighten people," Ewa Kulik explained. "It was imposed so the communists wouldn't lose their power. The Soviets would not have entered Poland because they were already intervening in Afghanistan. But it makes no difference. Jaruzelski did it for them."

In part, Jaruzelski did indeed impose martial law in order to decrease Soviet pressure, which had been building for fifteen months—one month short of the time Solidarity enjoyed a legal existence. With Red Army troops positioned on Poland's eastern border and threatening to invade, Jaruzelski once again seemed to be doing the Soviets' dirty work for them. But mostly he did it to regain his own absolute power over Poland, for he understood only too well that the greatest threat to his authority was not the Soviet Union, his external master, but Solidarity, his internal enemy.

When Jaruzelski handily overpowered Solidarity, he recaptured Poland and got the Soviets off his back. He won, and the Soviets got the clampdown they had been demanding—while claiming to uphold a "policy of peace." As Tina Rosenberg assessed it, for the Soviets and Jaruzelski alike, "Martial law was the culmination of decades of belief that Poland had no choice but to submit."[2]

The general doubtlessly understood that, given the constraints he faced (Western sanctions and so forth), his strongest suit over the long term would be not military force but the repudiation of Solidarity's legitimacy. Where the coup succeeded most effectively, once the armed intervention gave the government the upper hand, was in slamming the door on any future negotiations, thereby bring to a screeching halt the dialogue that had developed between the state and the society over the previous sixteen months. No more talks, no more hope for peaceful coexistence. Solidarity's hands were tied—for what was Solidarity without the state to provide its direct counterpoint, without its power to negotiate with the Communist Party? The male-dominated bottom line had bottomed out. Only the telerevolution could be salvaged, and its shining example, *Tygodnik Mazowsze,* was made by women.

This, then, was the history and mind-set that led Helena to tell me that, after martial law was imposed, only women could have led the revolution to its successful conclusion. The patient revolution was necessary because the men's impatient revolution had (among other things) helped trigger martial law. The men had one dominant "personality," the women another. The women's personality was suited to waging the revolution that martial law made necessary; and, in turn, the "soft" nature of Jaruzelski's martial law helped make the patient revolution possible.

In this next round, there could be no more fighting, not internally or externally, for the grass roots movement that had, after all, been premised on nonviolence. The democratic opposition had entered "the long, slow period when a revolution gestates," to use Lawrence Weschler's description. Now what was needed were "[p]atience, realism and consistency," as Michnik put it in his May 1982 communiqué from prison. "We must look for ways to develop civil society and not just undertake actions simply in order to be a nuisance to the 'junta,'" he urged. "A Polish democratic state will never be born if democratic structures do not exist beforehand in Polish society. And independent of the institutional success of the underground, a base of Polish democracy is being created today."[3]

In their hideouts, Helena and company took Michnik's call for "patience, realism and consistency" to heart and recast the movement. In lieu of the peaceful resistance of a self-limiting revolution, they organized the nonviolent *persistence* of a patient revolution. But patience is not an innately female virtue and doesn't really explain why women were best suited to manage a patient revolution. Nor is patience the first attribute that comes to mind when I think of Helena, Joanna, or Ewa, among others. But if, instead of thinking in terms of character traits, one applies the idea of a patient revolution to the specific organizing styles, structures, activities, and locations of resistance that came to define the underground, then Helena's reason for singling out women becomes apparent.

For the first time, Polish women's activism can be seen as undeniably central, not at all marginal, to the democratic opposition's strategies, structures, and activities. Without women, the underground would simply not have existed. No deputies, no *Tygodnik Mazowsze,* no couriers, no typists, no housing networks. When women took charge of the media (typically a male bastion of power, whether in a democracy or a revolutionary setting), an inordinate amount of power came into their hands, for the underground press gave Poland the promise and the possibility of incorporating the norms of a meaningful free press into a future free of communism. The DGO played a leading role in establishing the precedents for an independent press that was and remains vital to the quality of citizenship in Polish society.[4]

At the same time, the underground's survival also depended on the kind of day-to-day, task-oriented activism that was considered women's work. According to Barbara Labuda, their ability to roll up their shirtsleeves, to build teams, to arrange meetings and production schedules, to type and edit articles, to provide shelters, and to recruit volunteers was instrumental in the preservation of Poland's democratic will. "This was the *real* work," she insisted.

The "real work" did not appeal to men, as Władysław Frasyniuk, Barbara Labuda's Wrocław cohort, told the editors of *Konspira*. "Men . . . like to do spectacular things, make decisions, be important. If they're delivering a letter, it has to be to Bujak or Frasyniuk; otherwise, they won't do it. We've had quite a few guys who declared their willingness to help us at any time, but only if they have direct contact with the boss. In my opinion, the underground relies to a large extent on the quiet and sacrificial activity of women."[5]

In reality, the action of the patient revolution was carried out on several stages simultaneously, with overlapping casts of characters—working-class heroes and their union cells, intellectuals writing from prison cells, bibuła publishers and their publications, priests and their parishioners, women and their Floating Offices. Women played a mediating role among these groups, providing the community with social cohesion traditionally expected of Polish women in times of crisis. Matka Polka rose to the occasion, as she always did for Poland, enabling real women to help dispel some of the internal heat between men that had been acted out in Solidarity's legal period. With women's active presence in strategy sessions and on political committees, there were fewer fights. And men were not about to wage political fights against women as they did against each other.

Instead of conflict, the working-class heroes received direct, round-the-clock support from female intellectuals who were not threatening, as their male counterparts might have been. Seen not as intellectuals but as good Polish mothers, the women did not threaten "real Poles." Matka Polka's image provided "national comfort," to quote feminist theorist Isabel Marcus in conversation with me. The women themselves didn't mind this projection. It enabled them to keep the peace so that they could do what had to be done.

Although the cultural image of Matka Polka was used liberally, and without protest from the women, it did not, of course, adequately describe their real contributions. Nor did it accurately depict how they viewed themselves. They did not identify as "mothers" and had little in common with, say, Argentina's Madres de la Plaza, who mobilized in the 1970s and 1980s in the name of their missing children, human rights, and democracy. It would not have occurred to the Polish women to transform the individual suffering of Matka into a politically powerful collective identity such as the one the Madres represent. That would have made too strong a statement, given that their interest lay in diffusing politically charged identities and issues.

Helena and company insist that they knowingly opted for a non-threatening identity that would not ruffle anyone's feathers while simultaneously protecting their anonymity. It is possible that, beyond the possible threat it posed to security, one of the reasons they stopped using the code name Damska Grupa Operacyjna was because it conveyed a female consciousness that could have threatened the vulnerable male leaders in hiding and, in turn, weakened the women's position. The DGO were pragmatic realists. Through all the smoke and mirrors, they saw themselves as full-time, professional oppositionists; as editors, handlers, and communication experts; and as senior management to the men's board of directors. Simply put, they were fighting for the rights of citizenship for themselves and all of society—and they were obviously willing to do whatever it took.

"Whatever it took" included a willingness to forego assigning political importance to their work, for they knew it would ignite trouble. From the outset the *Tygodnik Mazowsze* women "resigned" themselves, to quote Joanna, in order to avoid touching off that spark. Later, as they got busy, they forgot about the whole issue and didn't think about it again.

So when I referred to them as the Founding Mothers of Polish democracy, some of the editors felt complimented while it made others uncomfortable. To my surprise, it turned out that none of the *Tygodnik Mazowsze* women regarded herself as a leader. Their similar views, as expressed to me throughout the 1990s, were best represented by remarks Joanna made in one of our conversations in 1991. "I think we had influence as each important newspaper has. It didn't matter that we were women. I think our personal influence was less. People saw us as a kind of support for the political leadership. I saw it the same way. I did not want to influence political decisions. The only way I influenced political decisions was that I am a professional stylist. I edited statements made by Solidarity leaders. I took care that an article would be shaped into good Polish and that the ideas would be clear. It is also an influence."

Words carry different meanings from one culture to another, and the interviews I conducted acquainted me with the tensions that cross-cultural differences in language can create. Certain words were like small land mines, particularly during the early years of my work. Before the Polish experience of democracy had progressed, some of the interviewees and I found that we had very different understandings of words such as *internationalism, leftist politics, feminism,* and *collaboration.* For many of them, these words held immediate, negative associations with communism, and when I used them in the early 1990s, they made people wince or fume. As I later learned, my choice of language sometimes made me appear either highly suspect or incredibly naive.

The word *leadership,* I discovered, sounded particularly totalitarian. Leadership evoked horror movie images of Hitler and Stalin—"evil monsters with thick, ugly moustaches," as one woman remarked. Rated high on the scale of reign-of-terror terms, *leadership* meant one-party rule, or power *over* people, in contrast to power shared by people. The word was tightly linked to politicians, power struggles, and corruption in an oppressed society where "Politics smell" and "Politics are dirty" were common phrases.

When I asked during the interview sessions held in the early 1990s, "Did you think of yourself as a leader?" or "Are you saying these women were leaders?" some irritated female interviewees snapped, "Polish women don't have to be leaders to get things done." A few others said, "You Western feminists are always looking for power struggles."

The leadership question was always provocative and elicited a range of emotional responses and little consensus over the years. But it wasn't only the negative associations with communism that ruled out women's identification with leadership. According to Polish novelist Izabela Filipiak, that was only a superficial rationale. "Look beyond the allegation 'communist,'" she instructed me, "and you will find a deeper root cause—our patriarchal code." Her words brought to mind the illustrative, though hardly common, example of Magdalena X's activist experience, for she was a woman who freely told me of her leadership ambitions and of the ways in which male oppositionists had consistently blocked her involvement.

One of the few Solidarity women to highlight the sexism within the opposition during her three decades of effort to participate, Magdalena understood that she was up against patriarchy, not communism. But after speaking openly with me in 1991 and 1998, she backed away in 1999 and tried to withdraw her interview from being published in Poland. She said she wanted to revert back into hiding. The intriguing story she told me, which scores of Solidarity women already knew about during the underground years (Barbara said they used to call her the "James Bond of the underground"), went like this:

When martial law was declared, Magdalena was organizing workers and farmers in her region and immediately went into hiding. She was eager to take the lead, but she believed that no one would allow a woman to be, as she put it, "the boss." Not one to back off easily, she told me that she invented a man whom she claimed to represent and set about delivering messages to activists in factories and universities from "Josef A.," an intelligent, extremely busy gentleman who had undertaken to organize the region. No one challenged her communiqués for about a year. Then people started to pressure Magdalena for a meeting with Mr. A. Implementing "phase two" of her outrageous scheme, she persuaded an old acquaintance, newly out of prison in another part of the country, to move to her city, to follow her instructions, and to serve as her figurehead. In this way, Magdalena said, she maintained control of the underground and, equally meaningful to her, finally had her chance to tell a male oppositionist what to do.

Without her straw man, Magdalena insisted, people would not have respected her initiative. She felt that she had the skills and confidence to develop an underground movement after the regime suppressed Solidarity but that sexism blocked her way. The ploy she developed was expedient; it was the simplest, quickest, and least threatening tactic for a woman who believed that political and gender oppression were two distinct issues.

Magdalena noted that her initiative had always been barred or ignored, beginning when she was in university. Yet she continued to avoid confrontation. "Why?" I asked her. "Because women can only wield power when we pretend not to have any. We were all invisible," she insisted. "Society is made of guises."

Magdalena tolerated this condition and to this day has not come forward to present the true story. Nor has the man who acted as her cover, though following the changeover, he was interviewed frequently about his role in the underground. Magdalena said he would tell reporters, "I headed our region, using a pseudonym invented by Magdalena X." He'd then proceed to describe his orchestration of the network with no further mention of his "loyal assistant." The man had identified so closely with the role, she concluded, that he had forgotten the real story. Now, she wishes that everyone would forget the real story.

When women told me the leadership question was irrelevant or said they had never thought about the "L-word," I believed them because, if they were adhering to traditional gender expectations without questioning them, then the question had no basis in their reality. At the opposite end of that spectrum, however, was a handful of women who gave me their analysis of the cultural prohibitions against female leadership or who declared emphatically that the *Tygodnik Mazowsze* editors had performed leadership roles. (And no, these respondents were not feminists.)

If the editors did not see themselves as leaders, then how did they define their roles? All the editors made similar assertions: "We did what we had to do." "We were all in this together." Women insisted that gender and leadership had nothing to do with their management of the underground. It became clear that, in the asking, my American heritage of individualism had rubbed up against the Solidarity legacy of unity. While declarations of "solidarity" were what shaped the opposition rhetoric of the time, for Helena and company it was a value each had truly internalized. Against the backdrop of an authoritarian system, the sense of communal belonging and the need for support were deeply felt values. Group power was more important than individual ambition.

I also realized that, in asking the leadership question, my American sense of entitlement had rubbed up against a Polish woman's sense of privilege and reward. If a Polish woman kept up the Matka

Polka image, she earned her privileged status, "but if she were to change the tenor of the presentation of self and step outside the culture, she would lose her male-ordained importance," Isabel Marcus stressed in conversation with me. "Women cannot be leaders or heroes in their own right." Thus, leadership was too dangerous a notion to entertain. Marcus's explanation helped me understand the frustration that some women expressed when I asked the "L-word" question.

The first time I asked Helena, back in 1991, if she had been a leader of the underground, she responded with a nonchalant shrug, "I did what I had to do. Everyone did." She wasn't defensive or annoyed, as others had been, and her answer made sense to me in light of what Ewa had called their group's "activity impulse." Helena had reacted to martial law by grabbing a hundred towels and reminding other activists not to cry over spilled milk. It seemed there was little room for introspection among activity impulse personalities. Thinking about Helena and how intensely she concentrated her energies on work above all else, I remembered that when people are staving off a political crisis they are usually busy acting and not thinking about their roles or identities or, least of all, of posterity. And I wondered whether, over time, Helena would reflect differently on her role and would, in retrospect, regard herself as a leader.

The following year, when I asked Helena the same question, her answer differed slightly and her tone was thoughtful and modest. "I suppose I have a talent for organizing things," she said. It was this subtle shift in her response that led me to wonder to what extent women's perceptions of their opposition experience would change over time and whether that change would correlate with the evolution of democratic thinking in Poland. Leadership seemed to be a likely site around which an evolving consciousness might be gauged. Would their attitudes change, and, if so, how?

After the experience of democracy had jelled, one woman or another would sometimes speak of leadership in positive terms, although her definition was still more singular in meaning than my own. By the mid-1990s, it seemed that leadership was no longer associated solely with the fading communist experience. It had become respected as a representation of participatory democracy.

"An electorate votes on its political leaders," Helena reminded me when we spoke in 1998. "The Solidarity leadership had been voted into power. They were the people's choice; therefore, they were the respected and recognized leaders." She stressed in this conversation that only an electoral process could determine political leaders, overlooking the point that every social group has its leaders. Helena—the consummate manager and community builder who set out to give thousands of people a sense of purpose and belonging and succeeded in doing so—failed to recognize the broader spectrum of social contexts that rely on leadership, from the media, civic organizations, and communities to businesses, universities, and grass roots groups. Remarkably, she did not identify herself as a leader of the patient revolution, which she had said women were best suited to manage. However, years later, in 2003, she did acknowledge that, after reading my analysis of the DGO's crucial role in bringing democracy to Poland, her mother had told her she thought that I was a wise woman.

In contrast to Helena and Joanna, Ewa did perceive women to be leaders, as she declared to me with great enthusiasm back in 1992. She readily identified with the political realm in which she had worked, first as Bujak's handler and later, in 1988, as a member of Warsaw's regional committee. She was part of a leadership circle that carried out political work; and that experience enabled her to feel like a leader, without a shred of embarrassment. Leaders were, by her definition, people who made political decisions and managed communities, organizations, networks, projects, and other people. Leaders inspired teamwork. They cultivated the individual talents and the best human qualities in others. So, when I asked her, "Were women leaders?" she exclaimed without missing a beat, "Definitely! For us, it was automatic. For example, it was obvious that Helena would take charge of the underground press because she had directed AS before martial law, and there were several women who had been doing AS with her." It was clear to Ewa that the AS women would take charge of the martial law crisis. "For most of us [the *Tygodnik Mazowsze* editors and Ewa] our leadership was a continuation. We were already active. Women aroused less suspicion than did men. Thus, it was probably also because of a vacuum."

Ewa also thought that women's leadership had been evident to others in the opposition as well. But if activists recognized that women had taken command, then why, I asked her, wasn't women's vital role also obvious to the Western writers who were reporting on the underground? She fired off another of her assured replies: "Because we were anonymous. We were working and all the credit was going to men, to the ones with well-known names who were the leaders." How, then, did Ewa explain the lack of acknowledgment after 1989? "Poland is a macho society. It must be men who are doing this and that—it is a myth. There were so few women in the Solidarity leadership before the underground, who would have believed it afterward? Women were at fault too. When women vote and they have a choice between a man and a woman, they usually vote for a man too. If the woman is politically active, it means that she is not normal. A normal woman should have a family. If she does not, something is wrong. Maybe she is divorced. Maybe she didn't succeed in her sexual life. She makes up for it in politics."

Listening to Ewa, I wondered if the stigma she described so well accounted for her DGO colleagues' shared reluctance to claim leadership roles in the Warsaw underground. So I asked if they denied their importance in order to avoid reproach. Why else, I wondered, would they downplay their contributions? "They are modest," Ewa replied.

Irena Grudzińska-Gross also provided me with insight into the question of whether these women were leaders. "A division of labor existed in the opposition, had always existed, that led Helena and the other women to treat their work as nonpolitical," she told me in 1991 over coffee in a Warsaw café. "They thought of themselves as organizers, not as political brains. Therefore, they assumed responsibility without attributing the level of authority to their activity that they should have applied. They believed in the notion of politics as belonging to the sphere of language, of pure ideas, and as of being expressed in declarations, communiqués, and so forth. Men made decisions about why and when to strike. These decisions were framed in the language of politics/freedom/emancipation."

Other than Barbara and Ewa, most of the women saw themselves as following through on the men's decisions. They did the work; they accepted responsibility for anything that went wrong; they understood the importance of their work. But, as Irena pointed out to me, "devising the means for transmitting these ideas was not regarded as political. The women in hiding who were producing and distributing information believed that they were subservient to this higher type of politics. They did not make any direct political decisions. Yet they had enormous influence, because they were the ones who conveyed information, who edited articles and decided what got printed. But they never took the power of coming forth and signing the declarations that were presented to the government."

"Only those few who were part of regional bodies," Irena went on, "such as Ewa Kulik in Warsaw and Barbara Labuda in Wrocław, were in a position to take that power. However, Barbara never put her name to any document because, as she said, only very well-known people signed them. The function of signing declarations was to let General Jaruzelski know that people of influence were behind certain decisions. Equally important, Solidarity's survival depended on people's trust in their known leaders. Helena never signed because she didn't want to expose her identity. Only Ewa signed communiqués from Warsaw."

"No one would have respected a movement led by women. That partly accounts for why we didn't sign our names to petitions," Barbara Labuda stressed. "Everyone assumes that men run things, in Poland and everywhere. People place greater trust in men, and they endow them with power more readily. The idea of a woman leader makes people laugh. That's true in the States as well. You can return to the West shouting, 'Women organized the underground!' but no one will believe you," she wagered. "Our strategy was too successful."

Barbara emphasized that people knew that women were leaders, because "everyone followed our instructions. No decisions were made without our involvement or approval. But no one assigned political value to our roles." Politics was understood in conventional terms, as representing the activities of elected officials or governments. Politics, good and bad, were considered men's business. Thus, women were not regarded as political actors because the accepted definition of politics did not recognize them. Only

Barbara believed that their invisibility as political agents was a social condition to be overcome. She experienced no feelings of ambivalence about her attempts to bring women into the public spotlight in 1989, though many of her colleagues were quite reluctant to relinquish the advantages of invisibility.

It seemed to me that Irena, Barbara, and Ewa had grasped the larger significance of women's part in Solidarity's success, while most of the other women, who had proven themselves to be brilliant, reliable lead actors, nevertheless saw themselves primarily in support roles. I am reminded of a statement made by U.S. Supreme Court justice Potter Stewart: "Leadership, like obscenity, is impossible to define, but we know it when we see it. Or do we?"

Perhaps it is only in retrospect, and in the context of democratic Poland and the continued prominence of *Gazeta Wyborcza,* that the true value of women's principal role in the shaping of an independent press, and thus the value of their leadership, can be fully appreciated. It seems to me that while the 1980s opposition introduced new organizers, events, strategies, and structures, including those led by women, the movement's values did not shift in consonance with the new directions undertaken. The movement did not consider the meaning of the changes of the 1980s while they were happening. Actions outpaced the shift in values that would have been needed in order to allow women's significant contributions to receive a proper accounting, a shift in values that would have led men to appreciate the patient revolution and the women who engineered it.

Whenever Barbara Labuda and I talked in the 1990s, she expressed her bitterness about this failing of her colleagues. "Poland owes a lot to the great numbers of women who worked but were left out of this beautiful history—the history of fighting for Polish independence." She went on to give a telling example: "In a few interviews following the Round Table negotiations, Zbigniew Bujak mentioned that he owed much to Helena, but that is not the same as saying that Helena Łuczywo created the underground."

8. "Our Romantic Model"
myth, literature, and women's place

By their own accounts, Solidarity women came from, and were sustained by, a long tradition of women's partisan activism that dates back to the turn of the nineteenth century. Between 1792 and 1795 Poland was partitioned by the Austrians, Russians, and Prussians, and its political autonomy was destroyed through the next 123 years, setting the stage for future rebellions and uprisings in Poland's name. The crisis of statelessness was continually addressed and the restoration of independence was fought for—by men and women both. This was unprecedented.

Polish women were first summoned to public duty in 1794 when General Tadeusz Kosciuszko initiated a (failed) rebellion to wrest Polish independence from the three imperial powers. General Kosciuszko was renowned for fighting in America's War of Independence before returning to Poland to wage a battle for freedom in his native land, and his decision to beseech women to "sacrifice for the homeland" was unprecedented. He also addressed the women as "fellow citizens," marking the first time in Polish history that women were publicly recognized as citizens of the nation. In response, women rallied to the call for aid and continued to do so across the next two centuries.

In the mid-nineteenth century, women figured prominently

among the rebel fighters during the 1830–31 and 1863 uprisings—indeed, a female conspirator in the 1863 uprising referred to it as a "women's war" in an interview with a Swiss journalist.[1] Polish women were active partisans during both World War I and II and, of course, were tireless oppositionists under communist rule.

Similar to the sentiments of many female Solidarity activists, Magdalena X told me: "Those of us who were activists in the Solidarity underground grew up in the Polish tradition, in which women had a sense of worth because she carried the burden of supporting her family and other families in times of war. It gave us a certain knack for knowing what to do. The tradition of our involvement is found in this literature."

However, the literary tradition in which Magdalena and company found their role models was a truncated, romanticized version of the complex role Polish women had played in their country's sociopolitical history. After accepting the postpartition invitation to be counted among their country's citizens, Polish women dove into partisan activities with gusto. But while the many women rebels these activities produced did find their way into the literature of their times, or wrote it themselves, the complete canon did not endure into the twentieth century. The most tenacious works depicting Polish women's role in society were those of male nineteenth-century Romantics such as the revered poet Adam Mickiewicz (1798–1855). The celebrated verses by the creator of Matka Polka enshrined the culture's most enduring female icon as the heroic mother who raises her sons to martyr themselves for the nation.

> O Polish mother!
> You should kneel before the Mater Dolorosa
> Look at the sword, which bleeds from her heart:
> The foes will make such wounds in your own heart![2]

The image of the Matka Polka, a mythic creature of male design, took hold of the collective imagination and assumed legendary proportions in the very era when real Polish women were awakening and reinventing their lives. Behind the fabled image of the self-sacrificing mother who sends her men off to war, nineteenth-century women identified with a diverse range of roles and experiences. They were patriots, conspirators, educators, writers, reformers, foot soldiers, and *emancipates*. The most evanescent works showed a far more complex and intriguing pattern that, from the late sixteenth century through to the twentieth century, centered around how Polish women have been forced to cope with the demands of personal, societal, and political survival in the midst of dramatic upheavals. This body of literature, depicting women's patriotic and feminist aspirations and the tensions therein, has only recently begun to be reconstructed by gender studies scholars.[3]

Taken together, the literature shows that, more than any other tradition or recurring pattern, it is the dramatic absence of men that defined women's participation in the struggles of each successive century. Whether permanent or temporary, whether by choice or by force, men's absence determined women's organizing styles, their political identities, their consciousness-raising experiences, and the conditions in which they were able to carry out patriotic campaigns and/or feminist pursuits.

The historical anecdotes and the various commentaries that report women's activism in the partition period are rich in revelation, not only in their portrayals of women's shifting consciousness in that turbulent century but also in how they shed light on the work of the women who coordinated the Solidarity underground more than one hundred years later.

Martial law revived an old tradition. I was learning what Polish women had done—have always done—in the absence of their men.

Like their male counterparts, the women who responded to General Kosciuszko's call for an uprising were members of the aristocracy. Poland was leaving the eighteenth and heading into the nineteenth century with its feudal economy and patriarchal social relations intact. The nobility made up close to 20 percent of the population, a larger proportion than elsewhere in Europe. The partitions stripped aristocrats of their wealth, lands, and political power and drove them into cities and towns to compete for employment in private enterprise, trade, transport, and public office.

Uprooted from their estates and family structures, the impoverished gentry gradually grew into an urban intelligentsia. For the women of this class, the terrifying rupture in their daily lives and norms also provided an unanticipated opportunity, for they were forced, for the first time, to seek education and employment outside the home. Within the family, which was the nobility's core socioeconomic institution, women occupied an elevated status made higher in accordance with lineage, and they customarily were the managers of their feudal estates—often in the absence of their men, who were frequently called away to perform military or political duties.

After the partitions, women suddenly had an opportunity—a pressing need as well—to assume a new position in society, but they also found themselves on undefined ground relative to their men, to the nobility's strict patriarchal codes, and to the society at large. This development opened the subject of emancipation to public discourse and linked it to the overarching challenge of the early partition years: how to ensure that the nation would survive in spirit and culture until paradise lost could be regained.

For women, it was clear that the answer to national survival lay in their emancipation, which meant education reform, a role in public life, and recognition of their status as citizens (albeit of an imaginary state). General Kosciuszko's call to his female "fellow citizens" to "sacrifice for the homeland" was a powerful one. As scholar Maria Janion has noted, once the possibility of citizenship was made available to women in exchange for their support of men's battles (a compelling bargain), women took the role and identity of "fellow citizen" most seriously. "Polish noblewomen, and then also women from educated families, felt acutely aware of their citizenship, as they took active part in the resistance during the partition times," Janion wrote in her 1996 philosophical treatise, *Women and the Spirit of Otherness*.[4] They took advantage of their new identity to argue for their emancipation and, further, to argue for education as emancipation's necessary precondition. Their demands developed not only because a window of opportunity had opened but also because the battles, poverty, dislocations, and absences of men produced unexpected hardships for which they were unprepared. They were forced into survival mode and had to learn to fend for themselves and their families.

But the grave material circumstances the noblewomen faced

were balanced by the fact that their fall in status had unburdened them of inflexible social roles. Even when her patriotic duties revolved around the roles and responsibilities conventionally associated with a woman's domain—that is, the family and the home—they and her identity had acquired new social implications. For example, according to Swedish historian Bianka Pietrow-Ennker, the family turned into a "stronghold of national identity during the whole time when Polish public life was hamstrung by the dictates of the partition powers."[5] Just as happened when martial law was enforced in 1981, many activities normally associated with public life turned inward, went home to that private sphere traditionally defined as women's domain. The home, much like the woman who maintained it, provided a safe space, both citadel and refuge, for political activities, cultural expression, and education.

"The general question of the education of children had an overtly political component injected into it," Pietrow-Ennker elaborated. "Poles came to view children as a sacred pledge against a future spent in national freedom. The task of raising the children in the spirit of Polish ideals fell to the woman. Women were to ensure that their children were raised as patriots, across sex lines, as coming saviors of the Polish nation. Thus, as a direct result of the partitions, the position of women in the family came to take on a new semi-political, semi-cultural significance."[6]

However, in order to properly educate their children and serve their country, women knew that they themselves needed to be educated. Even within the aristocracy, the education of girls had historically been discouraged. Taught by private tutors, girls in the last half of the eighteenth century were at most trained in French, music, and household management. Their meager studies fell short of adequate preparation for the postpartition expectations placed upon them. In the early nineteenth century, educational reform became their rationale for pressing for their emancipation.

While moving toward education and citizenship, however, these postpartition women were also enmeshed in a set of relationships between men and women that were both well established and (temporarily) fluid. Feminist historian Sławomira Walczewska points out that these gender dynamics, which persist to the present day, were rooted in aristocratic norms that she identifies as a chivalrous social contract between knights and ladies. "The most basic form of relationships between the sexes is the 'lady and knight ideal,'" she writes. "These relationships typically require men to be protective of their ladies, and women, in turn, to be obedient. The task of the man is to fight, protect and defend. Woman's task is complimentary: she is expected to support him spiritually, and give him rest and reward after his struggle. The ritualized system of expectations, which one sex holds out for the other, is socially and culturally sanctioned and gratified."[7]

Wałczewska attributes the preservation of these peculiarly durable gender dynamics to the fall of the Polish state. "[The partitions] shook the foundations of the nobility culture. . . . The knights were no longer capable of fulfilling their roles as defenders of their ladies. The ladies could no longer be a mainstay and a reward for the permanently frustrated and defeated knights. Nevertheless the chivalrous contract between the sexes consolidated itself as if in defiance of the political reality, creating a *residuum* in the cultural transformations over a span of two centuries."[8]

Poland had developed into what Bianka Pietrow-Ennker calls, perhaps too euphemistically, a "benign patriarchy." She writes: "[I]n all three provinces [the Russian-, Austrian-, and Prussian-ruled areas], women's efforts to improve their lot cannot be separated from the national struggle for freedom, and both grew hand in hand—especially since women's growing involvement in public life out of the home was an act of national self-affirmation. . . . [T]he reality confronting women was that their emancipation in political and social life had to be extracted not only from their own menfolk, but from the occupying powers as well. . . . As long as women took their place beside men in the freedom fight and raised children in the national spirit, the sex dynamics were 'benign patriarchy.' Women extended their activities into the public arena without male opposition. But only if they did not challenge all too radically the prevailing consensus on women's place in the social order."[9]

It is not surprising that for each gender the terms of patriotic duty were differently articulated, if not strictly adhered to. Men, it was commonly said, took up arms and poetry in defense of the nation. Women also fought with weapons and words, but their special rebellion against the imperial powers was to preserve the cultural heritage and to transmit it to younger generations so that "Poland will not perish, as long as Poles still live." And so a new tradition evolved out of partition—under the extenuating circumstances of war, insurrection, and foreign domination, political activism in the name of nationhood became *expected* of women.

As the nineteenth century progressed, social, economic, and political upheavals propelled women beyond the home and from behind their men's shadows into underground circles and public spaces. They educated and armed themselves, worked and conspired in concert with other women, and equipped themselves with the material and intellectual resources needed to continue and to diversify their challenges to foreign rule.

At the time of the 1831 November Rising to try to oust the Russians, women such as Emilia Plater, Antonina Tomaszewska, and Joanna Zubrowa donned military uniforms and fought the enemy. The poet Mickiewicz penned tributes to the Woman Knight—the fierce warrior who sacrificed her domestic duties to replace her wounded man on the battlefield and to face her death. The first women's organization to serve the patriotic cause was also founded that year. Called Towarszystwo Dobroczynności Patriotycznej Kobiet (Charitable Society of Women Patriots), it openly conducted philanthropic works, and after the rising was quashed, its members went underground to care for victims of political repression. Although their work was usually ancillary to or in support of the men's activities, the founding of women's organizations in support of nationalist causes represented a monumental break from earlier forms of involvement, according to Polish-born historian Bogna Lorence-Kot.[10] Previously, girls participated in secret study groups or women joined conspiratorial cells, most of which were directed and dominated by men. The women's organizations freed them from both this absolute dependence on men and social isolation.

But women also learned to act independently of men, because after each successive uprising there were fewer of them. After the 1830–31 uprisings, tens of thousands of men were exiled to Siberia. Some were accompanied by their families, but men were the primary victims of that ominous geography. At the same time, ten thousand Poles, including most of the intellectual and political elite (that is, men), fled to the West in the *Wielka Emigracja* (Great Emigration)—a mass departure from the Russian-controlled territories. The remaining population faced punitive taxation and reparation payments; were dispossessed of their property and belongings; paid penalties for relatives who were fined in absentia; and endured brutal censorship, police surveillance, arrests, and prison terms. Women outnumbered men in the now fractured communities and subsequently filled in for them at all levels—in the family, in the workplace, and in conspiratorial activities. In this way, the women kept the idea of freedom alive after 1831, just as women from the Class of '68 kept the idea of Solidarity alive during martial law.

In her research on patterns of women's activism during the partition period, Lorence-Kot perceived that "It must have taken time and generations to accept the loss of independence, to relinquish the hope of returning to the old structure, in which women served the family's interests. It must have taken time to accept, begin to understand, and eventually learn to effectively use the existing circumstances in asserting their will—in other words, to develop an oppositional style which suited women of that era and their newly minted loyalty to the nation."[11]

The next major uprising in the name of independence was in 1861, a year that, according to Lorence-Kot, "launched a growing and complex opposition movement by women in the Kingdom of Poland."[12] Two noteworthy developments were launched that year, Piatki (Fives) and National Mourning. Both echoed down the decades to the 1980s underground. Lorence-Kot told me that the Piatki organizing tactic that Helena Łuczywo had tried to implement at the start of the Solidarity underground was originally used by women to assist men's military activity against the Russians in 1861. Helena knew it had been instrumental during the anti-Nazi resistance, but she was apparently unaware that both the name and the tactic represented one of several networks that women built to pass information and supplies around the country in 1861. Lorence-Kot confirmed that, just as Helena had explained it to me, five people contacted five people, and then those five contacted another five people. Each group of five maintained contact with another group of five. The networks were responsible for collecting arms and uniforms, provided food and medical supplies, and transported weapons and information throughout Poland.

Just as women's anticommunist activism had evolved over several decades and generations, the women of 1861 built upon their own experiences and those of their predecessors—particularly the women's patriotic organizations of 1831—to create elaborate networks like Piatki. The Piatki structure fostered tolerance among social groups, crossing class, ethnic, and religious lines. Piatki leaders encouraged participation from Catholic, Jewish, Lutheran, and Russian Orthodox women, as well as from the gentry, teachers, governesses, other employed intelligentsia, students, actresses, and middle-class wives. The participants also crossed geopolitical borders to establish contacts with women in St. Petersburg and Moscow, as well as with groups of Polish émigré women in Paris, Prague, and the United States, all of whom helped to gather provisions and to smuggle them into the homeland.

The major development that unfolded in 1861 and came to be called the National Mourning captured my interest because it was a symbolic and mass-based effort that women conducted over a three-year period. On February 25, 1861, women in Warsaw held a public mass to mourn five people who had died during the most recent demonstrations against tsarist rule. The women in attendance all dressed in black and continued to do so at a series of subsequent public mournings held to commemorate the thirtieth anniversary of the 1831 uprising. For weeks the funereal silhouettes of women in black dominated the streets of Warsaw. By April irate tsarist officials had prohibited the wearing of black in public and even forbade merchants to display black items in their shop windows.

The ban was defiantly ignored. In fact, the symbolic National Mourning quickly galvanized new supporters, spreading through the Russian-, Austrian-, and Prussian-occupied provinces and even to Russia and Europe. By 1863 thousands of women had adopted the radical chic. It then became nearly impossible for the regimes to discriminate between those who were subversive and those who were "en vogue."

Soon tsarist authorities were provoked to ban black attire throughout their whole province, and their retaliatory measures proved more repressive than those taken by their Austrian and Prussian counterparts. A woman could be fined and jailed for wearing black clothing. Government officials whose wives were identified wearing black clothing would lose one month's salary per incident. Most seriously, tsarist police were known to open fire into crowds where black clothing was spotted. In July 1863, on the streets of Warsaw, men suspected of being government agents attacked women wearing black garments and tore at their crinolines with hooks. Leaders of the National Mourning responded by switching the color of resistance to gray. When police caught on, they penalized the wearing of gray apparel. The pattern was repeated with the color brown. Police even arrested a woman innocently dressed in green, charged her with wearing the color of hope, and fined her two hundred rubles.[13]

The National Mourning served purposes well beyond the merely symbolic. It was "an outward manifestation of an inner spirit unifying and sororitizing the women," wrote an anonymous chronicler of the period.[14] It was a clearly visible display of solidarity among women in opposition to the occupiers. As it also ran parallel to the organizing efforts of Piatki, the women of the two groups may have conspired together, according to Lorence-Kot.[15] The National Mourning may even have been extended in order to distract the authorities from other insurgent actions, such as those Piatki performed.

Thinking of this possible link brought to my mind similar patterns of women's activism in the Solidarity underground. For example, groups of elderly women used to create floral memorials to Solidarity, which they would display in public squares. This humble little ritual would infuriate the police, who would retaliate by trampling the flowers and chasing the women away. In response, the patient, persevering, audacious women would simply move their operations elsewhere and then somewhere else again, while the police trailed after them. The tactic was, in part, a ploy to distract the police from the more serious underground actions of the *Tygodnik Mazowsze* editors.[16]

By the 1863 uprising, women had become so integral a part of the resistance that a Swiss chronicler of the period, Franciszek L. von Erlach, would write: "Women were the true soul of the uprising." Women themselves said so, in the kind of defiant language that Anna Walentynowicz might have used during the 1980 Gdańsk shipyard strike. "If they want to avoid further uprisings, they will have to kill all of us women, one by one," a *partyzantka* (female partisan) declared to von Erlach, who had come to Poland to report on the latest uprising against the Russians.[17]

"Women's role in the current [1863] uprising is so unbelievably important that it seems inconceivable to a foreigner until he sees it himself. . . . Men representing every class and every belief had their opponents—but women were always respected, across the various divisions," von Erlach wrote.[18] He tracked the movements of partyzantkas on the streets and, literally, in the trenches. In several of his interviews with them, the women spoke passionately about their roles and the conspiratorial legacy that they inherited from their mothers. Having lived through the times of the November Rising (1830–31), von Erlach wrote, their mothers had given the partyzantka "ten times more energy and relentlessness than they themselves had possessed, even though they were already ten times more energetic than their mothers from the times of the partitions of Poland. They said that they would raise their daughters to be ten times more energetic and relentless than themselves. They didn't fear the threat of being sent to Siberia and there being married to strangers, and promised that even then, they will teach their children the love of Poland and the hatred of the oppressor from their infancy onward."[19]

While von Erlach's interviews were among the most vivid of the contemporary reports from which I gathered my information, he was not the only chronicler to comment on women's fierce participation in that revolt. Several tsarist authorities recorded similar observations. In his daily log, one high-ranking Russian military officer remarked upon Polish women's insurgency in a surprisingly complimentary fashion: "Among Polish men there are differences, and the men backslide because they tire of fighting and fall into paralysis, but the female population never changes and always maintains."[20]

At no previous moment in Polish history had women mobilized en masse in an array of such wide-reaching networks of elaborate design. Von Erlach reported that agitators armed themselves and fought in military squads or worked in underground cells, hospitals, organizations, schools, and homes. They continued the work of the Women's Committee, founded two years earlier, and its practice of working in groups of fives. The nineteenth-century partyzantkas worked as couriers, organized underground study groups for children and adults, distributed illegal literature, and supplied clothing and food to families of political prisoners. Some hid their men from the tsarist gendarmes, while others nursed the wounded. Still others replaced their men in military or conspiratorial operations or followed them to Siberian settlements, either voluntarily or by tsarist decree. A small number of partyzantkas were sent to Siberia on the strength of their own transgressions.[21]

Clearly, there were noteworthy consistencies between women's organizing styles during the failed nineteenth-century uprisings and those adopted by their Solidarity descendants. In both time periods, women banded together in all-female groups and engineered large-scale movements while men were in hiding, prison, or exile. They also acted independently and individually in spontaneous or symbolic acts of resistance and, at times, disguised themselves as men or hid behind male pseudonyms. Some women even ritualized their resistance by wearing gold bracelets in the shape of handcuffs, or they wore black enamel rings to symbolize their mourning for both family members and the nation. Such adornments were later echoed by the martial law fashion of wearing black enamel jewelry and buttons with symbolic images—a militant Virgin Mary waving a clenched fist, for example.

As one underground of women gave rise to another and then another, this long tradition of female conspiracy specifically legitimated Solidarity women's activist endeavors. It also helped to protect them in their political adventures and edgy life-styles—taking illegal action, living in hiding, and being single women, unwed mothers, or women without men. And, finally, the heritage worked to define the Solidarity women's female identities because there was nowhere else outside of this particular history where they felt they could readily have looked to for role models without being mocked or challenged—given that the feminist ideal was off-limits because the Communist Party had already appropriated it.

Transmitted to the Solidarity women by their mothers and grandmothers as well as in the classroom, the nineteenth-century legacy both reinforced the Solidarity women's sense of purpose and nourished their self-esteem. But that truncated legacy was not based on the substance of their predecessors' concrete contributions but on the myth that was created around them—largely by famous nineteenth-century male writers. Central to the myth were stories that glorified Matka Polka, the Virgin Mary, and the Woman Knight, but the selective literary legacy that endured emphasized only the self-sacrificing role of Matka Polka and obscured two other important roles—that of the woman warrior and the emancipate. "As an effect of romantic warrants, women grew accustomed to bearing the burden of family and political life in the shadows and in silence, for the sake of a sacrifice to be fulfilled," Maria Janion wrote.[22]

There is a certain resonance between the gender dynamics in the 1980s underground and the accounts of earlier women conspirators, such as those described in Edward Wolinowicz's 1863 paean of praise to the women of that year's uprising. In his view, they were "sensitive, self-sacrificing, passionate patriots, who always led in all the demonstrations and pulled youth after them, they smuggled literature, hid weapons, and then they hid the partisans. One had the impression that most of the men were so politically inept or hypnotized that they reacted too little to the female lead, and women among them, with youth in tow, decided everything."[23] This exaltation of female conspiracy is part of a pattern, which recurs from the partition era to communist times, showing women performing the role of unsung caretakers, while men were either absent or nominally in charge.

It was from perspectives such as Wolinowicz's that the *ciche bohaterki,* the "quiet, calm heroines," of the nineteenth-century revolts evolved and then became the *bezimienne bohaterki,* the "anonymous heroines" of the Solidarity era. "Unsungness" was the female way of conspiracy, and its reward—its unjustly meager reward—was mainly lofty praise at the expense of political gain.

Solidarity organizer Joanna Szczęsna was the first to tell me about the nineteenth-century role model and to introduce me to some of the histories and literature that formed the canon. She explained the tradition to me with great care: "A valued model in Polish culture is the strong, self-sacrificing Polish wife and mother, who supports her fighting men, her husbands and sons. Polish women have always been strong and supportive, perhaps more than in other countries." *Supportive, strong, self-sacrificing,* and *more than in other countries* are the key operative words in her description, and they are intended to be wholly complimentary.

It is easy to understand why young, female '68ers with rebel tendencies, growing up in colorless communist times, would revel in the forbidden histories of nineteenth-century nationalist insurrections. That's where they found heroines to emulate—brave fighting women who juggled child rearing with the hiding of partisans and decision making about everything. Reading about Polish revolts against the Russian Empire revealed that the Communist Party did not have a monopoly on images of strong, self-sacrificing women. The party's callused female icon, which in reality was emblematic of an exploited female labor force, was easily outmatched by the nineteenth century's partyzantkas, a composite—in the eyes of their male contemporaries who wrote of them—of Lady Liberty, Betsy Ross, Virgin Mary, Matka Polka, and Joan of Arc.

The partyzantkas exemplified female civic virtue, and I heard their attributes—such descriptions as "self-sacrificing" and "supportive"—repeated in many interviews. It later became clear to me that these iconic images from the past were the building blocks of what U.S. feminist scholar Isabel Marcus calls a "national truth." According to Marcus, the Polish romantic myth of the female comprises three iconic roles. "The cultural and historical trinity consists of a class-based tradition of ladyhood that is rooted in the culture of the Polish nobility; the popular cult of the Virgin Mary, suffused with traditional images of motherhood; and the gendered aspects of Polish nationalism, wherein women are honored minders of the hearth and transmitters of the cultural heritage, while men fight invaders and, when unsuccessful, are sent into exile."[24]

Marcus elaborates on the concept: "Just as the Virgin Mary is accorded special treatment and respect, so, too, it is said, are Polish women. . . . This view of women is rooted in the idea of Polish exceptionalism—that is, in the ability of Poles to survive and flourish as a nation and to preserve their culture in the face of repression. The gender-based claim to exceptionalism is understood as Poland is a society which is enlightened or civilized, rather than Asiatic or barbarian—a ready reference to Poland's eastern neighbor, Russia. In effect, cultural superiority in this context is manifested in the treatment of women."[25]

According to this line of reasoning, Polish society has a venerable tradition of being so good to its women that Poles do not need feminism.

With such a strong, spiritually imbued model to sustain them, it is no wonder that Solidarity women did not look to feminism for strength or illumination. And for all intents and purposes, the model of Polish women's self-sacrificing specialness seemed to have paid off in the era of Solidarity because national freedom was won and women stood triumphant on the side of victory. Someone had to play the supporting role, and these women did so willingly while perpetuating the honorable tradition of strength, self-sacrifice, and so forth. Men, in turn, appreciated and respected their contributions and made them feel special. When Joanna Szczęsna characterized the *Tygodnik Mazowsze* editors' true value as having resided in their support of men's roles, she was doling out the highest praise.

Granted that someone does indeed have to play the supporting role, to my ears, Joanna's homage to time-honored tradition obscured, perhaps negated, the true worth of the concrete, present-day leadership contributions that she and her cohorts made. Their real contributions to the growth of a civil society, and of a free press in particular, departed from tradition, and that altered course accounted for Solidarity's success, which was itself a marked departure from the Polish tradition of hopeless battles and tragic defeats. Cut off from the nineteenth-century legacy of feminist thought, they never developed their own gender discourse.

The emancipation discourse that blossomed in the late eighteenth and early nineteenth centuries expressed the real tensions that existed between what women of that era wanted for themselves and what they wanted for their country. According to feminist historian Sławomira Walczewska, nineteenth-century women writers explored a range of subjects—from individual freedom to the body, sex, and reproduction to participation in public life—and they were definitely trying to break free of the traditional relationships established between men and women. Two things situated these writers in the world histories of women's movements: their developing consciousness of a hierarchical social order in which women were subordinated to men, regardless of class, and the formulas they put forth for redress, which ranged from education to reform of marriage laws to political and economic equality.

The moral argument in support of women's education that was spearheaded by Klementyna Tańska in the early 1800s gave way to demands for equality between the sexes in the 1840s, as put forth by Narcyza Zmichowska and other members of the Enthusiasts, a proto-feminist group. The edification of women was also what informed Eliza Orzeszkowa's 1873 literary creation *Marta,* which was hailed as "*the* Polish novel of the century written by a woman about a woman," according to Bianka Pietrow-Ennker.[26]

Although nationalist obligations and economic and political hardships both stimulated and restrained the growth of emancipation initiatives, the pursuit of emancipation nonetheless continued well into the first decades of the twentieth century. In 1918 Poland regained its independence and established a republic, and in 1919 women won the right to vote. Very gradually, then, women accessed education, employment, and public life; new ideas and visions for self-improvement; and unprecedented experiences of autonomy and community outside the domestic realm.

As the heirs to two hundred consecutive years of very selective history dedicated to anchoring Poles to a nation-state that no longer existed, the Solidarity women knew very little of the significant body of Polish women's literature, which had been evolving since the close of the eighteenth century and about which scholars have recently written. The degree to which an emancipation discourse had developed in the nineteenth century had been greatly obscured for at least two reasons. First, in Poland, as elsewhere in nineteenth-century central Europe, the yearning for gender equality was commonly subsumed beneath nationalist struggles. The ensuing tension played itself out in Poland for 123 long years, and the rationale that national independence came first and women's emancipation would follow persisted into Solidarity's times. The second reason the emancipates languished in obscurity was that ignorance of them served the Communist Party's purposes. In asserting that feminism was a communist invention, the party could claim that it had brought feminist ideals to post–World War II Polish soil, that communism had emancipated Polish women.

The Solidarity women who didn't treat feminism seriously applied a mythic narrative to their experience that made little room for what Janion calls the Woman Fighter and completely ignored women's quest for emancipation.[27] The disconnection highlights the reality of twentieth-century Polish women's ultimate sacrifice: their own history and self-knowledge.

If the Woman Knight and emancipates got short rations at the banquet of history, Matka Polka's plate was full to overflowing. Adam Mickiewicz's poem "To the Polish Mother" immortalized her virtues, her impossibly perfect virtues.

> O Polish mother! If the radiant light of genius
> > Should kindle in your son's eyes
> If the pride and valiance of Polish heroes
> > Should shine from his childish brow
>
> O Polish mother! His games are bad for him
> You should kneel before the Mater Dolorosa
> Look at the sword, which bleeds from her heart:
> The foes will make such wounds in your own heart!
>
> . . . .
> Our savior when he was still a child in Nazareth
> > Fondled a cross whereon he would save Mankind
> O Polish Mother! You had better give your child
> His future playthings in his hands today.
>
> Bind his arms with chains when there is still time
> > And have him harnessed to a heavy cart
> So later he should not grow pale before a headsman's axe
> > Nor should he blush at the hangman's rope.

He will not, like knights of olden days
    Place a victorious cross in Jerusalem
Nor like the soldiers of the New World
Will he plough freedom's acres, water them with blood

. . . .

The only monument to his defeat
Will be the dried out gallow-wood
The only glory left—a woman's tears
And the long nightly talks of his countrymen.[28]

"Mickiewicz had a great influence on the way Polish women shaped their identity," Maria Janion wrote in *Women and the Spirit of Otherness*. "His ideal woman was a true patriot, combining pure feminine feelings with strength and courage, infinitely devoted to her husband and father. According to him, Polish women were closer to liberation than anywhere else in Europe. One of the first symbols of their equality was the fact that Polish women were punished for conspiracy and sent to Siberia on equal terms with men, after trials in military courts even. Mickiewicz thought Poland was so advanced in the question of women's emancipation because Polish women weren't fighting to liberate, but to sacrifice themselves. Transcending the woman's domestic role was comparable to a moral response to historical circumstances."[29]

However, as Maria Janion pointed out in conversation with me in 2000, the Matka Polka, like the cult of the Virgin Mary, is a remote ideal, against which real lives cannot be measured. The same holds true of another female icon that Mickiewicz conjured up. His Matka Polka shared the stage with his Woman Knight—the fighting woman who disguises herself as a man to perform the male duty of armed battle. Although the Woman Knight's hold on the collective imagination was not as visibly powerful as that of Matka Polka, she is memorably personified in his epic poem "Grażyna," which is about a semimythic Lithuanian princess of the late Middle Ages who dons her husband's armor to fight his enemies. Grażyna is killed in battle, and her husband, the prince, throws himself into the fire of her funeral stake.

Do you know whose remains
Are consumed on the pyre?—Total silence reigns—
A woman's. The armor is just a disguise
Of female graces but heroic pains.
Although I avenged her, we mourn her demise![30]

Grażyna was no emancipate, Janion underscores: "Mickiewicz always worshipped women as instinct, heart, emotional gust. His choice of heroines emphasized his idea of the instinctive character of national honor. Grażyna was not, and never pretended to be a leader. . . . [S]he never sought trouble, she fought in her husband's shadow, in his disguise. [At the end of the epic] Grażyna experienced tragic illumination—she recognized Fate and accepted it, and went to the very end, to meet her death."[31]

Sławomira Wałczewska adds provocative insights into Grażyna's mythic sacrifice.

When a man cannot cope with the role of a knight, a lady comes to his help. She takes the sword out of the knight's weakened hand and kills the enemy. By this act she sacrifices herself, as it is known that she herself must die as well. Although the enemy is dead, the sword-wielding lady is the enemy too—the enemy of the knight's male identity and the enemy of the long-established contract between the sexes, guaranteeing that law and order is maintained in social life. The enemy outside is actually less dangerous, as he is more easily identified. The enemy inside is a woman transgressing the boundaries of her gender role and taking over male competences. The punishment for gender treason and for breaking the male-female social contract may take one of two forms: death or oblivion. Death is a radical solution, but at the same time it is full of grace. The dead can be awarded with a poem, a statue, or a street by his name. When she dies, the Woman Knight does not question the contract between the sexes. She seals it with her death. The treacherous punishment of oblivion is worse . . . [and this] may have happened to the Solidarity women. They took over men's competence and they weren't killed. Therefore, their names must be erased from history. And those very men who were kept in hiding by the women who managed to do all the conspiracy work without them will do their best to obliterate them. The anachronistic contract between the sexes characteristic of the nobility and knighthood is to remain intact and unquestioned.[32]

The myth of the male hero profoundly influenced the social responsibilities that women, even during the communist era, were expected to take on, Janion told me in a 2000 interview.

In Romanticism, and it is very visible in Polish Romanticism, the main protagonist is the romantic hero. The romantic hero is in fact an emblematic hero. Everyone revolves around him. I became interested in the role the woman plays in the emblematic biography of the romantic hero. According to Joseph Campbell's interpretations in *The Hero with a Thousand Faces*,[33] the only role the woman plays is as an obstacle or as a temptation. Man has to overcome this woman to reach his great ideal.

In Polish Romantic literature, there is a similar strategy. The hero has to say good-bye to the woman to go to his grand duties, to the struggle for independence. It is a central motif in Polish Romanticism: "Farewell to blood, farewell to family."

This scheme was repeated in the first Solidarity revolution in the summer of 1980. The men were striking, enclosed in the shipyard. Women brought in bread, fruit, blankets. Usually they were not allowed inside the shipyard. The shipyard workers hung a banner on an outside wall, with an inscription that made reference to the motif of nineteenth-century uprising poetry, the martial motif of "Farewell to the Beloved." Romantic poetry was used as a message to loved ones. The banner said: "Poland's independence is your rival, woman." It meant more or less: "Women, don't interfere with us. We are fighting for Poland."

The original poem was written by a third-rate poet of the November 1831 insurrection. Here is the original verse:

Remember you are a Polish woman
It is a fight for Poland
And since you are a Polish woman

She is your rival
Remember you are a Polish woman
The fight is for the Polish cause
The duty—to defend it
 She is your rival. . . .
Remember that you're a Polish woman, that it's a fight for
 the country,
Poland's independence is your rival.[34]

There was one song, very popular among the shipyard workers in 1980, called "Song for a Little Daughter." The story told in this song is that Father cannot be with his little daughter while Poland is not free. While Poland is not free, his happiness is impossible. At one point in the poem, we learn that the hero didn't find happiness at home because there was no happiness in the motherland. His home and motherland were put in opposition. The message is that a man has to leave his home and sacrifice his life for his motherland. Everything was sacrificed for the motherland.

Thus, it is no wonder that we thought the struggle for independence was the most important act. It was our romantic model. We thought that the struggle for women's rights can begin only after we regain our independence. I myself represented this stance many times, unfortunately.

9. In the End, the Beginning
adjustments and new problems for women after 1989

In the mid- to late 1980s, though Jaruzelski was still in power, though martial law was still—de facto if not de jure—in force, the nature of society, and by extension of dissent, began to undergo a metamorphosis in Poland. Perhaps the most noteworthy change, as U.S. historian Padraic Kenney has stressed, is that the opposition was no longer solely identified with Solidarity.[1] Not only were the two terms no longer interchangeable, but Solidarity itself no longer dominated center stage. As both Solidarity and the party began to weaken in the mid-1980s—as they became less the sharply defined, well-understood entities they had been five years earlier—the power vacuum that would be filled in 1989 began to open. Then a critical moment arrived, a moment when Polish women had an opportunity to step forward and demand political power for themselves as a social group. Unfortunately, the barriers to empowering women on new terms within a new democratic society proved to be simply too high.

Beginning in the mid-1980s, just as the *Tygodnik Mazowsze* editors and other endorsers of the long march strategy had hoped, the Polish opposition blossomed and a vibrant civic life emerged. The country experienced an "almost bewildering pluralism of movements that defied the usual opposition categories," as one historian put it,[2] or a "permissible pluralism," in the words of another historian.[3] The underground press, led by the ever-consistent *Tygodnik Mazowsze,* helped to educate ever-widening sectors of the society in the language of human rights and democratic values. Cultural and civic activities branched out as a new generation of activists began to add its fearless voice and uniquely playful style to the arena of dissent. The familiar oppositionist triad of workers, intellectuals, and the Church was suddenly joined by environmentalists and nuclear disarmament activists, anarchists, punk rock bands, street theater performers—and Western-style human rights activists and feminists. The newcomers, preferring visible street action to secret meetings in factories and apartments, clamored for public space so they could insert their globally infused ideas into the brew of opposition discourse.

Although by 1988 these twenty- and thirty-somethings may have had little patience for underground conspiracies, the underground was nonetheless the tradition that had schooled them in dissent and had emboldened them. The younger oppositionists usually belonged to several groups simultaneously, reflecting their overlapping interests. For example, in addition to serving as the Polish liaison for Amnesty International, Małgorzata Tarasiewicz—who would also eventually head Solidarity's very short-lived Women's Section—helped organize many acts of civil disobedience, sit-ins, and happenings that were characteristic of the youthful movement called Wolność i Pokój (WiP) (Freedom and Peace). A native of the Baltic seaport town of Sopot, Małgorzata also socialized with the trade unionists who had birthed Solidarity at the Lenin Shipyard and traveled to campuses in Prague and Budapest to meet with fellow anarcho-environmentalists. She attended her first feminist consciousness–raising group while attending Gdańsk University in 1984. The group had been started by a Canadian visiting professor just that year.

The playing field for dissent had expanded from the fear-ridden underground into a joyful playground, a "carnival of revolution," to quote Padraic Kenney. "Anti-communism did not mean, to them, waging war against the regime, or even engaging in dialogue with the regime. In place of loathing of the regime, or the desire to reform it, came indifference. . . . The carnival ruptured the

Communist Party's monologue with a cacophony of insistent and derisive voices."[4] The more conventional forms of dissent persisted as well, of course, and originated from the revisionists, nationalists, and Catholic pacifists, as well as from the trade unionists and banned literati who made up Solidarity.

But Solidarity was no longer directing the show, and while some of the creative new forms of dissent had sprung from the shattered trade union movement, others emerged in *opposition* to Solidarity—whether to its narrow political agenda or to its need to be legitimized by a government that had already lost its credibility. There were also groups that paid no heed either to Solidarity or to the state.

After it shifted gears from a roaring trade union engine to a patient (r)evolution, Solidarity changed dramatically throughout the rest of the 1980s. Its mass-based membership of ten million dwindled to an eventual low of less than two million, and the party replaced Solidarity's trade unions with its own. The now diminished grass roots movement, based on "unity above all," continued to split internally over new issues, one of the more divisive of which was whether to remain underground or to go aboveground. Those who favored going public either were already openly politically active (Władysław Frasyniuk and Barbara Labuda were among this group) or had been freed in the general amnesty of 1986 and had little to hide now that they were known entities to the police (Ewa Kulik and her boyfriend, Konrad Bieliński, for example). In contrast, the *Tygodnik Mazowsze* editors doggedly protected their anonymity. Even though by 1987 they were all living aboveground and had since added a few men to their expanded team, the newspaper's Floating Offices remained one of the last holdouts of underground invisibility.

Tygodnik Mazowsze managed to stand its ground as a profoundly visible, durable, and concrete example of anticommunist resistance throughout most of the 1980s and continued to be a primary forum for reliable, regular news and public discussions. Activists didn't need to affiliate or identify with Solidarity in order to read it, and thus it successfully bridged one era of dissent to the next. Despite the defeats and changes that Solidarity endured, the newspaper's human rights discourse, rooted in the 1970s opposition, reinforced the intellectual underpinnings of 1980s activism. And even though the opposition was no longer dominated by Solidarity, Solidarity remained the symbol of resistance.[5] Its logo was everywhere, Lech Wałęsa continued to be its name and face, and *Tygodnik Mazowsze* was its messenger, informing and enlivening ever-broader and more diverse audiences.

The outpouring of dissent all across 1980s Poland, from major industrial hubs and university campuses to village market squares, attests to the fact that human rights principles, as discussed in the pages of *Tygodnik Mazowsze* and elsewhere, had been internalized by millions of individuals. Each new generation was less fearful of the state and its increasingly obsolete paradigm. Information was, indeed, light, and it was only a matter of time before civil society burst out of its communist seams.

It began in February 1988 with a new wave of food price protests and culminated in shipyard strikes that broke out the following August. The sleeping giant, Solidarity, awoke to steer the protests. The party had been on a downward spiral throughout the 1980s and would not be able to face down these strikers with either military force or consumer bribes. Without goods, profits, or legitimacy, the party had no more bargaining chips, and Jaruzelski's power had lost its sway. Poland's foreign debt had risen to forty billion dollars, and over 60 percent of the population lived below the poverty line. Jaruzelski couldn't even win a referendum he called in 1987 offering the society a more democratic public life in exchange for voting in favor of a 110 percent increase in basic commodity prices. The general actually acknowledged this defeat, which, in and of itself, was an incredible turnaround.

When the summer 1988 strikes broke out, Jaruzelski realized that the Communist Party could no longer rule Poland, and he looked exclusively to Solidarity to negotiate the sharing of power. Solidarity rose to the occasion, quickly resurrecting its male-dominated hierarchy. The ease with which the relationship between the Communist Party and Solidarity—dormant since the era of the Gdańsk Accords—was revived supports Padraic Kenney's assertion that the two rivals spoke the same masculine language, shared a "culture of masculinity and political logic."[6] As the men once again took their seats around the bargaining table, that commonality of language made it possible for them to broker the transition to democratic governance.

And what of the *Tygodnik Mazowsze* women at this historic juncture?

Another cucumber season was approaching in August 1988, and the *Tygodnik Mazowsze* editors were preparing to close up newspaper operations and join much of the rest of the country on vacation. Though they retained anonymity as the editors of *Tygodnik Mazowsze*, Helena and company now led seminormal lives, residing in their own homes, raising their children, traveling abroad, and generally taking advantage of the more tolerant times they had helped to usher in. Some editors had already gone abroad or to mountain retreats without telephones. Helena Łuczywo was preparing to return to Poland from the United States, where she had just completed a yearlong peace fellowship at Radcliffe College. Joanna Szczęsna had just begun a stay-at-home vacation in Warsaw, which she hoped would be filled with rest and relaxation, friends, and cultural pleasures.

While playing bridge one evening, Joanna heard a radio report that strikes had erupted in the Szczecin shipyards in northern Poland. A series of strikes had rumbled across the nation earlier that year, and now new ones had begun. At first Joanna pretended she hadn't heard the news. "Oh no, I am on vacation," she tried to convince herself. But by the third day of the strikes, the deputy editor of the country's preeminent underground newspaper could no longer ignore their significance.

The previous February, the government had announced a 40 percent increase in food prices, and, predictably, strikes had erupted in Silesia and Gdańsk that lasted until April. In a noteworthy departure from precedent, these strikes were organized by young workers who did not identify with Solidarity and who considered themselves more radical than their predecessors—angrier, more spontaneous and demanding, and less willing to compromise. They did, however, eventually bring in Lech Wałęsa to help them negotiate with the government.

The August strikes that interrupted Joanna's bridge game, however, were mostly Solidarity directed, and they quickly grew extremely aggressive and confrontational. As Joanna read it, a summer revolution was about to explode, and her journalist's heart hadn't beat so excitedly since Gdańsk in 1980. She decided to crank up the summer-dormant printing presses, to report on the strikes, and to put out an edition of the newspaper. "A strike that is not publicized cannot gain strength or be effective," she emphasized while telling this story. But with none of her fellow staff members in town to assist her, she would have to produce the newspaper herself.

Joanna made a checklist: go to the striking shipyards and also to the coal mines to which the protests had quickly spread, research and write all of the articles, collect production materials, organize the print production (the printing staff was also on vacation), and manage the distribution. She was determined to have the newspaper circulating on the streets in one week's time. Then an unprecedented problem arose. On Monday and Tuesday, as she traveled around Szczecin interviewing the strike leaders at the Warski Shipyard, she realized she would need to maintain contact with them after returning to Warsaw. No trusted friends were available to act as liaison with the strikers, so she would have to rely on the telephone. Despite the more lenient times, phones were still wiretapped, which still led to dissidents being arrested, and with strikes now heating up the political cauldron, one could not predict the nature of government intervention.

Breaking a fundamental rule of conspiracy, Joanna gave out her telephone number to strikers, telling them, "Call me. Call me at home." In the previous four years, Joanna had "never even called my best friend because I knew that the police bugged phones." Her decision to thus expose herself signaled a turning point for both Joanna and the underground. Knowing that *Tygodnik Mazowsze* was one of the last outposts of underground action and that the editors had chosen to remain anonymous, Joanna might have been risking the newspaper's future. But after two decades of activist experience, she trusted her ability to do the right thing. She said she had two motivations to give out her phone number. "First, it was the only way to get information because the underground network was not functioning. Second, I felt that I should support the strikers' activism. The miners were two thousand feet underground and needed help. I was the first person to produce information that several miners had gone on a hunger strike in the mine and would bomb themselves if no one came to talk to them."

Back at home, Joanna telephoned Radio Free Europe and Agence France Presse to get the word out internationally. Placing international calls, she told me, was difficult "not because of the police but because of Polish telephones." There was a slow and exasperating protocol for making long-distance or international phone calls throughout the communist era, which lingered through 1990. Though the call was usually put through in the middle of the night, Joanna did not find this problematic—she wasn't sleeping anyway. In order to fan the fires of revolution, she stayed awake nonstop for 120 hours. "Biology prepares women for sleepless nights," she commented in her characteristically understated manner. So does a legacy of Romantic mythology.

That Wednesday and Thursday Joanna worked on the newspaper in Warsaw. Thursday was her self-imposed deadline. On Friday she found people to print it and personally transported the boards to the various sites for print production. On Saturday morning, the first set of copies arrived at her home, and she arranged for them to be distributed to all the work sites in Gdańsk, Szczecin, and Silesia where people were striking. It was important to her that the strikers know that their protests were getting front-page coverage, that their demands and activities were being observed and recorded. On Sunday morning, when the various printers were ready to send the next delivery of papers, they called Joanna from public phone booths and asked in code, "Do you need fresh bread?" Friends she had recruited picked up the papers from her "bakery" and drove them to additional strike locations. By this time, Joanna was taking a shower every quarter hour just to stay awake. Otherwise, she told me, she would surely have fainted.

Several weeks later, the police raided Joanna's home, taking with them whatever remained of the twenty-five thousand copies that had been delivered there, but they did not take her. As she explained it, "By that time, the Round Tables were in formation, the pre-talks had begun." The government had acknowledged its weakness and called for open dialogue with Solidarity, offering to legalize it if Lech Wałęsa could get the workers to return to the job. It was an offer Wałęsa did not refuse.

The one-woman edition of *Tygodnik Mazowsze* was one of the last instances of large-scale underground action. With victory at hand, Joanna could finally sleep soundly, a happy ending to what she called "the last major action in my underground publishing career."

In my estimation, it was no exaggeration when Zofia Bydliń-ska—speaking not just of Joanna's herculean task but of the paper's career as a whole—declared to me with obvious pride, "It was thanks to us that the opposition evolved into the Round Table talks. In a way, the coming together of the Round Table was our newspaper's success. It was our activity in the underground, the way we animated other groups, it was the fruit of our activity. We influenced history."

The unsung heroines and their newspaper had done what they set out to do; they kept the idea of Solidarity alive, and they did so until the unbelievable happened, surprising even the newspaper's most prescient strategists. First in Poland and then in the rest of the Soviet Bloc, communist governments surrendered power peacefully.

Poland's women warriors had worked in partnership with their male counterparts for close to eight years. After allowing women to keep their seats of power warm for so long, would the Solidarity men move the women aside—again—now that they were preparing to negotiate with Jaruzelski and the party? Yes, indeed. Were women now differently positioned so that they might avert the men's power grab? Yes and no. Unlike 1980, by 1988 women held the power of numbers and influence necessary to make demands, but they lacked the drive and the know-how to exercise it.

When the women from the Warsaw underground formally came out of hiding in April 1989, all around them Poland was changing. Lech Wałęsa had by then formed the Citizens' Committee, made up of twenty-six Solidarity activists (only one of which was a woman), to meet with government officials to negotiate the end of commu-nist Poland. Party bureaucrats were already packing up their of-fices. The editors of *Tygodnik Mazowsze* saw the Round Table as the realization of the long-awaited goal—the legalization of Solidarity and the emergence of a democratic public life. "I never guessed that the repression would last for seven and a half years," Joanna told me in 1991. "But in terms of what we won, underground existence actually lasted a short amount of time."

"Many factors contributed to our success," Helena told me. "The times had changed. The government had weakened. Poland was in heavy debt. International human rights communities defended us. The pope supported us. Most of Poland supported us." The years of sacrifice and uncertainty seemed to have paid off.

The unsung heroines of the underground press broadcast their first public statement in nearly a decade. Identifying themselves openly and visibly in *Tygodnik Mazowsze* as the editors of their underground weekly, they stated: "We know very well how frail and unstable the present political structure is, how we cannot trust the declarations of the authorities, how high the risk is that we will lose what we had without getting anything in exchange . . . and yet it is a new situation. . . . To wait and see [if it was safe to come out] would mean for us giving up new, incomparably wider possibilities of acting in the name of the ideals we fought to achieve for years— the ideals of Solidarity."[7] Theirs was a historic and formal statement, which marked the end of *Tygodnik Mazowsze* and the beginning of a free press in Poland. The announcement was meant to encourage unity in the population, to push progress forward at a time when a show of solidarity, *their* show of solidarity, could effectively diminish the last vestiges of party resistance.

There was virtually no recognition accorded the editors of *Tygodnik Mazowsze* for their contributions to the changes now afoot— certainly nothing else that was said approached the level of credit Zofia Bydlińska had given them. A rare, perhaps the only, instance of simple acknowledgment appeared in a November 1989 *New Yorker* article by Lawrence Weschler, who wrote of these women, his friends: "It turned out that the overwhelming majority of these journalists who had been driving the regime crazy with their defiant irrepressibility were women."[8] Helena told me she had requested that he say no more than that about their work in the underground.

The grand, commemorative round table seated fifty-seven people and was used for the ceremonies that opened and closed the talks. Fifty-five delegates participated: twenty-six representatives of Solidarity and twenty-nine from the party, plus two observers from the Church. Adam Michnik, Grażyna Staniszewska, Bronislaw Geremek, Jacek Kuroń, and Tadeusz Mazowiecki joined Wałęsa and others as Solidarity delegates. The negotiations were organized into three main discussions: political reform, social and economic policy, and union pluralism. Four important terms were negotiated in the talks: to legalize Solidarity, to hold elections on June 4, to sanction Solidarity's electoral participation, and to create a newspaper for Solidarity's election campaign. There were also numerous sub-table talks on a variety of issues including health care, education, and the media.

Helena participated in the media sub-table talk, where she pushed for starting a daily newspaper. But that demand, she reported in one of the last issues of *Tygodnik Mazowsze,* "gained no response at the first meeting." Minister of Information Jerzy Urban preferred to discuss the regulation of paper supplies to the opposition, she reported. Showing little appetite for cooperation or compromise, Urban defined the "material foundation of the newly born pluralism: 'What's ours is ours; what's yours will be yours.'" One of Helena's colleagues reprimanded him for his miserly response, asking, "Why do you feel threatened? Is the world falling apart?"[9] Urban's rigid world was, indeed, falling fast. In the end, Solidarity won its uncensored press and supplies of paper too.

Gazeta Wyborcza (Election Gazette) was launched as the new voice of Solidarity just prior to the first real (half-free) election in Poland in fifty years, and starting with its eight-page premiere issue, the tabloid played a crucial role in the transition process. Timothy Garton Ash pondered the question of the paper's concrete contribution to Solidarity's election success in the pages of the *New Yorker:* "It's an open question. Poles had more than enough reasons to vote out the communists after so many years of non-elected communist misrule. But the paper decisively contributed to the next step: the appointment of a non-communist Prime Minister—the first in Eastern Europe since 1948—and the installation of General Jaruzelski as President, to reassure Moscow. It was the paper that first suggested this. In a characteristic division of labor, Michnik wrote the editorial advancing the radical proposal, while Helena thought up the historic banner headline: 'Your President,

Our Premier.' His article, her headline. With interventions like this, *Gazeta Wyborcza* wrote itself into the history of Poland's negotiated revolution."[10]

Back in the business of reporting what she thought of as real news and real politics—societal upheaval, change in governments, partisan conflicts, election campaigns, and power games—Helena Łuczywo no longer felt that her everyday reality was "actually very boring." As she told the *Radcliffe Quarterly* in 2000, "When the results of the June election began to flow in and Solidarity's victory became obvious [Solidarity won ninety-nine out of one hundred open senate seats], it was incredible and overwhelming. Even the military voted for Solidarity. Poland would never be the same after that. We knew then that the communist regime in Poland had no legitimacy. . . . [T]he election was something wonderful, something true. When it came, it was so much more important than the biggest strikes. That's why the newspaper is called *Gazeta Wyborcza,* because we were created to help Solidarity in the election. We thought about changing the name after the election was over. We did a poll among leaders about what the name should be, and then someone said, let's keep the name, just to commemorate the event."[11]

After the elections, the time for solidarity and "unity above all" ended. For some women, the "duty of politics" also ended, and it was now time to tend to career goals, education, health, and family. Solidarity's victory presented some of the unsung heroines with the long-awaited opportunity to concentrate on facets of their private and public selves that had been on hold during the underground years. Anna Bikont and Zofia Bydlińska joined Helena and Adam Michnik in establishing *Gazeta Wyborcza.* Along with working on the newspaper, Anna cared for her baby daughter, born in October 1988, in the last autumn of communist rule. Anna Dodziuk began work as a psychotherapist at a treatment center for alcoholics and gave birth to a daughter. Małgorzata Pawlicka and her husband, a Japanese journalist, moved to Japan for the next three and a half years, and upon their return she worked as a science editor for a major publishing house. Ewa Kulik, Joanna Szczęsna, Agnieszka Maciejowska, and Anka Grupińska, like many other women, finally found the time and space to assess their priorities and to recover from the psychic and physical stresses of the underground years. They also found that leaving Poland, leaving "all Polish problems behind," was an option each needed to exercise in order to realign their sense of self with a changing society. Of all the women interviewed for this book, only Barbara Labuda chose to campaign for political office. When I asked her why so few of her female colleagues had joined, or tried to join, her in Parliament, she fired off the terse reply, "Better to ask why some of us continue to go on!"

Just before the Round Table discussions began in February 1989, Joanna decided to leave Poland to study in the United States. When I asked her why she had left the country just as victory was at hand, she replied, "My input wasn't critical to the next phase of organizing a new government. I thought I would see the changes in Poland when I returned. It is impossible to be involved in everything."

She named three reasons why she applied for fellowships in the United States. First, it was her only opportunity to study English, which she felt would be impossible to master in Poland. "I was always too busy or tired in Poland to take a class," she added. She also needed medical treatment for a condition that Polish doctors had not been able to treat successfully. And third, she said, "I needed a break. I needed to leave all Polish problems behind me and lead a completely different lifestyle. I was sure that I had to get out for a while."

Joanna's application to Stanford University was sent to the U.S. Embassy in Warsaw, and soon embassy officers invited her to lunch. "I did not speak English, and my illness made it impossible to eat. My spine pressed on the nerve that is responsible for the stomach, which made eating all food difficult. Americans like to help. If I told the embassy that I am in my forties, I do not speak English, and I am too ill to eat, I thought that, at best, they might give me twenty dollars to take a taxi home. It was impossible to learn English in one night, so I decided that I would eat lunch. American cuisine is not my favorite. This was one of the bravest things I have ever done."

Admitted to Stanford, she left for the United States, and in two months' time her illness was healed. "Now I speak and read English and I eat everything," she told me when we met at her Princeton home in May 1991. "The two years in the United States have been the best years in my life. It was good for my son too." She returned to Warsaw soon after that meeting and resumed her editorial work on *Gazeta Wyborcza*'s weekend edition.

Ewa Kulik too emerged from the underground with a deep urge to step back from her previous life and regroup. "I was twenty-nine years old in 1989, and I wanted to figure out what to do with my life—work, politics, romance, everything." After the opposition's victory, her relationship with Solidarity activist Konrad Bieliński arrived at a crossroads. They needed time to consider whether they would create an aboveground life together or venture separately into the new Poland. "We thought that our underground relationship might have only been a 'marriage of convenience' and not real love. We finally decided to stay together, but for almost two years we weren't certain." In 1990 Ewa too left Poland—to study American literature at Boston University. Upon her return to Warsaw the following year, she began translating English-language fiction into Polish, which supported her while she sorted out her life. That same year she and Bieliński married.

I asked Ewa whether she ever planned to write about her experiences in the underground. She gave me the following reply.

When communism ended, we were so happy that it ended. Most of us were too busy to write our memoirs. We left it again for others to do it. I regret that I haven't written anything. Due to my obsession with security, I had destroyed every note and document that could have been used as evidence if discovered. *Tygodnik Mazowsze* also destroyed its papers for the same reasons. I never kept a diary during the underground years because police usually caught people by reading diaries in which names were identified. Today, it would be difficult to write about the underground because my memory would fail me.

Recently, I met with a lot of people from the underground at a party. I realized that all of them, who had contributed so much, had stayed anonymous. It is a pity, because they were anonymous then and they are anonymous now. It is important for the historical record and for their own personal satisfaction that their contributions be recognized.

Some people are disappointed with the new reality. They tell me, "We have all of these terrible problems now. Was it worth it to give up five years of our lives?" For me, it was worthwhile. I used to tell people, "Don't expect a medal. When it ends, you will get a kick in the behind." There is no profit to this work. I promised myself that I will establish my professional work outside politics. In a free democratic Poland, one might choose what they want to do now. Being involved in politics is not a moral obligation. In the underground, we were obliged to be political. Today, it is a free choice.

Agnieszka Maciejowska had joined the underground in February 1982, one year after completing her university studies. Having spent seven years in hiding—years in which she would otherwise have put her philosophy degree to professional use—she found the transition to an aboveground life to be slow, difficult, and filled with soul-searching questions—What next? What do I want? What am I qualified to do?—that echoed the sentiments of others I had interviewed. When we talked in December 1990, Agnieszka spoke somewhat bitterly, and certainly ironically, about her despair that she lacked the skills and experiences that prepare one to live in ordinary times. "Of what use are conspiratorial skills in a democracy—such as noticing when the police are following me? For people like me, who went to work for the underground immediately after getting our degrees, the opposition could be likened to a prolonging of our childhoods. We shared the strong conviction that we lived in absurd circumstances, and in such conditions it makes no sense to lead an adult life. And so we coped with the situation, playing and scheming and at the same time trying to oppose and change it in order to be able to enter adulthood. Somehow, it became a dead-end street."

Agnieszka continued, "After the Round Table discussions and the '89 elections, everything changed. The time for adulthood arrived, and it was difficult for me to adjust to the life of a grown-up. This is the real start of my adult life because I had studied longer than the average at my age, and then I went into the underground. Now I enter adulthood and find my feet stepping in puddles of mud." Agnieszka landed solidly on both feet, however, and five years later moved to Israel to work in the Polish Embassy.

Barbara Labuda had always chosen to pursue politics; she never felt it was an obligation. But when she expressed her desire to participate in the Round Table talks, her male colleagues rejected her. It was 1980 all over again; the men handed one another the perks and excluded women from the receiving line. The one female Solidarity delegate to the Round Table talks was Grażyna Staniszewska, a teacher and librarian who had been very active in both the legal and illegal structures of Solidarity in Bielsko-Biała, a small town in Upper Silesia.

Barbara realized that people who didn't get a seat at the Round Tables talks or at a sub-table talk would find it nearly impossible to run for office. She recalled her frustration with the situation in an interview in the *OŚKA Biuletyn:* "At the time, the criteria of gender was out of the question. . . . The political table, which I found the most attractive, was occupied only by men. Every time that I demanded my rights, I heard that there were other experts who would be more suitable for the negotiations. At last, only men participated in the debates. Certainly, it was possible to keep insisting, but the negotiations had already begun, and the list of participants had been created."[12]

In addition to Barbara Labuda, Ewa Kulik had also been passed over for participation in the Round Table talks, though each had been elected to her Regional Executive Committee, in 1987 and 1988 respectively. When I asked Ewa whether she would have joined the Round Table talks if an invitation had been extended to her, she replied, "I doubt I would have been invited since there were so many activists who had to be recognized by being invited. Most probably I would have assumed the role of a supporter and organizer of the Round Table talks on the part of the Solidarity leadership."

The selection of seats at the Round Table talks was highly competitive. Decisions were made on the basis of reward and recognition and at the expense of representation. According to Barbara, at the time no one thought to ask questions such as "Why is there only one woman at the Round Table talks?" or "Why won't Solidarity welcome in those women who want to participate?" As a result, the male-to-female ratio in the Round Table talks neither represented Solidarity's membership nor justly recognized the value of women's long-term contributions. Even nine years earlier, at the Lenin Shipyard, the presidium of the Inter-factory Strike Committee had boasted a larger number of female participants—three out of eighteen—in its August 1980 negotiations with the government. Apparently, as women's influence as activists increased during the 1980s, respect for the democratic principle of equality decreased until, by 1989, women reached a point where, as far as politics was concerned, they lacked freedom of choice.

As a consequence, neither women nor their interests were represented at the Round Table talks, thereby setting a precedent that compromised democratic representation from the outset. Women were again in the minority in the appointment of candidates to the parliament and the senate for the June 1989 elections—approximately 200 of the 2,500 candidates were women. Of the 460 persons elected to the parliament, only 62 were women.[13] "It worked in the underground for women to be in charge, but now it has backfired" was Ewa's pointed comment on the election. "We withdrew," Małgorzata Pawlicka told me, shaking her head. "Women sacrifice themselves too easily."

Barbara Labuda turned out to be the rare exception to the rule that Round Table participation was prerequisite to election to the Sejm, Poland's parliament. She was voted into the Sejm in 1991, representing the liberal Democratic Union in the Lower Silesia region, of which Wrocław is the capital city. As one of the few opposition women to enter the new political arena, when she surveyed the new playing field, she worried that, as the new democratic culture was being created, far too few women were showing political ambition or demanding to be represented. Barbara lobbied her Solidarity sisters to come forward with her and to make their roles in the underground known, but they shrugged her off. She was particularly frustrated with the influential *Tygodnik Mazowsze* editors, who did not recognize that women's entitlements needed to be safeguarded and that they, the editors, had the bargaining power to make political demands for themselves and for women as a social group.

Barbara alone understood that, without formal recognition of women's vital roles in the underground, Solidarity would not be obliged to include women in the Round Table talks or on election tickets. If women were thus excluded, it meant their involvement in political and public life could be restrained and they would be made too politically weak to counter measures that went against their interests. If women had organized into a politically powerful faction, they might, for example, have been able to quash the soon to be proposed abortion ban legislation before its advocates could gain strong backing. "In countries that had so-called revolutions," Barbara told *Ms.* magazine in the summer of 1990, "women were promised that their concerns would be addressed as soon as the 'more important' political and economic problems are solved. At least, women themselves shouldn't say, 'Let's wait, there are more important things now.'"[14]

Influential opposition women did not seize the moment to protest the draft bill because they weren't looking for an opportunity to seize. They had accepted and internalized their role as the support team for the men and carried it over into the new democracy. "Maybe we women were simply not solid enough. Maybe we did not want to be accused of pettiness and megalomania," Barbara told the *OŚKA Biuletyn*. "Maybe it is valuable to conduct a political analysis to explain why women gave up power. Certainly, most of all, it is a question of political ambitions. I happen to have them, and I want to participate in politics; besides, I know that I am not any worse than men and I should have equal chances. Secondly, it is a result of rejecting and shoving women away from power in Solidarity. . . . Of course, at the same time, we were also praised and flattered, but every time an issue of real power emerged, we heard: 'The boss? No, the boss will be Franek' [Frasyniuk]. This is the recurrent and permanent mechanism which, in my opinion, is derived only from the culture. I have always come out first in the election in Wrocław. I even felt bad about always winning over men. . . . We tried so hard and men abandoned us," Barbara concluded. "Women were rejected by Solidarity."[15]

Barbara became one of the few politicians to defend women's social and legal position under the swiftly changing conditions of democratization. As she had foreseen, women were among the first social groups to shoulder the unanticipated burdens of political and economic change. Beginning with the 1989 election, female representation in government dwindled from 20 percent to 14 percent, and the introduction of a free market economy threatened women's job security, maternity benefits, and other social service hallmarks of the old order that had benefited women. "The revolutions that toppled Communist regimes have left women in a paradoxical situation, only tenuously retaining equal rights," reported the *New York Times* on November 25, 1990.[16]

Privatizing the economy brought with it the elimination of childcare and maternity leave benefits and the implementation of a nationwide back-to-the-home campaign, which was pursued in the media, on the podium in Parliament, and in the parishes. The country's Catholic Church began to do the work of politicians. Immediately, and uniquely in Poland, democratic politics were riddled with the question of whether religious values and the rule of law would remain respectfully in separate spheres. Few people were prepared in 1989 to understand the Church hierarchy's agenda, apart from women such as Barbara Labuda and newly emerging feminist groups, who watched women's rights be among the first to be ruled out.

In a dangerous turn of events, reproductive rights were about to be outlawed. Shortly before the June 1989 parliamentary elections, the lower house of the Sejm began to debate draft legislation that would send women who got abortions and the doctors who performed them to prison for two years. "Women are going to lose something," Barbara warned very early on, "the right to abortion."[17] The ban was passed into law in 1993 and is still being forcefully challenged today.

Spearheaded by the Catholic Church and its political allies in the government, the antiabortion proposal seriously divided the Polish population just as people were forming their first political parties and grass roots organizations. "No recent debate in Poland has been comparable in emotional intensity, pervasiveness of discussions, or the depths of divisions it provoked," Warsaw legal scholar Małgorzata Fuszara emphasized in a seminal essay on the early abortion debates.[18] The news of the draft legislation shocked and horrified some women. Why was the government spending its time criminalizing a long-standing entitlement when it faced so many truly crucial matters? Other women were embarrassed that the new democratic leadership was interfering in their private affairs. Several women with whom I spoke in the early 1990s believed that such a law would never be passed. No comparable law had restricted Polish women's reproductive choices since the mid-nineteenth century. Warsaw sociologist Anna Titkow insightfully characterized what was going on as a "visible retrogression" to the customs, symbols, laws, and propaganda of the precommunist past in order to fill the ideological vacuum created by the party's withdrawal.[19] "Men were retaliating," cautioned Sławomira Wałczewska, "attempting to fortify the traditional social contract between the sexes, to win back their lost powers, and to show women where they belong."[20]

The proposed abortion ban finally brought feminism's time to Poland and did so under hostile, reactive conditions. Thirty independent, nongovernmental feminist groups formed in the wake of the antiabortion proposal, including, among the strongest, the Polish Feminist Association, Pro Femina, and Neutrum. The third group, Neutrum, actually focused on issues dealing with the separation of church and state. Its involvement in the abortion rights campaign encouraged some of its organizers to break away in order to establish the Federation for Women and Family Planning. Most of the women in these groups were new to feminism, though some had been active prior to the changeover, even back as far as 1980 during the founding of Solidarity.

Wanda Nowicka, now Poland's leading advocate of women's reproductive rights and health, described for me the process of what her U.S. counterparts might have described as her "radicalization." Wanda's life, work, and belief in the two institutions that had led the country out of communism were totally changed when the proposed abortion ban moved her from astonishment to outrage to activism. "Although I was never a member of the Church, in the 1980s I worshiped it as an external authority that was right and true, that represented democracy, freedom, and justice. Then it turned on us. Both the Church and Solidarity betrayed us. When the negative signs first appeared—with the proposal of the abortion ban—I could not believe that it was happening, that the whole Church establishment and all of Solidarity's leadership supported the ban. I thought that it must be the design of a few powerful individuals within each institution who were abusing its ideals."

"However, at some point—I don't know exactly when, but certainly by 1990—it was obvious that the Church was trying to fill the void after communism and control the society in the only 'right way,'" Wanda explained. "As for Solidarity, I always thought that since so many individual leaders were deeply connected to the Church, that they were in a difficult position because they could not really say 'no' openly or strongly. It was not acceptable to me, but I understood how it had happened. I always hoped that someone like Michnik would say, 'Stop it. It cannot go further.' But it went further and further. And then I had to suddenly face the fact that Solidarity was no longer Solidarity. It was a completely different force, which was struggling with the ideas of freedom and democracy. I had to face the negative undercurrents that had always been there, except hidden. The negative forces, which threatened women's rights, were not something new, which only developed after Solidarity won. They had always been part of the movement. I just hadn't seen them beforehand."

Wanda left her work as a secondary school teacher to head up the Federation for Women and Family Planning, which she continues to direct today. I asked her whether she had realized, when she started to organize in defense of reproductive freedoms, how daring it was to challenge the Church and how controversial the abortion issue would become. "I had no idea," she responded. "No, not at all. Partly I was naive because I knew I was right, and I thought that since I am right, we will win. I did not realize that our struggle would be so difficult and uncertain."

In a ferocious uphill battle, a dedicated band of activists protested that, in the purging of all things communist, reproductive rights were being scapegoated. Abortion was being used as a "bargaining chip," Małgorzata Fuszara pointed out, "traded away by the liberals" to ensure a political success in a time of uncertainty.[21] The human toll on women was ignored in this equation. The former Solidarity oppositionists were not seeing the issues pertaining to women's rights with the same clarity they had brought to bear when the issues at hand also caused men to suffer. Even worse, their adamant antiwoman stance was brazenly undemocratic, given that 70 percent of the populace identified as pro-choice. One million people signed a pro-choice petition that feminists presented to the Sejm in 1991, but this, like all other tactics, failed to turn the tide. The new government, which included many people who had once envisioned creating a grass roots movement called Solidarity, resisted women's organizing efforts and the show of support they rallied to safeguard their entitlements.

"[T]he anti-abortion law has become the first business card of the insecure young authority in Eastern Europe," Warsaw University professor of American literature Agnieszka Graff reflected in a 1999 Op-Ed piece published in *Gazeta Wyborcza*. "One of our Polish senators stated that focusing in that difficult period on the abortion issue, at the expense of other burning questions, resulted from the fact that abortion was believed to be an issue that could be 'handled.' . . . For the time being, it was not known what to do about the rampant inflation or how to reform the agricultural sector, but meanwhile it was possible to 'nationalize' female reproduction. Governments must have authority over somebody. The powers-that-be, in order to feel in power, must subordinate someone. In post-communist democracy women have turned out to be that someone."[22]

Part of the problem, Małgorzata Fuszara wrote in a 1991 essay, resulted from the Catholic Church's influence on the new political process and on antiabortion attitudes. "Candidates in the presidential and electoral campaigns feared losing the support of the church and often strive to win it. For the same reason, other groups and the press prefer to keep silent on the issue. Such silence suggests disagreement with the bill, accompanied by a fear of criticizing it openly."[23]

Poland is a country where political allegiances shift daily, and that was certainly the process going on after Solidarity replaced the communist regime. As the union's own cohesion began to rip apart and men like Adam Michnik and Tadeusz Mazowiecki, who became the interim prime minister, fell into popular disfavor, the Polish Catholic Church immediately vied for a political stake in the new government. Shedding its revolutionary, anticommunist garb, it easily reassumed its traditional, now somewhat moth-eaten robes. "The Church is being treated like a political party. Indeed, it is," sociologist Anna Titkow warned.[24]

Agnieszka Maciejowska observed in one of our interviews that it might prove to have been easier to rebel against the Communist Party than to defy the Catholic Church. "The antiabortion bill shows the kind of power that we learned to oppose and the kind of power we did not learn to challenge—we learned not to be afraid of the police and their pressure, but we cannot resist the pressure of the Church's power. For example, a senator who is an independent thinker nonetheless said in a *Gazeta Wyborcza* interview that he does not dare to say 'no' to the abortion ban. By the way, he spoke anonymously, requesting that his name not appear in the newspaper."

Joanna Szczęsna expressed shock and disappointment when we discussed the antiabortion bill during her stay in the United States in 1991. "When I read what our representatives said in the Sejm, I understood that I must become a feminist. It is so stupid, so anti-woman. Even open-minded people are ignorant. The abortion issue shows that, for our parliamentarians and other people, this issue is separate from women and women's fate. It is now so abstract that it is a pie in the sky."

In September 1989, in the midst of the backlash against reproductive rights, Solidarity made a different kind of move, one that seemed to signal a significant recognition of women's rights—the Solidarity National Commission called for the formation of a Women's Section of the union. Feminists immediately questioned the union's motivation, given that the call was hardly consistent with Solidarity's characteristic neglect of women's interests. The idea had come from the West and had been introduced by the Brussels-based International Confederation of Free Trade Unions (ICFTU), which had begun providing funds and aid to Solidarity in the 1980s and continued to do so as the trade union adapted to Poland's developing market economy. The ICFTU predicted that within the evolving economic context Solidarity's new issues and potential problems would likely resemble union experiences in Western countries. Based on this forecast, the ICFTU advised Solidarity to provide direct support to its female membership so women could organize around their specific demands and rights.

Małgorzata Tarasiewicz, the twenty-nine-year-old WiP activist from Sopot who had arranged my interviews in Gdańsk, was hired to coordinate the Women's Section. Though she had not been active in Solidarity, the Baltic trade unionists respected her. "I was very excited," Małgorzata told me in 1991. "I had always thought it was a pity that membership in Freedom and Peace was rather elitist and small in numbers. I also thought that women in the union were probably cut off from contacts, information, and power. I thought that if they had the opportunity to speak out, to meet independently from men, then they would finally have the chance to express what they really wanted. For me, the Women's Section meant the opportunity to empower women. In WiP, I was responsible for contacts with Western peace and human rights organizations. I used to meet with only a few women, who were university educated and with whom I shared common ideals. I wanted to learn what women representing the working class thought about their rights and their position in society. I viewed my new work in the Women's Section as a challenge and an unprecedented possibility to influence the developments in Poland."

The founding of the Women's Section in Gdańsk established several new advocacy precedents in postcommunist Poland. First, it encouraged working-class women to develop the organizational skills necessary to protect their economic and social rights. Hence, its very existence represented an opportunity to diversify the class base for postcommunist women's activism from urban, educated feminists in major cities such as Warsaw and Kraków to working-class women in industrial hubs such as Poznań and Łódź. With this advance, the range of women's issues expanded to include not only the consuming concern of that time period—abortion—but concrete labor and economic demands as well.

Second, the launch of the Women's Section positioned Gdańsk as another major center of women's organizing efforts. During the communist period, opposition activism in all the Baltic seaport towns had historically been male dominated in terms of both representation and interests. Until the formation of the Women's Section, women had largely been ascribed either invisible or symbolic status in Solidarity. This was particularly true in Gdańsk, where women such as crane operator Anna Walentynowicz could perform crucial roles in the 1980 strikes but not be elected to decision-making bodies. Moreover, the most influential women organizers of the 1980s opposition, such as Helena, Joanna, and Barbara, had not been based in working-class Gdańsk but were primarily Warsaw intellectuals and professionals.

With the founding of the Women's Section, Solidarity had recognized, for the first time, that women workers have specific labor concerns; furthermore, it had endorsed women's authority to formulate their own issues and programs. It remained to be seen whether the Solidarity National Commission would approve the demands made by the Women's Section, incorporate them into their statutes, and finally move beyond the perspective on women that was reflected in the Gdańsk Accords. While waiting, working-class women were going to get organized.

Comfortably ensconced in the Tri-City region, Małgorzata had the advantage of being familiar with and respected by activists of all ages and backgrounds in WiP, Solidarity, Amnesty International, and other groups. A skilled, sensitive organizer of people across class, ethnic, and gender lines, she was primed for the challenge of coordinating the Women's Section. Like other activists in her generation, her social consciousness was influenced by pre-1989 contacts with Western countries and with developing trends in the international human rights arena—for example, the articulation of women's rights as human rights. She belonged to a new generation of postcommunist democratic activists, who thought globally and acted locally and whose boyfriends could state sincerely and without a snicker that "a democracy that does not protect women's rights is not a democracy." Małgorzata; her boyfriend, Adam; and their circle of friends around the country represented Poland's future. But it was a future whose time had not yet arrived, as Małgorzata would soon discover.

In her new role, Małgorzata immediately contacted women in Solidarity offices in regions such as Łódź, Wrocław, Poznań, and Warsaw and organized the meetings that eventually created a women's network within the union. The founding meeting of what became known as the Women's Section was held in November 1989 and was attended by representatives from seventeen out of thirty-seven regions. Five more regions joined the committee in January 1990. The national women's decision-making body, called the Interim Presidium, consisted of the regional committees. Additional subcommittees were organized to address labor and employment, social welfare protection, health-care, and cultural issues. This momentous undertaking marked the first effort to organize women nationwide.

At the founding meeting, the group identified problem areas that it would target. As Małgorzata reported it: "The Women's Section called for Solidarity to establish a program to: 1) eliminate women's discrimination in employment, promotion, and remuneration; 2) conduct research on constitutional guarantees of equality; and 3) introduce social rights such as parental leave for both women and men, in order to overcome the custom that women are the only ones who are responsible for their households."[25] A homegrown program was taking shape, with Western support.

The organization agreed to survey its constituents to learn more about their needs and to arrange workshops to teach organizational, leadership, advocacy, and media skills. The media workshops trained women in fundamental communication skills such as how to speak to reporters and how to address important questions including, as Human Rights Watch reported, "why there are so few female union leaders."[26]

"We placed a strong emphasis on women becoming chairpersons, making reports of sessions and participating in the various working groups, so that they can follow through the whole process of how to organize a meeting or a seminar," Małgorzata explained in a 1990 interview with British researcher Anna Reading. "This is because we think that up until now, women have been benevolent observers of what had already been organized for them and not really participants."[27]

The question of women's union leadership was raised at a January 1990 meeting of twenty-two regional groups. According to Małgorzata's report from that meeting, "Very few participants knew the percentage of women members in Solidarność, nor even how many women were on the National Executive Committee. (There are none.) At the regional level, the percentage is slightly better, with up to 25 percent of some of the boards represented by women. In a few enterprises, 50 percent or more of the enterprise commissions are composed of women."[28] Women's Section organizers realized that women's awareness of concrete percentages would validate their sense of entitlement. Organizers consistently strove to build confidence and to raise consciousness among their members.

The weeklong January meeting refined the Women's Section's objectives—for example, concrete plans were made to recruit women's membership in Solidarity and to organize a two-year educational program on trade unions. Their resolutions called for equal pay for equal work; flexible work hours and part-time employment for women; an increase in the number of day-care centers; equal responsibility between spouses for domestic labor and childcare; and parental leave for fathers to care for sick children.[29]

However, all did not go smoothly in building consensus for the Women's Section's progressive program. Organizers were often met with resistance, which they understood to be rooted in prevailing cultural restraints or in the easily triggered aversion to the communist legacy. Małgorzata told Anna Reading, "When we put out publicity about the women's section, many people said, 'We don't want another League of Women and communism is finished, so why should we have a women's organization?' . . . It is also difficult to say that women should learn non-traditional jobs because then we hear, 'Yes, we've had women on tractors before.' That makes things very difficult . . . [I]t's the burden of the fifties and traditional attitudes toward women."[30]

Here was the first major barrier to empowering women on new terms and within the new space of a democracy. In the immediate aftermath of communism's collapse, notions of women's rights continued to be associated with the dismantled system rather than with democratic entitlements. Separating women's rights from the communist experience presented an unavoidable challenge— both to the Women's Section and everywhere that women's advocates were organizing in the postcommunist region.

Małgorzata's tactical response was to try to separate the organization's work from the communist legacy by cultivating an understanding of the Western model from which the Women's Section's distinctive program derived. "Poland is looking to the future. It is trying to imitate Europe. This is also in terms of the women's section: the women's section aims to show that we are European."[31]

Małgorzata's group collected women's statements for their surveys and reports, and in so doing they were, in effect, documenting a historic moment in women's evolving awarenesses of their identity and social position in a dramatically changing society. Such records provide a rich source of study into the meaning and implications of women's varying responses to democracy.

Among the things Małgorzata learned from these statements was that, in part, Polish women were not accustomed to asserting themselves to protect their social benefits and rights, "because women had not acquired them through their own efforts. Their privileges did not have a character of rights, but rather, took a form of charity," she told Reading. "Symptoms of discrimination present in their socially assigned role passed unnoticed by women."[32] Charity is not something Polish women would be likely to admit to needing or taking, for, Małgorzata continued, "In Poland to be a woman is to be proud. . . . [W]omen don't like the word 'discrimination' to be applied to them. They would do anything intuitively to fight discrimination, but they'd rather not say they are discriminated against. They don't use certain names—feminism and discrimination—but their demands are quite radical and they don't like the way the government is treating them; they feel they're not listened to by the government and by the union's leadership. They're angry because they don't really know how to push their ideas forward. That's why getting women organized and setting up a magazine and teaching women how to use the mass media is so important. It's giving women the tools to express what they think."[33]

The Women's Section, in both concept and practice, proved to be too far ahead of its time to survive. As had been true throughout most of Solidarity's history, 50 percent of its rank-and-file members were women, but when the union held its National Congress in May 1990, only 10 percent of the delegates were women. When that National Congress passed a resolution in favor of legal protection for the unborn, the Women's Section protested that the delegates had no right to adopt the resolution when women members had not been consulted. "We stated that issues of abortion should not be regulated by criminal law. We argued that, most of all, women should be the ones to make the decision," stated organizer Krystyna Politacha of Wrocław.[34]

In direct reaction to the National Congress, members of the Women's Section conducted referenda in factories in two regions. These showed that members supported the right to abortion. Krystyna, who surveyed Wrocław factories, reported: "Eighty to 90 percent of both men and women opposed the resolution. But I [conducted the referendum] against the will of the union and I was spanked for it."[35]

"The Women's Section did not fulfill the expectations of the union leadership because it was not a window-dressing organization," Małgorzata stressed.[36] (It was not the feared reincarnation of the League of Women after all.) She resigned on March 15, 1991. Her assistant was dismissed two weeks later. After Małgorzata left, she received telephone calls from Gdańsk Solidarity forbidding her to make contact with the Women's Committee. If she defied the ban, she was warned, she would be publicly disgraced.[37]

New York–based Human Rights Watch investigated the union's persecution of Women's Section members and issued its findings in a report on discrimination against women in Poland: "The union leadership expressed its unhappiness about these actions, both publicly and through conversations with Małgorzata. In the process, it was suggested to her that she should try to find a job with a feminist organization. At the same time, members of the Women's Section in regional offices were harassed. For example, according to Małgorzata, they were banned from representing the union abroad because 'they lack the proper moral spine.'"[38] That statement led me to conclude that the communist legacy's penetration of the Women's Section, bringing with it a rejection of feminism, was far shallower than its penetration into the Solidarity elite, bringing with it the practice of intimidation and slander.

Solidarity's Women's Section was dissolved in the spring of 1991, soon after Małgorzata was forced to resign. "The Women's Section spoke many times against the ban on abortion. As a result,"

Małgorzata asserted, "the organization was dissolved. It was accused of pursuing fractional policies and of attempting to destroy Solidarity from within."[39] According to Krystyna, "A great number of women quit their [organizing] activities after the Women's Section's dissolution. They came to the conclusion that they would not be able to push their way through."[40]

In 1999 Maria Janion reminded *Gazeta Wyborcza* readers about that disgraceful incident in Solidarity's none too distant past.

> I used to think through the end of the 1980s—and said so at a conference in Berlin in the late 1980s—that Western feminists had nothing to say to Polish women. I claimed that Solidarity must first fight for the freedom and independence of the whole society and then, together, we can take care of women's issues.
>
> A few years later, Solidarity did take care of women's issues, and we know exactly what happened, and in what manner it did so.
>
> In Poland, the woman is not an individual, but a family creature who should turn away from politics and take care of her home. The moment when I realized this was during the 1990 meeting of the Solidarity National Committee, which took on a bill to protect unborn children. It was the beginning of our male democracy.[41]

Not even willful firebrand Barbara Labuda could withstand the tides of antiwomen sentiment she encountered while on Poland's heady roller coaster of partisan politics. By marching in pro-choice rallies, organizing a parliamentary Women's Caucus, and protesting church-state alliances, she began to arouse the ire of her own—allegedly liberal—party, the Democratic Union. In 1992 she announced her withdrawal from Solidarity because, as she declared publicly, it had turned into a conservative, Catholic political organization under Lech Wałęsa's presidency (1991–95). When compared to Solidarity, the postcommunist communist party, called the Democratic Left Alliance (SLD), looked liberal to her.

Compared to those of other politicians of the early 1990s, Barbara's positions seemed radical, indeed extreme, largely because she challenged the inroads the Church was making into Polish politics. "It behaves like a super-political party," she declared, referring to the way the Church openly supported constitutional sanctions of the state's Christian values, religious education in the classroom, restrictions on divorce and abortion, a ban on Sunday shopping, and the inclusion of language in a new media bill that would ensure the media's respect for Catholic values. It also lobbied successfully for the reclamation of Church property seized by the former government—though thousands of Poles with individual property claims found themselves ignored or overruled. "I know the Church will never accept me because it is anti-feminine by nature, and I am not a handsome tall man," Barbara announced defiantly in *Gazeta Wyborcza*.[42]

Although neither her progressive positions nor her bravado lost her any popularity with the people, especially in Wrocław, and she won two more parliamentary reelections (in 1991 and 1993), Barbara met with increasing disfavor in the eyes of the Church leadership and the Democratic Union.

Barbara became a "negative heroine of the homilies, a woman who spreads corruption, and is called Satan's daughter," *Gazeta Wyborcza* reported in an interview with Barbara in 2000. "A flower pot filled with excrement shatters the window of her Wrocław apartment. She is too often asked: 'How many times did you have an abortion and did you have pangs of conscience as a result?'"[43] The one time a priest asked her this question in an unruly meeting, she responded: "How many times have you masturbated? Such questions are hurtful and insulting, aren't they? You can see my response is equally as awful as your question."[44]

Barbara Labuda was speaking out at a time when her former Solidarity peers—who made up the majority of the Democratic Union membership—had ceased to do so. When she took to criticizing the Democratic Union in the press for its lack of democratic process, the party began a process that the press called "Awantura o Basia" (The Disturbance over Barbara),[45] the title of a well-known children's book in Poland. The Democratic Union accused her of disloyalty, self-aggrandizement, and hysteria, and her membership was suspended for six months. Not long after her suspension, Barbara proposed to establish a committee to examine the government's agreement to return property and monies to the

Catholic Church. That was more heresy than her political party could tolerate, and they began a move to expel her on the grounds that she hadn't paid her membership dues—which, of course, she hadn't done after being suspended.

"There was no room left there for independent views," Barbara told me. The abolition of the previous government's censorship policies, one of the first parliamentary initiatives on which she worked, didn't save her from the Democratic Union's vehement rejection of her political positions. The party to which she had once felt the strongest of emotional bonds, the Solidarity-based Democratic Union, ousted Barbara Labuda in 1996.

10. Filling in the "Blank Spot"
the public discourse on women

From 1989 to 1999 a growing number of women's rights advocates struggled to be heard as a new opposition voice in Poland but were effectively silenced by the right-wing majority in Parliament before their voices could reach the mainstream public. Then, at the end of that decade of concerted efforts by women in the universities, the government, and at the grass roots level, public interest in gender discrimination suddenly awakened. Something touched the nerve that the feminists had been working so long to expose.

In March 1999 Warsaw feminist Agnieszka Graff was watching the televised parliamentary debates on a draft bill that would guarantee the equal status of women and men. The relatively liberal side, which she supported, talked about international conventions and the Council of Europe's recent findings that Poland's government was violating women's human rights. The other side lined up in defense of "real Poles" and talked about Matka Polka and the Creator, who had designed "the natural law as the most certain guarantee of social justice." Agnieszka, a lecturer on American literature at Warsaw University, fumed as she watched the majority conservatives rudely interrupt their opponents with laughter, jokes, and comments on the absurdity of proposing laws that would respect the Universal Declaration of Human Rights more than the Bible's creation myth. She felt strongly that people needed to be reminded that Poland had *already* ratified human rights–related documents.

Not long after the debates, Agnieszka sat down at her computer to draft a paper she was scheduled to present at an academic conference on why the early writing of second-wave American feminists had been so disruptive in the United States. What emerged instead was the first feminist manifesto to go mainstream in Poland. Published in *Gazeta Wyborcza* that June, the essay ignited a human rights debate in the Polish media that utterly disrupted the status quo and continues to this day.

That debate might not have spread as it did had certain combustible ingredients not already been close at hand. These included a decade of persistent feminist organizing; mounting government violations of women's human rights; the acceptance by a developing independent media of its responsibility to investigate gender-discriminatory government practices; and growing popular disaffection with an extremely conservative body politic. This concatenation of circumstances finally allowed women's issues to enter the limelight and gave feminists the opportunity to challenge the terms of political debate. And the ensuing media debate, many feminists told me, would itself have been impossible even two years earlier because, at that time, neither women's analysis nor their skills in public discourse were sufficiently honed to captivate an audience outside of their own circle.

Agnieszka's deeply affronted anger was hardly universal among women in 1999, even within the circle of former underground activists. Without the support of more "moderate" advocates such as Barbara Labuda and a few sympathetic staff members at *Gazeta Wyborcza,* Agnieszka might not have had a mainstream public forum that summer. From the outside, it initially appeared to me that the sixties generation women—those who had created an independent press but did not themselves use it to discuss women's rights—had passed along their vehicle for public education (that is, access to *Gazeta Wyborcza*) to younger women like thirty-year-old Agnieszka in the service of raising gender awareness. I soon learned, however, that most of the older generation women, except Barbara, were uncomfortable with the notion of passing the torch to young feminists. They didn't want to be identified in any way with the feminists, as Joanna Szczęsna and Anna Dodziuk explained to me later that summer of 1999.

When I traveled to Poland for the tenth anniversary of the revolution, I met with Barbara Labuda once again. To the shock of her longtime colleagues, after her ouster from the Democratic Union, she had been invited to join President Aleksander Kwasniewski's cabinet. Although she did not join Kwasniewski's party, the SLD, she did accept the position, which provoked an ongoing national controversy. "I really understand people who read my joining of Kwasniewski's cabinet as a betrayal of the Solidarity ideals," she told *Gazeta Wyborcza*. "This was tough on my entire family, especially on my brothers, who are also Solidarity activists. . . . Today, I don't feel that my old party is my 'us.' Nor do I call the SLD my 'us.' Today, my 'us' is made up of individuals, not parties."[1]

"Such are the paradoxes of democracy!" she said when I asked her about her incongruous alliance. "The postcommunists look to be liberal; the democrats do not." But she insisted that I understand that she is a Western-style democrat with Polish-bred antiauthoritarian antipathies and would never be a card-carrying communist. She awaits a truly liberal party.

In 1999 Barbara was still of two minds about her nation's break with its iron-fisted past. On the one hand, she was proud. "Beginning in 1989 we shattered everything that meant the old regime, especially the monopoly on information, organizations, economics, and politics." On the other hand, she said, "the only thing that saddens me is the renaissance of conservative attitudes. The moment all borders opened and we became exposed to the world, we realized, for the first time, that we are not progressive after all. We are afraid of different views than those held by ourselves, and of differences in race, ethnicity, class, and gender. How to convince people that a new democratic order does not come about simply by introducing the rules of a market economy? How to cultivate a liberal consciousness in a country that prefers free trade to free choice?"

The topic of free choice—that is, abortion rights—had become increasingly contentious since Barbara first championed it in Parliament ten years earlier. The Church continued to assert its authority in political matters, and Barbara discussed why it held so much sway over even liberal-minded politicians. "Many people from the old days of opposition feel so indebted to the Church and the Polish pope for their support in the 1980s," she explained, "that they become paralyzed when it's time to vote or lay down laws that serve justice, which is not always the same as serving Church positions. People are stuck in what I call 'gratitude syndrome.'"

But the majority of the population had indeed thought to vote against the Church when they voted out Lech Wałęsa and voted in the postcommunists in the 1995 elections. Kwasniewski's SLD won the presidency not because Poles were nostalgic for the old communist system but because they saw Wałęsa's limitations in the face of the Catholic Church's overbearing political interventions. Yet not even the SLD, whose platform ran counter to the Church's political agenda, directly criticized the religious fundamentalism.

The politicians and the public were not necessarily on the same page when it came to the power of the Church. According to the pollsters, in 1998–99 most of the estimated 95 percent of the population that had been baptized were not churchgoers, 70 percent continued to favor abortion, and Poland showed the highest condom sales in Europe. In speaking for the public, Barbara Labuda took on the Church more openly than most and in so doing fueled outrage. (Cardinal Glemp, head of the Polish Catholic Church, announced that he would not visit the presidential offices as long as Barbara was in residence.) To Barbara, it was simply "a historical necessity."

"My problem is that I am much more in tune with Western parties, like the Socialists in France or the Democrats in the United States. In Poland I am regarded to be an extreme radical, which indicates that it is not me who is extreme but the Polish situation," Barbara explained. And while the Catholic Church is part of that situation, Barbara stressed that it is not the Church but the fact that Poland remains in the throes of an identity crisis that is the real problem. In 1999 the country was still grappling with fundamental questions such as What is citizenship? What is a parliamentary democracy? Where do the boundaries lie between religious and legal norms? Barbara did point out important accomplishments to me, however: "Poland has demonstrated its commitment to democracy and continues to develop an appropriate political culture. Today, with economic conditions stabilizing and our inclusion into NATO, we are more securely situated in Europe."

When I interviewed Helena Łuczywo to get her tenth anniversary perspective, she spoke with greater enthusiasm than did her more battle-scarred former underground colleague. "The free press is much more interesting now and so is the world we now live in. It is infinitely more interesting than the world under communism. Today's world is full of shades and conflicts, and people behave in so many different ways. Yesterday's world was, frankly, boring. The mission of our newspaper is much more complicated than what we had in the 1980s, even though this may sound banal and cliché. Now, more than before, we are devoted to building the institutions of democracy, a free market, and peace with our neighbors through NATO and the European Union. These sound like simple goals, but if you go into each of them, they become very complicated."

"We got used to the luxuries of democracy very quickly," Helena continued. "It feels natural to have a free media, a parliament, and free elections every half a year. However, it's human nature to complain, and people do. After the free press started in Poland, people began to notice its faults. A similar reaction to the free market occurred as well. After years of empty shops, once the shops were full, people said it was too expensive compared to what people were earning so they complained again. They forgot how great it feels to have available goods to buy."

The post-1989 era had been very good to Helena. *Gazeta Wyborcza* had become Poland's paper of record, and when it went public in 1999 the London stock market appraised it at a value of US\$800 million, making Helena one of the wealthiest people in Poland. Under communism, she had had her freedom and little else, but she invested it in building publishing skills that produced incredible profits under the new market economy. She continued, however, to lead a modest life-style in her same apartment, which she now shared with Wanda Rapaczynska, the newspaper's publisher and a friend since high school. And she continued to work day and night.

"Working on the underground press, we devoted 80 percent of our time to hiding from the police and other such things that wasted our energies," Helena explained. "Now we can devote our time and energies to growth instead of draining ourselves. I am most proud of the media institution we created and the way we stuck together with no serious conflicts, which is one of the most important reasons why we are successful. And we have by far some of the best reportage in Europe."

Throughout the 1990s *Gazeta Wyborcza* was Poland's most popular mainstream forum for public debate on social issues. And so in 1999 it was the medium of choice for the unprecedented and lengthy debate on feminism and the debunking of the male myth of Solidarity that was triggered by Agnieszka's essay. Its placement in the June 20 Sunday Op-Ed section was comparable, in terms of prestige, to the front page of the "Week in Review" section of the Sunday *New York Times*. To their credit, the *Gazeta Wyborcza* editors recognized the need for a mainstream editorial debate on women and chose to give the explosive essay prominent coverage. It's doubtful, however, that they foresaw the consequences.

An avid reader of Western feminist theory, Agnieszka, who was educated in Poland, in the United States, and at Oxford, had noted a peculiar current running through Polish democracy—an outright aversion to and rejection of liberalism that was influenced by both Polish Catholicism and nationalism. There was a direct link, she felt, between the way the 1980 Gdańsk Accords located women's interests in the home and family (that is, the best solution to their problems was to strengthen their domestic role) and the 1989 Church-backed proposal to ban abortion.

When Agnieszka sat down to write her essay, she was already exceptionally well versed in the details of how her country's "male democracy" had failed to enfranchise women. After winning the antiabortion battle in 1993, each conservative parliament thereafter continued to vote down proposed laws that would safeguard women's rights. By 1999 Poland's violations of women's human rights could no longer be excused as random breaches of justice. Polish women's advocacy organizations and several international agencies had called attention to the systemic discrimination that was causing government policies and practices to be monitored by commissions of the United Nations, the European Commission, and the United States. The list of abuses was long and reflected threats to almost every aspect of women's political, economic, and civic rights.

For example, in 1999 women earned 30 percent less, on average, than men, although their level of education was higher. Employers in both the government and private sectors openly admitted that they were afraid to hire young women because they were likely to become pregnant and take maternity leave. Not only had it become harder for a Polish woman to find a job, but it was much easier for her to lose one. Sixty percent of the unemployed were women; they were the first to go in cases of group redundancies, based on the assumption that men would support them. The Government Plenipotentiary on Family Matters, the principal government agency created to represent women's interests, denied that these and other such statistics indicated gender discrimination.

Meanwhile, politicians continued to introduce privileges likely to further limit women's chances in the job market. Proposals to extend fully paid maternity leave and to maintain the five-year gap between men's and women's retirement ages (sixty-five and sixty, respectively) made hiring women increasingly unattractive financially. A public awareness campaign against domestic violence, which attracted Western media coverage in 1997, was suddenly discontinued because, according to government sources, it promoted divorces and undermined the authority of Polish husbands and fathers. Because Poland had one of the strictest abortion laws in Europe (limited to incidents of rape and incest, when the mother's health or life is threatened, or if there is damage to the fetus), women's access to contraception and prenatal testing was extremely restricted, particularly in rural areas. Without any public debate, antiabortion rhetoric had even entered the canons of Polish law when the word *fetus* was quietly replaced by *conceived child* in the penal code and when the bill on a children's ombudsman defined the child as "any human being from conception to the age of 18."

"We've had no success in changing the law, but we do manage to inform the international community about the reality," Wanda Nowicka, the persevering executive director of the Federation for Women and Family Planning, told me in February 1999. "They listen to women's organizations, and they know what we are talking about, whereas in Poland, the government simply ignores us." As Barbara Limanowska, director of OŚKA, a national women's information center, observed clear-sightedly to me in 1999, "Women's rights are not treated as important because women are not yet taken seriously as an electorate. Therefore, we don't count."

Polish feminists had filed their statistics and grievances with the European Commission, the UN Human Rights Committee, and the U.S. Department of State, hoping that international attention and reprimands would help to legitimize their work at home. Each of those entities issued a separate report in 1999 concluding that the Polish government had violated women's human rights, but conservative politicians turned up their noses at the reports, alleging that they imposed "foreign" ideologies such as feminism. "Today, the West should be learning from us how to treat women right," parliamentarian Urszula Wachowska huffed[2] as she joined other conservatives in sending an official "hands off" message to the international community. The message was simple: Poland is special. Its long tradition of chivalry and hand kissing, the cult of the Virgin Mary, the myth of the patriotic Polish mother make it immune to international conventions that safeguard women's human rights. "As for the European recommendations . . . we respect them . . . but they are not an order," stated parliamentarian Tadeusz Czymanski.[3]

By 1999 Church-backed conservatives seemed unbeatable. Liberal-minded parliamentarians from the SLD and Freedom Union (formerly the Democratic Union) failed to establish serious discussions because conservative parties such as the Solidarity Action Party (AWS), the political offspring of Solidarity the trade union movement, dominated the debates on the floor of Parliament. For example, during the March 1999 discussion of the draft bill on the equal status of women and men, the tone was set by proclamations such as this one by AWS parliamentarian Ewa Sikorska-Trela.

> Mr. Speaker! Ladies and gentlemen, Honorable Members! Women have always been and are still treated well in Poland. They have been given all due respect and honorable titles have been bestowed upon them. They have always had every opportunity to seek professional, academic and political careers. They

can fulfill their destinies in many places and on many levels. We are proudly referred to as "The Polish Mothers" to emphasize the significance of our role in sustaining the Polish family and the nation itself. . . . God has created man and woman and He designated different roles for each. We should not improve upon the decrees of our Lord. . . . We cannot demand rights, which are already determined as part of natural law. Every person is born free and equal, so we must not ask for more equality to be legislated. Equality is just *there.*[4]

It was the television broadcast of this particular political circus that triggered her treatise on "why Poland makes a national pastime out of mocking feminism," Agnieszka told me in an interview after its publication. "The essay wrote itself. It was very personal, the first I felt I really had to write."

"Let's not have any illusion that Polish patriarchy is making a transition to democracy," Agnieszka wrote.

It is young and robust, with its claws dug deep into the floor of the parliament, or maybe into the soil beneath the parliament. It talks from a position of strength—to the extent that it can afford silliness and plain old stupidity, garrulity and vainglorious pontificating, pretending in-your-face that it just doesn't know who you're talking about. Indeed, what have we heard from the parliamentary opponents of the equal rights bill?

Discrimination, which should more aptly be called "natural difference between the genders," has always existed, it's with us now and will remain so. And that's a good thing. This is what our young Polish democracy is all about. When communists ruled, women were driving tractors and had abortions, but now the situation has returned to normal. Poland is on its own, Polish males are virile, and Polish women are feminine again.[5]

From her arguments on the government's absurd defenses of gender discrimination, Agnieszka turned her incisive pen to the ways in which the rise of a male-dominated democracy formed a reaction to the distortion of gender roles and the breakdown of "normal" social life and family that occurred under communism.

The era of the so-called "real socialism," often described as an "interruption" in the life of Polish society, was felt to be a time of humiliation and domestication of the Polish male, tantamount to his symbolic castration. . . . As our national mythology has it, long ago, we used to be brave, chivalrous warriors, fathers of families, in a word, True Males. The communist party (the witch! the bitch! the wench!) sent this male into internal exile, turning the true male into a hen-pecked backyard gardener or do-it-yourselfer. . . . Yes, the new man had an opportunity for political activity, but that only meant servility, careerism, conformism, ultimate debasement. And the woman? The national mythology says: Under communism, the Woman was fighting for survival. That's why shopping was referred to as "hunting" for goods, although it remained a woman's chore. The story indicated that real socialism was an abnormal world, a world turned upside down, in which it's the women who did the hunting. . . . In a society so deeply patriarchal, the story about the reversal of gender roles is the clearest metaphor for chaos. . . . The myth became permanent in our collective imagination as if it were obvious truth.[6]

And then Agnieszka turned her attention to the Solidarity myth of a male revolution, a mutual interest of ours, though we had not yet communicated at that time. "If communism emasculated the Polish male, Solidarity empowered him to become virile again. O yeah, Solidarity, that was Manly Talk, Manly Business." But the men could not have had their conversations without the movement's women, Agnieszka pointed out. At that point she drew upon my own research, citing my 1995 article in the Kraków feminist journal *Pełnym Głosem*.[7] "Penn's . . . article was shocking, yet Poland's national press was completely silent about it. . . . Women did plenty of things in the Solidarity movement. It was not a coincidence, though, that the female leaders of the Solidarity underground whom Shana Penn interviewed kept insisting that their function was purely supportive, that even if they temporarily served as leaders . . . they were ready to enter their contribution into a scenario in which struggle was only what men do."[8]

Agnieszka knew she would infuriate some of her readers when she challenged Solidarity's legacy.

Even though I may sound unconvincing if not outright iconoclastic, I propose that the great upheaval that was Solidarity, on the symbolic level, was an act of restoring the patriarchal order that had been disturbed by the totalitarian system. . . . Poland's new freedom was tantamount to liberating men from their domestic exile, at the same time relegating women to "their place."

No matter what really happened, Solidarity was, symbolically and in our collective memory, a great male rite of passage. The fact that its history began with Anna Walentynowicz has been virtually deleted from the movement's mythology; it remained somewhere in the background, as an anecdote, a sort of apocrypha.

It has been accepted that the moment in which the mustachioed Lech Wałęsa, acting in a manly manner, jumped over the fence to enter the Gdańsk Shipyard was the proper beginning of Solidarity history. The Mother of God in his lapel—the Black Madonna, Queen of Poland, that femininity rendered unreal and disembodied—constitutes the revolution's holy blessing, its path toward the *sacrum*. At the same time, the "Wałęsa moment" is a reminder that in order for the ritual to become complete, real womanhood must be completely pushed out from the mythology of the Solidarity movement.[9]

Not simply an appeal to the nation to confront its sexist treatment of women, Agnieszka's document was framed as a high-level feminist conversation with Polish society. It also included a valuable critique of feminist strategy, particularly as it related to the EU, which Poland hoped to join in the near future. The Polish feminist movement, she wrote, "has been much too centered on the government's negotiations with the EU and not enough on building a popular base of feminist support." The most frequently quoted part of this argument contends that Poles "are mistaken if we think the European Union will solve our discrimination issues. I fear that the EU is willing to accept gender discrimination as the cultural specificity of Poland, and that they will say in response: 'The French have their cheeses, the British have their queen, and the Poles have their discrimination against women.' And so, we have to deal with the sexism ourselves inside Poland and not depend on outsiders. The

EU negotiations are mainly on economic issues, and in the end, the bottom line is not gender; it simply is not important enough."[10]

Agnieszka tested a draft of the essay at the academic conference where she had been expected to speak on U.S. feminism. Attendees gave her a standing ovation. Friends encouraged her to publish the paper in *Gazeta Wyborcza,* where it was sure to be "truly explosive," as one friend remarked. Agnieszka, however, was dubious. "I thought *Gazeta* would reject the essay because it was too radical, too academic. In part, I feared going public with my viewpoints."

The Sunday after the article first appeared, *Gazeta Wyborcza* printed two attacks on Agnieszka's analysis of Solidarity as a great male rite of passage. In addition, her praise of my study led Solidarity women who felt that Agnieszka had attacked them personally to submit harsh and unfair rebukes, which were published in subsequent weekend editions. One of the writers accused Agnieszka of being "ideological," which is a code word for "communist" and one of the nastier epithets in postcommunist Poland. Former underground editor Joanna Szczęsna penned a furious response, which frankly surprised me. Joanna's editorial set off an ongoing—and, I think, artificial—controversy between "the feminists" and "the Solidarity oppositionists," which I discuss in detail subsequently.

Throughout the summer of 1999 the assaults against Agnieszka were met with a flurry of letters and opinion pieces in her defense and in defense of feminism. These carefully crafted essays appeared in *Gazeta Wyborcza* and other national publications, and they outnumbered the antifeminist arguments submitted for print. Even though several pieces from the feminist camp were rejected (they later appeared in the Kraków feminist journal *Zadra*), the *Gazeta Wyborcza* readership was treated to an unprecedented flow of discourse that read like an introductory course on gender studies.

By mid-July, the debate had become so compelling and exhilarating that I flew to Poland to investigate its impact. I also planned to meet with those Solidarity protagonists who, like Joanna Szczęsna, had apparently misunderstood points I had made that were based on my early interviews with them.

When I arrived in Warsaw, it was immediately clear that "woman" had become a subject of national debate and new and exciting questions were being asked. Had Solidarity women been excluded from the historical record? Was the democratic opposition sexist? Could a foreigner's analysis be trusted? Are women's rights being violated today? Does Poland need feminism? Several original players in Solidarity weighed in with their interpretations and reinterpretations of what had happened during the time of the country's opposition to communism. Others, differently placed in relation to the democratic opposition, presented divergent viewpoints that dared to deconstruct the society's historical treatment of women. Both sides fed the unanticipated national dialogue.

The debate appealed to some people and incensed others, and it certainly caused greater fury than Agnieszka had intended. Some praised her as a courageous truth teller: "Solidarity turned away from women, and this is a fact," Maria Janion wrote in a *Gazeta Wyborcza* editorial. "Agnieszka Graff was brave to have said it. . . . It is sad that people who dare to say this out loud are being stigmatized as ideological."[11] Novelist Izabela Filipiak, writing in *Gazeta Wyborcza* in late July, addressed the "importance of passing along the heritage—cultural and political—[of the Solidarity women's model] from mothers to daughters." Otherwise, Izabela emphasized, "women cannot progress without knowing our history."[12]

However, like Joanna, several other Solidarity women—Helena Łucyzwo, Anna Dodziuk, and Magdalena X among them—were not pleased. They objected to having had their activist roles discussed in public by a person with whom they were not acquainted, and some were not interested in serving as inspirational sources for younger women. They did not want to claim heroine status, and those who had edited *Tygodnik Mazowsze* certainly didn't want their all-female team to be cast as a cadre of feminist heroines, and Joanna said so in print. Several women, including Joanna, Anna, and Magdalena, even rejected invitations to meet with women's groups in person to try to resolve the conflicts that surfaced as the national debate progressed. In addition, because she had quoted passages from my article, Agnieszka was charged with having been misguided by a foreigner.

Małgorzata Fuszara, whose gender studies courses at Warsaw University are a breeding ground for feminists, told me why she felt the debate had proven to be so powerful. "Younger generations of Polish men and women were not involved in anticommunist opposition history. In Poland, generations coexist as if belonging to two worlds, two systems. Our youth barely know the recent past, which culminated in the Solidarity revolution of 1989. Thus, the important but overlooked role of Solidarity women was revelatory for many. It is precisely this history which has dramatically reoriented the entire society."

"It mattered the way I hoped it would matter," Agnieszka said with measured pride when I asked her to characterize the impact of her manifesto.

In addition to the ongoing media debate, Polish feminists experienced a second watershed moment in the summer of 1999, a moment that both supported and expanded upon the debate. That July the UN Human Rights Committee had released its report citing gender discrimination as one of the most serious forms of human rights abuse in Poland. When the government failed to translate that English-language document into Polish for public consumption, the Federation for Women and Family Planning, under executive director Wanda Nowicka, made the Polish translation and distributed it to the media, the ministries, and the nongovernmental organization (NGO) community. Shortly thereafter, the document's conclusions were reported in the national mainstream press, and for the first time, according to Wanda, who had cooperated with the UN committee, "Polish society absorbed the message that 'women's rights are human rights.'" This made it possible for women's NGOs to build an unparalleled coalition with the Helsinki Committee, Poland's leading human rights organization, and to garner continued press coverage in *Gazeta Wyborcza* and elsewhere.

"*Gazeta Wyborcza* was the first major publication, but not the only one, to realize that women's issues sell newspapers," remarked Izabela Filipiak. Liberal newspapers had to begin to take note of recurring legal and political violations of women's rights, especially during the wave of international attention. And according to the women I interviewed, there was plenty of disconcerting news to report. In 1999 alone, Polish women suffered several major legal and political setbacks: the passage of a discriminatory retirement law, the parliamentary defeat of draft legislation to establish a commission on gender equality, and the suspension of sentence for the rapist of a fourteen-year-old girl.

Gazeta Wyborcza's coverage of feminist issues appeared in editorials, news sections, and the special weekend women's magazine *High Heels,* which Helena had started in April 1999 to compete with the monthly fashion magazines. Although *High Heels* generally focused on fashion and cosmetics, once the media debate on gender took off, its editors increased the number of features by or about leading Polish women. Controversial columnist Kinga Dunin appeared bimonthly in *High Heels,* questioning everything from marriage, labor discrimination, contraception, and pension plans to the magazine's compromising name. And the "letters to the editor" pages provided ordinary women with an opportunity to publish their ideas and feelings about feminism, women's social position, their bodies, and personal life experiences.

Public space was opening up to women and their interests, and soon a cornucopia of articles, columns, editorials, roundtable discussions, and interviews with and profiles of feminists began to appear in a variety of venues, including the national dailies, the elite cultural review *Res Public Nowy,* the feminist quarterly *Zadra,* and Polish editions of *Marie Claire* and *Cosmopolitan.* I recall being both impressed by and envious of the extent of this coverage because there has never been a comparable phenomenon in the United States—for example, a thirteen-week-long discussion of women's issues in the *New York Times.*

Polish feminists such as Agnieszka Graff, Małgorzata Fuszara, Izabela Filipiak, Wanda Nowicka, and cabinet member Barbara Labuda found that they had a whole new set of publishing options in which to present tactical appeals to women nationwide, and they learned to make use of the media in innovative, influential, and playful ways. Arguments appeared in print between feminists and Solidarity women, neocommunist women, right-wing politicians, and organized Catholic women. There was even an exchange between Wanda Nowicka and Cardinal Józef Glemp, although he was apparently unconvinced, as Church leaders continued their verbal assault on individual feminists and their issues.

Poland's feminists took pains to figure out how best to make themselves heard and understood. The women's movement was, and is, made up of activists and academics, and several women stressed to me that both are equally important in a country where gender studies scholarship and civic activism are relatively new, postcommunist phenomena. It is also a society that holds its intellectuals in high esteem and revels in the written word, which is why feminists created an intellectual circle of academics and activists who met regularly to refine their critique of Polish democracy. They met in seminars, at conferences, and informally each month at OŚKA's office in Warsaw, and many of the articles that flooded the editorial desks at *Gazeta Wyborcza* and other media had already passed through numerous drafts and critical reviews at such gatherings.

"This matters," OŚKA director Barbara Limanowska pointed out, "especially because people who publish on the antifeminist side make weak arguments, mixing judgments with emotions and lacking sound evidence." The fact that the feminists' arguments were seamless and exciting also helped capture and hold readers' attention. As Barbara Limanowska saw it, two main obstacles had traditionally blocked public interest in gender issues. "One is the lack of information and concrete facts; the second is the absence of a language in which to talk about gender." As an information clearinghouse, OŚKA aims to overcome both problems by producing fact sheets, press releases, and reports for public, media, and government consumption. With the information and facts available, the needed language can develop.

It also helped that the feminists scored a major coup early on in the debate when Maria Janion published on their side. The "Simone de Beauvoir of Poland" silenced Agnieszka's critics with a brilliant analysis of the Polish roots of "male democracy" in which she wrote: "Solidarity turned away from women, making them understand clearly that they are not welcome in places where there are no longer national fires to extinguish, but where there is now money, privilege and power."[13] Spoken by Janion, such ideas could no longer be ignored.

When I asked several editors and reporters why *Gazeta Wyborcza* had decided to publish Agnieszka Graff's article, I realized that Barbara Limanowska's reasoning had been particularly sound. The article was smart and literary, they said, well argued, a representative voice of a younger, more liberal generation. Deputy editor Piotr Pacewicz said it was among the very few pieces to appear on his desk that clearly argued the ways women are discriminated against. The editors also felt that the time was ripe, that their readers were ready to listen. "It is important to be radical," Pacewicz said. "I understand that feminists must be radical because the exponents of a rising ideology and new values have to be radical, because that is their strength. But when you are too radical, you lose your arguments because people stop listening to you, because it is always one argument, and life is a little more complicated. The world is like it is; we can improve it. But when you are too radical, a general public cannot understand you."

Piotr Staśinski, who edits *Gazeta Wyborcza*'s "Opinie," or Op-Ed, section, made the final decision to publish Agnieszka's article. He said he went with it because it opened his eyes for the first time to the possibility that Solidarity had in fact been a paternalistic movement, and he had never thought about that point before. Unfortunately, he also told me, the debate didn't get very far. To his mind, it became repetitive, and the articles by Maria Janion and Kinga Dunin didn't excite him. I replied that the debate had unfolded like an introductory course on gender studies for the general population and that great worth could be found in that alone. He accepted my notion but was neither deeply convinced nor forthcoming about why.

Staśinski was wrong to think the journalistic debate failed to create a broad perspective on women's situation. It is evident from the opinion polls subsequently published in *Gazeta Wyborcza* and elsewhere that the readership absorbed, and in many cases internalized, two fundamental messages: first, that gender discrimination exists in Poland whether or not you call yourself a feminist, and second, as Wanda Nowicka had highlighted, that women's rights are human rights. But in addition to successfully creating a positive perspective within the general population, the debates also set off a storm of unanticipated controversy between two select groups of powerful women.

In the autumn of 1999 Agnieszka told me she had envisioned that her article would result in a hearty discussion where people would present their arguments and "agree to disagree." She and I were both concerned that instead the summerlong debate had triggered needless controversy because it arbitrarily divided women who held many values in common into two groups—those who identified first as feminists and those who identified first as Solidarity oppositionists—and pitted them against one another. But the split was not black and white, and in their essays and editorials, some of the Solidarity women expressed feminist views, while some of the feminists described their experiences as Solidarity members. This may have contributed to the breakdown in communications that lasted well into 2002.

The commotion in question was perhaps first set off by Joanna Szczęsna's editorial, which appeared in *Gazeta Wyborcza* shortly after Agnieszka's article first came out. "I don't like the fact that I am called to the blackboard by Graff . . . to serve as an illustration of the thesis that Polish history was falsified by men," Joanna stormed. She continued,

> I . . . am grateful that there is not yet in our country a habit of reading feminist literature. . . . I remember that fragment of my conversation with Shana Penn that was transformed into the strange pretension that the "Central Committee overlooked women." While describing the realities of oppositionist activity, I recounted how gender stereotypes functioned in society, and therefore in the Security Service as well, and how these attitudes had been helpful for us. One has to come from a country that has, fortunately, never needed to know anything about conspiracy in order to turn this ideologically innocent description into an accusation of discrimination. . . . Dear feminist colleagues—And what if one were to rub one's eyes and look at the thing from the perspective of, for instance, a social movement,

where one doesn't work for oneself but for the team, plays different more or less prestigious roles and is still happy that even though there are leaders, there are no bosses. . . . It doesn't mean that I failed to notice the discrimination of women in PRL [communist Poland], nor does it mean that I tried to idealize relations between genders in the opposition movement. . . . However I considered feminism a needless luxury in those days, when I preferred to get involved in activities against the use of physical violence by the police rather than in a struggle for the equal distribution of policeman's blows. . . . It happened that once in my life I had to put out lots of fires, but please believe me, it was not because of gender discrimination that I didn't become a fireperson. I didn't become one because I didn't want to be one.[14]

There can be a great distance between lived experience and the observation of that experience. At times, the distance is unbridgeable. The research that I had published in Poland, and to which Agnieszka's article made reference, clearly did not resonate with some of my interviewees' sense of themselves and their experiences. How one feels when inside an experience can reasonably differ from how one recounts it; and how that recounting is heard or studied by someone on the outside can further distance the actor from her act. For example, based on their stories, I regard some of the Solidarity women as heroines, though they did not view themselves as such. But while attributing heroism did not feel accurate to some, others agreed with my assessment. These differences lay at the heart of the communication breakdown that played itself out in the pages of *Gazeta Wyborcza*.

I made an effort to help bridge those differences and began by submitting an Op-Ed to *Gazeta Wyborcza* called "Heroes and Heroines." It became part of the summer's media debate on July 10, 1999.

I am honored to have my work discussed in Poland, where the experiences I recorded took place, and where I had hoped my research on women's contributions to Solidarity would find both its deepest resonance and dissonance. . . . The experiences of those women and men who played crucial roles in building Solidarity are radically different from American social change experience. It takes time—has taken me time—to penetrate Polish culture and absorb its inherent meanings for the people who both shaped and were transformed by political resistance to authoritarian rule. . . .

As I studied the underground and listened to women's stories, my own preconceptions shifted. Originally, I wondered why most women did not draw attention to gender dynamics in the opposition, or why others spoke to me about sex discrimination within the ranks but did not and would not make the subject a point of contention with their colleagues. I sought answers, and the ones I found altered my perspective. As Joanna Szczęsna points out in her recent article, feminism is a luxury within an authoritarian context. However, there is more to say.

I think that the loyalties people forged, along with the stigmatization that a whole generation of young men and women experienced for their involvement in the '68 student demonstrations, had rendered awareness of gender inequalities insignificant when compared to other, more imminent human rights violations. I think this occurred, not only because people thought in the black-and-white terms of "us versus them" (the people versus the state), but because men and women from the '60s generation had suffered similarly the loss of the rights and privileges that were associated with normal life. . . . Although I think an argument can always be made to rationalize why gender awareness is not urgent, given the fact that such thinking had not permeated the opposition milieu, I respect this. I also respect the invaluable contributions that women made to build and sustain a collective vision of a democratic future.

Sadly, the history of Solidarity remains under-analyzed. To ensure the integrity of the historical record, a fuller examination demands attention from within Poland, which is only appropriate. . . . Joanna Szczęsna is right to question why Agnieszka Graff only relies on my work and has not sought out the Solidarity women who are still a "live source of information." I am disappointed that Szczęsna, who read a draft of my manuscript, never directly challenged my ideas as did others, which would have helped me advance my thinking. I invite such dialogue, even today.

Now that Poland is building a democracy, does this mean that feminism's time has arrived? No more a luxury (no more excuses!), but a valid mode of inquiry that has never aimed to explain the whole world, but does raise important questions about how women and men, and feminine and masculine, are socially constructed.[15]

Though the three-month debate may have been disruptive, it stimulated the Solidarity heroines and me, and through my concerted outreach efforts it got us reading and discussing my manuscript together. Our goal was to find a mutual understanding of my representation of their recollections against their experience and to discuss how I had understood the memories I had recorded. The purpose was not to alter the text but to broaden our understanding of the text, and the exchanges went on for over a year, from 2000 into 2001. In the end, one might say we agreed to disagree and did so respectfully.

The summer 1999 debate was followed in the fall by public discussions at the Federation for Women and Family Planning and at OŚKA. I presented my research at one of the OŚKA discussions and was delighted when, afterward, writer Izabela Filipiak announced her plan to begin a Memory Project and invited students to record women's experiences in Solidarity. Her aim was to develop the research topic that I had initiated and thus encourage Polish studies of the subject. Inspired to participate in the Memory Project, one of Izabela's students, Ewa Kondratowicz, later interviewed around a dozen Solidarity women, and the collected interviews appeared as *Szminka na sztandarze* (Lipstick on the Banner), published in 2001.[16] It was extremely gratifying that the "fuller examination . . . from within Poland" that I had called for in my editorial had been launched so quickly. I felt that it was one of the more positive outcomes of the 1999 debate.

On the negative side, in addition to creating a split between "feminists" and "Solidarity women," the debate also exposed a division among liberals at a time when an ultraconservative parliament was in power. While internal conflicts can potentially weaken political options, the former Solidarity activists and feminists did not necessarily view themselves as having aired an *internal* conflict because they had never formally identified as belonging to the same camp, even though most of them supported the Freedom Union in 1999. The media debate accentuated the differences between them at a time when political foresight might have motivated them to band together. Two years later, they witnessed the dramatic defeat of the only real liberal party, the Freedom Union, in the Sejm elections and felt profound remorse. The September 2001 election results produced a gaping void in liberal leadership and challenged Poles to rethink their priorities and possibilities and to consider forging new alliances among like-minded individuals and groups in politics, the media, and social change movements—including the feminists among them.

By January 2002 it seemed possible that the conflict laid open in 1999 was gradually being laid to rest. New publications and discussions were informing the general public that women had indeed played vital roles in the democratic opposition. For example, Władysław Frasyniuk told the *OŚKA Biuletyn* in a September 2001 interview: "Women were active in political issues in the PRL times. It's a phenomenon that has not yet been described. Women constituted the organizational core of the opposition. They were active in the most important spots—for instance, Helena Łuczywo was the boss of *Tygodnik Mazowsze,* and Barbara Labuda wielded an important function in Wrocław, just as Ewa Kulik did in Warsaw."[17]

Throughout that January, a new flurry of exchanges in *Gazeta Wyborcza* regarding the restrictive abortion law brought Solidarity women and feminists together in unanticipated ways. First, Izabela Jaruga-Nowacka, the government's plenipotentiary for the equal status of men and women, raised the issue of possibly reforming the abortion law. Her comments were immediately countered by Bishop Tadeusz Pieronek, press secretary for the Catholic Church. To paraphrase, the bishop asserted that the only reason to revisit the abortion law would be to change it into a total ban. Ignore the feminists, Pieronek urged readers, because "feminists, as rigid as communists, do not even dissolve when treated with hydrochloric acid."[18]

OŚKA immediately protested the bishop's abusive language in a letter to *Gazeta Wyborcza*. This, in turn, unleashed writer Dominika Wielowieyska, whose feminist-bashing contribution to the growing turmoil can be summarized as follows: The bishop is famous for his wit, which everyone knows, except for feminists, who are dogmatic, intolerant, and have no sense of humor.

The public display of mudslinging needed to be stopped. In a "Page Two" commentary, Helena, who rarely contributed her own editorials, commended Minister Jaruga-Nowacka for having informed the public of the need to reform the abortion law. Her "stance and her utterances are perfectly fitting within the framework of a normal democratic debate, which is welcome in every country. Furthermore, I do not think that her standpoint should be defined as a cement-like feminism, which won't alter even if treated with hydrochloric acid. Apparently, it was a joke made by Tadeusz Pieronek, the bishop renowned for his sharp sense of humor. It seems to me that it wasn't one of his funniest."[19]

Helena also praised OŚKA as "the organization known for years now for its useful activity in support of unemployed women and of equal status for men and women, as well as against violence at home. OŚKA got trapped in the hydrochloric acid metaphor." Helena went on to point out, "However, it is no wonder that Polish feminists behave defensively at times. Too often they hear of being dogmatic and intolerant, now even from *Gazeta Wyborcza*. The fact is that Polish feminists are often right and often they are the only ones with courage. That's why I put forward a cheerful appeal: more feminism, less hydrochloric acid."[20]

Over that weekend and continuing into the next week, Polish friends sent me email messages about Helena's statement. Some expressed surprise, others delight that she had defended OŚKA. People also appreciated that she had condemned the use of violent language in a public forum. Certainly she had not spent all those years living under siege in order to have to tolerate the manipulation of the media by representatives of the post-1989 Church and Parliament, among others. But most interesting to all was the fact that her commentary marked the first time she had openly supported feminism. In celebration, the Kraków feminist group eFKa quickly printed T-shirts reading, "More feminism, less hydrochloric acid!"

On December 13, 2002, Poland and nine other candidate countries were invited to join the EU. The date, of course, was laden with historical significance for the Poles. The invitation was a signal victory for the governing SLD, which had steered the EU accession negotiations. In the name of "One Europe," the postcommunist SLD had even managed to win over some of its pre-1989 adversaries—among them Adam Michnik and Catholic primate Józef Glemp. The SLD recognized that the prospect of Europeanization could inspire the Polish imagination in ways that the Internationale never could.

The new political theater revolved around Prime Minister Leszek Miller, mastermind of the EU negotiations and former Politburo member. Miller performed a notorious role in imposing martial law in 1981 and continued to insist, without apology, that the coup had saved Poland from Soviet intervention. His "lesser of two evils" perspective has been grudgingly acknowledged, in retrospect, by many Poles who forgave Miller his past transgressions. After winning the 2001 parliamentary elections by an unexpectedly narrow margin, the SLD had lost confidence in its ability to capture a majority "yes" vote on the EU referendum scheduled for June 2003. In contrast to its postcommunist counterparts elsewhere in the former Soviet Bloc, the SLD adopted an astonishing formula for success—abandon ideology. Religion was no longer the opiate of the people; the party could drop its traditional anticlerical stance in order to court the Polish Catholic Church's help in rallying the "Euroskeptics"—that is, the mostly churchgoing farmers and peasants who justifiably feared that EU membership would cost them their livelihoods.

The Church, in turn, welcomed the opportunity to carry out the Vatican's affirmation of EU integration as a means to Christianize the continent. Well, why not? shrugged Prime Minister Miller. "God is already present in Europe." Eventually, Glemp and his bishops even went so far as to appeal to the SLD to insert language about God and Christianity into the EU constitution.

But when Poles had voted the SLD into power in 2001, they also were voting the Church-backed Solidarity party out of power, so why Miller's party now believe it needed the support of an institution that promised to "bring Polish values to Europe" was not an easily answered question. Protection of "unborn life" and woman's "maternal dignity" were the bargaining chips on the table when the Church and the postcommunists struck their deal. Even though the SLD had vowed, when seeking women's votes in the 2001 election, to liberalize the country's severely restrictive abortion law, in 2002 Miller promised church leaders that, in exchange for their support, all talk of such liberalization would be shelved. This secret agreement also included a freeze on discussion of other social issues, including sexual abuse within the Church.

Recognizing that secrets are hazardous to the health of an open society, feminists became Poland's courageous code breakers. On International Women's Day in March 2002, they deftly "outed" the collusion between church and state in a petition to the EU Parliament that was signed by one hundred prominent Polish women, including Wisława Szymborska, recipient of the Nobel Prize in Literature, and film director Agnieszka Holland. The DGO were conspicuous in their absence, though other important, former oppositionists such as author Anka Grupińska, and Irena Grudzińska-Gross were listed. Helena Łuczywo regretted that, as she saw it, her role in the media precluded her signing the petition, which asserted: "Women's rights are being bought and sold behind the scenes of Poland's integration into the EU. The church will support EU integration in return for the government closing the debate on the reform of the anti-abortion law." For most of the prominent women who signed, this marked the first time that they publicly supported a feminist issue and joined forces with feminist groups.

Even the media had colluded in silencing the public debate, Agnieszka Graff, one of the petition's organizers, told me. She recalled being harangued by a well-known television journalist to whom she had submitted the petition. He yelled at her, "Are you mad? Do you want us to lose our chance of getting into Europe? There couldn't be a worse moment than now to bring up abortion. I have a kid, I want him to be a European. You are completely irresponsible."

Opinion polls at the time showed that over half the population opposed the antichoice law, so why did the postcommunists and even the liberals buckle under religious pressure? Agnieszka attributed it to the "postcommunists' exaggerated view of the power of the Catholic Church." As she saw it, "First of all, the postcommunists don't really grasp the peculiarity of Polish Catholicism because they are not part of it. Most of them were raised outside of Church influence. Second, it does not cost the SLD anything to be 'careful' with the Church, since they never intended to risk such conflict. The cost of their cowardice is paid only by women—five hundred dollars per illegal abortion multiplied by an estimated one hundred thousand illegal abortions annually. The ban on abortion has humiliated thousands of women, turning them into outlaws, forcing them to seek help illegally. But women's needs don't count politically in Poland since there is no gender gap in voting like you have in the U.S."

Barbara Labuda's "gratitude syndrome" also played a role, however. Many Polish politicians and citizens felt a profound sense of obligation to the Catholic Church for its heroic, prodemocracy activism under the former authoritarian regime. This has given the Church an incredible political advantage to tilt Poland's social and moral compass toward Rome more than Brussels. In so doing, the Church no longer represents a liberating force; instead it coerces the country into compromising democracy.

The exposed secret pact became ever more transparent after the negotiating team returned home from the EU summit in mid-December 2002. On December 16, SLD secretary-general Marek Dyduch broke ranks with the president and prime minister to announce: "We are not giving up our campaign promises regarding the right to abortion. We are talking about this today because we do not want the Catholic Church to feel deceived, since it supports our efforts to join the EU. However, after the referendum, we will begin to liberalize the anti-abortion law, which we know is unacceptable to the Catholic Church."[21]

Was the secretary-general as "mad" as the feminists? President Kwasniewski and Prime Minister Miller instantly refuted his "deeply unfortunate" remarks, underscoring that reform of the abortion law should not be connected with the referendum on EU accession. The two issues should indeed remain separate, responded reproductive rights advocate Wanda Nowicka, but her reasons differed from the administration's. "We don't want to wait until after the referendum to press for reform of a law that jeopardizes the lives of women and children," she told me. "The law's tenth anniversary is this January [2003]. Ten years is long enough."

Moreover, added Małgorzata Tarasiewicz, who coordinated a nonprofit sector program monitoring Poland's implementation of EU gender equity laws, the EU's "laws and regulations mainly focus on economic issues. There is no binding law on abortion, although the EU Parliament passed a resolution last July urging member states and candidate countries to legalize abortion," she told me in an interview. "Polish women can expect the adoption of EU safeguards against employment discrimination and sexual harassment, but abortion remains a national problem that, for now, we have to resolve ourselves."

President Kwasniewski issued a rebuttal, saying that the national problem was actually demographic. "Poland's birthrate is terribly low. This is the issue that requires serious consideration." This claim shocked the feminists on two counts. For one, the birthrate had not increased at all in the ten years that the prohibitive abortion law had been in effect. Low birthrates comprised an ongoing concern across Europe, but most countries had not restricted abortion in response, which would put a punitive tax on women's lives. Nor could feminists understand why a postcommunist president was using the pronatalist rhetoric of a rightwing ultranationalist. Feminist groups appealed to him in a press release, stating, "The need to change the abortion law has been noticed by the most important international institutions such as the UN Committee for Human Rights (1999), the UN Committee for Economic, Social and Cultural Rights (1998 and 2002), and the European Parliament (2002). It is hard for us to understand why that which is visible from afar eludes the attention of our head of state." Well versed in both national dynamics and international human rights conventions, the feminists possessed a clearsighted view of democracy and understood the benefits of joining the EU.

The SLD should have kept its promise to women, but instead it faced the costly outcome of having struck a devil's bargain with the Church, for in reaction to the president's and prime minister's statements denouncing the secretary-general, enraged Church leaders demanded that they put their antiabortion comments in writing. Then the Polish delegate to the Commission of the Bishops' Conferences of the European Community (COMECE) called for the EU Parliament to add to the Accession Treaty a special ad hoc protocol that would prohibit reform of the abortion law. Additionally, he forewarned that the subject would be of top priority at the next meeting of the Mutual Commission of the Polish Episcopate and the Government. In the old communist era, the Church had been forced to negotiate with the government, but now it played its hand openly. Up against an inflexible institution and its ultimatums, the SLD had backed itself into a corner.

Feminists were among the first to realize that the Church was not the "collective hero unblemished by compromise or weakness," to quote journalist Jarosław Anders, that most Poles believed it to be. As a national myth, the Church is equally, if not more, revered than Solidarity, and few but feminists stood up to it early on. Now, however, many more people appear to be becoming disillusioned with the Church. As Anders wrote in *Foreign Policy* in the summer of 2003, "[T]here has been a visible anti-clerical reaction, with griping about the church's political meddling and a rapid secularization of a large part of Polish society, especially among the young. Witness the recent polls showing that 52 percent of Poles with college degrees believe the Church has too much influence on Polish life. Poles may still be a religious people, but fewer of them define their religiosity according to Catholic dogma and church attendance. . . . The Church is rapidly squandering its moral authority. . . . An open vigorous debate on the Church's political legacy in Poland is overdue."[22]

The rest of Polish society may now be ready to join in the public conversations started by women in 1989. Since then, it has continued to be the case that women's consciousness changes but the laws do not. When women were polled in 1989 and 1990, the majority indicated a desire to stop working, to leave the labor force, and to return to run their households and families. But an opinion poll taken in the spring of 2003 reveals that a decisive majority of Polish women express satisfaction with their professional work and that almost 60 percent declare that they would never give up their job, even if their husbands were making enough money to support them. Over 70 percent of the women polled said that professional work carries more social prestige than does sacrifice for home and family. More than half the poll respondents preferred the partnership model of marriage and family life.

Given these figures, one might ask, with journalists Joanna Pogórska and Justyna Kapecka, "Is Matka Polka still alive?" Writing in May 2003 in the weekly newsmagazine *Polityka* (a former communist publication that today is comparable to *Newsweek*), the journalists responded,

In these times of freedom, the Matka Polka stereotype is limited to procreation and domesticity. For some politicians, Polishness means at least four children per family. Even though Matka Polka is slowly disappearing, its existence still reinforces the assumption that femininity is defined by maternity. Recently, young readers of [the fashion magazine] *Twoj Styl* were discussing the stereotype in an Internet chat. The discussion most of the time led to one question—to have or not to have children? Some of the readers were willing to give up their careers for children; others in reverse; and others were trying to combine both. But all of them were stressing that they want to have a choice. The stereotype of Matka Polka is an image that is put right into their faces by the priests, by their neighbors (the nosy female neighbor plays an important role in Polish society), and their aunts when they postpone their decisions of maternity. When the discussion led to a more detailed definition of Matka Polka, they contributed the following features: faithfulness to the church, obedience to a husband, devotion to household chores, as well as handiness connected to permanent tiredness. Women always knew how to do things but always were so tired because they had to do so many things all the time.[23]

Also addressed in the Internet chat, Pogórska wrote, were aspects of sexuality and desire. Polish women are taught that sex and desire are animal emotions that Matka Polka denies for herself— or, rather, she rises above them. To support her points Pogórska quotes from "The End of Matka Polka's Career?"—an article by writer Anna Witkowska. "The marriage bed serves procreation and not her recreation. Matka Polka closes her eyes and does it only for the homeland. It is not in the style of Matka Polka to do purely hedonistic things. Even her pastimes are usually active. Community gardening, gathering raspberries for juice for kids, shopping." At the end, Pogórska and Kapecka add, "How many of us know how to darn or cook edible *flatchke*? This is not the most important but one of the unquestionable reasons for us to give up the ethos of Matka Polka and become who we are—the daughters of Matka Polka, *Córki Matka*. We are not domesticated but we are her daughters." The journalists explain, "Matka Polka wrote a beautiful page in Polish history. She is one of the icons of the fight for independence. But in normal times she doesn't work. Her authority and power are only superficial, illusionary. They are limited to four walls of a house. So maybe we should send her to a museum and start praying that we will never need her again."[24]

Not all young Polish feminists want to banish Matka Polka. Agnieszka Graff, whose anthology *Świat Bez Kobiet* (World Without Women) became the first feminist best-seller in Poland in 2002, told me, "We need [Matka Polka], we value her." In 2000 Agnieszka created an imagined interview with Mickiewicz's enduring role model, one that envisions her in a whole new incarnation. It was performed at an International Women's Day *manifa* (happening) that year and was later published in the Polish edition of *Cosmopolitan*.[25] In the performance, a recognizable, but newly feminist, Matka Polka emerges from underground to join the March 8 festivities, announcing vehemently that she has "HAD ENOUGH!" She has sacrificed too many sons and daughters to wars, socialism, the underground, and the antiabortion laws. When told that Parliament's "lawmakers keep saying that the role of Matka Polka is very special," she replies: "If they like this role so much, let them take it. I don't want it any more. For that matter, now I'm going to look after myself."[26]

It is only fitting, I think, that I close with a final reference to Helena Łuczywo, Founding Mother of both *Tygodnik Mazowsze* and *Gazeta Wyborcza*. Though I recall that Helena had early on expressed dismay about the then-proposed antiabortion legislation, she continued to distance herself from feminist topics. She had had little exposure, until the UN released its 1999 report, to blatant violations of women's human rights or to the vital advocacy work that independent, grass roots feminist groups had undertaken to improve women's lives and to safeguard their entitlements. By the time Helena wrote her unprecedented "More Feminism" editorial, the Polish women's movement had become one of the strongest new movements in Eastern and Central Europe, and as a woman who deeply reveres democratic practices, she honestly acknowledged it as "courageous and often right."

It is through experience and access to information, after all, that feminist values make sense. Information is indeed light, as free press pioneer Helena Łuczywo has shown us through her lifelong dedication to throwing open the doors of her country, which has been culturally isolated and in the dark for more than forty years.

One social change legacy that she and the Damska Grupa Operacyjna represent—the one Ewa Kulik called their "activity impulse"—also characterizes the effective, rapid-response capacities of Polish feminists, who have managed, most impressively, to educate the public about core gender equity values. "Whatever women do not win for ourselves, we do not have," Kraków activist Sławomira Walczewska stressed to me. That "activity impulse," so crucial to creating and sustaining a patient revolution during the communist era, continues on today, where it is more widely understood as exercising responsible citizenship.

In this era of dramatic change, as an increasingly well-informed citizenry begins to separate feminism from its outmoded communist context, Polish society is demonstrating a remarkable capacity for reinvention.

Appendix

I. *The following pieces are excerpted from several of the key Op-Eds that generated the summer 1999 media debate in* Gazeta Wyborcza, *beginning with Agnieszka Graff's lead essay, "Patriarchy after Sexmission."*

Agnieszka Graff, "Patriarchy after Sexmission"
(*Gazeta Wyborcza,* June 19–20, 1999, 20–23)

. . . In the Shadow of Male Leaders

We often hear that the attitude towards women in Poland and other Eastern European countries after '89 is a peculiar "paradox" and a momentary deviation from the democratic default. In time, we are told, gender will cease to exclude half of the population from political involvement because that's "the logic of democracy."

Not so, says British political scientist Peggy Watson. This view results from premature generalization of the history of Western democracy. In democracy, "the difference," any difference which is natural or regarded as natural, such as gender, color, etc., eventually loses it political relevance as a determinant of political identity and a basis for political participation or exclusion. This scenario played well in South Africa, leveling racial concerns in the political discourse and in political divisions. In Eastern Europe, however, both the initial situation and the outcome have been quite different.

Inherent in the communist system was the radical denial of any political significance of "the difference." It's not that everybody was equal, but that any difference perceived as "natural," such as gender, social or ethnic background, wealth or age did not determine the level of political participation. Everybody was equally helpless, so there were no groups identifying themselves as victimized minorities.

A few years ago a feminist periodical published in Kraków [*Pełnym Głosem* (In Full Voice)] printed an article by Shana Penn about women in Solidarity. It was both shocking and carefully ignored by Poland's national media. The author interviewed several women playing important roles in the opposition movement who, to the very end, remained in the shadow of the male leaders. It was clear from what they told Penn that they had no feminist consciousness and no feelings at all of being discriminated against, although the gender discrimination was obvious to Penn as an American.

Those women could not have any feminist consciousness because the fact of being a woman failed to be their starting point in forging a political identity. According to Peggy Watson, this was because during communist rule in Eastern Europe, gender was not perceived as a politically meaningful difference. "It's curious," according to a Hungarian commentator quoted by Watson, "that in the midst of a deep economic crisis and political chaos, when essential social transformation was needed, what emerged in almost all the post-communist countries as the basic problem was abortion."

It was by no means a "paradox." To the contrary, it was in this way, by re-establishing the gender difference and subjecting the female body to restrictive laws, that the newly elected parliaments asserted their power. A Polish senator remarked that focusing on abortion during this difficult early period, while neglecting other more urgent matters, resulted from the fact that abortion was regarded as something that "can at least be dealt with." "We will socialize those bellies," replied one of the authors of the anti-abortion bill to the slogan "My belly is mine," shouted by women protesting in front of the Diet building. The antiabortion law became the first challenge to be addressed by the emerging, self-conscious new Eastern European government.

At that moment, nobody had a clue about how to deal with three-digit inflation or how to bring changes to agriculture, but meanwhile they could "socialize" female reproductive organs. To be happy and productive, a government must have someone to govern and subjugate. In the post-communist Polish democracy, women have been singled out for this role. . . .

. . . Everything Is Just Fine

Let's summarize [what our legislators tell us]: There is no discrimination; OK, there is discrimination, but we know how to deal with it; unfortunately, we don't know what discrimination is. Those three lines of thought are incompatible with each other, but they were useful nevertheless in helping to quash the equal rights bill in the Diet after its first reading. Its defeat was due neither to logic nor to facts at hand, because the right cannot claim to have either.

The Right made obvious mistakes that should have spelled defeat for them. One of the few statistics they quoted was that 62 percent of Poles believe that the current constitutional language is sufficient and 63 percent believe that the path to public office is wide open to both genders. Now it's easy to see that 63 percent is not much over one half. If we admit that many of the 63 percent are males, we can see that most women in Poland do feel discriminated against.

The Right was so sure of its success that they didn't even prepare their speeches. They didn't have to, because none of the arguments heard on the Diet floor actually had any impact. What did have an impact was a belief shared by the ruling right AWS party, a large proportion of the [liberal] Freedom Union and, surprisingly, the [postcommunist left] SLD. Only [extreme right fringe] Rep. Janusz Korwin-Mikke actually voices this belief aloud on occasion: Discrimination which should more aptly be called "natural difference between the genders" has always been there, it's with us now and it will remain so. And that's a good thing. This is what our young Polish democracy is all about. When communists ruled, women were driving tractors and had abortions, but now the situation has returned to normal. Poland is on its own, Polish males are virile, and Polish women are feminine again.

... The Miraculous Transformation

... This version of the last 20 years of Polish history—which I am presenting here and which was presented before me by Shana Penn and Peggy Watson, though they placed emphasis elsewhere—is not commonly known, obviously. Accepting this interpretation of history would involve overly painful demystification of that period in which, according to the obligatory version, the Poles went through a sort of miraculous transformation. We were great, noble and in solidarity with each other. We felt good.

Unlike Shana Penn, I am not surprised that women agreed to serve in their supportive roles without any protest and, with a few exceptions, without even a sense of being harmed. . . . I am not surprised by all this mainly because I experienced similar situations myself and only several years later, after plenty of reading and not without strong inner resistance, did I feel bold enough to reinterpret that experience in terms of gender relations. However, during those days when I was participating in those events as a teenager, this approach to the issue would have been absurd to me.

The Game, Fiction and Pretenses

In 1987, as a seventeen-year-old "oppositionist's" girlfriend, I was dragged away from a rally against my will when it seemed as if the police would soon start clubbing the protesters. On one hand, I was furious; on the other, I knew that the bruises which the guys would have from that combat would be worth more in their own eyes, and also in my eyes, if I first let myself be carried away from the battleground. I knew that if I DID NOT BOTHER THEM when they were FIGHTING FOR POLAND, then I would be given MY reward.

Today I am convinced that those skirmishes with the riot police, and the follow-up stories about their atrocities, constituted a ritual in the student anticommunist community and that male identity was forged in that ritual. Who made up the category of "the others" at that time? "The other" was not so much the "enemy" (who was not even so dangerous during communism's waning period), but mainly the woman, standing agog with admiration, on the side. By allowing myself to be carried out from that rally, I enacted—not quite consciously, but well—the "Damsels and Knights" cultural scenario, the history of which is described by Wałczewska. I became briefly mixed up in the ranks of the knights, but after being called to order, I easily agreed to return to the role of the damsel, as I was anxious to receive my reward as promised in the contract between the sexes in the culture of noble knights.

The reward for participation in the game is sweet indeed: spectacular romantic gestures, care, protection from violence, plus clear definition of one's own role and the certainty that one is all one is supposed to be. Enacting their concern, expectation and admiration for the manliness of their boyfriends, the girls from that community created their own female identity. To a certain degree, we identified with the elevated, sanctified ideal of womanhood that is the myth of The Polish Mother.

I believe, however, that while we women maintained an ironic distance toward our "womanly" roles, the guys clearly took their roles quite seriously. They were *into* their masculinity, or at least wanted it to be real; our femininity was, to a large extent, a masquerade. That was not a coincidence. A unique characteristic of female identity deeply cherished by women who have fallen prey to the Polish patriarchy, is the conviction that it is all a game, fiction and pretense. We, women, are convinced of our men's hidden weakness. We believe that they need our recognition and acknowledgment of their own superiority and that we give it all to them of our own free will so that—at least in our fantasies—we actually have control over the entire game. Asked by Shana Penn, [one activist] replied in an unusually traditional way: "Because we, as women, can exercise authority only as long as we pretend that we don't have it. All of us went unnoticed. Society is made up of appearances."

In democracy, however, there is no invisible power. Pretense no longer defines the society. That is why believing in the feel-good myth according to which "men are in charge of the world and women are in charge of the men" did not serve us well after the 1989 government takeover. If the Solidarity period was an era in which the identity of "man as politician" was formed, then democracy has established itself overtly as a "man's world."

Joanna Szczęsna, "Ladies, Knights and Firepersons"
(*Gazeta Wyborcza,* June 27, 1999, 22–23)

Without going too deeply into detail, I'd venture to say that I have earned a notation in my biography that could be recognized as feminist. Indeed, if something like a feminist personality or temperament exists, then I am possessed of such. It has even been passed down to the next generation, for the first person to notice my feminist proclivities was my son, when, years ago, he and I went to an exhibition of medieval torture instruments. I have no idea why we decided to go there. For both of us, reading the descriptions was just as interesting as viewing the exhibits. The carefully prepared legends announced that most of the instruments were meant to be used on women—the insufficiently humble, the disobedient, those too ambitious for their times or too energetic. When, pale of face, we hurriedly left the exhibition, my son groaned pathetically: "Wow, I've got the feeling that you and Grandma wouldn't have escaped torture in those days."

Unlike Agnieszka Graff I am not a feminist. I only tend to be one from time to time—whenever, for example, I encounter real signs of gender discrimination, oppression of women, and violence (which aren't that uncommon in Poland after all). Or when I meet someone who is a kind of "male chauvinist" (which isn't a rare event in Poland either). However, I immediately stop considering myself a feminist when I read texts like Agnieszka Graff's "Patriarchy after Sexmission." It doesn't seem to me that discrimination against women and the gender power struggle can explain every alarming occurrence in contemporary Poland. I do not accept feminism as a master key to explain the world.

I appreciate the role that the feminist movement plays in contemporary Poland and also feel gender solidarity, and I would probably never feel the need to engage in this controversy, even with feminism's most extravagant factions, if it were not for the fact that I feel that Agnieszka Graff has involved me personally. Both Danuta Winiarska and I were used to illustrate the thesis that the last twenty years of Polish history have been falsified by men whose perfidious conspiracy has deprived the women, who were involved in secret "Solidarity" activities, of the fruits of their victory. Thus deprived, women couldn't enter the political stage of liberated Poland, and—in accord with the stereotypical self-image of their gender—they modestly left the limelight for the men.

Agnieszka Graff supported her challenging thesis with quotations from an article, "National Secret" (published a few years ago in a Kraków feminist magazine "Pełnym Głosem"), written by American feminist Shana Penn, who interviewed the editors of "Tygodnik Mazowsze." Agnieszka Graff writes that she regrets that Penn's text met with no significant response in Poland. I—as one of its heroines—am, however, grateful that there is not yet in our country a habit of reading feminist literature. Sometimes it's really hard to recognize oneself as described by even the kindest feminist. "Both in her life style and writings"—Penn writes—"Szczęsna pays attention to cultural blinders. In spite of communist rhetoric guaranteeing women equality, the Central Committee [PZPR] failed to notice them. . . . Women were neglected both by the Party's leaders and by men acting in 'Solidarność.' . . . [They] depreciated their influence in leading resistance to the revolutionary turning point."

Remembering Shana Penn's kindness to me, I have no reason to think that she tried to make a fool of me. However, this paragraph perfectly reflects what happens to reality when predetermined viewpoints are applied to it. Shana Penn came to Poland with a ready thesis, which Agnieszka Graff adopts: the women involved in [anticommunist] conspiracy failed to notice gender discrimination within the resistance movement (for they lacked feminist consciousness), discrimination which, for Shana Penn as an American woman, was visible at first glance.

It's understandable that, given her upbringing in a different culture and her unawareness of Polish reality, an American feminist can create such odd paragraphs as the one above. Still, it is strange that a woman educated in Poland didn't find it suspicious and that, instead of quoting her foreign colleague, she felt no need to contact the primary sources, who are still alive, after all. But that is what happens if ideology blinds a person to the rest of the world.

It so happens that I recall that fragment of my conversation with Shana Penn that was transformed into the strange pretension that "the Central Committee overlooked women." While describing the realities of oppositionist activity, I recounted how gender stereotypes functioned in society, and therefore in the Security Service as well, and how these attitudes had been helpful for us. One has to come from a country that has, fortunately, never needed to know anything about conspiracy in order to turn this ideologically innocent description into an accusation of discrimination.

Still, those are really just mere details. Danuta Winiarska is in a much worse situation, for she appears in Shana Penn's and Agnieszka Graff's story as a kind of demonic manipulator who, while hiding behind a male pseudonym, controls everything in one of the regions.

Agnieszka Graff writes that, when she was once an "oppositionist's girlfriend," she was carried away from a demonstration against her will just as the clashes with police were about to start. Today she interprets that event as follows: "I reenacted the cultural screenplay titled 'Ladies and Knights.' . . . For a moment I had gotten into the knights' ranks, but after being called to order, I agreed very easily to get back and play the lady's role. . . ." When I was in quite a similar situation of physical threat, I felt something completely different; and please do not try to make me believe it was because of my lack of feminist consciousness. In August 1988 I was in the Szczecin shipyard named after Warski. After rumors spread about the imminence of a police crackdown, the minister of internal affairs, Andrzej Milczanowski, assigned a big shipyard worker to me and made him responsible for my security. This gesture seemed to me very elegant and practical (I had materials for the secret press with me), and it did not offend my human dignity in any way. I may be uttering some kind of feminist heresy, but I think that a woman, in contrast to a man, has the fortune to be able to play both lady and knight. . . .

This doesn't mean that I fail to notice the discrimination against women in the Polish People's Republic. It doesn't even mean that I try to idealize relations between genders in the opposition movement. However, I considered feminism a needless luxury in those days. I'd rather get involved in activities protesting the use of physical violence by the police than in a struggle for the equal distribution of a policeman's blows.

Both Shana Penn and Agnieszka Graff regret—also on my behalf—that women who were able to organize the structures of the underground conspiracy and lead it did not get involved in politics after 1989. (The example of Barbara Labuda shows that they did, if they wished.) The wonder is that it didn't cross Penn's and Graff's minds to imagine how it was possible for women, who had been able to express their determination and strong personalities when it was necessary, to immediately allow themselves to be pushed off stage.

And so I'd like to submit a personal declaration. It happened that once in my life I put out lots of fires, but please believe me, it was not because of gender discrimination that I didn't become a fireperson. I didn't become one because I didn't want to be one. . . .

Maria Janion, "For Your Freedom and Ours"
(*Gazeta Wyborcza,* July 4, 1999, 20)

. . . Agnieszka Graff's article was not an attack on Joanna Szczęsna for choosing to be a journalist over a politician. On the contrary, Graff's purpose was to show the great and forgotten role of [this] woman and other women in Solidarity.

. . . Therefore I cannot agree with Joanna Szczęsna that the result of removing women from politics was the result of individual choices. They did not enter the Sejm (Parliament) in the same way they did not enter the fire departments. Individual choices do not change the greater dynamic that Graff described. Solidarity turned away from women making them understand clearly that they are not welcome in places where there are no longer national fires to put out, but where there is money, privilege and power.

Zofia Kuratowska of the left part of the Democratic Union, who was outspoken about gender discrimination, did not want to be a candidate for the Senate and left the country, because she said she could not communicate with male colleagues of Solidarity who had changed their views so dramatically after 1989.

Feminism is an attempt to understand the mechanisms that legitimate and propagate the unequal distribution of power in society. It is also a personal development path that allows for one to return to the sources of female authority. The point is not to cut the self off from one's heritage or from world culture, but to find a way to express female experience and restore its meaning in the culture at large.

My own path is to discover more and more the feminine element in what I do. I slowly developed my feminist interests over the last few years. Thanks to this, I have reassessed my own path of development and notice the importance of female friendships and networks between different generations of women. There is a great bond connecting me to my female teachers and students. And now I try to help my students develop this spark of creativity. Earlier my ideals had been broadly human. I speak to humans. But in the past few years I left the philosophy of universalism and became fascinated with the philosophy of difference. What happens beyond is an attempt to create a new subjectivity, which perhaps will be truly human. But we will not reach this truly human identity by pretending that gender does not matter. The new identity must be an identity after the breakthrough of difference.

Dominika Wielowieyska, "A Turtle and a Women's Question" (*Gazeta Wyborcza,* July 1, 1999, 19)

. . . The Right to Choose

Do we really need—following Agnieszka Graff's example—to worry about the fact that university presidents, outstanding thinkers or high-ranking officials are mostly male? Somehow I am not disturbed by that. There are many admirable women who are specialists in their domains. But do we really need to compete in the statistics race: how many women can we find here or there?

The key question is whether a woman indeed has the right to choose. And the rest should be left to each one of us alone. Professional fulfillment does not have to equal a dazzling career. The fulfillment of a woman does not have to equal a profession. What is important is that every choice is conscious. Feminists complain that they are unjustly accused of being anti-family. I don't think they are. The problem is that they create a certain image of a woman, that she is appreciated only if she has a career.

My Belly . . . Is Civilization's Problem

I've learned from Agnieszka Graff that in the new Poland men decided to oppress women and—instead of taking care of raging inflation or economic crisis—they passed an anti-abortion law. Let's begin with the good news: inflation has been controlled, as has an economic crisis. Abortion became the subject of a grand national debate in Poland mainly due to the fact that a number of MPs and a large part of the society see abortion as a crime. The debate, although unusually long and at times too stormy, took place in a relatively peaceful atmosphere, compared for instance to what also takes place in the USA today.

It's amazing that feminists feel entitled to represent all women on this issue and that they do not want to realize that some of us do not accept their way of thinking. I strongly object to putting abortion under the category of restriction of women's rights. This problem does not boil down to stating that "my belly belongs to me." I don't say that my belly doesn't belong to me. The question is: can the life growing inside be destroyed without any restrictions? I'm far from passing categorical judgments on specific cases and specific decisions women make. I don't know—and I humbly admit it—what is the best way of solving legal problems with regard to abortion, although I'm inclined to the view that the right to abortion should be very restricted.

I'm only saying that, for me, the question of abortion and of our approach to it is one of the very important questions about the character of our civilization. It is a test, proving whether—and how—we can cope with such sensitive issues. It is a significant problem of a sociological, philosophical, religious, and—most importantly—moral nature. And finally—it is a prelude to considering the limits that ought not be crossed by humans, a prelude to considering the moral aspect of the achievements of geneticists, of cloning people and of many other questions. Do we allow ourselves full freedom in manipulating the process of the creation of life? Won't this freedom turn against us at some point?

II. *In 2000 the Polish edition of* Cosmopolitan *published the following monologue by Matka Polka as transmitted to Agnieszka Graff.*

Agnieszka Graff, "Against the Current"
(*Cosmopolitan,* May 2000, 30)

Matka Polka. There could be no shade of doubt. It was Her. Powerful, dignified, and at the same time warm and familiar. And only a little grotesque in her large blue apron. She emerged as if from under the ground at the International Women's Day demonstration on March 8th in Warsaw's Stare Miasto [Old Town]. With her came the smell of mothballs, gunpowder and pierogi with cheese.

- Welcome! We're glad you could come here.

- Sure I could come. I left pierogi on the kitchen counter and came running to be here. I even plastered posters all over the city—"I've HAD ENOUGH"—with the signature of Matka Polka.

- You've had enough? Why? And how did that come to be?

- It started awfully long ago, darling. The eighteenth or nineteenth century, I can hardly remember it. They wrote poems about me. That I hum patriotic songs over the child's cradle, and that I help my motherland when she needs it. Well, I was helping her. I bore sons and I sent them off to fight. When one was dead, another went. If he was killed too, I would send the third one to take revenge, and so it went. I could hardly keep pace.

- But it's a beautiful role. Honorable.

- Maybe it's honorable, but what about all those sons I gave birth to? What about all the worries I had? Everybody thinks that I find pleasure in all this suffering and sacrifice. And I've just HAD ENOUGH! Later, my child, there were the uprisings. Again, for every uprising I had to supply sons. One would tear bed linen for bandages. One would go to Siberia. One would enlighten the people. One would manage the estate. And if there was such need, one would go to the barricades, too. Various things happened.

- And how do you like the newest history, oh dear Mother?

- To this second war, dear girl, I sent not only sons, but daughters as well. They were nurses. They ran in the canals. I fought a little myself too. But when they finally erected the Warsaw Uprising monument, they forgot about me. What they put there was this poor creature with a baby, and the brave fighter shielding her with his manly arm. But I'm not on the monument. So where's justice?

- And what happened after the war?

- Don't you remember, baby? Are you that young? One would build socialism. One would drive the tractor. I rather enjoyed that, actually. But later there were mainly queues. On March 8th one would be given a coupon for pantyhose and a tulip, you know, to show that woman is a human being too, and a supporter of the socialist motherland at that. They have even founded a hospital-monument for me. What were all those monuments for? I will never forget all the times I spent queuing, cooking, doing laundry, ironing, giving birth! And then there was the underground. One would print and distribute *samizdat* papers, one would throw leaflets. And when the fellows went to prison, me and my girl-friends would build the underground ourselves. And now they say, one and another, that they were fighting and the lovely ladies served them tea. History likes to repeat itself.

- Well, but now you should be happy, dear Mother. We have pro-family policy, they speak very well about you up there. . . .

- I wouldn't curse my worst enemy with such friends! They will do me in with all this care and respect. My nerves won't take it. They are closing down kindergartens and creches! They stopped financing contraceptives! There were going to be those hostels built for women who are troubled by their fellows, there was even money from the West. And now they tell us we don't need them. I sent my children to school, to learn something useful, and they tell them rubbish about harmful condoms. And all this allegedly for my own good! This is too much, I've had enough!

- But in the Parliament the lawmakers keep saying that the role of Matka Polka is very special.

- If they like this role so much, let them take it. I don't want it any more. For that matter, now I'm going to look after myself. But first I'll go and finish my pierogi!

And she disappeared. There was no time to say good-bye. Only for a moment one could still smell mothballs, pierogi and gunpowder in the air.

III. *The following excerpt is from a review of my book,* Podziemie Kobiet, *which was published in Poland in 2003.*

Zuzanna Siemieñczuk, "In a dangerously convincing way, Podziemie Kobiet *changes our familiar, historical perspective . . ."*
(<www.Merlin.pl>, April 8, 2003)

It is easy to be skeptical about a book on Solidarity written by an American author. But it is much more interesting to change for a moment into an innocent, unprejudiced reader, and to listen to this supposedly well-known story being told in another voice—which is what Prof. Maria Janion encourages us to do in her foreword to *Podziemie Kobiet.* "Shana Penn's book is a thrilling tale of extraordinary deeds by the heroines of the underground." That's just one way of describing the book in a sentence—if we were willing to create another heroic legend. However, such a statement would be an oversimplification in terms of this unusual narrative, whose substance and language carry nearly the same weight. The author and her protagonists seem to be using entirely different discourses. When Penn asks a question, her interlocutors try not only to answer it, but also to make it understandable to this woman, who is apparently unaware of the Polish realities if it occurred to her to ask about such things.

Yet what they never appreciated was the author's insight and her actual knowledge. It is enough to check the book's bibliography to set this misapprehension right. Penn's feminist perspective is disturbing, as it doesn't allow the reader's thoughts to take their usual course. It might be irritating, but it does make one think. The reactions of women interviewed over 10 years ago and of the readers today are the same: why introduce divisions now? Didn't we all share Solidarity? Well—was that the fact? *Podziemie Kobiet* traces another map of the Opposition. Setting the male heroes aside, it concentrates on the female experience, "women's own ways," a female perspective.

Paradoxically enough, it is most difficult to bring this very perspective out into the daylight—it is very shy, becoming aggressive only when attempts are made at appreciating and presenting it to the public. . . . And that's precisely what Shana Penn managed to do. As if, while assuming the position of a laywoman, she innocently tricked her interlocutors into telling her some amazing stories under the disguise of a patient lecture. There is an irresistible impression of a psychoanalytical effect in this book—as if the women telling about their oppositional activity didn't fully realize their position in those times' power system. Shana Penn gives an interesting diagnosis.

Naturally we don't have to agree with it—it's only a hypothesis. Nevertheless, her vision cannot be denied cohesion and logic. The testimony of *Podziemie Kobiet* complements the picture of history we know from textbooks and critical studies. Thanks to Shana Penn, Solidarity women have finally come out of hiding.

Notes

Introduction

1. Father Popiełuszko was murdered by the secret police in 1984.

2. Prior to the birth of Solidarity in 1980, anticommunism was called the opposition; from 1980 to around 1985, the opposition and Solidarity became interchangeable terms; and in the remaining years of communist governance—1986 to 1989—the opposition expanded beyond Solidarity due to the initiatives of a new generation. At this point it was again called the opposition or prodemocracy movement.

3. Padraic Kenney, *A Carnival of Revolution: Central Europe 1989* (Princeton: Princeton University Press, 2002), 15.

4. Timothy Garton Ash, *The Polish Revolution* (London: Trinity Press, 1983), 285.

5. Ibid.

6. Although I quote Lawrence Weschler and Timothy Garton Ash extensively throughout this book, I relied significantly on many other Western journalists and scholars who have published about the Solidarity experience and whose works appear in the bibliography. Weschler's and Garton Ash's accounts, however, struck me as both credible (in that their portrayals agreed with the accounts I gathered from the Solidarity women) and particularly well written, succinct, and accessible. Because these authors are journalists rather than academics, their reports and books were widely read in the West and played a prominent role in informing public opinion about events in Poland.

Nonetheless, like so many other observers, they too overlooked women's important contributions and the role that gender dynamics played in shaping the opposition.

7. See chapter 1.

8. Maciej Łopinski, Marcin Moskit, and Mariusz Wilk, eds., *Konspira* (Berkeley: University of California Press, 1990). *Konspira* was originally published in Poland in December 1984, when the interviewees were living underground.

9. Lawrence Weschler, "Afterword," in *Konspira,* ed. Łopinski, Moskit, and Wilk, 253.

10. Tina Rosenberg, *The Haunted Land: Facing Europe's Ghosts after Communism* (New York: Random House, 1995), 220.

11. Barbara Jancar, "Women in the Opposition in Poland and Czechoslovakia in the 1970's," in *Women, State, and the Party in Eastern Europe,* ed. Sharon Wolchik and Alfred Meyer (Durham, NC: Duke University Press, 1985), 169–70.

12. Pronunciations: Anna Bikont: Anna BEE-kahnt; Zofia Bydlińska: Zofia Bead-LIN-ska; Anna Dodziuk: Anna DODE-juke; Ewa Kulik: Eva KOO-leek; Helena Łuczywo: HEL-lena Woo-DZHEH-voh; Małgorzata Pawlicka: Mah-gore-ZHA-tah Pahv-LEETZ-ka; Joanna Szczęsna: Yo-AHN-na SH-CHez-na.

On my first two trips to Poland, in June–August 1990 and December 1990–January 1991, I learned about the Warsaw women's role in creating the paper and the underground network that made it possible. Much of my research during the spring and summer of 1991 focused on following up on this subject. For much of the next decade I studied the implications of their political use of invisibility on both the Solidarity past and the democratic present. I was curious to also observe how the rapid political and economic changes under way would affect each of their lives as well as women as a social group. I continued my research and interviews during subsequent trips to Poland, in May–June and October 1992, with follow-up interviews conducted between 1993 and 2003. Through 1996 I conducted fieldwork in Poland while serving as the executive director of the Network of East-West Women, an international nonprofit organization that supports the postcommunist region's women's movements. Between 1996 and 2000 I studied the independent media in Poland, while serving as media relations director at the United States Holocaust Memorial Museum in Washington, D.C. With the generous support of an Open Society Institute Fellowship between 2000 and 2003, I completed the research, interviews, and writing of this book, dividing my time between Poland and California. I have also interviewed many émigré Polish activists and scholars residing—either temporarily or permanently—in the United States. I first published some of the Solidarity women's stories in *Journal of Women's History* in 1994 and in *Pełnym Głosem*, a Kraków feminist journal, also in 1994. Based on my interviews, I've since published several more articles in the United States and Poland and one Polish-language book, *Podziemie Kobiet* (The Underground of Women), in addition to the present volume.

13. Anna Husarska, "From Hellholes with Love," *Media Studies Journal* 13, no. 3 (fall 1999): 44.

14. Anna Husarska, "Up From the Underground," *New York Times* Sunday book section, October 8, 1989, 1.

15. Jancar, "Women in the Opposition," 168–85.

16. Lawrence Weschler, *Solidarity: Poland in the Season of Its Passion* (New York: Simon and Schuster, 1982), xv–xvi.

17. Jay Rosen, "Civil Society and the Spirit of 1989: Lessons for Journalists, from East to West," *Media Studies Journal, "After the Fall"* (fall 1999): 118.

18. Timothy Garton Ash, "Helena's Kitchen," *New Yorker,* February 15, 1999, 34.

19. See chapter 8.

20. Maria Janion, "Foreword: Amerykanka w Polsce," in *Podziemie Kobiet* by Shana Penn (Warsaw: Rosner i Wspolnicy, 2003), 6.

21. See Bogna Lorence-Kot, "Konspiracja," in *Women in Polish Society,* ed. Rudolf Joworski and Bianka Pietrow-Ennker (Boulder: East European Monographs, 1992).

22. See Belinda Brown, *The Private Revolution* (London: Hera Trust, 2003); Padraic Kenney, "The Gender of Resistance in Communist Poland," *American Historical Review* 104 (April 1999): 399–425; Kristi S. Long, *We All Fought for Freedom: Women in Poland's Solidarity Movement* (Boulder: Westview Press, 1996); and Anna Reading, *Polish Women, Solidarity, and Feminism* (London: Macmillan, 1999).

23. I traveled with my friend and colleague Dr. Dorien Ross on my first trip to Central Europe in the summer of 1990. Dorien interviewed Anka Grupińska at that time for research on ethnic identity and resistance. I conducted several interviews with Anka in December 1990, January 1991, January 2000, and April 2000. Most of her experiences that are told in this book were recorded in the winter of 1990–91.

24. Shana Penn, "Tajemnica państwowa," *Pełnym Głosem,* Kobiety w Solidarnośći (Special Issue: "Women and Solidarity") (Kraków: eFKa, Jesien 1994).

25. Agnieszka Graff, "Patriarchat po seksmisji" [Patriarchy after Sexmission], *Gazeta Wyborcza* (Warsaw edition), June 19–20, 1999, Świateczna [Weekend] section, 22. See chapter 10.

Chapter 1

1. Kenney, "The Gender of Resistance," 401.

2. Freedom and Peace was a mid-1980s opposition movement, mainly peopled by younger generations of activists, who engaged in acts of civil disobedience, sit-ins, and happenings. Their activism was informed by Western peace and human rights movements.

3. Neal Ascherson, *The Polish August* (New York: Viking Press, 1982); Garton Ash, *The Polish Revolution*.

4. Ascherson, *The Polish August*, 145; Garton Ash, *The Polish Revolution*, 46.

5. Flora Lewis, *Europe: A Tapestry of Nations* (New York: Touchstone, 1987), 403.

6. Ibid., 393.

7. Hanna Krall, "Perhaps People Aren't Bad After All . . . ," in *The Strike in Gdańsk, August 14–31, 1980*, ed. and trans. Andrzej Tymowski (New Haven: D. H. Back Press, 1981), 33.

8. Ibid., 34.

9. Ibid., 35.

10. Ibid.

11. See chapter 3.

12. Garton Ash, *The Polish Revolution*, 28–29.

13. Irena Grudzińska-Gross, *The Art of Solidarity* (Staten Island: International Popular Culture, 1985), 7.

14. Garton Ash, *The Polish Revolution*, 29.

15. Zbigniew Gluza and Katarzyna Madoń-Mitzner, eds., *The Days of Solidarity* (Warsaw: KARTA Center, 2000), 5.

16. Garton Ash, *The Polish Revolution*, 32.

17. Ibid.

18. Ibid.

19. Lech Wałęsa, *A Way of Hope* (New York: Henry Holt, 1987), 115–16.

20. Gluza and Madoń-Mitzner, *The Days of Solidarity*, 8. See also Paweł Smolenski, "Alina Pieńkowska—To Oppose When You Need To," *Gazeta Wyborcza/Wysokie Obcasy* (Warsaw edition), August 12, 2000, 6–13.

21. Gluza and Madoń-Mitzner, *The Days of Solidarity*, 9.

22. Tymowski, *The Strike in Gdańsk*, 2.

23. Gluza and Madoń-Mitzner, *The Days of Solidarity*, 18.

24. Garton Ash, *The Polish Revolution*, 41.

25. Ibid.

26. Jancar, "Women in the Opposition," 174.

27. Jancar, "Women in the Opposition," 169–70; Renata Siemieńska,

"Women and Social Movements in Poland," *Women and Politics* 6, no. 4 (1986): 5–35.

28. Jane Atkinson, "The Woman Behind Solidarity: The Story of Anna Walentynowicz," *Ms.*, February 1984, 96.

29. Lynne Olson, *Freedom's Daughters: The Unsung Heroines of the Civil Rights Movement from 1830 to 1970* (New York: Scribner, 2001), chapters 5–7.

30. Roger Cohen, "Ten Years Later," *New York Times,* November 7, 1999, 71, <http://www.nytimes.com>.

31. Agnieszka Graff, "Patriarchat po seksmisji," 22.

Chapter 2

1. Janion, "Foreword: Amerykanka w Polsce," 5.

2. Agnieszka Grzybek and Barbara Limanowska, "Polityka to jest bitka. Wiwiad z Barbara Labuda" [Politics Is a Struggle: Interview with Barbara Labuda], *OŚKA Biuletyn* 2, no. 11 (2000): 25.

3. Ibid.

4. "No Sacred Cows: Halina Filipowicz Interviews Anna Bojarska," *Women's Review of Books* 7, nos. 10–11 (summer 1990): 4.

5. Anna Reading, *Polish Women, Solidarity and Feminism* (London: Macmillan, 1999), 201–2.

6. Ewa Hauser, Barbara Heyns, and Jane Mansbridge, "Feminism in the Interstices of Politics and Culture: Poland in Transition," in *Gender Politics and Post-Communism,* ed. Nanette Funk and Magda Mueller (New York: Routledge, 1993), 262.

7. Jancar, "Women in the Opposition," 177.

8. Lawrence Weschler, *The Passion of Poland* (New York: Pantheon Books, 1984), 146.

9. Hauser, Heyns, and Mansbridge, "Feminism in the Interstices of Politics and Culture," 261.

10. Rosenberg, *The Haunted Land,* 188; see also 192. Note that Wałęsa held moderate views, which positioned him with the KOR intellectuals and not with the predominantly working-class radicals.

11. Jarosław Anders, "Did the Polish Catholic Church Commune with Communism?" *Foreign Policy* (July–August 2003), 99.

12. Rosenberg, *The Haunted Land,* 189.

13. Grudzińska-Gross, *The Art of Solidarity,* 45.

14. Wojciech Jaruzelski, "Przemówienie radiowe i telewizyjne wygloszone 13 grudnia 1981 r" ["Broadcast declaration of the imposition of martial law, December 13, 1981"], <http://www.geocities.com /wojciech_jaruzelski/ proklamacja>.

15. Grudzińska-Gross, *The Art of Solidarity,* 47.

16. Rosenberg, *The Haunted Land,* 184.

17. Ibid., 188, 203.

18. Jaruzelski, "Przemówienie radiowe i telewizyjne wygloszone."

19. Grudzińska-Gross, *The Art of Solidarity,* 47.

20. Andrzej Tymowski, *Solidarity under Siege* (New Haven: D. H. Back Press, 1982), 22.

21. Jadwiga Staniszkis, *Poland's Self-Limiting Revolution* (Princeton: Princeton University Press, 1984), 320.

22. Tymowski, *Solidarity under Siege,* 22.

23. Ibid., 29.

24. Weschler, *The Passion of Poland,* 92.

Chapter 3

1. Weschler, "Afterword," 253.

2. Helena Łuczywo et al., interview by Jane Rosenthal, "Special on Solidarity," *All Things Considered,* National Public Radio, October 25, 1981.

3. Ibid.

4. Wałęsa, *A Way of Hope,* 41.

5. Irena Grudzińska-Gross, "Stars in the Gutenberg Galaxy: 1989 and the Polish Émigré Press," *Media Studies Journal* 13, no. 3 (1999): 3.

6. Monika Krajewska, essay in possession of the author, 1–2.

7. See "The Kuroń-Modzelewski Open Letter to the Party," in *From Stalinism to Pluralism,* ed. Gale Stokes (New York: Oxford University Press, 1991), 108–14.

8. Timothy Garton Ash, "Letters from Warsaw," *New Yorker,* February 15, 1999, 34.

9. Grudzińska-Gross, "Stars in the Gutenberg Galaxy," 4–5.

10. Ibid., 5.

11. Adam Michnik, "A New Evolutionism, 1976," *Letters from Prison and Other Essays* (Berkeley: University of California Press, 1985), 135–48.

12. Joanna Szczęsna, "Wkościele św, Marcina" [In St. Martin's Church], *Zapis* 4 (1977): 38, 41.

13. Ibid., 40.

14. Ibid.

15. Ibid., 49.

16. Ibid., 41.

17. Ibid., 43.

18. Ibid.

19. Ibid..

20. Ibid.

21. Helena Łuczywo et al., interview by Rosenthal, *All Things Considered.*

Chapter 4

1. Łopinski, Moskit, and Wilk, *Konspira,* 47.
2. Jane Cave, ed., *Poland Watch No. 6: The Church of Poland and Solidarity* (Washington, D.C.: Journal of the Poland Watch Center, 1984), 97.
3. Ibid., 98.
4. Ibid., 99.
5. Joanna Szczęsna, "Women in the Opposition," essay in possession of the author, 1991, 5.
6. Garton Ash, "Letters from Warsaw," 35.
7. Grudzińska-Gross, *The Art of Solidarity,* 49.
8. Ibid., 48.
9. Ibid.
10. Ibid.
11. Ibid.
12. Ibid., 51.
13. Ibid., 52.
14. Ibid., 53.
15. Rosenberg, *The Haunted Land,* 277.
16. *Tygodnik Mazowsze,* vol. 2, February 11, 1982, 1–3. The translation into English made use of the one done by Andrzej Tymowski in *Solidarity under Siege.*
17. Grudzińska-Gross, *The Art of Solidarity,* 49.
18. Cave, *Poland Watch No. 6,* 97.
19. Ibid.
20. Grudzińska-Gross, "Stars in the Gutenberg Galaxy," 5.
21. Ibid., 4.
22. Grudzińska-Gross, *The Art of Solidarity,* 52.
23. Weschler, *The Passion of Poland,* 149.
24. Grudzińska-Gross, *The Art of Solidarity.*
25. Cave, *Poland Watch No. 6,* 98.
26. Dominika Suwik, "Tygodnik Mazowsze and Gazeta Wyborcza" (Warsaw, 2001), 3, essay in possession of the author.

Chapter 5

1. Kenney, "The Gender of Resistance," 408.
2. Ibid., 409.
3. Ibid., 410.
4. Szczęsna, "Women in the Opposition," 3.

5. Krajewska, essay, 1.

6. Szczęsna, "Women in the Opposition," 3.

7. Rosenberg, *The Haunted Land,* 215.

8. Ibid., 222.

9. Ibid., 223, 224.

10. Helena Łuczywo et al., interview by Rosenthal, *All Things Considered.*

11. See Katherine R. Jolluck, *Exile and Identity: Polish Women in the Soviet Union during World War II* (Pittsburgh: University of Pittsburgh Press, 2002): 1247.

12. Irena Grudzińska-Gross, review of Jolluck, *Exile and Identity, American Historical Review* 108, no. 4 (October 2003): 1247.

13. The identity of the "real Pole" had negative connotations when used by extreme nationalists in Solidarity to distinguish themselves from the urban-based, often Jewish-born, intellectuals such as Adam Michnik and Helena Łuczywo, whose commitments to nonviolent tactics were opposed by the nationalists at critical times.

14. Adam Michnik, "On Resistance," *Letters from Prison and Other Essays,* 54.

15. Ibid.

16. Ibid., 56.

17. Anders, "Did the Polish Catholic Church Commune?" 100.

18. *Tygodnik Mazowsze,* October 13, 1982, 1.

19. Weschler, *The Passion of Poland,* 187.

20. *Tygodnik Mazowsze,* May 26, 1983, 1.

21. Szczęsna, "Women in the Opposition," 7.

22. Ibid., 8

23. Ibid., 1.

24. Ibid., 6.

25. Jancar, "Women in the Opposition," 174.

26. Szczęsna, "Women in the Opposition," 7.

Chapter 6

1. Anonymous, "Prisoner of the Month: Ewa Kulik," *Tygodnik Mazowsze,* vol. 178, August 15, 1986, 2.

2. Ibid.

3. Krajewska, essay, 1–3.

4. Ibid.

5. Łopinski, Moskit, and Wilk, *Konspira,* 144.

6. Ibid., 151.

7. Ibid., 157.

8. Ibid., 158.

9. Ibid., 159.

10. Ibid., 160.

11. Ibid., 161.

12. Ibid.

13. "Prisoner of the Month: Ewa Kulik, Tribute by Jan Lityński," *Tygodnik Mazowsze,* vol. 178, August 15, 1986, 1–2.

Chapter 7

1. Adam Michnik, "The Polish War," *Letters from Prison and Other Essays,* 29–30.

2. Rosenberg, *The Haunted Land,* 222.

3. Adam Michnik, "On Resistance," *Letters from Prison and Other Essays,* 55.

4. Marcus, in conversation.

5. Łopinski, Moskit, and Wilk, *Konspira,* 159.

Chapter 8

1. Franciszek L. von Erlach, *Partyzantka w Polsce w r. 1863 w swietle wlansnych obserwacji zebranych na teatrze walki od marca do sierprnia 1863 roku* [Partisan Struggle in Poland in 1863 in the Light of Personal Observations, Collected in the Theatre of War from March till August 1863], Tlum. J. Gagatek i W. Tokarz (Warsaw: Wydawnictwo M. Arcta, 1918), 234.

2. "To the Polish Mother," by Adam Mickiewicz, translated by Agnieszka Graff for the author, from Mickiewicz, "Do Matki Polki," in *Wiersze* [Poems] (Warsaw: Czytelnik, 1970), 322–24.

3. See Maria Janion, *Kobiety i duch inności* [Women and the Spirit of Otherness] (Warsaw: Wydawnictwo Sic!, 1996); Sławomira Wałczewska, *Damy, rycerze i feministki. Kobiecy dyskurs emancypacyjny w Polsce* [Ladies, Knights, and Feminists: Women's Emancipation Discourse in Poland] (Kraków: Wydawnictwo eFKa, 1999); Lorence-Kot, "Konspiracja"; Bianka Pietrow-Ennker, "A Historical Introduction," in *Women in Polish Society,* ed. Jaworski and Pietrow-Ennker.

4. Janion, *Kobiety i duch inności,* 78, 79.

5. Pietrow-Ennker, "A Historical Introduction," 12.

6. Ibid., 13.

7. Wałczewska, *Damy, rycerze i feministki,* 93–94.

8. Ibid.

9. Pietrow-Ennker, "A Historical Introduction," 11.

10. Lorence-Kot, "Konspiracja," 36.

11. Ibid., 37.

12. Ibid., 36.

13. Ibid., 31–35.

14. Ibid., 35.

15. Ibid., 37.

16. Szczęsna, "Women in the Opposition," 7.

17. von Erlach, *Partyzantka w Polsce w r. 1863,* 233.

18. Ibid.

19. Ibid., 233–34.

20. Ibid., 234.

21. Ibid.

22. Janion, *Kobiety i duch inności,* 99.

23. Lorence-Kot, "Konspiracja," 44.

24. Marcus, "Dark Numbers," essay in possession of the author, 5.

25. Ibid., 6.

26. Pietrow-Ennker, "A Historical Introduction," 11.

27. Maria Janion, interview by the author, September 18, 2000.

28. "To the Polish Mother."

29. Janion, *Kobiety i duch inności,* 96–99.

30. "Grażyna," in *Poems by Adam Mickiewicz,* ed. George Rapall Noyes (New York: Polish Institute of Arts and Sciences in America, 1944), 237.

31. Janion, *Kobiety i duch inności,* 86–87.

32. Sławomira Walczewska, "Gdie Kobiety?" *Nowe Ksiazki* 7/8 (2003): 29.

33. Joseph Campbell, *The Hero with a Thousand Faces* (Princeton: Princeton University Press, 1972).

34. The poem appears in Janion, *Reduta: Romantyczna poezja niepodległosciowa* [Romantic Era Poems of Independence] (Krakow: Wydawnictwo Literackie, 1979), 169–70. The title of the anonymous poem is "Pozegnanie" [Farewell]. It was reprinted in Janion's book from an anthology of patriotic poetry: *Poezja powstania listopadowego,* ed. A. Zielinski (Wrocław: Biblioteka Narodowa (BN I, 205), 1971), 236–37.

Chapter 9

1. Kenney, *A Carnival of Revolution,* 4–5.

2. Ibid., 4.

3. Gale Stokes, *The Walls Came Tumbling Down: The Collapse of Communism in Eastern Europe* (Oxford: Oxford University Press, 1993), 121.

4. Kenney, *A Carnival of Revolution,* 4, 5.

5. Stokes, *The Walls Came Tumbling Down,* 121–22.

6. Kenney, "Gender of Resistance," 408.

7. *Tygodnik Mazowsze,* vol. 290, April 1989, 1.

8. Lawrence Weschler, "A Grand Experiment," *New Yorker,* November 13, 1989, 65.

9. Helena Łuczywo, "What Is Ours Is Ours—On the Mass Media Table," *Tygodnik Mazowsze,* vol. 283, February 22, 1989, 1–2.

10. Garton Ash, "Helena's Kitchen," 36.

11. "Interview with Helena Łuczywo," *Radcliffe Quarterly 2000,* <http://www.radcliffe.edu/quarterly/200002/justice-10.html)>.

12. Grzybek and Limanowska, "Politics Is a Struggle," 25.

13. Siemieńska, "Women in the Period of Systemic Changes," 75.

14. Slavenka Drakulic, "In Their Own Words: Women of Eastern Europe," *Ms.,* July–August 1990, 43.

15. Grzybek and Limanowska, "Politics Is a Struggle," 25.

16. Celestine Bohlen, "East Europe Women Struggle with New Rules, and Old Ones," *New York Times,* November 25, 1990, E1, E2.

17. Drakulic, "In Their Own Words," 43.

18. Małgorzata Fuszara, "Abortion and the Formation of the Public Sphere in Poland," in *Gender Politics and Post-Communism,* ed. Nanette Funk and Magda Mueller (New York: Routlege, 1993), 241.

19. Drakulic, "In Their Own Words," 25.

20. Wałczewska, *Damy, rycerze i feministki,* 11.

21. Fuszara, "Abortion and the Formation of the Public Sphere," 243.

22. Graff, "Patriarchat po seksmisji," 22.

23. Fuszara, "Abortion and the Formation of the Public Sphere," 243.

24. Drakulic, "In Their Own Words," 26.

25. Małgorzata Tarasiewicz, "Kobiety w NSZZ Solidarność" [Women in the Solidarity National Commission], *Pełnym Głosem* 1, summer 1993, 32.

26. Joanna Weschler, "Hidden Victims: Women in Post-Communist Poland," *Human Rights Watch Report* 4, no. 5 (March 1992): 6.

27. Reading, *Polish Women, Solidarity and Feminism,* 197.

28. *Report on the Sixty-first Meeting of the Women's Committee,* International Confederation of Free Trade Unions, Brussels, March 22–23, 1990, 6.

29. Ibid., 7.

30. Reading, *Polish Women, Solidarity and Feminism,* 196.

31. Ibid.

32. Ibid.

33. Reading, *Polish Women, Solidarity and Feminism,* 198.

34. Rozmowa z Krystyna Politacha, "To nie jest walka, tylko dobijanie sie o swoje prawa," List do Rzecznika Raw Obywatelskich, *Pełnym Głosem* 1, summer 1993, 32.

35. Politacha, "To nie jest walka, tylko dobijanie sie o swoje prawa," 35.

36. Tarasiewicz, "Women in the Solidarity National Commission," 30–31.

37. Ibid., 33.

38. Weschler, "Hidden Victims," 5–6.

39. Tarasiewicz, "Women in the Solidarity National Commission," 33.

40. Politacha, "To nie jest walka, tylko dobijanie sie o swoje prawa," 36.

41. Maria Janion, "Za waszą wolność i naszą" [For Your Freedom and Ours], *Gazeta Wyborcza* (Warsaw edition), July 4, 1999, Świateczna [Weekend] section, 25.

42. Jarosław Kurski, "Barbara Labuda," *Gazeta Wyborcza* (Warsaw edition), March 11, 2000, 12, <http://www1.gazeta.pl/kraj/1,34311,138541.html>.

43. Ibid.

44. Ibid.

45. Ibid.

Chapter 10

1. Kurski, "Barbara Labuda," 12.

2. Graff, "Patriarchat po seksmisji," 22.

3. Ibid.

4. Ibid.

5. Ibid.

6. Ibid.

7. Penn, "Tajemnica państwowa."

8. Graff, "Patriarchat po seksmisji," 23.

9. Ibid., 23.

10. Ibid.

11. Janion, "For Your Freedom and Ours," 25.

12. Izabela Filipiak, "Ciekawosc wlasnego zycia" [Curiosity towards One's Own Life], *Gazeta Wyborcza* (Warsaw edition), July 29, 1999, Świateczna [Weekend] section, 13.

13. Janion, "For Your Freedom and Ours," 25.

14. Joanna Szczęsna, "Damy, rycerze i strazak" [Ladies, Knights and Firepersons], *Gazeta Wyborcza* (Warsaw edition), June 26–27, 1999, Świateczna [Weekend] section, 22.

15. Shana Penn, "Bohaterowie i bohaterki" [Heroes and Heroines], *Gazeta Wyborcza* (Warsaw edition), July 10–11, 1999, Świateczna [Weekend] section, 20.

16. Ewa Kondratowicz, *Szminka na sztandarze. Kobiety Solidarnośći 1980–1989* [Lipstick on the Banner: Solidarity Women, 1980–1989] (Warsaw: Wydawnictwo Sic!, 2001).

17. Magdalena Grabowska, "Zeby miec na samolot, trzeba wiedziec,

ile kosztuja kalesony. Wywiad z Wladyslawem Frasyniukiem" [Interview with Władysław Frasyniuk], *OŚKA Biuletyn,* no. 2 (2001): 15, 22.

18. Helena Łuczywo, "Mniej kwasu, prosze" [Less Acid, Please], *Gazeta Wyborcza* (Warsaw edition), January 26–27, 2002, 2.

19. Ibid.

20. Ibid.

21. "Poland Celebrates," *Rzeczpospolita,* December 16, 2002.

22. Anders, "Did the Polish Catholic Church Commune?" 100.

23. Joanna Pogórska and Justyna Kapecka, "Cien Matki Polki: Kobiety u nas rzadza, ale sie z tym nie afiszuja" [Shadow of Matka Polka: Polish Women Lead but They Don't Want to Show It], *Polityka,* 21, February 24, 2003, <http://polityka.onet.pl/162,1120664,1,0,2402-2003 -21,artykul.html.>

24. Ibid.

25. Agnieszka Graff, "Against the Current," *Cosmopolitan,* May 2000, 30.

26. Ibid.

Selected Bibliography

Polish History

Andrews, Nicholas. *Poland 1980–81: Solidarity versus the Party.* Washington, DC: National Defense University Press, 1985.

Ascherson, Neal. *The Polish August.* New York: Viking Press, 1982.

Borowski, Adam, and Miroslawa Latkowska, eds. *Solidarność—20 lat historii.* Warsaw: Volumen Publishing House, Tysol Ltd., 2000.

Brown, Belinda. *The Private Revolution.* London: Hera Trust, 2003.

Cave, Jane, ed. *Poland Watch No. 6: The Church and Solidarity.* Washington, DC: Journal of the Poland Watch Center, 1984.

Davies, Norman. *God's Playground: A History of Poland.* Vol. 2, *1795 to the Present,* Oxford: Oxford University Press, 1981.

Garton Ash, Timothy. *The Polish Revolution.* London: Trinity Press, 1983.

Gluza, Zbigniew, and Katarzyna Madoń-Mitzner, eds. *The Days of Solidarity.* Warsaw: KARTA Center, 2000.

Gluza, Zbigniew, Katarzyna Madoń-Mitzner, and Grzegorz Soltysiak, eds. *W stanie.* Warsaw: KARTA Publishing House, 1984.

Gross, Jan Tomasz. *Polish Society under German Occupation: The General-gouvernement, 1939–1944.* Princeton: Princeton University Press, 1970.

Grudzińska-Gross, Irena. *The Art of Solidarity.* Staten Island: International Popular Culture, 1985.

Hayden, Jacqueline. *Poles Apart: Solidarity and the New Poland.* Portland: Irish Academic Press, 1994.

Human Rights Watch. *Hidden Victims: Women in Post-Communist Poland.* New York: Human Rights Watch, 1992.

Janion, Maria. *Kobiety i duch inności* [Women and the Spirit of Otherness]. Warsaw: Wydawnictwo Sic!, 1996.

Janowska, Żdzisława, Jolanta Martini-Fiwek, and Zbigniew Goral. *Female Unemployment in Poland*. Warsaw: Friedrich Ebert Foundation, 1991.

Jawlowska, Aldona. "Za szklana sciana," *Pełnym Głosem*. Kobiety w Solidarności (Special Issue: "Women and Solidarity"). Kraków: eFKa, Jesien 1994.

Jaworski, Rudolf, and Bianka Pietrow-Ennker. *Women in Polish Society*. Boulder: East European Monographs, 1992.

Jolluck, Katherine R. *Exile and Identity: Polish Women in the Soviet Union during World War II*. Pittsburgh: University of Pittsburgh Press, 2002.

Karpinski, Jakub. *Countdown*. New York: Karz-Cohl, 1982.

Kaufman, Michael. *Mad Dreams, Saving Graces: Poland: A Nation in Conspiracy*. New York: Random House, 1989.

Kenney, Padraic. *A Carnival of Revolution: Central Europe 1989*. Princeton: Princeton University Press, 2002.

———. "The Gender of Resistance in Communist Poland." *American Historical Review* 104 (April 1999): 399–425.

Lewis, Flora. *Europe: A Tapestry of Nations*. New York: Touchstone, 1987.

Long, Kristi S. *We All Fought for Freedom: Women in Poland's Solidarity Movement*. Boulder: Westview Press, 1996.

Łopinski, Maciej, Marcin Moskit, and Mariusz Wilk. *Konspira*. Berkeley: University of California Press, 1990.

Michnik, Adam. *Letters from Freedom*. Berkeley: University of California Press, 1998.

———. *Letters from Prison and Other Essays*. Berkeley: University of California Press, 1985.

Nowicka, Wanda. *The Anti-Abortion Law in Poland*. Warsaw: Federation for Women and Family Planning, 2000.

Noyes, George Rapall, ed. *Poems by Adam Mickiewicz*. New York: Polish Institute of Arts and Sciences in America, 1944.

Penn, Shana. "National Secret." *Journal of Women's History* 5, no. 3 (1994): 55–69.

———. *Podziemie Kobiet* [The Underground of Women]. Warsaw: Rosner i Wspolnicy, 2003.

———. "Tajemnica państwowa." *Pełnym Głosem*. Kobiety w Solidarności (Special Issue: "Women and Solidarity"). Kraków: eFKa, Jesien 1994.

Prins, Gwyn. *Spring in Winter*. New York: St. Martin's Press, 1990.

Rachwald, Arthur. *In Search of Poland: The Superpowers' Response to Solidarity, 1980–1989.* Stanford: Hoover Institution Press, 1990.

Reading, Anna. *Polish Women, Solidarity and Feminism.* London: Macmillan, 1999.

Ruane, Kevin. *The Polish Challenge.* London: British Broadcasting Corporation, 1982.

Siekierski, Maciej, and Christopher Lazarski. *Polish Independent Publications, 1976–1990: Guide to the Collection in the Hoover Institution Archives.* Stanford: Hoover Institution Publications, 1999.

Staniszkis, Jadwiga. *Poland's Self-Limiting Revolution.* Princeton: Princeton University Press, 1984.

Szczęsna, Joanna. "Wkościele św, Marcina" [In St. Martin's Church]. *Zapis* 4 (1977).

―――. "Women in the Opposition." Essay in possession of the author, 1991.

Szporer, Michael. *The Great August: Conversations with Solidarity.* University Park: Pennsylvania State University Press, 2005.

Torańska, Teresa. *"Them": Stalin's Polish Puppets.* New York: Harper and Row, 1987.

Tornquist Plewa, Barbara. *The Wheel of Polish Fortune.* Lund, Sweden: Slavonic Department, University of Lund, 1992.

Tymowski, Andrzej. *Solidarity under Siege.* New Haven: D. H. Back Press, 1982.

―――, ed. *The Strike in Gdansk, August 14–31, 1980.* New Haven: D. H. Back Press, 1981.

von Erlach, Franciszek L. *Partyzantka w Polsce w r. 1863 w swietle wlasnych obserwacji zebranych na teatrze walki od marca do sierpnia 1863 roku* [Partisan Struggle in Poland in 1863 in the Light of Personal Observations, Collected in the Theatre of War from March till August 1863]. Tlum. J. Gagatek i W. Tokarz. Warsaw: Wydawnictwo M. Arcta, 1918.

Wałczewska, Sławomira. *Damy, Rycerze I Feministki.* Kraków: eFKa, 1999.

Wałęsa, Lech. *A Way of Hope.* New York: Henry Holt, 1987.

Wedel, Jane. *The Private Poland.* New York: Facts on File Publications, 1986.

Weschler, Lawrence. *The Passion of Poland.* New York: Pantheon Books, 1984.

Central and East European/Russian History

Crampton, R. J. *Eastern Europe in the Twentieth Century and After.* New York: Routledge, 1994.

Einhorn, Barbara. *Cinderella Goes to Market.* New York: Verso, 1993.

Funk, Nanette, and Magda Mueller. *Gender Politics and Post-Communism: Reflections from Eastern Europe and the Former Soviet Union.* New York: Routledge, 1993.

Garton Ash, Timothy. *The Uses of Adversity: Essays on the Fate of Central Europe.* New York: Random House, 1989.

Havel, Václav, et al. *The Power of the Powerless.* New York: Palach Press, 1985.

Rai, Shirin, Hillary Pilkington, and Annie Phizacklea, eds. *Women in the Face of Change: The Soviet Union, Eastern Europe and China.* New York: Routledge, 1992.

Renne, Tanya. *Ana's Land: Sisterhood in Eastern Europe.* Boulder: Westview Press, 1997.

Rosenberg, Tina. *The Haunted Land.* New York: Random House, 1995.

Rothschild, Joseph. *Return to Diversity.* New York: Oxford University Press, 1989.

Rueschemeyer, Marilyn. *Women in the Politics of Postcommunist Eastern Europe.* Armonk: M. E. Sharpe, 1994.

Scott, Hilda. *Women and Socialism: Experiences from Eastern Europe.* London: Allison and Busby, 1976.

Sommer, Mark. *Living in Freedom.* San Francisco: Mercury House, 1992.

Stites, Richard. *The Women's Liberation Movement in Russia: Feminism, Nihilism, and Bolshevism 1860–1930.* Princeton: Princeton University Press, 1991.

Stokes, Gale. *From Stalinism to Pluralism.* New York: Oxford University Press, 1991.

———. *Three Eras of Political Change in Eastern Europe.* New York: Oxford University Press, 1997.

———. *The Walls Came Tumbling Down.* New York: Oxford University Press, 1993.

Tismaneanu, Vladimir. *The Revolutions of 1989.* New York: Routledge, 1999.

Verdery, Katherine. *What Was Socialism, and What Comes Next?* Princeton: Princeton University Press, 1996.

White, Stephen, Judy Batt, and Paul G. Lewis. *Developments in East European Politics.* Durham, NC: Duke University Press, 1993.

Wolchik, Sharon, and Alfred Meyer, eds. *Women, State, and Party in Eastern Europe.* Durham, NC: Duke University Press, 1985.

Index

209–11, 266; and post-1989 discourse on women, 305, 315, 322–23; pre-Solidarity activism, 45, 115–16, 124; pronunciation of name, 342n. 12; and *Tygodnik Mazowsze,* xi, 10, 103, 150, 152, 154–55, 157–58, 160, 168–69, 172–73, 314; as underground leader, 27, 98, 101–9, 133, 166–68, 177–78, 192, 248, 348n. 13; on women oppositionists, 226–27, 229, 236–37

Łuczywo, Łucja (daughter of Helena), 103, 211

Łuczywo, Witold (husband of Helena), 103, 210–11

Maciejowska, Agnieszka, 107–8, 216–18, 272, 275–76, 283

Madoń-Mitzner, Katarzyna, 344n. 15, 344nn. 20–21, 344n. 23

Madres de la Plaza (Argentina), 231–32

Magdalena X (pseudonym), 23, 121–22, 152, 234–35, 242

Mały Konspiracja, 161

Man of Iron (Wajda), 71

Mansbridge, Jane, 78, 82

Marcus, Isabel, 74, 236, 254–55

Marie Claire, 307

Marta (Orzeszkowa), 256

martial law: communication control during, 103, 158–59; and feminism, effect on, 78; German occupation as analogy, 162–64; and imprisonment of oppositionists, 3–4, 8, 184, 195–96; 1981 implementation of, 3, 88–97, 137–41; 1982 "suspension" of, 197; 1980s (mid to late) weakening of Communist Party, 262; as "normalization" campaign, 167–68, 196, 228–29; underground education during, 72; underground press during, 96, 101–4, 142, 148–62, 185 (see also *Tygodnik Mazowsze*); women oppo-

sitionists' responses to, 9–10, 88–90, 94, 96, 97, 112, 138–41, 182, 228

Marx, Karl, 118–19

Matka Polka (Polish Mother): and Communist Party, 26, 184; as cultural icon, 16, 81, 258; in post-1989 discourse, 293, 301, 321–22, 329; and Solidarity, 231–32, 253; in "To the Polish Mother" (Mickiewicz), 257–58

Mazowiecki, Tadeusz, 271, 282

media, Polish: and post-1989 era, 28, 298, 294; and Solidarity's legal period, 72, 106–7. *See also* press, underground; *individual publications*

media, Western: and post-1989 Poland, 299; and Solidarity movement, 2–5, 50, 165, 194; and Solidarity women, 6, 13–14, 238

Media Studies Center, 13

Media Studies Journal, 11, 130, 173

Memory Project (Warsaw), 313

Michnik, Adam: early activism of, 117–18, 122–23; and *Gazeta Wyborcza,* 13, 101, 271–72; and post-1989 Poland, 282, 316; as Solidarity leader, 8, 16, 86, 90, 151, 193, 227, 230, 271, 348n. 13; Western media portrayal of, 2, 64; and Workers' Defense Committee, 43–44, 133

Mickiewicz, Adam, 119; *Dziady,* 123; and Matka Polka ("To the Polish Mother"), 16, 242, 257–58; and Woman Knight ("Grażyna"), 247, 258–59

Mieszko I (king), 7

Milczanowski, Andrzej, 332

Milewicz, Ewa, 97

Military Council for National Salvation. *See* WRON

Miller, Leszek, 316–18

Miłosz, Czesław, 119

MKS. *See* Inter-factory Strike Committee

Solidarity Press Agency (Agencja Prasowa "Solidarność"; AS): content of, 106–7; methods of production, 107–8; as police target, 140–41; women's management of, 9, 11, 102–3, 107–8, 110, 237

Solidarity underground, 4; Damska Grupa Operacyjna role in, 141–44; formation of, 98–99, 102–4; gender dynamics within, 179, 220–26, 230–31, 253; infrastructure of, 153, 198, 200–202; and 1988 food price strikes, 265–68; as non-representational of opposition (mid-1980s), 262–65; and past underground movements, 162, 167; regional variations, 137; strategies for success of, 169–70, 226–27; and Temporary Coordinating Committee, 192–98, 218–22; Western support of, 165, 194. *See also* Damska Grupa Operacyjna; *Tygodnik Mazowsze; individual underground leaders*

Solidarity women. *See* Solidarity leaders (women)

Solidarity Women's Section, 263, 283–90

Solidarność. *See* Solidarity

Sopot, Poland, 44, 55, 95

South Africa, 326

Soviet Union: denunciation of Israel, 124; invasion of Czechoslovakia, 92, 129–30; invasion of Hungary, 41, 92; occupation of Poland (World War II), 35–38, 198–99; and Polish Communist Party, 92, 166, 186–88; and Solidarity, 86–87, 104; "thaw" following Stalin's death, 40–41

Stalin, Joseph, 36–37, 40, 188. *See also* Soviet Union

Stanford University, 273

Staniszewska, Grażyna, 271, 276

Staniszkis, Jadwiga, 96

Staśinski, Piotr, 309

Stewart, Potter, 240

St. Martin's Church (Warsaw), 135–36

Stokes, Gale, 346n. 7, 350n. 3, 350n. 5

strikes: debates on effectiveness of, 193–94; 1970 food price, 34, 42, 43, 47–48, 52; 1976 Radom and Ursus, 43; 1982 (in wake of martial law), 94–97, 191, 193–94, 196–98; 1987–88 food price, 265–68; and 1989 Round Table discussions, 4. *See also* Gdańsk shipyard strike; "Polish August" strikes

student protests (1968). *See under* '68ers

Suwik, Dominika, 176

Świat Bez Kobiet (Graff), 322

Szczecin, Poland, 95, 152, 266–68, 332

Szczęsna, Joanna: and Damska Grupa Operacyjna, 109; on feminism, 75, 202–3, 295, 330–33; "In St. Martin's Church," 134–36; on martial law, 138–40, 228, 269–70; personal life of, 209–11; on police treatment of women, 42, 184; and post-1989 discourse on women, 304, 310–12, 330–33; post-1989 life of, 272–74, 283; pre-Solidarity activism, 45, 128, 131–36; pronunciation of name, 342n. 12; and Temporary Coordinating Committee, 192; as *Tygodnik Mazowsze* editor, 10, 27, 98–99, 152–57 passim, 160–61, 173–74, 177–78, 266–69, 332; on *Tygodnik Mazowsze*'s gendered tactics, 181, 183, 201, 203, 232, 349n. 16; on women oppositionists, 203–5, 253–55

Szlájfer, Henryk, 123

Szminka na sztandarze, 313

Szumiejko, Eugeniusz, 221

Szymborska, Wisława, 119, 317

Tańska, Klementyna, 256

Tarasiewicz, Małgorzata, 31, 263, 284–90, 319

Wałęsa, Danuta (wife of Lech), 52

Wałęsa, Lech: lack of women in advisory circle, 62, 64; pre-1980 activism, 43–48; and 1980 "Polish August" strikes, xii, 52–53, 56, 58, 106; as 1980–89 Solidarity leader, 16, 30, 33, 59, 61–63, 84–87, 90, 155, 191, 197, 266, 268, 303; and 1989 Round Table negotiations, 269, 271; 1991–95 presidency, 290, 296; and Nobel Peace Prize, 171; Western media portrayal of, 2, 5

Wall Street Journal, 4

Warsaw, Poland, 19–21; "feminine" nature of underground in, 137, 152; and martial law, 95, 137–40; and 1943 Jewish Ghetto Uprising, 21, 171; and 1944 Warsaw Uprising, 21, 37, 188; Parliament Hotel, 68; pre-Solidarity opposition in, 44, 133–36, 249–50; as Solidarity underground hub, 9–10, 22, 88, 98, 102, 147, 149, 151; and Temporary Coordinating Committee, 192–93, 195; and underground press, 45, 101, 148, 174

Warsaw Pact, 40, 41, 124, 129

Warsaw Underground Headquarters, 151

Warsaw University: and anti-Semitic purges, 85; and Polish feminism, 77, 80, 293, 306; and student oppositionists, 118, 123–24

Warski Shipyard (Szczecin), 267, 332

Watson, Peggy, 325–26, 328

Way of Hope (Wałęsa), 106

Weber, Max, 119

Weschler, Joanna, 351n. 26, 351n. 38

Weschler, Lawrence, 2, 341n. 6; on martial law, 3, 97, 227–28; on Solidarity men, 5–6; on Solidarity's underground, 13, 98, 103, 174, 197, 229; on Solidarity women, 79, 270

Western media. *See* media, Western

Who's Who in Solidarity, 72

Wielka Emigracja (Great Emigration), 248

Wielowieyska, Dominika, 315, 334–35

Wilk, Mariusz, 342n. 8, 346n. 1, 348nn. 5–12

Winiarska, Danuta, 305, 330, 332

WiP. *See* Wolność i Pokój

Witkowska, Anna, 321–22

Wojtyła, Karol. *See* John Paul II

Wolinowicz, Edward, 253

Wolność i Pokój (WiP; Freedom and Peace), 31, 263, 284–85, 344n. 2

"Woman Knight," 253, 257–59

women, Polish: and communism, 24–26, 67, 73, 75–76, 80, 188–91, 199, 252, 257, 301–2; and emancipation discourse, 255–57; and feminism, resistance to, 73–76, 235–36; and Polish Romantic myths, 242–43, 253–55, 259–61; in post-1989 era, 18–19, 278–90; and Solidarity's legal period, 66, 83; Solidarity underground's dependence on, 199–202, 204–5. *See also* feminists, Polish; Solidarity leaders (women); women oppositionists, Polish

women oppositionists, Polish, xi–xiv; anonymity of, 27, 238–40; and feminism, xiv, 14–15, 23–27, 74–75, 200; gendered tactics of, 181–84, 190–91; importance of illegal press to, 8; and "leadership question," 66, 233–40; Penn's interview process with, 21–27; personal lives of, 208–18; and Polish Romantic myths, 16–18, 242–43, 253–55, 259–61; and pre-Solidarity opposition movements, 114, 183, 241–58; and Solidarity beginnings, roles in, 32, 50, 56–58; and Solidarity leadership structures, scarcity within, 9, 60–65; and Solidarity underground, as crucial to, 9–10, 141–44, 179–80, 191, 200–205,